A History of

Western Philosophy

PHILOSOPHY FROM THE AGE OF POSITIVISM TO THE AGE OF ANALYSIS

by

A. Robert Caponigri

UNIVERSITY OF NOTRE DAME PRESS
Notre Dame   London

Library of Congress Catalog Card Number: 63-20526
Manufactured in the United States of America

To Three Songs With Words,
Victoria Marie, Lisa Marie, Robert John,
And to the One Who Wrote
the Lyrics,
Winifred

TABLE OF CONTENTS

Part I
The Age of National Imperialism

Introduction   3

Chapter I Philosophy and Life   5

    Introduction   5
    A. Vitalism and Neo-Vitalism   5
    B. The Philosophy of Life   11

Chapter II Historicism   24

    Introduction   24
    A. Wilhelm Dilthey   26
    B. Georg Simmel   29
    C. Max Weber   30
    D. Ernst Troeltsch   33
    E. Oswald Spengler   35
    F. Friedrich Meinecke   38
    G. Arnold Toynbee   39

Chapter III Pragmatism   43

    Introduction   43
    A. The Five Masters of Pragmatism   46
        1. Charles Sanders Peirce   46
        2. William James   49
        3. John Dewey   53
        4. George Mead   57
        5. Ferdinand C. S. Schiller   60
    B. The Italian School   61

Chapter IV Materialism: Scientific, Historical, and Dialectical   64

Introduction   64
A. Scientific Materialism   65
     1. Radical, Humanistic Materialism   65
     2. Psychophysical Materialism   68
     3. Monistic Materialism   71
     4. Evolutionary Monistic Materialism   73
B. Historical Materialism   74
C. Dialectical Materialism   78
     1. The Germinal Ideas of Dialectical Materialism as Identifiable in Historical Materialism   78
     2. Friedrich Engels and the Formulation of Dialectical Materialism   79
     3. Nikolai Lenin   82
     4. Joseph Stalin   85
     5. Some Further Developments of Dialectical and Historical Materialism   87

Chapter V Realism and Naturalism   90

Introduction   90
A. English Realism and Naturalism   91
B. Realism and Naturalism in America   102
     1. Genesis and Polemical Phase of Realism in America   102
     2. The First Constructive Phase: Neo-Realism   103
     3. The "Six"   104
     4. The New Realism: A Cooperative Philosophical Undertaking   105
     5. Transition to the "Critical" Phase   106
     6. The Critical Realism of Roy Wood Sellars   107
     7. Essays in Critical Realism   107
     8. Lovejoy and *The Revolt Against Dualism*   108
     9. The Systematic Phase of Critical Realism   108
C. The Naturalism of Woodbridge and Cohen   113

Chapter VI Neo-Scholasticism   118

Introduction: Scholasticism and Neo-Scholasticism   118
A. Pre-Thomistic Neo-Scholasticism   120
B. Thomistic Neo-Scholasticism   125
  1. *Aeterni Patris:* Occasion and Character   125
  2. The Great Centers of Development   126
  3. Basic Characteristics and Present Tendencies
     in Neo-Thomist Philosophy   130
  4. The Transcendental Method in Neo-Thomism   139

Chapter VII Phenomenology   152

A. Preliminary Definition   152
B. Edmund Husserl: Life and Works   153
C. Antecedents of Phenomenology   154
D. The Phenomenological Doctrine   155
  1. Disengagement from Brentano   155
  2. The Rejection of Psychologism and the
     Intuition of Pure Phenomenology   156
E. Developments of Phenomenology   171
  1. Alexius Meinong and the Theory of Objects   171
  2. Nicolai Hartmann   173
  3. Max Scheler   176
F. Continued Influence of Phenomenology   180

Chapter VIII Bergson   183

Introduction   183
A. Bergson and Positivistic Evolution   184
B. Time and Freedom   185
C. Matter and Memory   186
D. *Elan Vital* and *Creative Evolution*   188
E. Intuition   192
F. Morality and Religion   193

Part II

The Post-Colonial Age

Introduction　　　　199

Chapter I The Philosophy of Action　　　　201

    Introduction: Intrinsic Character of the
        Philosophy of Action　　　　201
    A. John Henry Cardinal Newman　　　　204
    B. Léon Ollé-Laprune　　　　208
    C. Maurice Blondel　　　　212
    D. Lucien Laberthonnière　　　　219

Chapter II Absolute Historicism and Actual Idealism　　　　223

    Introduction: The Revival of Idealism in Italy　　　　223
    A. Benedetto Croce　　　　223
        1. The Seminal Phase: To 1902　　　　224
        2. The Philosophy of Spirit　　　　226
        3. Development Subsequent to the Philosophy
           of Spirit　　　　233
    B. Giovanni Gentile　　　　237

Chapter III Existentialism　　　　248

    Introduction: Inception and Distribution　　　　248
    A. Existentialism in Germany: Jaspers and Heidegger　　　　254
        1. Karl Jaspers　　　　254
        2. Martin Heidegger　　　　263
    B. Existentialism in France: Marcel, Sartre, and
        Merleau-Ponty　　　　276
        1. Gabriel Marcel　　　　276
        2. Jean-Paul Sartre　　　　285
        3. Maurice Merleau-Ponty　　　　294
    C. Existentialism in Italy: Nicola Abbagnano　　　　297

Chapter IV Philosophy as Analysis of Language　　　　301

    Introduction　　　　301
    A. The Anticipatory Phase: Peirce, Moore, Russell,
        Wittgenstein as Pupil of Russell　　　　304
    B. The Continental Phase: The Vienna Circle
        and Its Adjuncts　　　　306

1. Origins and Organization 306
2. Philosophical Aims and Themes of the
   Vienna Circle 307
3. Salient Ideas of Central Figures of the
   Vienna Circle 309
C. The British Phase 314
D. The American Phase 324
1. American Developments of Logical Positivism 325
2. American Developments of British Analytic
   Philosophy 328

Chapter V Contemporary Spiritualism 330

Introduction 330
A. The Philosophy of Spirit in France 331
1. Louis Lavelle 332
2. René Le Senne 335
B. Christian Spiritualism in Italy 339
1. Armando Carlini 340
2. Augusto Guzzo 342
3. Felice Battaglia 343
4. Michele Federico Sciacca 346
5. Luigi Stefanini 348

Name Index 353

Subject Index 359

Introduction

Our basic reason for undertaking the authorship of this work is to promote the return of the history of philosophy to its rightful place of honor and usefulness in the academic program. This return is long overdue; it is becoming painfully clear that philosophy cannot be pursued in an historical vacuum. Indeed, in a very real sense philosophy is identical with its history and torn from this context it loses its particular character and force.

Philosophy pursued in an unhistorical or ahistorical manner cannot help but warp the individual and social consciousness at whose heightened refinement it is aimed. To pursue philosophy, one must either enter into the rich heritage of its history or run the risk of falling victim to a kind of speculative barbarism.

The form of these works has been determined by the authors' conviction that the history of philosophy itself can be fully appreciated only when taken as a basic element in the whole cultural complex of the West. Philosophy is not a specialized but a pervasive discipline. It finds its interest everywhere in the life of the spirit and it takes form as a response to all of the needs of the spirit. Philosophy is never a *part* of a culture but a pervading influence and mode of awareness. For this reason, in these volumes the chief architectural principle has been to place philosophy as firmly as possible in the cultural context, seeing it in this living relation to all the interests of culture and the life of the spirit.

It is our belief that the division of the work into five volumes and the articulations of the history of culture within which the history of philosophy has been placed is justified and even demanded by that history itself and has nothing artificial or contrived about it. For this reason, the student and the general reader will, we believe, be able to relate the flow of philosophical speculation directly to what he already knows about the general architecture of the history of Western Culture and will immediately experience the history of philosophy as an enrichment in depth of his cultural consciousness. It is hoped that the student will come to perceive that it is precisely the quality of its philosophical experience which gives an age its special character and it is precisely its philosophical discontent which, stirring in one age, prepares and induces the vast labors which usher in a new.

While the volumes have been so planned that they may be read profitably by the general reader, they have a special orientation toward the academic world of the classroom. It is the authors' conviction that the basic book used in an academic course ought to be the meeting ground for the minds of both teacher and student. To this end, both will find that these volumes contain something which suits their particular needs and functions.

The particular need of the student is background; he can profit little from any contact with even the best of teachers unless he brings the richest possible preparation to this encounter. Therefore, these volumes are addressed to him in the hope that he will be drawn into them by a natural and spontaneous response. Frankly, we hope that the student will enjoy reading them and not find that reading a chore.

The need of the teacher, by contrast, is for an instrument of focus; something which will enable him, in the limited time at his disposal, to select the points of greatest impact with the student mind and those which will bring about the most significant student discussion and mutual exchange. The flexible construction of these books should meet this need. The teacher may assess and evaluate the whole and/or parts according to his own needs and interests and select for treatment in the classroom those articulations which will give him the greatest direct access to the minds of his students. In this process of selection, the volumes may be used as a guide to serve him by indicating the structure of the history of philosophy. They do *not* undertake *to make that selection for him* or dictate to him, by their structure, what his selection should be. He too, it is hoped, will enjoy teaching with this book (note we carefully avoid saying *teaching this book*) because it ministers to his own irreplaceable activity and does not dictate or constrain it.

In the text, reference to original sources and to the best secondary sources has been constant. In every way the authors have made an effort to place the student in contact with these sources in the context in which they will be most beneficial. In addition, lists of supplementary readings have been appended at important junctures. The quality of these reading lists should be clear from the start. They are not mere bibliographical lists nor are they "outside readings" in the current, vague sense of that term. These readings have a utilitarian purpose; they are closely related to the process of the narrative of the text itself. It is the authors' hope that as specific issues arise in class discussion, corresponding readings may be found which may extend the discussion or give it direction and emphasis. Again, it is hoped that the composition of studies will always be made a part of the student obligation in any course in the history of philosophy. The supplementary readings are so planned that the student will find in them direct help in the researching, planning and composition of such papers.

In closing, the authors would emphasize again one salient point: they hope that from these pages the reader will derive above all a renewed sense of the universal relevance of philosophy to the life of the mind and of the spirit.

Philosophy is above all a humanistic pursuit in the basic sense of that term; namely, philosophy takes for its own all that touches man. Only when seen in this perspective can philosophy be appreciated and enjoyed. Only in this way will it inevitably be recognized by every man as the supreme human discipline, the one activity of mind and spirit from which he cannot isolate himself and still achieve stature and maturity as a human being.

Notre Dame, Indiana   A. ROBERT CAPONIGRI
                                                              and
                                                    RALPH M. MCINERNY

PART I
THE AGE OF
NATIONAL IMPERIALISM

Introduction

The movement of positivism and the influence of the idea of evolution had scarcely reached the peak of their ascendent movement when the countermovements to which they were to give rise made themselves felt. The general rubric under which these countermovements are gathered by the best historians of the period is *idealism*. Obviously so vague a term cannot be taken as a positive guide as to what was transpiring during the last third of the nineteenth century. What confronts the observing eye is in fact a vast tangle of currents and movements, which only with difficulty can be separated into its constituent strands. A significant thread which does, in some degree, advance this work of disentanglement is the distinction between the retrospective and the perspective movements of thought.

The earliest signs of this general unrest under the dominance of positivism and, to a lesser degree, under that of evolutionism, is the appearance of certain "neo" currents, e.g., neo-Hegelianism, neo-Kantianism, neo-scholasticism. "Neo" movements in the history of thought, as Croce has pointed out in his *Discorsi di varia filosofia* (Vol. I, p. 107), are not merely ineffective, but nearly always spurious. Movements under this rubric are more significant as indications of the need of fresh speculative effort than as restatements or as revitalizations of older positions. The reason for this is not far to seek nor difficult to comprehend. So closely is any movement of thought bound to the historical and cultural circumstances of its first emergence that its transfer to another period of history must prove a fatal operation, productive of something stillborn. For each period naturally is alive with its own and not a past life and therefore conscious of urgent problems which were not the problems of an earlier age or of "perennial" problems in a form in which they were never before encountered. The neo-movements of the nineteenth century certainly exhibit this abortive character. Despite the great resources of speculative acumen and historical erudition, as well as great (though as yet unformed) sensitivity to the spiritual and speculative needs of the time, they are inert bodies, culturally ineffective. Sometimes, inevitably, they are productive of deeper insights into the original perceptions of the movements

3

of which they purport to be the reincarnation. But when these insights are analyzed they prove to be ultimately of historical and not speculative value.

But this phase of the nineteenth and early twentieth centuries did not exhaust itself in such revivalist efforts. It exhibits much more significantly an élan of its own, that is, a genuinely vital speculative drive which, while in touch with history, is in vital and not merely mimetic relation to it. The philosophy of Bergson may be taken as symbolic of this positive thrust of the period, though of course not exhaustive of it. The appearance of phenomenology, the struggle toward relevant spiritualism, even the naturalism and realism of the period, all bear marks of this fresh and vibrant speculative life. It is for this reason that this period, despite the tangled physiognomy it presents, immediately communicates a sense of vitality which makes it one of the most interesting phases of the age.

CHAPTER I

Philosophy and Life

Introduction

The phenomenon of life, under all of its aspects, has been a constant preoccupation of western thought. In the nineteenth and early twentieth centuries, however, this interest became especially intense and motivated considerable philosophical reflection. This intensification of interest was due to the renewal and rapid development of the biological sciences, which for some centuries had lagged behind the development of the other natural sciences. Other forces also contributed to this increased interest, for example, the strong romantic current, in which the concept and sentiment of life held a central place. In any event, the philosophical reflection on life now took on considerable importance and exercised wide influence on all aspects of culture.

Two basic forms of this reflection may be distinguished. The first was occasioned directly by biological concerns and was scientifically orientated; this form is called *vitalism* and its later phases (which will concern us most) *neo-vitalism*. The second was inspired by romanticism, though the cultural presence of the biological sciences and especially of evolutionary philosophy contributed to its accentuation and to the variety of subforms in which it was expressed. This form is oriented toward life as *lived experience* (*erlebnis*), toward life, not as an objective and observable phenomenon in the natural order, but as an inwardly experienced movement to which the subject of reflection has direct and immediate access. To this form of philosophical reflection the term *philosophy of life* is assigned. The specific characteristics of each form will be examined more closely and their representative exponents given fuller review.

A. *Vitalism and Neo-Vitalism*

The generic term *vitalism* is employed to designate all of those doctrines which were concerned to deny that the phenomena of life, in its biological aspects, could be reduced to physico-chemical processes. Thus, the definition of vitalism is essentially dialectical and presupposes the prior effort to effect such a reduction. In its more positive aspect, vitalism becomes the effort to identify that principle or complex of principles by which life is essentially distinguished and hence rendered incapable of reduction to physico-chemical processes. On the whole, it must be recognized that vitalism was more successful in the first than in the second of these efforts; i.e., it could more readily point out the differing characteristics of each order than discover any essential principle which positively characterized life in its autonomy.

The distinction, which is both theoretical and historical, between vitalism and neo-vitalism rests on the basis of this effort to demonstrate the irreducibility of the phenomenon of life to physico-chemical processes. In the widest sense, all of those classical theories which had identified life with the soul and had sought to establish its independence from material forces might be called vitalistic. This use is very broad, however. In a more precise sense, the term *vitalism* is reserved for the efforts of philosophers and men of science of the late eighteenth and the early and middle nineteenth centuries to establish an independent *life-force* as the principle of all life-phenomena and to underline the complete autonomy of that force with respect to physico-chemical processes. This life-force was variously described and depicted; its autonomy was the single point which was common to all such descriptions. It was characteristic of vitalism to suggest that, because of the autonomy of the life-force, it and the phenomena of life did not lend themselves to scientific investigation. The essence of life must necessarily escape such strict determination.

Vitalism and neo-vitalism are directly, though in different ways, related to an event in the history of biochemical research. The synthesis of urea in 1828 demonstrated the possibility of producing organic compounds or substances in the laboratory. Thus, the early vitalistic point of view regarding the prospects of scientific investigation of life-phenomena was clearly discredited. The absolute disunity of the organic and the inorganic orders had been refuted by scientific means. *Neo-vitalism* may be said to have its origin in this fact. The scientific study of life now at least had to be admitted, if not placed at the center of the problem. Nevertheless, neo-vitalism was not prepared to recognize the reducibility of life to chemical-physical processes. It continued to hold that life was sustained by a principle proper to itself. This principle in turn was characterized in various ways: for example, as *élan vital* by Bergson, as *entelechy* by Driesch, as the *dominant* by Reinke. A fatal difficulty attached to this persistent attitude; it involved the postulation of an inaccessible and unknowable element as the explanatory principle of the phenomena of life, a situation universally recognized as unsatisfactory.

The basic questions which concern vitalism and neo-vitalism have been ably summarized. They number four: 1) whether life-phenomena can be investigated by the methods of science with profit and without fundamental distortion of the evidence; 2) whether vital phenomena can be adequately explained by physico-chemical laws, so that no further principles of explanation must be postulated; 3) whether living organisms can in principle, if not in fact, be artificially produced or synthesized in the laboratory; 4) whether life could have originated naturally or historically, for example, by evolution from nonorganic matter, or whether it must be traced to a special providential design, even to a special creative intervention. The replies offered to these questions present a synoptic view of the problematic and doctrinal range of vitalism and neo-vitalism.

The reply to the first question was divided. Classical vitalism was inclined to deny that vital phenomena could be investigated by scientific means with any profit and even to hold that the application of this method must result in distortion of the data and the evidence. After this position had been called into doubt by the synthesis of urea, neo-vitalism, representing a transformation of the older position, seemed inclined to look favorably on such investigation, though still holding that it could achieve only limited results and that some other principle had to be postulated in order to account for the specific character of life-phenomena.

The reply to the second question remains consistently negative and is, in fact, the specific hallmark of both vitalism and neo-vitalism. The difficulty inherent in this position did not inhibit the constant renewal of efforts to formulate such a principle, for the complexity of life-phenomena seemed to justify the attempts. The major difficulty lay in the fact that any such principle necessarily eluded the conditions which would enable it to confront scientific explanation directly. It remained inexplicable and inaccessible in itself, and its power to explain the phenomena of life seemed, therefore, postulatory rather than evidential. We shall examine one or two of these principles below in an attempt to clarify both the motive which inspired these efforts and the limitations under which they labored.

The third question also met with a firm negative reply. The production of life under artificial or laboratory conditions was held to be not only contrary to achieved fact but impossible in principle. The negation rested, of course, upon the basis of the complexity and transcendency of the specific characteristics of life-phenomena. Nevertheless, the denial was subject to certain doubts and ambiguities. The passage from the fact that science had not produced life under controlled conditions to the statement that it *could not* do so and the prophecy that it would *not* be able to do so seemed illicit. *Ab esse ad posse valet illatio.* However, *ab non esse ad non posse non valet illatio.* One can argue from a fact to its possibility, but one cannot argue from the nonexistence of a fact to its impossibility. Again the instance of urea was important. What ensued was *methodological* materialism as a guide to the scientific investigation of life-phenomena. This position held that, while certainly life-phenomena have characteristics proper to themselves, distinctly different from the physico-chemical characteristics by which they are always accompanied, this difference does not constitute a gap that is unbridgeable in principle. Methodological materialism held that, given this situation, there is an obligation (based on the theory that the most economical explanation is the most satisfactory) to proceed on the assumption that scientific method could lead to an adequate explanation of vital phenomena, until evidence to the contrary would dispell its pretensions.

With the definitive elimination of the hypothesis of spontaneous generation through the work of Pasteur, the final question seemed to admit of only the following possibilities. Life could only come to be through either the direct or the indirect creative act of God. Since it involves a special creative act, the appearance of life in the universe is not natural. With regard to this creative act, two hypotheses are possible: first, that it is a direct intervention at a given point in the history of the universe and, second, that it is a continuous process immanent in, but differing in principle and action from, natural process. Neo-vitalism, on the whole, leaned toward this second hypothesis, which found precise and eloquent formulation in Bergson and others.

In order to view these possibilities more concretely, the doctrines of representative figures of neo-vitalism should be examined. A number of representative figures suggest themselves, the most prominent being Bergson. As special attention will be given to his thought in another chapter, attention here might be directed to the theories of Reinke, Ostwald, and Driesch.

The contribution of Johannes Reinke (1849–1931) lies in his theory of "dominants," which is developed in several of his numerous works on botany and biology and their relation to philosophy. Of these works the most instructive is perhaps *Einleitung in die theoretische Biologie* [Introduction to theoretical biology], 1901, which saw a number of subsequent editions. The evident musical association of the term is carried out by Reinke's view that the principle of life is, above all, a principle of harmony and order. This thought is suggested by the manifest complexity of vital phenomena as well as by their immanent finalistic structure, which precludes any mechanistic explanation and fosters the introduction of quasi-aesthetic notions. These dominants are spiritual in nature in the precise sense that they cannot be reduced to physico-chemical laws. Nevertheless, they can be formulated in laws, just as laws of music can be formulated without the supposition that they can be reduced to or identified with laws of acoustics. These dominants account for the organizational patterns of organic processes, and in fact of all life-processes. They cannot be known by any direct process of observation, but only indirectly, by observing their effects. They operate finalistically and not mechanically to produce the effects that may be observed. In a word, for Reinke, organic life is aesthetic in structure, similar to a work of art, and the processes it involves are ruled by principles which resemble aesthetic principles more than any other kind of explanatory schemata. These philosophical reflections did not prevent Reinke from adhering to methodological materialism.

The specific form of neo-vitalism advanced by Wilhelm Ostwald (1853–1932) is given the name *energeticism* (cf. *Die Energien* [Energy], 1908; *Lebenlinien* [Patterns of Life] 3 vols., 1926–27; 2nd ed. 1932–33). As a matter of fact, energeticism was a broad theory in physical chemistry which Ostwald applied to the specific phenomena of life. His basic problem involved the transformation of energy. In addressing this problem, he reached an antimaterialistic position. He held that the fundamental element of reality is energy. Matter itself must eventually be identified as energy. In his theory of the order and classification of the sciences, Ostwald holds that energy is the most general concept available to the physical sciences, while the biolological sciences avail themselves of the concept of life. However, just as matter must eventually be identified with energy, so too must life be identified and defined through energy.

The crucial idea would seem to be his notion of free energy, which distinguishes a living system from a physical system. The physical system is one in which energy has reached a state of equilibrium; the energy input and the output are equal. The fact that the universe itself is not such a system provides the framework both for Ostwald's anti-materialism and his specific form of vitalism. A living system is an economy of free energy. It utilizes the free energy in the universe as a whole, such as that released by the sun, and it employs this energy in a pattern which transcends the patterns exhibited by physical systems, precisely in those ways which have led life to be called creative and free. Free energy is energy which is not subject to the law of the diminution of energy as stated in the second law of thermodynamics.

By general consensus of historians and critics, Ostwald's philosophy of life-phenomena is not entirely self-consistent and clear. Its implications, however, seem clear enough for him to be placed definitely in the vitalist current; for he consistently maintains the irreducibility of life to material and mechanistic processes, while offering a concept of life which would meet the demands of scientific method and at the same time avoid that "agnosticism" which afflicted other concepts, such as Reinke's theory of dominants.

The term *vitalism* is more directly associated with the name of Hans Driesch (1867–1941) than with any other thinker, but even in his case it is necessary to make the concept more precise. His vitalism is, more specifically, *entelechism*. His work *Ordnungslehre* [Theory of order], 1912, provides a limit-basis for entelechism. Driesch defines philosophy as "the knowledge of knowledge" or, better perhaps, the knowledge *that* one knows; thus, it has its basis in the self-conscious reflection of the "I" or subject, the reflective act by which the "I" knows that it knows. The essential element of this self-conscious act and the knowledge it produces is order, for this knowledge is a kind of order or an ordered whole. Consequently, his first speculative problem is the general theory of order. Basing his thoughts on Kant's theory of the categories, Driesch develops a theory of order to embrace the whole of the nonorganic world. When he comes to the living organism, however, he finds it necessary to introduce certain basic modifications into his theory. The organism cannot be reduced to the patterns of order exhibited by the inorganic world. This is equivalent to saying that its principles are not mechanical or that the organism is not a machine. In order to account for the system of life-phenomena exhibited by a living organism, it is necessary to recognize another factor: the *entelechy*.

Driesch's characterization of this entelechy is complex. In the first place, it is an entirely *natural* principle; he has no intention of making life the manifestation in nature of a principle transcendent to nature. Nevertheless, the entelechy operates in such wise as to countervene certain basic laws of nature as established in his own theory of order, for example, the principle of the conservation of energy. Again, the entelechy is extraspatial, though it acts only in space. Similarly, it is suprapersonal and supraindividual, though acting and manifesting itself only in the individual organism which appears in time and space. The best insight into the mode of operation of the entelechy is provided by the analogy of man. Nevertheless, the entelechy as formative principle is proper to the species, so that the individual becomes both its realization and its limitation. Like human behavior, the entelechy of all living forms is finalistic. The end toward which it works is both immanent to the individual organization and transcendent to it. The entelechy generates the form of the individual and directs its organized energies to the activities of life, but, in so doing, it serves the transcendent end of the species, which is its own conservation and realization through the reality and activity of the individual. From the point of view of the general definition of vitalism given above, Driesch's doctrine must be considered to be clearly and economically formulated. The irreducibility of life to the processes of physical nature is clearly established, even while the absolute immanence of life to nature is emphasized. The entelechy of life lifts nature to a level of self-transcendence without negating its basic properties.

B. *The Philosophy of Life*

Vitalism addressed life as given objectively in nature, in biological forms. For it, life was an objective fact and process, like any other given in nature. It attempted to explain life in this form in accordance with the principles of the philosophy of nature. Its chief effort was directed, first, to establishing the fact that life could not be reduced to physico-chemical processes and, second, to determining the nature of the principle which might account for life in this objective order.

In contrast, the point of departure of that group of theories and ideas to which the term *philosophy of life* is applied lies in the notion of life as *erlebnis*. Life as *erlebnis* cannot be approached as a "given," an object presented to us "from without" for contemplation, observation, or scientific analysis; it is neither a perception nor a representation. On the contrary, it is present to us as an "interior" process which we "live through" and in which we become immediately and interiorly present to ourselves. The structure of life as *erlebnis* is just the opposite of passivity before an "external" world which imposes itself upon us. It involves a sense of active participation and interior dynamism. Its form is finalistic, looking forward to an end-value to be realized and achieved. It is a generating and creative "thrust," pregnant with realities yet to be realized, which are not ends transcendent to the subject of life but values and goals constitutive of it. The philosophy of life is concerned to understand life in this sense, a task manifestly different under almost every aspect from that which confronted vitalism.

Two speculative tendencies can be perceived in the "philosophy of life." The first is the tendency to find in life as *erlebnis,* as interiorly sensed tension and dynamism, the basic explanatory principle of all other phenomena, while making life itself the term of an interior intuition which cannot be explained but only apprehended. This has frequently been considered the "irrationalistic" or "mystical" tendency in the "philosophy of life." It is dubious, however, whether these adjectives can be applied to it in any strict sense. It must be kept in mind that, even when the philosophy of life places the life principle beyond reason and maintains that it transcends any analysis, this is done by an act which is itself rational. The recognition, itself the result of a rational act, that the ultimate principle of reality lies beyond reason does not render a philosophical point of view "irrational"; neither does it render the principle thus apprehended and characterized "irrational." Such a position bears a direct relation to reason by the very fact that the recognition of its transcendence is an act of reason. To judge the matter otherwise is to confuse *rational* with *rationalistic*.

The second tendency of the "philosophy of life" is to bring life itself, as *erlebnis,* within the scope of some rational principle of explanation which, in its logical status, would be clearly transcendent to life. This tendency is more traditionally philosophical, for its seeks to "explain" life itself, in the form of *erlebnis.* Nevertheless, it too seeks to stop short of that point at which it would become rationalistic, that is, would demand that reason encompass life rather than appear as a manifestation, perhaps the supreme manifestation, of life. However, neither of these tendencies appears in its pure form in any of the representatives of the philosophy of life. The philosophical effort is always to clarify life through rational reflection, while realizing that the life thus clarified is itself the ground of reason.

While the philosophy of life is a phenomenon chiefly of the late nineteenth and early twentieth centuries, its history extends much further into the past. Though present as a possible point of view, expressed only in tentative and fugitive forms, throughout the history of western thought, it assumes a positive and characteristic configuration during the romantic period. The concern of romanticism to vindicate, against the unilateral rationalistic tendencies of the Enlightenment, the "pre-rational" or "pre-logical" powers of the soul—imagination, sentiment, etc.—first generates this configuration. Romanticism's desire to place the organicity of nature in relief against the mechanicism of the Enlightenment also contributed to this effect. The name of Giambattista Vico takes on great importance in this context, for his reconstruction of the "poetic mentality" of man pioneered the entire romantic movement. While he placed his analysis of the poetic character in the perspective of a history whose dynamic is toward the dominance of the rational powers of man, the actual effect of his thought was to restructure the whole of human presence, making these poetic or pre-rational powers of the soul the permanent matrix of all its other activities. Johann Gottfried Herder, in his *Ideen zur Philosophie der Geschichte der Menschheit* [Ideas for a philosophy of the history of mankind], stresses the continuity between the inorganic and organic processes of nature and places man's consciousness at the center of the entire process, revealing it as living and dynamic, not static and dead. The genial though fragmentary work of Goethe's youth: *Die Natur* [On nature] accentuated the immanent finality of all living forms and the inner creative dynamism which constitutes their essence, thus evoking profound pantheistic reverberations. Finally Schelling, especially in such works as his *Bruno, oder über das natürliche und göttliche Prinzip der Dinge,* embraces conscious and unconscious alike within the divine life and holds that the mediation of that divine life in human consciousness may take intuitive-artistic as well as logico-conceptual form.

Against the background of these developments in romantic philosophy, the post-romantics Schopenhauer and Nietzsche formulated philosophical positions which have been called, with complete justice, the paradigms of all subsequent forms of the philosophy of life. In their philosophies, life is presented as continuous and unlimited creative power under the aspect of will. This creative power generates all forms and values from its own resources and in this process is impelled by its own inner dynamism to constantly transcend itself through the dissolution of the concrete forms and values in which it is expressed and the creation of new ones. Above all, this creative power is presented as ultimately incommensurate with, though always immanent in, the order of concrete forms and values which it creates; thus, life cannot be identified or explained through them, but only they through it. In Schopenhauer this line of philosophical speculation bred an ultimate pessimism which led to an ascetic negativism toward life itself, while in Nietzsche it produced the mystical exaltation of the superman; but the basic pattern remains the same, and it is this pattern, and not the diverse attitudes, which becomes paradigmatic for the philosophy of life. Later forms of the philosophy of life will add one important note, however; the humanistic note; for man will be recognized as the *locus* of life, at least in its highest and most creative form. Life will reveal itself, not as a quasi-natural power which stands against man even while it achieves its ends through him, but as the concrete life which man himself *lives through,* in both his individual and his collective experience.

In its exaltation of life, the philosophy of life, in its later developments, advances claims which seem to run counter to many of the classical attitudes of western culture. Thus, in its formulation as the will to life and to power, it will claim, in the name of the creative power of life, to transcend moralistic limits, to place man, as Nietzsche so dramatically phrased it, *beyond good and evil,* at least as these concepts had been traditionally understood. Emphasizing strongly the all-embracing character of life as *lived experience,* it will seem to denigrate the power of reason to transcend experience and to give transcendental order to life itself. Reducing all values to the fundamental level of the creative power of life, it will seem to some to demolish all boundaries between the achievements of various cultures in history, uncritically equating, for example, the primitive art of native African tribes with the highest expressions of European art simply on the ground that the former too is an expression of life, in some ways an even clearer and more direct expression because it is unmediated by the debilitating processes of reason and reflection.

Aestheticism achieves a new status because life is basically *expression*, intuitive expression and lyrical expression, as Benedetto Croce says, and all other forms of life must be mediated through expressive forms. Hence, life and art are profoundly *one,* and the function of art is to heighten and intensify the *experience of life.* An element of mysticism creeps in, an effort to communicate with life in its pure unmediated flow, an effort to lose in that primitive and all-embracing movement the burden of mediated, and hence limited and exclusive, forms of life. Sometimes, emphasis is given to the experience of life in collective forms, as in the French writer Guyau, while at other times the concept of culture as the true level of life expression leads to a fresh interest in cultural process in itself and in its historical forms, as in the German theorists of culture like Wilhelm Dilthey and Georg Simmel. The German writer Ludwig Klages will give special emphasis to the secondary role of intellect in the process of lived experience, thus giving occasion to the charge of *irrationalism* (though the distinction between irrationalism and anti-intellectualism would seem to be elementary). Finally writers like the Spaniard Miguel Unamuno will give an heroic-religious-tragic character to life as it is lived through both by the individual and by collectivities, and his more realistic countryman José Ortega y Gasset will stress the existentialistic and pragmatic elements in life processes.

As it might already have been gathered from these observations, many of the thinkers who contributed to the philosophy of life are associated even more closely with other philosophical postions and concerns or have achieved such personally distinguished positions that they demand monographic treatment rather than mere inclusion in a wider movement. The latter is the case with Schopenhauer, Nietzsche, and Bergson. The former is the case with Simmel and Dilthey, who are more amply considered under the rubric of historicism and philosophy of value. Consequently, consideration will be restricted in this chapter to a selected number of thinkers who are identified principally or exclusively through their contributions to the philosophy of life: the French philosopher Guyau, the German psychologist and characterologist Klages, and the interesting group of Spanish thinkers—Unamuno, Ortega y Gasset, and the very able disciple of the latter, Julián Marías.

Jean-Marie Guyau (1854–1888), in his brief and troubled years, lived an intense philosophical experience which found expression in a number of works which have become fundamental texts of the philosophy of life. In addition to his brilliant doctoral thesis on utilitarian moral doctrine, the most important of these are *Esquisse d'une morale sans obligation ni sanction* [Outline of a moral doctrine without obligation or sanction], 1885, and *L'irréligion de l'avenir* [The irreligion of the future], 1887. He also contributed to the discussion of aesthetic ideas in relation to the philosophy of art in *Problemes de l'esthétique contemporaine* [Problems of contemporary aesthetics], 1884. Guyau conceived of the process of *erlebnis* primarily in collective terms. It is only at the collective level that life achieves truly creative intensity. By contrast, the life of the individual appears attenuated and, in isolation, relatively impotent. The chief striving of the individual is to increase the intensity and creative efficacy of his life through identification with the life of the group at some level and in some form. In this way Guyau transposes all of the classical problems of philosophy into social terms and categories. The essential value of individual life is its capacity to expand, to transcend itself, and to become an integral element in the social complex. In this process of social identification, its creative power is intensified.

The three forms under which the creative power of the individual is released in the collectivity are art, morality, and religion. Art is the basic form of creativity in life. The very form of life in its creative dynamics is rhythm, harmony, expression. Art and life are absolutely one in their creative actuality. The form of the collectivity likewise is a free creative force with harmony its supreme good and end. With regard to art, Guyau writes that the solidarity and the sympathy existing among the different parts of the self seem to constitute the first grade or level of aesthetic emotion, while social solidarity and universal sympathy seem to constitute its most elevated and complex form. There is no aesthetic emotion without an object through which one enters into society, attributing to it personality, unity, and life. Just as art is the immediate expression of the free creative rhythm of life itself and has no inner principle save that freely created form, so morality within the social group is the pursuit and generation of harmony and is equally free from arbitrary constrictive rules or from forms of obligation and sanction.

Religion is the highest form of the creative harmony of the human collectivity. In religion it is the creative force of life itself that is worshipped. Here the free nature of this activity is most clearly manifest. Constriction and obligation are terms opposite to religion. The future (Guyau shares the intense faith in the future which so many of his contemporaries—Renan and Taine, for example—exhibit) will see the emergence of a religion in which the true object of worship is recognized as the creative life force itself and the form of which will be harmonious realization of that power in all the forms of human solidarity and sympathy.

The contributions of the German psychologist and philosopher Ludwig Klages (1872–1956) to the philosophy of life were made in the course of a life of intense study and teaching which touched on many fields. They found expression in his chief work, *Der Geist als Widersacher der Seele* [The mind as adversary of the soul], three volumes, 1929–32. The essence of this work is a vitalistic and anti-intellectualistic vision of the world in which the exaltation of the spontaneous creativity of universal life is set in contrast to intellectualism, utilitarianism, technicism, bourgeois culture, and weaker forms of aestheticism.

The more positive reflections of Klages's philosophy are incorporated in a general psychological anthropology. Man's life is compounded of three principal factors: *Leib* (body), *Seele* (soul or *anima*), and *Geist* (spirit or mind). These are three manifestations of the underlying immanent principle of life and stand in diverse relations to it. The body is most directly related to life, for the life-forces flow through it with the least mediation of reflection and ego-formation. Soul is the complex of instinctive appetites, attitudes, and activities which arises within and mediates the body. Within soul there emerges a primitive self, which is farther removed from the direct flow of the life-force than is body but which, at the same time, is capable of activities beyond the range of mere bodily processes. But soul still enjoys the advantages of body because, by its relative proximity to the primitive life-force, it is fixed and ordered in its processes and, hence, not open to deviation and error, to catastrophe. Spirit represents the synthesis of rational activities. It is the seat of the self-conscious subject, the "I." It is capable of a range of activities closed both to soul and body, including that all-important process of self-rectification, which is the basis of progress but which at the same time lays spirit open to error. Error here is not merely logical error; it is a fatal deviation from the direct movement of the life-force. Hence, in every "higher" achievement of progress and culture, dependent upon spirit, man is open also to the risk of error in an ontological, and not merely logical, sense. The basic rhythm of creative life activity consequently involves a circularity of movement through these levels. Man is ever seeking to move forward to the higher reaches of consciousness toward progress and its accompanying risks of thwarting the movement of creative life; at the same time he always seeks to recover direct contact with the primitive life-forces, to refresh himself in their undeviating and inerrant movement.

The techniques for regaining contact with the direct movement of the creative life-force without surrendering the "higher" activities entailed in progress and culture are fundamental to man's life. The most important among these is art. Art is the spiritual form under which the primitive life-force can be present to the "self" in both its native directness and its spiritually available form. Art makes it possible for the self to vibrate in direct conformity with the rhythm of creative life without losing its own identity, without regressing to the level of instinct and unconsciousness. It is, therefore, simultaneously an "exaltation" or sublimation of the primitive life-force and a refreshment from within of the somewhat "precious," fragile, and perilous processes of the higher consciousness. Art is, therefore, the great mediating form of life and the basis of all culture.

Morality also mediates the self and the life-force. The norms of life cannot be mere abstract enactments of reflective reason. They must be rooted in the movement of life itself. They must bring the primitive life-force to consciousness at the level of reflective activity. Hence, they cannot be that purely juridical type of moral enactment and prescription which has so often appeared in western civilization. They must be free, vital, creative norms. To secure these norms the self must return to the wellsprings of vibrant primitive life movement, there to discern the real ends of life and at the same time raise that life-principle to the level of conscious activity and progress.

In addition to this analysis of man's own life processes, Klages elaborated a theory of *character*. The essential note of this theory is that character resides in a certain proportion or ratio of the three constitutive elements which he had distinguished. This is true both in individuals and in collectivities, such as nations. Character in the individual is reflected in all his particular modes of expression down to his handwriting; character in its collective form is reflected in cultures and civilizations with their collective modes of awareness and expression. Klages is concerned with the classification of character types in individuals and groups of individuals as well as with the characterization of cultures. His reflections on this level enjoyed considerable influence and can readily be discerned both in German psychology and in German theories of culture, for example, that of Oswald Spengler. Through his presentation of these concepts, Klages becomes one of the leading figures of that movement which came to be called "neo-romanticism" and which also finds expression in writers such as Leopold Ziegler and Hermann Count Keyserling.

The Spanish thinkers of the much-discussed (and sometimes doubted) "generation of '98" responded with surprising alacrity to the solicitations of the philosophy of life. There can be no doubt but that this philosophy touched a profound need in their own culture, for they had been weighted down with the social and intellectual traditions of centuries, among which the canonized scholastic philosophy, in forms which had been especially cultivated in the Iberian peninsula, carried peculiar authority because of its relationship with Catholic theology. Therefore, this culture, in its moment of reawakening, proved especially receptive to the notions of spontaneous life-force and its endowment of creativity and self-renewal. The "generation of '98" was a generation in revolt against that burden of tradition, against the archaism and isolation which it imposed upon Spanish culture. What it needed most was the sense of life within itself, of creative potentiality.

The figure of Unamuno towers above all the others of this generation. He was in every respect an individualist, a man who impressed upon everything he touched the mark of his own temperament and genius. This is true in a very special way of the expression he gave to the current of thought called the philosophy of life. Miguel Unamuno (1864–1936) spent his mature life as professor of Greek at the University of Salamanca, which he also served as rector. But this status ill-defines his true activity, his role in Spanish culture, or the character and quality of his philosophic thought. His true activity was a cultural and spiritual Socraticism, directed both upon himself and upon his nation and culture. His role in Spanish society and culture was that of awakener and "gadfly," to use the image which Socrates applied to himself; Unamuno sought to "sting" the "great horse" of Spanish society into an awareness of its own spiritual sloth and to compel it to enter the modern world of ideas.

Unamuno, a brilliant writer and an accomplished poet, is the author of many arresting works. His prose places him in the forefront of essayists in the Spanish language. Among his longer and more sustained efforts, two stand out: his *Vida de Don Quijote y Sancho* [Life of Don Quixote and Sancho], 1905, a "commentary" on the chief figures of Cervantes' great work, and his *La agonía del cristianismo* [The agony of Christianity], 1931 (a French version was published in 1925 during Unamuno's period of exile). Unamuno's thought, especially as contributing to the philosophy of life, finds its most comprehensive and finished expression in the work most closely associated with his international fame, *Del sentimiento trágico de la vida en los hombres y los pueblos* [The tragic sentiment of life in men and peoples], 1913, subsequently translated into many languages.

This work opens with a protest against the way classical philosophy, especially the philosophy of the schools, deals with man. That philosophy, through its abstract and universalistic mode of procedure, becomes, in Unamuno's view, the philosophy of Homer's "no man"; it does not touch the pulsating heart of human life and existence, the

individual man of "flesh and bone." His aim is the creation of a philosophy which will have its roots in human existence, in the immediate
pulsating life of the individual and the historically identifiable group,
and which will have its ultimate effect on the same plane, by transforming that existence itself and not by making universal and empty
statements about a "being" and a "life" which no man and no people
have ever experienced in their "flesh and bones." He turns, therefore,
to the examination of life as it actually is in the existing man, the concrete "I" who lives, hungers, learns, agonizes, and, ultimately and
most importantly, *dies.*

How does life reveal itself there, in the burning depths of the self-
consciousness of the existing individual? Following a clue from Spinoza, he finds that life is essentially a *conatus,* an intrinsically limitless
and illimitable *thrust* toward being and existence. He is careful to
point out that this thrust is not toward an abstract "being" or toward
the existence of another but toward the infinite perpetuation and
enrichment of the individual concrete life of the existing subject and
person. It is the thrust toward life everlasting, toward the everlasting
fulfillment of all of the possibilities of concrete existence, which is, in
its very essence, infinite possibility. His is, in this way, one of the most
unqualified exaltations of life to be found in all the literature of the
philosophy of life. Immediately, in the midst of this exaltation, however,
a contradiction arises. It is not an abstract, "logical" contradiction; like
existence itself, it is completely concrete and immediate. That contradiction is *death.* The individual knows, just as surely as he knows the
infinite expansiveness of the life within him, that his own concrete
person must die. Human existence is thus, for Unamuno, enclosed
within this iron parenthesis, the infinite thrust of life and the ineluctable
fatedness of death.

In this context, the *conatus* of life transforms itself into the thirst
for immortality. Man's thirst for immortality is the whole sense and
essense of man. How can he escape the jaws of death? How can he
transcend mortality in response to the divine thrust of life within him?
If he cannot, his tragedy is stark and unrelieved. He is an infinity
enclosed within an horizon of non-being, of death.

At this juncture in Unamuno's thought, God appears. He appears
as the concrete possibility of breaking the enclosing circumference of
death. But he does not appear as a *deus ex machina.* He does not
appear as an external principle which rescues man, as in the old Greek
tragedies some extrahuman force would intervene to resolve an almost
intolerable tension. The God who appears upon the horizon of Unamuno's thought is concrete, existent, and as full of contradiction as
man's own condition. He is the living Christ who came into history,

who lived and died and rose again but whose whole divinity is mystery.

In the Christ, the tragedy and the divine comedy of man's existence are worked out. Since he was man, he bore in his being the contradiction of infinite being and ineluctable death, and by rising again, he broke that concrete contradiction in his concrete existence. The life of Christ—his life, his agony, his death and resurrection—is no *idea;* it is a concrete existence. Therefore, Christ does not mediate human existence like a Platonic idea; he mediates it as confronting mystery and contradiction. The life of Christ contains all the hope and all the despair that man can know, hope in its embrace and despair before its contradiction as deep and as profound as that which reigns within ourselves. Therefore, Unamuno's thought does not reach any logical conclusion. It comes to rest, not in *The Tragic Sense of Life,* but in the long poem which Unamuno addressed to the Christ on the Cross in the moment of death, the poem entitled *El Cristo de Velázquez.* Here the whole inner power of Unamuno's reflection is released in incomparable lines in which he seeks from the lips of the dying God the word which will fulfill the life within man.

José Ortega y Gasset (1883–1955) is in many ways a more finished and accomplished philosopher than Unamuno, though he lacks the intense perceptiveness of the latter. He possesses Pascal's *esprit de finesse* in an exceptional degree. His rich and extensive bibliography has a uniformly high quality, even though much of the work was composed under great tension. To choose one of his writings as most representative of his thought is hardly feasible. Although he never composed a work of great extension, the books comprised of groups of his numberless articles exhibit a remarkable coherency within themselves and an equally remarkable consequence and continuity of thought and insight. Among those which have achieved the widest audience are: *España invertebrada* [Invertebrate Spain], 1921; *La deshumanización del arte e ideas sobre la novela* [The dehumanization of art and ideas on the novel], 1925; and *La rebelión de las masas* [The revolt of the masses], 1930. His strictly philosophical acumen is perhaps best displayed in the less known essay *La idea de principio en Leibniz y la evolución de la teoría deductiva* [The idea of principle in Liebniz and the evolution of deductive theory] (*Obras Completas,* Vol. VIII, 1958).

It has become something of a ritual to say that the thought of Ortega y Gasset can be summed up in a phrase for which he showed considerable predilection: "I am myself and my circumstance." There is indeed truth in these words if they are understood in their complex significance. Others, however, find the living center of his thought in the concept of the *vital reason (razón vital).* Both of these phrases remain rather opaque, however, unless one pierces to the insights which sustain them. These insights link Ortega most intimately with the philosophy of life, of which he must be recognized as one of the most clear-sighted and moderate exponents.

The basic reality for Ortega is life. For him, as for Unamuno, life is not grasped as some universal natural process but as the concrete life of the human individual existent, the life which the individual must live through. His first task is to examine the structure and the dynamics of that life. It is in the context of this examination that the first phrase quoted above takes on meaning, for it describes the structure and dynamics which he discovers. The individual discovers himself immediately as "I," the concentrated center of a life to be lived. But this "I" does not turn the subject which pronounced it back upon himself so as to enclose him within a solipsistic existence; on the contrary, it exhibits immediately a projective structure, which sends him *beyond* himself, though always in quest of himself and of his own reality. This projective is the "circumstance" of which Ortega speaks. He conceives this circumstance, not as something alien that is *given* to the individual, but as something intimately constitutive of him, so much so that it forms part of his definition of himself: the self is the self and its circumstances. This circumstance extends itself forward into a "prospective" or "perspective" which opens before the individual existence as the path of the possibility of his being. This is Ortega's conception of his world: the prospective of possibility which opens before the individual as the path of realization of his life, his *reality*. This world is obviously not the world of nature, a *given* that is already formed and presented to man; it is the world which man achieves and realizes. And in achieving this world, man realizes himself, brings to reality the life that is in him.

Not even the structure of the world as possibility, however, is *given* to man. It remains to be discovered *by* him. The quest for truth is the quest for the unveiling of the possibilities which actually constitute his world. The truth in itself is the actual "unveiling" of this possibility and is the concrete reality of man's *circumstance*. The primary act of man is this unveiling; the self-constitutive act of man is his assumption of his world, his "taking up" of the real possibility that is his. This is a self-creative act in the order of life, because prior to his act that world as possibility is a mere projection; after and through that act, it is living reality, the self in its concreteness.

The uncovering of truth or the assumption of the world is not a spastic or impulsive act for Ortega but an act of *reason*. The very nature of the operation makes clear, however, the notion of "reason" that is involved. It is not, manifestly, the intellect of classical anthropology and psychology. That "intellect" operated in function of an objective order. The reason which unveils the truth to man operates in function of the life within him, in function of his vital preoccupation with the structure and range of his real circumstance. It is, therefore, in Ortega's term, "vital reason," reason functionally related to life. This vital reason does not expend its force in the formation of abstract concepts or images of things; it expends itself in the construction of the true perspective of life: the life of the individual as life-project and the life of mankind as history and culture, within which the prospective of the individual life finds its place.

One of the basic and constitutive elements of the possibility of the individual prospective is the possibility of life with others. This is not an abstract possibility, which may or may not be fulfilled. It is a constitutive possibility which therefore belongs to the truth of the individual life. The realization of this possibility neither diminishes nor transcends the individual; it *fulfills* him, both in the order of his actuality and in that of his responsibility. The social prospectus represents the extension of the range of life itself. Specifically, it is the theater for the realization of possibilities which are rooted in the individual but which transcend his own power of realization. Society is the theater for the realization of historical values, the values of culture, and these values redound to the enrichment of the individual existence.

Ortega exercised a decisive influence in Spanish culture. Every philosopher of stature owes him a direct debt. He has been fortunate in those who have undertaken to continue his work and to maintain the force of his doctrine in current culture. Chief among these is Julián Marías (b. 1914), a very able mind in his own right and the author of numerous authoritative works, particularly the *Introdución a la filosofía* [Introduction to philosophy], 1947, translated into English as *Reason and Life* (Yale, 1956). In this work his master's thought is not only expounded with force and clarity but is developed and extended to a range of problems which Ortega himself had not touched.

Readings

I. BIOLOGICALLY ORIENTED VITALISM AND NEO-VITALISM

Bertalanffy, L. *Problems of Life: An Evaluation of Modern Biological Thought.* New York: Wiley, 1952.

Driesch, Hans. *The History and Theory of Vitalism.* Translated by C. K. Ogden. London: Macmillan, 1914.

Koren, H. *Introduction to the Philosophy of Animate Nature.* St. Louis: B. Herder, 1955.

Lillie, R. S. *General Biology and Philosophy of Organism.* Chicago: Chicago University Press, 1945.

Loeb, J. *The Mechanistic Conception of Life.* Edited by Donald Fleming. Cambridge, Mass.: Belknap Press of Harvard University Press, 1964.

Mitchell, Peter C. *Materialism and Vitalism in Biology.* Herbert Spencer Lecture, 1930. Oxford: Clarendon Press, 1930.

Neal, Herbert V. *Vitalism and Mechanism.* Lancaster, Pa.: Science Press, 1934.

Tansley, A. *Mind and Life: An Essay in Simplification.* London: Allen & Unwin, 1952.

Wheeler, Leonard R. *Vitalism: Its History and Validity.* London: Witherby, 1939.

II. PHILOSOPHY OF LIFE

Barea, A. *Unamuno.* Cambridge, England: Bowes & Bowes, 1952.

Bourke, Vernon. *Will in Western Thought.* New York: Sheed & Ward, 1964.

Ducasse, C. J. *Nature, Mind and Death.* LaSalle, Ill.: Open Court, 1951.

Ferrater Mora, J. *Ortega y Gasset: An Outline of His Philosophy.* New Haven: Yale University Press, 1963.

Huertas-Jourda, J. *The Existentialism of Unamuno.* Gainsville, Fla.: University of Florida Press, 1963.

Lacy, Allen. *Miguel de Unamuno: The Rhetoric of Existence.* The Hague, Paris: Mouton, 1967.

Read, Herbert. "High Noon and Darkest Night: Some Reflections on Ortega y Gasset's Philosophy of Art." *Eranos-Jahrbuch,* XXXIII (1964), 51–69.

Rudd, M. T. *The Lone Heretic: A Biography of Miguel de Unamuno y Jugo.* Austin: University of Texas Press, 1963.

Sanchez Villasenor, J. *Ortega y Gasset: Existentialist.* Translated by J. Small. Chicago: H. Regnery, 1949.

Sinnott, Edmund W. *The Bridge of Life: From Matter to Spirit.* New York: Simon & Schuster, 1966.

Valdés, M. *Death in the Literature of Unamuno.* Urbana, Ill.: University of Illinois Press, 1964.

CHAPTER II

Historicism

Introduction

The term *historicism* has taken on such varied and sometimes inconsistent associations in ordinary usage that clarification of its meaning in the context of philosophy becomes immediately necessary. A precise, and at the same time inclusive, definition of the term as it possesses specifically philosophical meaning may be formulated as follows: Historicism is the employment of historical categories in the analysis, interpretation, and explanation of reality, in the conviction that these categories alone are adequate to that end.

This definition immediately raises the question of what is meant by a historical category? This question is more difficult, but it may reasonably be answered: A historical category is a principle of being and of discourse, the elements of which are becoming, time, consciousness, ideality, and finality. Of these, the most basic is becoming, while all the others inhere in it or appear as qualifications of it. What is historical is that which becomes; but becomes in a certain way, i.e., through a temporal process which is impregnated with consciousness. This consciousness in time is the residence of an ideality, an order of ideas, which defines prospectives.

The notion of a historical category may be illustrated by the concept of progress (without subscribing to the *validity* of this concept). In the notion of progress all the elements of a historical category seem to be present: Progress involves becoming, but a becoming which moves toward ideal ends, consciously apprehended and valued, through a temporal process which is immanent in consciousness. These characteristics would seem to distinguish the historical category clearly from other categories which share some of the same elements. For example, it distinguishes historical change and process from evolutionary process, which lacks the elements of consciousness, ideality, and finality; evolution remains a natural category. Even more clearly, it distinguishes historical process from all natural processes of change

24

which are capable of mechanistic explanation. To these other categories of explanation, historical categories stand in various relations. But historicism, as a philosophical position and method, appears only when the historical category, as defined above, is taken as ultimate and other categories are related to it in some subordinate manner.

Western philosophy may be said to be overwhelmingly naturalistic in the categories of analysis, interpretation, and explanation with which it has chosed to approach reality. For this reason, philosophical historicism must be accounted a latecomer in the history of philosophy. Perhaps the most painstaking account of philosophical historicism is the two-volume work of Friedrich Meinecke *Die Entstehung des Historicismus* [The origin of historicism], 1936, though the similar investigations of Wilhelm Dilthey and Ernst Cassirer also possess great importance. (Meinecke and Dilthey also appear as major figures in the speculative development of historicism.) Meinecke has found first evidences of the historicist attitude in the Enlightenment, especially in the more independent thinkers of that period; Voltaire, Herder, the champions of *Sturm und Drang*, Lessing, and finally Goethe. Of these thinkers, Herder, in his chief work, *Ideen zue Philosophie der Geschichte der Menschheit* [Ideas for a philosophy of the history of mankind], comes closest to a truly historicist attitude, for he tries to make the historical categories ultimate; his actual development of these categories retains strong naturalistic elements, however, as Kant acutely points out.

The period of the first florescence of philosophical historicism is romanticism. All of the major figures of romantic philosophy exhibit elements of the historicist attitude in philosophy; the formation and employment of historical categories is central to their speculative efforts, although none of these thinkers asserted the ultimate character of these categories without conditions and reservations. Thus, Fichte may be said to be the first creator of historical, if not historicist, philosophy. The articulation of historical categories reaches a certain level of refinement in his thought, and a conscious and perceptive effort to employ them is maintained. Schelling is even more decisive in the development of such categories, especially in his important work *System des transzendentalen Idealismus* [System of transcendental idealism], where he treats sensation, intuition, reflection, and will as ideal temporal moments in the movement toward absolute consciousness. Finally, the historicist attitude in romanticism reaches its most finished expression in Hegel. The historical categories are not only developed with great clarity and precision, but their ultimate character is also affirmed. All of these positions may, within this perspective, be considered forms of proto-historicism, and the last of such proto-forms would correctly be recognized in historical materialism.

The term *historicism,* however, is reserved within the history of philosophy for that manifestation of the historicist attitude which appeared, principally in Germany, in the second half of the nineteenth century and the first decades of the twentieth. Its chief representatives are Wilhelm Dilthey, Georg Simmel, Friedrich Meinecke, Max Weber, and Oswald Spengler. In England it finds a related figure in Arnold Toynbee, while in Italy Benedetto Croce and Giovanni Gentile are sometimes associated with this current of thought. Since this last association is dubious, Croce and Gentile are treated separately in the present volume (Part II, Chapter II).

Historicism is radical in the way it sustains the basic historicist thesis; that is, in this context the historical categories are truly ultimate categories for the description, explanation, and interpretation of reality. On the other hand, it is less holistic and absolutistic than earlier forms of historicism as represented by Hegel's philosophy of history or historical materialism. Both of these had imagined that history was impregnated with a univocal meaning; that it therefore possessed a single, immanent unity throughout its course, leading to the realization of an absolute value; and that, with the realization of this value, history would be completed and come to a close.

With respect to this point of view, the newer current of historicism has been called *relativistic,* but this term must be employed with the utmost caution and should perhaps be abandoned completely. It is closer to the truth to say that: 1) history is *pluralistic* in its value potentials, i.e., it is the theater for the possible realization of many values; 2) the process of history is *open-ended,* i.e., it is not moving toward some definite period of realization which would close history, but is an infinite process within which value systems are both realized and dissolved; and 3) since history does not point toward the realization of a single absolute value, the lines of historical development may be distinguished both pluralistically and in terms of succession, e.g., of epochs. To designate this rather complex attitude by a blanket term like *relativism* is obviously obscurantist. Each of the representative figures of historicism develop this complex of insights in a distinctive manner and, as a consequence, the true configuration of historicism can be appreciated only by the examination of the thought of each of them in turn.

A. *Wilhelm Dilthey* (1833–1911)

Dilthey was trained in philosophy and came eventually to occupy the chair of Lotze in this discipline at the University of Berlin; he was a man of vast culture, attracted to the study of art, manners, society, and ideas. His philosophical activity took on an original quality when he turned his speculative talents to the field of culture and sought to reach philosophical principles governing culture as the existential form of man's individual and collective life. Especially important are his early works on the German poets and historians of the romantic period and his essays on Prussian history and the history of anthropological ideas during the fifteenth and sixteenth centuries.

This original speculative enterprise first appeared in the form of a "critique of historical reason" on the model of Kant's "critique of pure reason." (It should be noted, however, that Kant's "critique of judgment" is a critique of his own treatment of "pure reason" and anticipates in some respects the problems which become central for Dilthey.) His first treatment of this project was the essay which he submitted for his admission into the teaching profession, *Versuch einer Analyse der moralischen Bewusstseins* [An essay in the analysis of the moral consciousness] (in Wilhelm Dilthey, *Gesammelte Schriften*, 14 vols. [Stuttgart: Teubner, 1913–66], VI, 1–55). Opposing Kant's ethical formalism, he found the principle of ethicalness in the concrete consent of conscience, thus clarifying the difference in the historical forms which ethical judgments could assume. The project is carried forward in the intermediate essay *Uber das Studium der Geschichte der Wissenschaft vom Menschen, der Gesellschaft und dem Staat* [On the study of the history of the science of man, society, and the state], 1875 (*Gesammelte Schriften*, V, 31–73). The definitive work for the formulation of his historicism is *Einleitung in die Geisteswissenschaften* [Introduction to the sciences of mind] 1883 (*Gesammelte Schriften*, I, 3–429), which has been translated into many languages. The chief propositions of this historicism or science of the mind may be summarized in the following manner.

Philosophy must begin with history and not with "nature." The reason adduced for this proposition is strikingly similar to Vico's position: nature can be studied only "from without" and hence cannot really be known; the human socio-historical world, as the creation of the human spirit, can be known from within, and through it the human spirit knows itself. The historical science of the human mind cannot have an *aprioristic* or metaphysical basis; it must be based on concrete experience of the individual and of the human collectivity. The object of this science is not an "external object" but the "internal" reality immediately *lived through* by the human spirit. For this reason, Dilthey placed great emphasis on *psychology*, conceived neither as an experimental and objectifying science in which the human spirit and its expressions would be turned into quasi-natural objects nor as a formal science concerned only with the abstract forms of human experience, but as a *Realpsychologie,* a science of the concrete content of historical *lived* experience.

In this psychology, a crucial question for Dilthey was the relation between the lived experience of the individual and that realized collectively in history. He discovers a *structural connection* which relates them vitally. The sciences of spirit must follow simultaneously the individual and the collective patterns. Thus, Dilthey found great importance both in biography and in the history of ideas in cultural periods, exemplified in his study of the idea of man in the Renaissance. In a controversy with Windelband he denied the latter's distinction between "idiographic" and "nomothetic" sciences and held that the sciences of spirit must employ a special hermeneutic and critical technique directed upon the historical expressions of the human spirit (art, social institutions, *mores,* sciences and disciplines, philosophies, *Weltanschauungen*). Thus, for him, historical knowledge becomes the description, *ab interno,* of the way in which the human spirit brings to fruition over a temporal span the possibilities inherent in it. The bearer of this historical-temporal process is society, but the individual also plays an important, frequently paradigmatic role (cf. his *Life of Schleiermacher* [*Leben Schleiermachers, Gesammelte Schriften,* XIV, pts. 1 and 2] which illustrates this principle).

Since this is the case, the basic philosophical problem becomes the elaboration of the historical categories, among which he enumerates temporality, historicity, meaning, and development. These categories are not *a priori* forms; rather, they are rooted in life itself and express the structural forms of life in its temporal continuity. Conscious of the danger of "relativism" in his position, Dilthey makes especially clear that it is the continuity of these forms, in and through patterns of cultural change in various epochs, that constitutes the basic structure of history and of the self-knowledge of the human spirit.

The last task which Dilthey envisages for the science of the human mind as the supreme philosophical discipline is a "philosophy of philosophy." (This term was destined to have considerable historical fortune and to gain in significance and use.) This discipline would concern itself with the inner principle of the formation of *Weltanschauungen* or world-intuitions. Such structures were not, for Dilthey, merely conceptual structures; they were concrete cultural complexes, expressed and lived out. To understand their coming-to-be and the manner in which they acquire concrete meaning is the task of "philosophy of philosophy." In this discipline, the supreme trilogy of moments embraces experience, expression, and comprehension.

With the passage of time and the increasing study given to this movement in the history of philosophy, Dilthey has, through his great insight, cultural preparation, and speculative power, emerged as the most significant representative of historicism.

B. *Georg Simmel* (1858–1918)

Simmel is known primarily for his contributions to sociology. In his concern with sociological problems he was led to devote considerable reflection to the problem of history. With Dilthey, he perceived that these problems could not be addressed in the same manner as problems in natural science and the philosophy of nature but demanded a method corresponding to their own intimately historical character. His chief contribution to the literature of historicism is his *Die Probleme der Geschichtsphilosophie* [The problem of the philosophy of history], 1892. Elements of interest in this same context can also be found in *Lebensanschauung* [The intuition of life], written in 1918, near the end of his life.

Simmel's early philosophical formation had been influenced by neo-criticism or neo-Kantianism. Consequently, his general philosophical reflections tended to emphasize the place and efficacy of *a priori principles*. Approaching the problem of history and its method, however, he reveals an altogether different tendency. He does initially state the problem of history in terms reminiscent of Kant, setting out to determine first the possibility of history and historical knowledge. As his views progress, however, he not only rejects the *a priori* in the historical and historiographical order but actually goes far beyond Dilthey in the direction of historical "relativism." While Dilthey denied that there could be any *a priori* principles of historical knowledge, nevertheless, he did stress the importance of the continuity of historical forms. By contrast, Simmel seems to render even these forms relative. According to him, the historian does not address reality as an order of objects already formed and established, with an independent character. His concern must be with life as it has been lived in its immediacy. He must seek to produce or evoke a "theoretical image" of the experience. This image is by no means a copy of that reality; it is, rather, an interpretration of it, a rendering of its *meaning*. The problem then is that of the principles which govern the formation of this image.

One might have expected Simmel to assert at this point that these principles, at least, are *a priori*. In fact, some commentators believe that he does this. However, they would seem to be deceived by his language. He does indeed call the principles which govern the formation of the historical image the *a priori* of historical science; but it is clear from this passage (*Die Probleme,* p. 33) that he is simply constructing an analogy with Kant's principles. His actual account

maintains their empirical character. Since his principles are psychological, it is psychology which functions in historical science like the
a priori. The historical categories which enter into the constitution of
the historical image are themselves subject to variation. Immersed as
they are in history, they are bound to alter with history. It follows that
history is interpreted according to a variety of categories and hence is
represented in a variety of images. This difference is both successive,
one interpretation following another in the process of history and
dialectical, in the sense that, in any period, history may be interpreted
from a number of different points of view, all of which may have a
certain empirical basis in historical process. Therefore, Simmel denies
that there can be any laws of historical process.

Similarly, he rejects the view, so dear to the philosophy of history,
that history can be dealt with *as a whole* and that its total meaning can
be determined in some univocal sense. More important for his own
concern with sociology is the fact that these reflections on history make
it clear that the nature or meaning of society as a whole cannot be
determined. The aim of sociology must be the more modest one of
determining the forms of association in which the relations between
individuals crystallize. This concern with forms of association differentiates sociology from the social sciences, which are concerned with the
content of social phenomena. His book on the problem of the philosophy of history was completely reworked by Simmel and published as
Vom Wesen des historischen Verstehens [On the essence of historical
understanding] in 1918. The position assumed is not substantially
altered.

The theme of *Lebensanschauung* links Simmel more closely with
that current which has been called the "philosophy of life" than with
historicism; yet it does contain some insights which bear upon the
present question. Chief among them is his insight concerning the continuity of life through historical process. Life proceeds through history
by positing itself in limited forms, only to transcend these and to posit
itself in wider and profounder forms, thus establishing a process of
continuity and progressive self-enrichment. Through this process it
reveals itself as "more-than-life." History is concerned with both of
these aspects: with the successive self-transcending forms of history
and with the continuity of life which reveals itself in and through this
succession. Thus, Simmel's thought shows an affinity between these
two currents, the philosophy of life and historicism.

C. *Max Weber* (1864–1920)

Weber was primarily a sociologist, and perhaps his work belongs
more properly to the history of that discipline. But he also extends the

insights of historicism into the area of sociology and social ethics and, in doing so, reveals many aspects of that philosophical position as yet unsuspected by its original contributors. Since it is axiomatic that a philosophical position is of interest not only in its internal articulation but also in its influence on the other areas of culture and inquiry, his inclusion here seems not only justified but necessary. Weber's work takes three fundamental directions, which, while not always closely related to each other, are expressive of the various interests which drew him: political, sociological, and methodological. Only the writings in the last area are of concern here, for in them the relation to historicism becomes most directly apparent.

For placing in relief both his positive and negative relations to historicism, the most informative of Weber's works is *Kritische Studien auf dem Gebiet der kulturwissenschaftlichen Logik* [Critical studies on the logic of the sciences of culture] 1906, in *Gesammelte Aufsätze zur Wissenschaftslehre* (Tübingen, 1951, pp. 215–290). Weber agrees with historicism in its recognition that the object of the historical and social disciplines or sciences is *individual* in character. The point of departure for the social sciences is the real, and hence individual, form of social life in its relation to other forms and in its manner of proceeding from other social states of culture. He immediately introduces certain qualifications as to the nature of this individuality. This individuality does not belong to the object in itself; it is, rather, the result of the *individualizing choice* or selection which lies at the root of historical and social inquiry. The investigator selects his object from among a large number of other possible objects of investigation because he considers that one meaningful and those others relatively insignificant.

But what is it that gives *meaning* to an object? On this point Weber seems to adopt the position of Rickert that the historical character of an object resides in its relationship to a value; it is the value which gives meaning to the object. But again a question arises: Is this value something inherent in the object, for example, the manner in which it embodies a transcendent value? Not for Weber. Value, like individuality and objectivity, is assigned to the object by the investigator. Hence, the constitutive relativity of criteria and the inevitable unilateralism of all historical investigations. In Weber's view, every discipline constitutes its object in this way; it is not the objective relations prevailing among things or events which give them interest, but the conceptual relations in the problems perceived by the investigator. While reality is not problematic in structure, the scientific study of reality is, and objects achieve interest, meaning, and relevance in relation to that structure.

For these reasons, knowledge of the historical-cultural world is always knowledge from a certain point of view. The investigator stands at the center of such knowledge and is the determinant of its form, scope, and quality. Without the ideas of value that are proper to the investigator, there would be no principle for the choice of material and no meaningful knowledge of historical-social reality in its concrete and individual character. It is the investigator's faith in his values which gives direction to his inquiry. The investigator selects objects and assigns the relation to value which gives them meaning. Does this mean then that all historical-social research and investigation is hopelessly relative to this subjective factor, the investigator? This is not Weber's conclusion. The process is subjective, but the *results* are not. In the case of significant research, the conclusions will prove to be objectively true for all competent judges, all those who are seeking the truth.

What then is the basis of this objectivity? In replying to this question, Weber seems to desert the position of historicism and take up one which historicism would seem to have banished: causality. This desertion is only apparent; what actually takes place in Weber's thought is a modification of another concept of historicism, namely, *understanding* of the historical-social object. For historicism, this understanding had been intuitive, immediate, even emotive. This constituted, in Weber's view, a serious weakness in that position. He accepts the notion of understanding as the form of knowledge proper to historical studies, but he insists that this understanding is the result of a process of interpretation of the object which involves causal explanation. But the historical-social sciences employ the causal procedure in a way quite different from that in which it is employed in the sciences of nature. According to Weber, the latter proceed by subordinating facts as examples to concepts of species and to formulae. The historical-social sciences proceed by choosing, among the unlimited range of possibly relevant factors which might qualify as historical objects, a finite or limited number of such factors which constitute a specific or limited field of research. This choice is also founded on the values which originally direct the research. Among the elements thus chosen and organized into a casually related series, historical science proceeds to look for a system of relations which can be verified and controlled. This system of relations yields the basis for *objective possibility*, which is, for Weber, the ultimate category of historical explanation.

Connected closely with the notion of objective possibility is Weber's theory of *ideal types*. As concrete examples of *ideal types* he offers *Christianity* and *capitalism*, the concepts of *church* and *state*, and the constitutive concept of political economy. The essential characteristic of these ideal types is that they are never found in reality in their ideal purity. Nevertheless, they are, in origin, empirical concepts which have achieved, through theoretical exploration, a transcendence of the very empirical basis upon which they have been formed. From the point of view of this ideal transcendence, they become means of understanding that empirical reality, not in its purely empirical character, but in its *possibility*. Thus, the ideal type "capitalism" makes it possible for us to understand, on ideal grounds, how historical capitalism could come to be; and similarly for Christianity, the state, etc. Through the construction of ideal types, which are schema of objective possibility, historical science escapes from the threat of subjectivity and becomes at once a science of objectivity and of comprehension.

Weber finds this idea of historical social-science best realized in sociology. Sociology rests upon the objective dimension of the historical and spiritual world. Thus, in his scheme it takes the place held by psychology in the thought of Dilthey. In this objective dimension of historical-spiritual life, sociology seeks the specific *attitudes* which characterize human action. These *attitudes* would seem to be supreme examples of ideal types, far wider in scope than the examples adduced earlier by Weber. Weber distinguishes four such attitudes: the rational attitude with respect to ends to be achieved, the rational attitude with respect to values, the affective attitude and, finally, the traditional attitude. These attitudes constitute conceptually pure types of possible human action and reaction. Though never found in their pure form in empirical reality, they are empirically grounded and provide the interpretative schemes within which empirical reality of the historical-social order can be cast.

The full appreciation of Weber cannot, of course, be based simply on these methodological reflections. One must turn to his other works such as his famous *Die protestantische Ethik und der Geist der Kapitalismus (The Protestant Ethic and Spirit of Capitalism)* in *Gesammelte Aufsätze zur Religionssoziologie* (Tübingen, 1947, pp. 17–206). His methodological reflections nevertheless possess considerable intrinsic interest, since they place him in the line of philosophical historicism and also exemplify philosophical reflections on its problems from the viewpoint of one engaged in concrete research in the area of history and culture.

D. *Ernst Troeltsch* (1865–1923)

The speculative path of Ernst Troeltsch might be described as passing from transcendence to historicism, then back to transcendence by way of the dissolution or transformation of historicism from within. His entire career was conducted, not as a purely speculative venture, but in function of his activity as a historian of religion. He was seeking the inner *rationale* both of his work as a historian and of the specific historical phenomenon with which he was concerned: Christianity. The chief documents of this career are *Die Absolutheit des Christentums und die Religionsgeschichte* [The absolute character of Christianity and the history of religion], 1901; *Der Historismus und seine Probleme* [Historicism and its problem], 1922, the first part of a projected work touching on the logic of the history of philosophy; and *Der Historismus und seine Überwindung* [Historicism and its transcendence], 1924, comprising five lectures which were never delivered. We may follow his thought through the three stages indicated above.

As a historian of Christianity, Troeltsch is confronted by an ineluctable dilemma which provides the context of all his reflection. On the one hand, he saw the claim of Christianity to be a supernatural revelation, an intervention from above into history which hence claims to be, in its essence, transhistorical. On the other hand, there was the task of writing the history of this reality, which, despite its alleged suprahistorical character, appears in history. This is the problem which preoccupies him in *The Absolute Character of Christianity and the History of Religion*. The termination of this phase of his thought may be stated as follows: Troeltsch rejected the Christian claim as presented by traditional supernaturalistic thought, the view of Christianity as a supernatural, and thus suprahistorical, event penetrating into history but having no organic connections with the processes of history. He recognized that in this sense no history of Christianity was really possible. Nevertheless, he did not abandon the insight into Christianity as *an absolute value in history*. Thus was born his essential speculative problem, which was at the same time his essential practical problem as a historian: How can historical process be the locus, the vehicle, the bearer of absolute value?

The second phase of his career is characterized by an adherence (never absolute or uncritical) to historicism. In this phase he recognizes the totally historical character of every reality of culture and of every value; art, law, the state, religion—all are completely immanent in history. He accepts, at this point, the view attributed to Dilthey that the fundamental historical category is individual totality, totality as individual. Even more, the historical reality of that individual lies in the *value* which it *realizes* in itself in a unique and unrepeatable manner. It is not the brute *givenness* of the individual historical reality, i.e., the Roman empire, etc., which validates it before the historian. It is instead the fact that this individual is the locus of the realization of a value in a unique manner. This aspect of historical reality opens the path to the transcendence of historicism, i.e., to the reply to his initial question, how can history be the vehicle of absolute and transcendent value?

In his third and final phase Troeltsch seeks to establish his own thesis (or synthesis): The absoluteness of value and the relativity of all historical reality *coincide* perfectly. In other words, the values in history (even in their relative forms) establish the presence of absolute value in history. He supports his conclusion by this reasoning: The sole historical category is individual totality. But the individual totality is established by the fact that within it a value is realized in a unique and nonrepeatable manner. This value has both its relative and its absolute aspect. It is relative in the sense that it is wholly realized in this individual; it is present in history only in and through the reality of this individual totality. Thus, the value of religion is realized wholly in the historical reality of a specific religion, Christianity. But is the value which is thus realized itself something relative? On the contrary, for, if this were to be held, the value of the unique, historical individual would be destroyed. Its whole value lies in the fact that in it an absolute value is realized in time. Were this not the case, the uniqueness of historical reality would vanish. Thus it is in the heart of historical reality, the unique individual totality, that the pure relativism of historicism is overcome. Here also, the task of the historian is made clear. He is seeking the absolute value which is realized in the relative historical form.

E. *Oswald Spengler* (1880–1936)

The most celebrated document of historicism is, without doubt, Spengler's two-volume *Der Untergang des Abendlandes (The Decline of the West)*, 1918–22, which bore the significant subtitle *Sketch of a Morphology of World History*. The controversy which these two volumes occasioned can barely be imagined today, though they have lost little of their engaging character.

Spengler's theory is the outstanding example of *naturalistic* historicism. Although he opens his work with a distinction between the *natural* and the *organic* orders, it is clear that he is distinguishing between two orders within nature, the *mechanical* and the *organic*. These constitute two different orders of objects and invite two different methods of investigation. The former is the realm of *what has already come to be*, the second of *becoming* or of *life*. The former can be comprehended through a mechanistic logic which concerns itself with causal necessity, exhibiting itself in universal laws which, in turn, can be mathematically expressed; the latter is governed by an *organic necessity* which looks not to the universal and uniform but to the singular, that which is unique and cannot be repeated. With the other historicists, Spengler holds that the latter realm can be penetrated only through "lived" experience, intuitively, immediately. Nevertheless, it is clear that he is dealing with two orders of nature and two orders of necessity, for even in the organic realm he seeks the objective, necessary laws or patterns and not the freedom of movement of spirit. The central and controlling image of his work is the biological organism. The unit of history, the *culture,* is for him an organism. He seeks to study its morphology. Since he distinguishes a plurality of cultures, it is a *comparative morphology* of cultures that he seeks.

Culture, Spengler believes, is not a universal fact of human history; on the contrary, it is something rare and magnificent. In the entire span of history only eight *cultures* can be distinguished: the Babylonian, the Egyptian, the Indian, the Chinese, the Graeco-Roman (which he calls "Apollonian"), the Arab (which he calls "magical"), the western European (which he calls "Faustian"), and finally the Mayan of Central America. History, properly speaking, concerns these cultures and these alone; all that exists outside of them in the human order is "historyless" (*geschichtslos*), without historical significance. Spengler is concerned, in the first place, with the internal form of each of these cultures and, secondly, with the relations possible between them.

Treating each culture as a living organism, Spengler affirms that, like every living organism, a culture is born, follows an inexorable pattern of inward growth and decline and, *literally,* dies. He uses two analogies to describe this inner life-movement of the culture: the seasons of the year and the ages of man. In its life process, each culture realizes all of the possibilities which it has within itself. Having realized these, it moves inexorably toward decline and death. He defines the final stages of a culture, as *civilization.* Civilization may be compared to that final and galvanic heightening of the vital processes which inevitably precedes and heralds death. It consists in a super-refined expression of all of the possibilities within the culture, of which only the superior individuals within the culture are capable. Like the heightened flush on the cheeks of the moribund, it is the unmistakable harbinger of the end of the culture.

Spengler considers each culture a monad; it is a unique reality entirely enclosed within itself. At the center of each culture stand the ideals, values, and forces which compose it. These together form the inner life-system of the culture. As a life-principle, this system has absolute value within the culture but no meaning or value outside of it. Each culture has its own proper metaphysics, its art, science, and morality. There is no universally valid metaphysics, morality, art, or science, but the one cultivated within each culture is absolutely necessary and meaningful for that culture. These do not constitute specific realizations, within different cultures, of transcendent values; they are completely immanent to the respective culture. There is Faustian and Apollonian truth, but no *Truth;* there is Faustian and Apollonian beauty, but no absolute *Beauty.* Within the culture, there is no real possibility for choice; all is fixed by the necessity according to which its possibilities are realized, exhausted, and extinguished. Spengler calls this necessity *destiny.*

Though these cultures are monads, each enclosed within itself, they, like the monads, have "windows;" i.e., certain relations are possible between them. None of these relations are direct; according to Spengler all are analogical. Two kinds of relations would seem to be important. The first is suggested by the fact that Spengler can speak of an art, a science, a philosophy, etc., proper to each. To the degree that he can speak of these completely distinct manifestations under a single title, that title forms one basis for a relation of comparison and contrast between them. Spengler would admit this grudgingly or not at all. He would insist that a pure nominalism is involved here; the sameness of name implies no sameness in the thing designated. Like all nominalisms, however, his reveals certain flaws. The fact that he employs the terms in this dialectical and comparative manner points to the transcendent order of their significance. The second point of contact between the monadic cultures is Spengler's concept of "contemporaneity." This is based on the fact that every culture traverses the same path of birth, growth, florescence, and decay, each in its own unique way. Though entirely disparate in absolute time (calendar time), the moments of the cultures can be correlated with one another. Thus, Spengler says that Plato and Aristotle are the "contemporaries" of Kant and Goethe, for they represent corresponding moments in the internal development of two different cultures, the Graeco-Roman (Apollonian) and the western (Faustian).

Spengler comes finally to the theme announced in his title. Why does he speak of the "decline" of the West? It is because, when he turns his diagnostic powers on the present and actual condition of the West, he finds that it is now in that moment in the history of cultures which he has called "civilization." The present age of the Faustian culture shows all the earmarks of this stage. Its life has taken on the heightened flush of the moribund. For that reason Spengler predicts its imminent and inevitable extinction. This leads him to a point of prophecy: What will succeed the culture of the West? He has no methodological bases for such prediction since every culture has an absolute beginning; however, he discerns the emergent form of a new culture in the "heartland" of the Eurasian landmass, which may eventually prove to be Russian culture.

F.   *Friedrich Meinecke* (1862–1954)

Meinecke was a historian of modern Germany. In this field he continued the tradition of Ranke and Troeltsch. He came to a philosophical consideration of history and the problems of historiographic method through his effort to master not only the techniques but the inner principles of his discipline. Even in his concrete historical works, the strain of philosophical reflection is already present. For example, he bases his interpretation of modern German history on the realization within it of the synthesis of the principles of *Kratos* and *Ethos,* power and spiritual values. His philosophical perceptiveness within the process of history undoubtedly led to the selection of the theme of his most important historical work, *Die Idee der Staatsräson in der neueren Geschichte* [The idea of reason of state in modern history], 1924. The works in which his ideas about historicism and the ontology and methodology of history are expounded are *Die Entstehung des Historismus* [The origin of historicism] (2 vols.), 1936, *Vom geschichtlichen Sinn und vom Sinn der Geschichte* [On historical meaning and the meaning of history], 1939, and *Zur Theorie und Philosophie der Geschichte* [On the theory and philosophy of history], 1965.

Being a historian, Meinecke naturally approaches the phenomenon of historicism in a historical manner; his purpose, however, is philosophical. In the opening pages of *Die Idee der Staatsräson* he had already laid the ground for his own proper interpretation of historicism. The polarity between power and ethicalness, or energy and spiritual value, delineated there is given a truly philosophical from in *Die Entstehung des Historismus.* This form is the contrast or polarity between values and history. Meinecke sees the beginnings of historicism in the dissolution of the tradition of natural law. This philosophy was the last in the order of historical values to conceive human reason itself as eternal and atemporal. The rise of historicism involved the temporalizing of human reason itself, its immersion in history. Human reason became a historical principle which assumes various aspects in various historical periods. As a consequence, the process of valorization in history is similarly relativized. The transcendent values represented by the eternal and atemporal reason of natural law and classical philosophy are, like that reason, immersed in history and its flux.

Meinecke doubts the validity of this conclusion. Is it true that values are rendered relative by being immersed in history, by becoming the historical objects of a historical reason? He does not think so. Following Goethe, he comes to a conclusion that is quite opposite, namely, that temporalization itself involves relation to the eternal and the infinite. To develop this thesis he has recourse to the dialectic (such an intimate factor in German romanticism) between finite and infinite. The merit of romanticism, he holds (in contrast to the abstract rationalism of the Enlightenment), was precisely the fact that it placed finite and infinite in a dialectical and polar relation, dissolving that abstract, exclusive antithesis which separated them in the Enlightenment. The essence of this dialectic is the perception of the finite as the vehicle of the infinite and of the abstractness of the infinite as outside the concretizing situation of the temporal and historical moment. Values in history, though realized according to conditions of time and finitude, are always transcendent and absolute values. There exists between these terms a constant tension which can never be finally resolved either by the temporalization of the absolute or by the dissolution of the temporal in the eternal and absolute. This creative tension yields the very reality of history. Meinecke directs the attention of the historian toward this precise moment of polar tension, the prototype of which he had already perceived in his intuition of the German spirit as the synthesis of power and spirituality, *Kratos* and *Ethos*.

G. *Arnold Toynbee* (b. 1889)

Toynbee's monumental work *A Study of History,* twelve volumes (1934–1961), is probably unique in the English language. It is the only work of this character which can be placed on an equal footing with similar efforts on the Continent. In its form and temper it takes the mind back immediately to the work of Spengler. But Toynbee is no imitator of Spengler; he has both points of affinity and points of polemical difference with Spengler, which deepen to principles of interpretation. The main point of affinity is the common assumption that the proper object of historical study and investigation is the unit of historical reality, the *civilization.* They are also in agreement on the formal object of this type of inquiry: the formation of a morphology of culture, the study of the laws of its initiation, growth, and decline. Toynbee is critical, however, of what he considers Spengler's *apriorism* and proposes instead to conduct this study on empirical (i.e., documentary) grounds. This difference in method leads to an important difference in the very conception of the unit of investigation, the civilization. While Toynbee may employ the organic metaphor, he understands it much more loosely than does Spengler. The civilization is not a totally determined unity as it is for Spengler; rather, for Toynbee, it is a vast complex of more or less contingent and free relations between individuals and inferior collectivities in which the binding cords are systems of communication and the impulsive and propulsive principle is ultimately man's initiative action.

These affinities and differences are clearly reflected in the positive development of Toynbee's ideas. The insight that civilization has its origin in the initiative action of men leads him to consider the problem of origins seriously. He criticizes theories which would subject such beginnings or initiations to rigorous deterministic principles, such as environmentalism, whether physical or sociological, or theories of race, reminiscent of Gobineau. Instead, as an adequate, or at least a working, conception of the initiative process of civilization, he proposes *challenge and response.* It is the environment which provides the challenge to the human group, and the nature of the result will always reflect this challenge. But the kind of response with which men will react to this environmental challenge is not subject to rigid prediction, although some generalization upon it is possible when sufficient empirical evidence can be adduced. A civilization will arise when the response given is effective, when a balance is achieved between the environment and the free or nondeterminable response. Thus, a civilization is a creation of freedom, but not of unlimited freedom; rather of freedom responding to the challenge of an environment, which challenge gives limits and context to freedom and is the ground of its effectiveness.

It would be incorrect to compare the challenge of which Toynbee speaks to a *problem,* as some historians and critics have done, or the civilization to a *solution* of that problem. The solution of a problem is always commensurate to the structure of the problem. But the response of which Toynbee speaks is creative and incommensurate with the challenge; it creates values which transcend the entire process. Therefore, he would not hold that the values created within one civilization are restricted in meaning and value to that civilization. He finds firm support for all of these affirmations in the cultural experience of the West. Since civilizations are unities but not closed systems, relations between them are possible and may be empirically determined and classified. Toynbee emphasizes such intercultural processes as imitation, affiliation, and apparentation.

While Toynbee holds to the notion of a life-process within the civilization, involving it in beginning, growth, and decline, he holds this thesis in a much more flexible manner than Spengler had. Since the civilization has its life principle in a free and creative, though finite, response to challenge, it also possesses within its resources the power of self-correction, recuperation, etc., which make its life-pattern flexible. The internal process of decline can be arrested, and external threats can be creatively met and conquered. Spengler's notion of destiny has no counterpart in Toynbee, its place is taken by a concept of creative, though limited, freedom of action.

The detailed analyses which Toynbee presents as illustrations and support of his theses need not concern us, but it should be noted that they are amazingly rich and perceptive throughout the extended volumes of his work. Especially perceptive is his treatment of classical civilization, from the study of which he approached the entire project of his work. It is also notable that he assigns a privileged place to Christianity as a bearer of civilization, for he finds in the Christian view of man that regard for creative freedom which is the principle of his own construction and interpretation.

Readings

Books

Croce, Benedetto. *History as the Story of Liberty*. London: Allen & Unwin, 1941.

Dilthey, Wilhelm. *Pattern and Meaning in History: Thoughts on History and Society*. New York: Harper & Row, Harper Torchbooks, 1962.

Geyl, P., Sorokin, P., and Toynbee, A. *Pattern of the Past: Can We Determine It?* Boston: Beacon, 1949.

Hodges, H. A. *The Philosophy of Wilhelm Dilthey*. London: Routledge & K. Paul, 1952.

_____. *Wilhelm Dilthey: An Introduction*. London: K. Paul, Trench, Trubner, 1944.

Hughes, H. S. *Oswald Spengler: A Critical Estimate*. New York: Scribner, 1952.

Jerrold, D. *The Lie About the West: A Response to Professor Toynbee's Challenge*. London: Dent, 1954.

Klibansky, R., and Paton, H. J., eds. *Philosophy and History: Essays Presented to Ernst Cassirer*. New York: Harper & Row, 1963.

Mayer, J. P. *Max Weber and German Politics: A Study in Political Sociology*. London: Faber & Faber, 1943.

Mandelbaum, Maurice. *The Problem of Historical Knowledge*. New York: Liveright, 1938.

Parsons, Talcot. *The Structure of Social Action*. Glencoe, Ill.: Free Press, 1961.

Popper, Karl R. *The Poverty of Historicism*. Boston: Beacon Press, 1957.

Spykman, N. J. *The Social Theory of Georg Simmel*. Chicago: University of Chicago Press, 1925.

Simmel, G. *Sociology of Georg Simmel*. Translated by K. H. Wolff. Glencoe, Ill.: Free Press, 1956.

Troeltsch, Ernst. *Der Historismus und Seine Probleme*. Gesammelte Schriften Vol. III. Tubingen: J. C. B. Mohr, 1912–1922.

Weingartner, Rudolph. *Experience and Culture: The Philosophy of Georg Simmel*. Middleton, Conn.: Wesleyan University Press, 1962.

Articles and essays

Bendix, R. "Max Weber's Interpretation of Conduct and History." *American Journal of Sociology*, LI (1945–46), 518–526.

Blyth, J. W. "Toynbee and the Categories of Interpretation." *Philosophical Review,* LVIII (1949), 360–371.

Engel-Janosi, Friedrich. "The Growth of German Historicism." *Studies in History and Political Science,* LXII (1944), no. 2.

Gerth, H. H., and Mills, C. W., eds. "Introduction," *From Max Weber: Essays in Sociology.* London: Oxford University Press, 1947.

Geyl, P. "Toynbee's System of Civilization." *Journal of the History of Ideas,* IX (1948), 93–124.

Hayek, F. A. "Scienticism and the Study of Society: The Historicism of the Scientifistic Approach." In *The Counter-Revolution of Science.* Glencoe, Ill.: Free Press, 1952.

Lee, Dwight E., and Beck, Robert N. "The Meaning of 'Historicism.'" *American Historical Review,* LIX (1953–54), 568–577.

Meinecke, Friedrick. "Zur Theorie und Philosophie der Geschichte." *Werke,* VI (1957–62).

Rand, Calvin G. "The Meanings of Historicism in the Writings of Dilthey, Troeltsch and Meinecke." *Journal of the History of Ideas,* XXV (1965), 503–518.

Stark, W. Introduction to *Machiavellism: Doctrine of Raison d'Etat and its Place in Modern History,* by Friedrich Meinecke. Translated by D. Scott from *Die Ideen der Staatsrason.* New Haven: Yale University Press, 1957.

White, Hayden V. "On History and Historicism," in *From History to Sociology,* by Antoni Carlo. Translated by Hayden V. White. Detroit: Wayne State University Press, 1959.

White, Morton G. "The Attack on Historical Method." *Journal of Philosophy,* XLII (1945), 314–331.

CHAPTER III

Pragmatism

Introduction

Pragmatism has come to be called *the* American philosophy. It has been recognized as the first original contribution of American thought to western philosophy; prior to its appearance, philosophy in America had been derived from European thought. The American historical and cultural experience found voice in pragmatism, formulating insights which were the direct fruit of its own reflection, and pragmatism has been recognized as the single philosophy which has penetrated American culture at all levels and in all its forms. In such figures as Oliver W. Holmes, Louis Brandeis, and Benjamin Cardozo, it effectively influenced juridical thought; through James Robinson, Charles Beard, and others it acted on history and political science; through Thorstein Veblen on economics and social thought; through C. I. Lewis, P. W. Bridgman, and Ernest Nagel on the philosophy of science. In the areas of aesthetics, philosophy of religion, and education, its influence is discernible in the work of Horace Kallen, Edward Scribner Ames, and William Kilpatrick. It not only originated in, but effectively operated upon, American culture as no other doctrine could be said to have done.

Pragmatism could not, however, be called American in an exclusive sense. It enjoyed European manifestations as well. These not only showed an original impetus and character but, in their turn, exercised a certain amount of influence on certain aspects of the American doctrine. To illustrate this last point, we may point to the fact that Peirce was influenced in his final formulation of pragmatism by his contact with the Italian group about the journal *Leonardo*. Thus, though deeply American, pragmatism is in fact a common direction in western thought at this phase. Its origin must be traced to a common cultural experience, which may indeed have been felt with singular force in America but which formed part of the European milieu as well.

The common experience which provides the cultural setting of

43

pragmatism was the criticism of idealism. (The term *revolt* has frequently been employed in this connection, but it is obviously too
strong.) Certain qualifications must be made to clarify this statement.
The idealism in question was, in England and America, that which has
been identified in another chapter as neo-Hegelianism. In England this
idealism was represented by such figures as Edward Caird, Thomas
H. Green, Bernard Bosanquet, and Francis A. Bradley; in America by
William T. Harris, James E. Creighton, G. S. Morris, and, above all,
Josiah Royce. In Italy, it was the idealism represented by Bertrando
Spaventa, Augusto Vera, Bernardino Varisco, and Piero Martinetti,
as well as that which was beginning to take form in the writings of
Benedetto Croce in the journal *La critica*. The criticism of idealism by
pragmatism was not an attack from without but a process of revalua-
tion from within. It was rooted in the conviction that idealism did not
have the capacity to cope with the emergent problems of the intellectual life, and its purpose was to achieve an intellectual reconstruction.
Thus, Dewey spoke of pragmatism as a part or aspect of a general
movement of intellectual reconstruction (*The Influence of Darwin on
Philosophy and Other Essays*, 1910). In Italy, the same project of intellectual reconstruction formed the program of the *Leonardo* group,
through whose efforts, and in contact with American pragmatists, the
Italian form of the doctrine took shape.

A certain interest has always attached to the origin of the term
pragmatism, especially as this process affects the philosophical position
(or positions) involved. Charles Peirce is generally credited with having
brought the term into currency and giving it its basic orientation.
In an article explaining the term (cf. *Collected Papers*, Vol. V, p. 1),
Peirce makes specific reference to the appearance of the term in Kant.
In his *Critique of Pure Reason* Kant had selected the adjective *pragmatic* to designate a practical rule under certain definite conditions:
"I call pragmatic the practical rule (law) derived from happiness as
its moving principle (a rule of worldly wisdom). . . . It is based on
empirical principles because only from experience can I know what
inclinations there are to be satisfied and which are the natural causes
which might procure their satisfaction." He goes on to say that "when
I do not know with certainty the conditions under which an end may
be achieved, I call the accidental belief, which is, however, the basis for
using certain means, *pragmatic* belief" (cf. *Kritik der reinen Vernunft*,
B 523–524, A 534). In his *Anthropology* he goes on to distinguish
anthropology from the pragmatic point of view and the same science
from the physiological point of view, stating that the pragmatic regards
man under the aspect of what "as a free agent he can accomplish in
the world" (cf. *Anthropologie in Pragmatischer Hinsicht abgefasst*,
Vorrede).

All of these Kantian allusions are present, in one degree or another, in the employment of the term to designate this new current of thought. Peirce rejected the term *practicism* because the term *practical* had such a moralistic association in Kant's thought. His inclination toward the term *pragmatism* came from the Kantian view of man operating freely *in the world,* under empirical conditions, for the satisfaction of ends, the means to which may or may not be the objects of certain knowledge. The *situation of man* implied in the Kantian use of the term offered the most vivid suggestion and the strongest impulse for the selection of the term *pragmatism.* It would seem true to say that pragmatism, through all its convolutions, remains substantially faithful to this basic insight. Against this background, any attempt to define it in more vulgar terms of utility, etc., are clearly inadequate. The term refers to an insight into the entire situation of man in the world of experience and the way in which he makes his way in it. Under certain pressures Peirce was later to option for the variant *pragmaticism;* the conditions leading to this preference will be mentioned in the discussion of his own thought.

The positions designated by this term proliferated so abundantly that Lovejoy spoke of the "thirteen pragmatisms" in the famous essay by that title in the *Journal of Philosophy* for 1908. In a protesting reply W. P. Montague, in the same journal for the following year, maintained that there were really only four or five typical forms of pragmatism and then alleged that pragmatism was really only one doctrine comprising all of the four or five typical doctrines (cf. "May a Realist Be a Pragmatist?"). In the same journal, Max Myer heightened the confusion by holding that there were not really different types of pragmatism but that every form of the doctrine implied all the others (cf. "The Exact Number of Pragmatisms," 1908).

Amid all this confusion and proliferation, one must ask whether it is possible to isolate certain constants which characterize pragmatism. The reply is affirmative if one does not insist upon too simple a description. The constants which are present through all its variations, and which may therefore justly become the basis for a firm view of what pragmatism is, are two: an effort to construct a viable theory of truth and of reality (sometimes called pragmatism's metaphysical aspect) and an effort to formulate a theory of meaning (called its methodological aspect). When Peirce refined the term *pragmatism* into *pragmaticism,* it was the latter constant that he was trying to emphasize. However, for a full understanding of these constants, they must be placed in the context which had been developed by Kant. To fill out this picture, some historians have emphasized the relation of pragmatism to classical English empiricism, noting that, for classical empiricism experience was essentially past experience, while experience for pragmatism is essentially *openness to the future*. Peirce concurs in this reflection. However, it should also be noted that these elements of empiricism and futurism are already present in Kant's use of *pragmatic*. For any further understanding of what pragmatism is *concretely*, it is necessary to turn to the doctrines of the individual pragmatists and to consider directly the kinds of undertakings in which they were engaged.

A. *The Five Masters of Pragmatism*

Pragmatism, we may conclude from the foregoing, is what the pragmatists did. As a consequence, we can with greatest expectation of profit, consider in turn the thought of the five acknowledged masters of pragmatic thought. These are Charles Peirce, William James, John Dewey (whose special form of pragmatism will receive the further designation *instrumentalism*), F. C. S. Schiller, and George Mead. We can then devote some attention to the Italian form of pragmatism, which, while it developed in association with the American and English forms, assumed a very distinctive character.

1. Charles Sanders Peirce (1839–1914)

Peirce published relatively little during his lifetime, but at his death left a vast quantity of manuscripts which through successive editings have made his thought available and established his influence in many fields. Morris R. Cohen published selections from these manuscripts together with some of Peirce's best articles in *Chance, Love and Logic*, 1923 (2nd ed. 1956). A more inclusive selection was presented by Charles Hartshorne and Paul Weiss in *Collected Papers of C. S. Peirce* (6 vols.), 1931–35, while still further selections were edited and published by Justus Buchler as *The Philosophy of Peirce*, 1940, and *Philosophical Writings of Peirce*, 1955.

Peirce was essentially a logician, and his work must eventually be judged from the point of view of his contributions to this field. His "pragmatism" develops as an integral part of his logical thought. His conception of logic, however, was very large and included elements which others might assign to psychology and metaphysics. To see the scope of Peirce's interest we may consider his thought under the following headings: 1) the theory of signs; 2) the theory of the categories; 3) tychism, the theory which some have called Peirce's metaphysics.

The theory of signs, or *semiotic*, forms the first major articulation of Peirce's logical investigations. According to this theory, all human thoughts are signs. For this reason, they are essentially representative and referential; i.e., they present something to consciousness, and they must be referred to something other than themselves. The referential aspect of signs is basic. This reference may be direct or indirect, i.e., with or without the mediation of another sign. Again, it may be *denotative* or *symbolic*. It is denotative when the sign indicates or points to the object materially, in its givenness. It is symbolic, or representative, when it needs to be interpreted by another sign. The latter is called an interpretative sign.

The whole process of interpretation is one of the most important and suggestive aspects of Peirce's thought, promising decisive contributions in many areas, for example, in all areas of study resting upon documents; at the same time, it is admitted by seasoned students of his thought to be among its most difficult aspects. The process of interpretation is open-ended in Peirce's view; i.e., the interpretative sign, in its turn, needs to be interpreted by another such sign, without the possibility of arriving at any final interpretation. Interpretation, as a process, may take three forms: emotive, energetic (perhaps *kinesthetic* would be more precise), and logical. Peirce seems to conceive of the possibility of the same sign being susceptible to some or all these forms of interpretation. On the other hand, from the point of view of his pragmaticism, the "energetic" interpretation takes on considerable importance, becoming interpretative of the others. The emotive interpretation resides in the sentiment or emotive state which is aroused in the subject by the presence of the sign. Peirce remarks that this emotive response is never absent in any sign experience. The energetic interpretation resides in the action, of whatever kind, physical or mental, with which we respond or react to the presence of the sign. The third, or logical interpretation, resides in what Peirce calls the conceptual meaning of the sign.

At this point Peirce's pragmatism begins to emerge. It might be expected that the conceptual meaning of a sign might be another concept in the logical order. However, this is not the case. The conceptual meaning has not only the general value of the pure concept but also a conditional and a terminal aspect. Its conditional aspect resides in the fact that it induces a mental attitude which is a disposition to action. The conceptual meaning of the object and sign tend to dispose man to act in a certain general way when certain general circumstances present themselves to him. Its terminal aspect resides in the fact that, being a principle of action, this meaning does not need further interpretation. The relationship between the conceptual meaning of the sign and object and a situation of action would seem to constitute the seminal form of Peirce's pragmatism or pragmaticism.

What does Peirce mean by action? It is clear that the action he has in mind is not any physical operation, but the "action" which is identical with inquiry or investigation. The end of this action is to replace the irritable state of doubt with one of persuasion, or, in other terms, to establish a belief. Belief is a habit or a rule of action. The value of belief and the distinction among beliefs may be determined only on the basis of the rules of action to which they give rise. Beliefs put an end to doubt by creating the rule of action; hence, the character of this rule of action determines the character of the belief.

Peirce recognizes a number of different ways in which beliefs may be established: the way of tenacity, of authority, and of apriority. These have one property in common; they are inerrant and can neither be denied nor corrected. To all these, however, he prefers the scientific mode of inquiry. The scientific method, in contrast to those noted, is characterized by two traits: It is fallible and it possesses within itself the means of correcting its own errors. It is a controlled and controllable method, and its possibility of control is based on the nature of the method itself. But the end of scientific inquiry is like the others, to establish beliefs which are habits or rules or action, primarily in the order of investigation itself.

From this conception of action as inquiry and inquiry as the establishment of belief on the basis of a method which is at once fallible and self-corrigible, Peirce establishes the pragmatistic criterion of meaning. How is the meaning of a belief to be established? The only means would be to consider the foreseeable effects which that belief may have upon action. Peirce himself says that in order to work out the meaning of a thing, we must determine the habits which it produces, because what a thing means is the habits which it implies (*Collected Papers*, VI, 400). Thus, the conception of an object proves to be the sum of all the practical effects, i.e., the dispositions or rules for action which that object may have, actually or possibly. This does not justify the vulgar conclusion that truth and utility are one. Truth remains for Peirce conformity, the conformity of a sign to its object. This relation of conformity is not static but dynamic; it is the end-product of that continuing process of inquiry which is both fallible and self-corrective. Thus, Peirce's pragmatism and pragmaticism proves to be no common form of utilitarianism, but a logical theory, concerned strictly with the problems of truth and its attainment. It would also seem, from an ontological point of view, to be a theory of objects. Under no conditions would it justify that sophistical attitude which would subjugate truth and inquiry to practical concerns.

Peirce's conception of the categories has been called Platonic. He admits that all knowledge begins with the senses. However, categories, concepts, and scientific laws have a dual aspect. On the one hand, they are "beings of reason," constituted in their individual character by an act which he calls "hypostatic abstraction"; on the other, they are real beings, not, to be sure, because they subsist beneath appearances or phenomena, but because they act in nature. Peirce distinguishes three categories: primacy, secondness, and thirdness. Primacy designates being or existence independent of every other thing. Secondness designates being or existence relative to another thing, the reaction against something else. Thirdness means the mediation through which a first and a second are placed in relation. The first is chance, pure logical possibility; the second is law, the past, the submission or subjugation of the first to law and actualization; the third is becoming, the real potentiality of our experience and of nature itself.

The metaphysical view to which Peirce came as a result of these logical reflections has been called *tychism,* deriving from the Greek term for *chance.* The basis of tychism is the renunciation of all forms of "necessitarianism," whether in the world or in the process of science. Necessity is not the basis of a rational consideration of the world. The world, for Peirce, is the realm of pure chance; at the same time, it is the seat of those regularities or uniformities which provide the objects of scientific inquiry and which can be expressed as laws. But these uniformities must themselves be considered as casual, as related to chance more than to any rigid necessity. They do not exhibit any total order in nature. They are revealed in nature to scientific investigation, but, like all the results of scientific investigation, they are subject to error and correction.

2. William James (1842–1910)

Just as pragmatism has been called the American philosophy *par excellence,* so William James, with whose name that philosophy has been most closely associated, has been called *the* American philosopher. From one point of view, this is strange, since his education was primarily European. From another, it is entirely just, for his was a philosophy which could only have appeared on American soil and which directly reflected major traits of the American cultural character.

James's preparation and interests ranged over a wide field. Turning from an original engagement in art, he became, successively, a student of chemistry, a student and teacher of physiology and psychology, and finally a professor of philosophy. None of these experiences are irrelevant for an understanding of his mind; in his thought they achieved a highly personal, highly distinctive, and highly significant synthesis. He possessed none of the mental and stylistic traits of the typical philosopher. The unsystematic character of his thought, like that of his studies, has become legendary. Nevertheless, there exists a certain inward unity to all he thought and wrote.

A comparison, no matter how brief and superficial, between the thought of James and that of Peirce seems to offer ample justification for the charge that there are many pragmatisms and no single pragmatism. The center of Peirce's interest was science; James's chief concern was life, in the active dynamic sense of the term. This difference is reflected directly in the quality of their pragmatism. Peirce's is a logical theory. The pragmatism of James is a vital theory, a theory of how life must be lived and how thought may serve that living. Nevertheless, there is a certain affinity between them. This affinity lies most clearly in their mutual sense of the openness and dynamism of human experience, in the laboriousness of the task of knowledge, and in the tenuousness, fallibility, and necessity for self-corrective powers in its results. Finally it resides in the priority which both are prepared to assign to action, although that action for Peirce was preeminently the action of scientific inquiry itself, while for James it was action in the world, moral action, religious affirmation.

By quite universal consent of students of his thought, the first intimations of James's pragmatism are to be discovered in his first work, his only really systematic work, *The Principles of Psychology* (2 vols.), 1890. In this work he gives the psychic life of man that open structure to the future, that inner dynamism, which lies at the heart of all his thought. The pursuit of future ends and the choice of means to reach them are the sign of the presence of mind. We do not attribute mentality to sticks and stones, because they do not seem to move in view of something. This "in view of something" marks reflective action as the model of all active mental life, and James emphasizes the purposive structure of it. He conceives life as a complete cycle from passiveness before stimuli to the final action of the responding agent, and the stages between—sensibility, thought, reflection, etc.—all exist in view of that reaction. As he says in *The Will to Believe and Other Essays in Popular Philosophy*, 1897, the volitive part of our nature dominates the rational as well as the sensible part, and perception and thought exist only in view of action, of conduct. Like Peirce, he holds that at the heart of every action lies a belief; in fact, he goes a step further and is prepared to hold that serviceability to action is the measure of the truth of belief.

In this respect, the difference between Peirce and James becomes clearer. Peirce had taken science as the one absolute, the one process which, though structured pragmatically, could not be submitted to practical evaluation. But James holds that science is to be measured by the same criterion as all belief. When it does not serve the ends of human conduct, science lacks all meaning and purpose. Science itself is action with a view to the service of human ends. It is not the passive recognition of objective facts. It breaks up the order among phenomena and reorders them in ways foreign to their natural state. It simplifies and establishes schemes of prediction. Simplification and prediction are human values because they serve the ends of human action, and, hence, in establishing them science shows its own serviceability to human conduct and its own subjection to the pragmatic criteria of meaning, value, and truth.

Is man, then, entirely free with respect to his beliefs, free, that is, to choose any beliefs which serve his ends without further regard to conditions? James does not think so. Instead, he establishes certain norms which a belief has to meet before it can be adhered to. In *The Will to Believe* he identifies these norms as three: 1) that the hypothesis set up by the belief be one which cannot demonstrably be shown to be either true or false; 2) that it be a living hypothesis, one which makes a real appeal to the agent involved; 3) that it be important, that is, makes a real difference in the life of the agent and is not concerned with trivial things. If these conditions or norms are met, the agent has the right to believe without waiting for any demonstration. To be sure, in doing so, he is assuming a risk, the risk that he will eventually be proved in error. But, James argues that the same risk attaches to nonbelieving in the same circumstances, because nonbelieving is identical with believing the negative of the original belief. Belief and nonbelief carry the same burden of risk, but belief possesses one advantage over nonbelief which makes it always preferable: it can bring about its own verification, whereas nonbelief cannot. Hence, belief belongs to the dynamism of life in a way that nonbelief does not. All values are to be realized only on the basis of the belief that they are possible; and this belief always remains a belief.

James is ready to apply these fundamental persuasions to the various areas which have drawn his attention. Thus, with respect to the problem of knowledge, he seeks to refine this pragmatism by applying it more directly to the circumstances which surround and condition men's pursuit of knowledge and truth. James holds that the quest for truth cannot be restricted to what can be objectively established. Even in the absence of empirical objects it is right to believe. This is so because belief in a certain proposition makes it possible for the one who believes to overcome doubt and achieve an inner calm to which introspection gives empirical testimony. The will to believe here has the power of scientific truth. Human action cannot always, if ever, wait upon scientific demonstration. To do so would be to invert the dynamic order of thought and life.

Yet a difficulty inheres to this point of view which James never finally resolves. If conduct be taken as justification for belief, does this not warrant believing indiscriminately? James replies to this difficulty be introducing the notion of success: The belief is true which leads to successful action. But the concept of success is manifestly no clearer than the situation it is called upon to clarify. The question of the kind of success, success in what sense and what order, still remains to be established. The readers who looked to *Pragmatism*, which James published in 1907, for clarification of this problem were disappointed; as many critics have observed, in that work he oscillates between many possibilities, making appeal to some of Peirce's earlier writings without taking account of the distinction between pragmaticism and pragmatism which Peirce had introduced precisely to clarify such points.

James essayed one of the most telling tests of his pragmatism in dealing with religion, a phenomenon of capital importance in his thought. The relevant work in this relation is the *Varieties of Religious Experience*, his Gifford lectures for the year 1901–1902, published the following year. Here he gives a pragmatic view of religious beliefs which culminates in an assertion of the authenticity of the supraempirical realities which are the objects of religious beliefs. He begins with the nondemonstrability of religious beliefs, the point at which his pragmatism itself begins. He establishes the reality of these beliefs on the basis of the modes of action or conduct which they induce in their agents. On the same basis he establishes their truth, i.e., their value for action; they are true because the attitudes and modes of action they support have a reassuring and calming effect on the believers. He goes still further to maintain that the objects to which such beliefs refer, i.e., God and other supraempirical entities, must be accepted as real because they are the correlates of the entire process.

In the ontological order James came to a position which he called pluralism. This position is related to another insight which established a certain affinity between his position and that of the spiritualistic philosophers. James himself indicated this affinity, especially with the thought of Bergson. The essence of pluralism lies in its denial that the universe possesses a higher unity or totality. This position is maintained polemically against the monism of the neo-Hegelian school, which postulated a unity in the universe which is not subject to empirical verification. The pragmatic analysis of action and truth makes it clear that the world can only be composed of independent entities capable of the kind of liberty, choice, belief, and action which James's pragmatism postulated and, indeed, was confident could be established on empirical grounds.

The independence of the constituent entities of the universe with respect to each other does not destroy their effective unity; they can still enter into meaningful relations with each other. This unity must be established on pragmatic bases and runs the risk inherent in belief and action. But James's pluralism is not a metaphysical dogmatism; it is the legitimate consequence of empirical reflection. James underlines this point by calling it an empirical pluralism and associating it directly with that other aspect of his thought which he called its "radical empiricism." The work in which this spiritualistic ontology is developed, *A Pluralistic Universe*, became one of the best known of his writings. The doctrine seems to have political and social consequences, which James points out, noting that social life, political order, and progress depend, not on the existence of an overarching unity in the world, but on the free pragmatic collaboration of such independent entities as his theories envisaged.

3. John Dewey (1859–1952)

The great differences which exist between the thought of James and Peirce make it clear that pragmatism was never a doctrine or a school. It was rather a current or tendency of thought which developed independently in a number of thinkers with only tangential (though important and fruitful) contacts between them. This conclusion is strengthened even more by a consideration of the thought of John Dewey. By no stretch of the imagination can Dewey be thought of as a member of a movement or school. He is an independent thinker whose development is controlled entirely by its own inward logic. This process led him to share the current in which James and Peirce also moved, but he developed its principles in a manner all his own. He refined the method of pragmatism into a coherent method of philosophical research in many areas and made it yield rich results wherever he applied it.

Dewey had a very broad conception of the work of philosophy. It was not, for him, a specialized area of research with a restricted concern and limited promise. It was, above all, an instrument of social criticism and construction or reconstruction (a favorite term with him). It was a method of attack upon the inconsistencies and even contradictions of American society and culture. It served this end, however, not by providing a set of social dogmas (as, for instance, Marxism did), but by developing an instrument or method of inquiry and resolution. It was this view of the work of philosophy which made his "instrumentalism," for a period at least, *the* American philosophy, touching on every major area of social and cultural life and bringing into each its own basic principles.

It was noted above that the revolt against idealism provided the matrix for the development of pragmatism. This is especially true in the case of Dewey. His particular formulation of pragmatism, to which the name *instrumentalism* was given, developed not so much against, as within, neo-idealism. Instrumentalism represents an extreme transformation of certain germinal ideas of the idealism which Dewey imbibed at Johns Hopkins University from such teachers as G. S. Morris. In many ways, the designation *instrumentalism* was unfortunate, for it evoked the image of intelligence as an instrument of manipulation and led to the confusion of his position with a mere utilitarianism. The truth would seem to be that Dewey's pragmatism always retained the impress of its idealist origins. Consequently, to understand his thought it is necessary to follow the process by which his own position developed, a dual process of inner criticism and assimilation from without.

The first stage of this process involved a problem which Dewey perceived at the heart of neo-Hegelianism. The problem was as old as Hegel himself: the relationship between spirit and nature. This had been a touchy point in Hegelianism and involved the entire status of the natural sciences. By Dewey's time, because of the immense progress in these sciences, the problem was more acute than ever. In the Hegelian view, nature emerged at the negative moment of the life of the Idea: the moment of otherness, which spirit had to posit in order to return to itself in the fullness of dialectical self-consciousness, the moment of its complete contemplation of itself. Dewey's approach was different. The moment of nature, of otherness, of objectivity, could not remain negative. The testimony of modern science made this impossible. Nature had to become positive, the objective moment in which spirit fulfills itself, the order in which the work of spirit, which Hegel tends to consign to a dubious interiority, becomes objectively expressed and realized. Therefore, the self-conscious activity of spirit, reason, could not remain contemplative, as it tended to do in Hegel. It had to have a dynamic, creative relation to the order of nature in which it was realized. Finally, the relationship between them, as a consequence of these reflections, could no longer be dialectical, for it was the dialectical process which turned spirit back upon itself and rendered it contemplative, if not narcissistic.

All of these considerations form the premises of Dewey's form of neo-idealism, to which, it has been suggested, the term *practical idealism* might be applied. It leads up to his statement in the *Psychology* of 1887, the best expression of this period. Spirit, he avers, is not a passive spectator of the universe; it always produces certain effects, and these effects are objective to the degree to which all historical facts can be objective. In the domain of intelligence, the effects of spirit are language and science; in the domain of will, social and political institutions; in the realm of sentiment, art; finally, in the area which concerns the self in its entirety, religion. The term *historical* is especially important in this context, for in Dewey's view it is clearly not just the effects of spirit which appear in the objective order of history. To hold that would be to make spirit immanently transcendent to its own effects. It is spirit itself which is realized in the historical order of culture and which, therefore, itself possesses the form of history. Spirit evolves in history and, through its objective achievements in history and culture, conquers its own interiority, not the spurious interiority of contemplation which Hegel had assigned it, but the authentic interiority of effective operation within the objective order. In other words, Dewey's view of spirit and intelligence is already practical and instrumental, although he remains within the circle of idealist thought. The first form of his instrumentalism represents his personal reformulation of idealism.

By this line of thought Dewey had progressed to the extreme limits of idealism; or, more precisely, he had stretched that doctrine to the point where it could no longer contain the thrust of his own thought. This was especially true of the conception of intelligence. The Hegelian viewpoint, even as interpreted by neo-Hegelianism, did not provide the theoretical grounds for the notion of this agent intelligence. Dewey had to look elsewhere for testimony to support his insight. It was at this point that he encountered the thought of William James in *The Principles of Psychology*. The encounter was decisive. Dewey found in James precisely what he needed to clarify his own position: fresh support for the evolutionary and instrumental view of intelligence and, a more basic ally, the organic view. In the *Psychology*, Dewey felt, James not only treated with extreme clarity the psychology of ideas but constantly referred these ideas to their organic origin in the body. Intelligence has a natural history. It arises in the tensions and disequilibria which emerge as the organism seeks to adapt itself to and realize itself within its environment. Intelligence emerges within the life of the organism in response to these exigencies of adaptation because it has a function to fulfill within the life of the organism. When the organism finds itself in a situation of disequilibrium and uncertainty before its environment, the intelligence acts to reduce this disequilibrium and relieve this uncertainty. It does this, however, within the behavior of the organism; in fact, it is but a special mode of that behavior. Thus, in its very origin intelligence is practical, instrumental.

It is necessary to understand clearly what Dewey intended by the term *instrumental* as applied to intelligence. As has been noted, the term is in some ways unfortunate, for it evokes an equivocal image.

His analysis is directed toward dispelling this equivocation. The adjustment of the organism to its environment is not simple accommodation. The activity of the intelligence in the economy of the organism's life is anticipatory; it involves anticipation of future consequences and determination of potentialities, and it structures or orders the activity of the organism in the present to these future conditions and possibilities. Through this perception of possibilities and anticipation of futurities, intelligence structures present action with meaning, meaning which will be spelled out in terms of the organism's behavior in the contingencies for which intelligence prepares it. There is no question of "instrumentality" in any manipulatory or accomodational sense. It carries rather the sense of vital reason, a reason which renders present action more enlightened in view of its orientation to consequences, potentialities, and future exigencies.

Dewey justifies this account of the character of intelligence by an analysis of moral behavior. But his ultimate purpose looks beyond. He says that the real purpose of his theory has been to transfer the characteristic heretofore reserved to moral judgment and action to science and ordinary knowledge. Ordinary knowledge exhibits the same instrumental character which he had discovered in his interpretation of idealism in the light of James (and James in the light of idealism). Furthermore, science exhibits the same structure even more clearly than ordinary knowledge. Many of the older dualisms fall before this insight; for example, the dualism which he had long felt to be intolerable, between fact and value, in which science is deemed value-free. Dewey sees the instrumental moment as inherent in all investigation. This gives rise to his final concept, that of inquiry. *Inquiry* expresses better than any other term the living center of Dewey's idea. Inquiry indicates the place and function of intelligence in the total life of spirit, the inner dynamics of its mode of operation, and the form of spirit itself in its most vital moment. The concept of inquiry is developed most adequately in his work *Logic, the Theory of Inquiry,* 1938.

Dewey uses his theory of inquiry to address a large range of problems, in fact, all of those which fall within the scope of culture as it is understood in the West. His thought has been compared to a "summa" of the Middle Ages, though it might with greater felicity be compared to the Hegelian idea of the encyclopedia of the philosophical sciences. He stated the instrumentalist conception of the role of philosophy as early as 1910 in *The Influence of Darwin on Philosophy.* The first task he undertook in the light of this conception was the reconstruction of logic itself. The writings in which this project is carried out run from the early *Studies in Logical Theory,* 1903, to *Logic, the Theory of Inquiry.* In such works as *The Quest for Certainty,* 1929, he takes up the all-important issue of the nature of scientific knowledge. He considers the relation of the objects of science to those of common sense and the relation of scientific judgments to judgments of value. His *Art as Experience*, 1934, has been called the best introduction to his thought. In seeking to clarify the nature and function of art, to which he assigns a vital place, Dewey clarifies such central notions as "experience," successfully dissipating all the equivocations which might lead to the confusion of instrumentalism with utilitarianism. Ethics, as noted, was one of his earliest concerns and continually a central one; it forms the theme of *Ethics*, 1908 and 1932, and of *Human Nature and Conduct*, 1922. In *Democracy and Education*, 1916, *School and Society*, 1899, 1915, and *Experience and Education*, 1938, he confronts the problems of the school. In a later work, *A Common Faith*, he addresses the basic problem of religion. Dewey comes closest to a synthesis of his views in *Experience and Nature*, 1925. Here the ideas which he had been developing since his earliest philosophical experience are projected in masterly fashion and reveal the basically systematic form of his thought. The idealist in him never died.

Dewey's influence underwent some eclipse after 1930. In historical perspective, however, he must be accounted the most influential philosopher to appear in America. A renewed interest in his thought is manifest in the literature appearing about it. But the eclipse has not been without effect. The approach to his thought has undergone a basic change. No longer does his philosophy offer a faith and a program, as it once did. It now belongs to history and is studied with a view to determining its proper place in the perennial movement of philosophy.

4. George Mead (1861–1931)

George Mead was Dewey's colleague in Chicago during a period that seems most important for the formation of the basic ideas of pragmatism. Charles Morris, who edited one of Mead's books (*Mind, Self and Society*, 1934), has made a comparison of the two men which has become classic; he says that Dewey gave amplitude and vision to pragmatism but Mead gave it analytic depth and scientific precision. Mead published only a few articles during his lifetime, and after his death his manuscripts and lecture notes formed the basis of the four books edited by his disciples and colleagues: *The Philosophy of the Present*, edited by A. E. Murphy, 1931; *Mind, Self and Society from the Standpoint of a Behaviorist*, edited by C. Morris, 1934; *Movements of Thought in the Nineteenth Century*, edited by M. Moore, 1936; and *The Philosophy of the Act*, edited by C. Morris *et al.*, 1938.

Morris' statement may be conceded at least regarding Mead's intent; his analytic power cannot be questioned. One of the tasks to which he applied it assiduously was the clarification of the notion of experience, absolutely central to pragmatism. Dewey often pointed out that the relationship between the organism and the environment is not unilateral but bilateral. Thus, in describing how a problem is resolved, he states that such resolution demands the modification of the milieu which obstructs the projects of the organism, as well as the modification of the patterns of behavior of the organism. Organism and milieu act upon each other. Mead adopts this point as central to his thought and carries the analysis of two-directional conditioning to a new stage of refinement. From this emerges the seminal idea of experience; for, as Mead writes in *Mind, Self and Society,* since organism and ambient determine each other reciprocally, it follows that the process of life, to be adequately understood, must be considered in terms of their interrelations (p. 129). Experience is the name for the general field of such interactions. Within experience, thus understood, problematic areas arise which involve the functioning of these interrelations. These problematic areas are the direct concern of the pragmatic analysis of experience.

The concept of experience is transcendental; it applies to all natural processes. But Mead is chiefly concerned with human experience. Here the specific form of this bilateral conditioning process is *sociality.* Human experience is social in all its aspects. This is true of human perception, for example. The thing which one person perceives may be perceived by others. Both the object of perception and the act of perception have this social character. (Sociality, in Mead's sense, seems to have many affinities with Kant's "transcendental.") The social quality of human experience is revealed even more clearly, in Mead's view, at the level immediately superior to perception: *symbolization.* The objects of perception may be assumed to exist independently and only to be perceived socially, thus taking on the character of sociality as a result of being perceived. But the process of symbolization *constitutes* its objects; these objects have no "prior" existence but exist only in the social context. Here, Mead sees the constituting social process in its elemental form. Gesture and language, two forms of the symbolic process, are entirely social in themselves and generate an order of existence which is entirely social. As a consequence, meaning takes on social form for Mead, and he assigns a social character to such concepts as logical universality and necessity. Universality, in the logical sense, is the intention of directing a symbol indifferently to all members of an indefinite group. Necessity is the act of accepting certain elements of a symbolic situation as the conditions for evoking the response sought.

This is the context which Mead employs to clarify the basic concepts of mind, self, and society. All of these terms are strictly social in their origin and meaning; outside the context of sociality they are not comprehensible. Mind is the relation of the organism to its situation, which is mediated by a group of symbols. This would seem to mean that mind resides in the power to use symbols in such a way that the same symbols can be used in the same way by other members of the group. A language would illustrate this, for use of language and thought seem to become identified. Mind is thus an entirely social, never a private, process. Self, too, is wholly social in origin and character. Within the self, Mead distinguishes the "I" and the "me," using one to define the other. The "me" is the organized complex of the attitudes of others which one takes up as one's own. The "I" is the organism's response to such attitudes (values, etc.). The "I" thus has a new element, which may be called freedom and personality, because its response to those attitudes are its own in a new sense. It has to respond self-consciously or the responses would not be its own; it would then not be an "I" and, hence, not a self. There is another, more precise aspect to this freedom that is inherent in the behavioral process. No matter how the "I" considers its reaction to those attitudes, the reaction itself, with its proper qualities, is not a part of experience until it actually takes place. Thus, the "I" generates experience in a way quite proper to itself.

When he passes to the idea of society, Mead associates the notion of *institution* with the "me." The institution is the internalized form of the common responses of a group to common situations. The institution is a structural principle both of society taken in itself and of society taken in its concrete constituent members, the "me" of each member of the group. Within the self the relation of the "I" to the "me" may vary from subject to subject and, apparently, within a given subject at different moments of its history. This variable relation constitutes personality. Finally, even "private" experience, which Mead recognizes, is social in character and origin, and this in a dual sense. First, the area of the private can only be traced out in relation to the area of the social; without social structure, the concept of private experience would never even emerge. Secondly, the private experience itself takes on social form; the subject of the private experience becomes an object to himself and carries on colloquy with himself through a system of symbols which he both creates and interprets. Society takes its formal structure from the trilogy of mind, "I," and "me." The essence of society would seem to reside for Mead in processes of social control, especially those which are sometimes called "internalized." When the individual is able to take upon himself, into the structure of his "me," the norms or attitudes of the group and execute them in the character of his "I," actively and, in a certain limited sense, freely, society in the full sense of the term emerges.

5. Ferdinand C. S. Schiller (1864–1937)

The independence of the various thinkers within the current of pragmatism is again shown in the thought of F. C. S. Schiller. This philosopher gave his particular presentation of the attitude of pragmatism the name *humanism*. He is entirely justified in this, it would seem, for his specifically pragmatic utterances are developments and refinements of an earlier humanistic assertion.

His humanism is established in his earliest and only really organic book (the others are all collections of essays), *The Riddles of the Sphinx*, 1891. This book postulates three realities: world, man, and God, which it relates in a peculiar evolutionary form. The world consists of interacting entities. Among these, man occupies a privileged place because he alone is the observer, participant, and interpreter of the actions and reactions of all other agents. Through him—that is, through his observation and participation—these actions and reactions become a universe which has a structure of becoming, a history. Thus, all the agents of that universe achieve reality in it through man. This includes man himself, who asks of himself most insistently the question which he puts to all other beings: What am I? His reply is fundamentally Protagorean: I am the measure of all things, of those that are, in that they are, and of those that are not, in that they are not. Thus the humanist assertion takes form in Schiller: Man is, and the world is in and through man and has the form which man gives it.

Schiller draws close to the position of pragmatism when, within this framework of humanism, he approaches the problem of knowledge. Since man is the measure of all, Schiller rejects the notion of a transcendental logic or ontology which would be the measure of man, the first in the order of truth and the other in the order of being. Both are made immanent to man's presence and assigned a status and function there. Thought becomes an instrument in the service of man's reality. A "pure" reason is unthinkable. Reason is man's own concrete and psychological process of thought, which serves his ends. At the basis of every form of knowledge there is an emotional postulate, and at the basis of every process of reason there is a practical need being served. Schiller extends this insight to the theory of logic and science. Formal and traditional logic serve no end; they are without meaning. The only authentic logic is that of concrete human thought. Even science conforms to his analysis of concrete thought; it is postulation and practical and, when it comes to know itself, lays no claim to transcendental status.

Schiller's humanism and logical pragmatism fuse into one in his Protagoreanism. His defense of Protagoras in such writings as *Studies in Humanism,* 1907, and *Plato or Protagoras,* 1908, had an element of exaggeration about it but also a kernel of significance. It is the application of the "man the measure" thesis first to the moral realm and then to the ontological. In each case, the transcendental order of good and of being are not only questioned but reconstructed in pragmatic, humanistic terms. Protagoras, he contends, defines the natural basis of man's activity and of his attitude toward truth. A proposition is objectively true when it leads to a satisfying action within the world which supports or receives such an action. This is the moral rule. But reality itself is subject to a similar rule. There is no norm of reality which is transcendent to human experience. All affirmations of the real are mediated through man's thought, emotion, and action and are asserted relative to it. This in turn leads Schiller to adopt a problematicism and a probability theory of knowledge. The structure of existence, as man's experience testifies, is problem. The function of thought is resolution of problems. But all such resolutions are relative and not absolute. Experience and truth itself are open-ended. (Cf. *Logic for Use,* 1929; *Our Human Truths,* 1939; Reuben Abel, ed.: *Humanistic Pragmatism: The Philosophy of F. C. S. Schiller,* 1966.)

B. *The Italian School*

Pragmatic philosophy had its most significant continental resonance in Italy. This is somewhat astonishing since, objectively considered, the philosophical tradition of the peninsula would hardly seem to dispose Italian culture favorably toward pragmatism. But such an objective evaluation would be faulty; there was in Italian culture an element which responded to pragmatism. Even Croce at one time went to some pains to establish a certain affinity between his thought and that of Dewey. The chief literary organ of Italian pragmatism was the review *Leonardo,* which was published during the years 1903–1907. It attracted at least occasional collaboration from a wide range of writers of very different temper. Both Peirce and James appeared in its pages, as did Schiller. In it the highly polemical but gifted writers Giovanni Papini (1881–1956) and Giuseppe Prezzolini (b. 1882) conducted lively controversies. Though pragmatism was but a passing phase in their careers, their contributions were lively and perceptive. Papini attached himself particularly to the thought of James, while Prezzolini drew eclectically from all the American pragmatists elements which he found attractive and to which he gave a highly personal formulation (cf. *Il mio pragmatismo* [My personal pragmatism], 1905). The most philo-

sophically able of the Italian pragmatists, however, attached themselves
to the work of Peirce and sought to establish a pure logical pragmatism, in Peirce's sense, as opposed to the meaning of logic in Dewey
and in Schiller. It was in *Leonardo* that Peirce made the distinction
between pragmatism and his own logical concern, which he preferred
to call "pragmaticism."

Giovanni Vailati (1863–1909) was a logician and mathematician, a
disciple of Peano. He was interested in the theory of scientific method,
especially as it involved mathematical procedures. His writings were
brought together in the volume *Scritti* [Writings], published in 1911
(but incomplete). Attaching himself to the thought of Peirce, he tried
to clarify the contribution pragmaticism might make to the theory of
the nature of mathematics and scientific procedure. He rejected the
charge of subjectivism alleged against pragmatism, at least as touching Peirce, and saw pragmatism as an invitation to cast the affirmations of science in a form which would clearly indicate the experiments
or procedures to which we must have recourse in order to test their
truth (cf. *Scritti*, pp. 921–922). Mario Calderoni (1879–1914), Vailati's pupil, developed his teacher's ideas in the direction of an "experi-
mentalism" in science. He interpreted the "practical consequences" of
which pragmatism spoke as referring to the scientific experiments to
which science must turn in order to test its conclusions.

This experimentalist direction is developed more fully by Antonio
Aliotta (1881–1964), editor of *Logos*, with greater attachment to the
thought of William James. Combating the neo-idealism which was
then acquiring dominance in Italian thought, Aliotta developed a pragmatism and a pluralism which owed much to the American writer. He
placed major emphasis on the notion of *experiment* as the sole and ultimate test of truth. Experiment involves the testing of alternative means
toward an end as well as their evaluation and revision in view of their
capacity to advance the end. He considered this method applicable not
only in science and ethics but in philosophy itself. He said of philosophy
that *history* was the theater of its experimentation, as the laboratory is
that of the scientist and lived experience that of the moralist.

Readings

I. GENERAL WORKS
   Books
Madden, E. H. *Chauncy Wright and the Foundations of Pragmatism.*
   Seattle: University of Washington Press, 1963.
Thayer, H. S. *Meaning and Action: A Critical History of Pragmatism.* Indi-
   anapolis: Bobbs-Merrill, 1949.

Essays and articles

Kennedy, Gail, ed. *Pragmatism and American Culture.* Boston: Heath, 1950.
Lovejoy, Arthur O. "The Thirteen Pragmatisms." *Journal of Philosophy,* V (1908).

II. Particular Philosophers

A. *Charles S. Peirce*

Ayer, Alfred J. *The Origins of Pragmatism: Studies in the Philosophy of C. S. Peirce.* San Francisco: Freeman Cooper, 1968.
Boler, J. F. *Charles Peirce and Scholastic Realism.* Seattle: University of Washington Press, 1963.
Murphey, Murray G. *The Development of Pierce's Philosophy.* Cambridge, Mass.: Harvard University Press, 1961.
Wennerberg, Hjalmar. *The Pragmatism of C. S. Pierce: An Analytical Study.* Copenhagen: W. K. Gleerup, Lund, Ejnar Munksgaard, 1962.
Wiener, Philip P., and Young, F. H. *Studies in the Philosophy of Charles Sanders Peirce.* Cambridge, Mass.: Harvard University Press, 1952.

B. *William James*

Allen, Gay W. *William James: A Biography.* New York: Viking, 1967.
Brennan, Bernard P. *The Ethics of William James.* New York: Twayne Publishers, 1968.
Moore, Edward C. *William James.* New York: Washington Square Press, 1965.
Perry. R. B. *The Thought and Character of William James.* 2 vols. Boston: Little, Brown, 1936.
Wild, John. *The Radical Empiricism of William James.* Garden City, N. Y.: Doubleday, 1969.

C. *John Dewey*

Bernstein, Richard J. *John Dewey.* New York: Washington Square Press, 1966.
Geiger, George R. *John Dewey in Perspective.* New York: Oxford University Press, 1958.
Nissen, Lowell. *John Dewey's Theory of Inquiry and Truth.* The Hague: Mouton, 1966.
Thayer, H. S. *The Logic of Pragmatism: An Examination of John Dewey's Logic.* New York: Humanities Press, 1952.
White, M. G. *The Origin of Dewey's Instrumentalism.* New York: Columbia University Press, 1943.

D. *George Mead*

Pfuetze, Paul. *Self, Society, Existence.* New York: Harper & Row, Harper Torchbooks, 1961.

E. *F. C. S. Schiller*

Abel, Reuben. *The Pragmatic Humanism of F. C. S. Schiller.* New York: King's Crown, 1955.
Gullace, Giovanni. "The Pragmatic Movement in Italy." *Journal of the History of Ideas,* XXIII (1962).

CHAPTER IV

Materialism: Scientific, Historical, and Dialectical

Introduction

Materialism is one of the recurrent positions in western philosophy. Some, like Santayana, maintain that it is the primordial philosophy: that which immediately recommends itself to man when he takes his first steps beyond "animal faith." Others, like Plato and all "idealists," see materialism as the primordial "anti-philosophy," which must be exorcised before philosophy can come into possession of itself. In either case, materialism is a constant presence in western thought. One of the periods in which materialism sought to establish itself as the dominant philosophy was the nineteenth century. In this period it emerged in a number of sophisticated forms—scientific, historical, and dialectical. These constitute the subject of the present chapter. Before considering them directly, a few notes on the general notion of materialism will provide helpful background.

Materialism establishes "matter" as the first principle of all reality, both existentially, i.e., in the order of actual existence, and explicatively, i.e., in the order of explanation. Essential to every materialistic system, consequently, are a specific *concept* of matter and a *monistic* dynamism. From the philosophical point of view, the second is the more important.

Somewhat paradoxically, such a monism can arise only in the context of a pluralism: the possibility that two or more first principles are conceived as possible. The monistic tendency seeks to reduce such a pluralism. This picture is complicated by the fact that no single, univocal concept of matter has emerged in the history of philosophy.

There are, consequently, as many materialisms as there are concepts of matter. It is also to be noted that there is a fairly direct relation between the status of materialistic systems and that of the physical sciences. While the physical sciences do not of themselves incline toward philosophical materialism (indeed, to many they seem to incline, rather, to a spiritualism), most systems of philosophical materialism have tended to rest their case upon a concept of matter which, they felt, was supported by the natural science of the day.

This general pattern applies to the materialisms of the nineteenth century. The concepts of matter upon which they rest all claim to be supported by the natural science of the day. (The natural sciences, as such, obviously, are not to be held responsible for these claims.) Scientific materialism rests its case most heavily on this claim and stands in a direct line of development with science. From a philosophical point of view, the central factor in historical materialism is its claim to be scientific and to be related to matter as presented in scientific theory. Dialectical materialism is an attempt to restructure the world of matter, as supported by the notion of matter developed by contemporary science, on the dialectical principle, both as a support for and with a certain independence of historical materialism. The present chapter will follow this pattern of order and deal successively with scientific, historical, and dialectical materialism, keeping in mind the intricate relations between them.

A. *Scientific Materialism*

If materialism, taken generally, in the nineteenth century is not simplistic, scientific materialism is even less so. Within it, there must be distinguished four constitutive movements, namely, radical, humanistic materialism, derived from the Hegelian left (cf. Volume IV, Part I, Chapter V); psychophysical materialism; monistic materialism (so called, not because the monistic tendency is exclusive to it, but because it is present in a more direct and less sophisticated way); and finally evolutionary materialism.

1. Radical, Humanistic Materialism

Radical, humanistic materialism derives, as has been noted, from left-Hegelianism. Its emergence involves a radical inversion within the Hegelian system. The first stage of this inversion concerns the relation of system and method. In the Hegelian philosophical system, the structure of doctrine had been primary; the method, the dialectic, was instrumental. Left-Hegelianism accepted the dialectic as method but dissociated it from the system as doctrine, equating philosophy with the exercise of the dialectic in whatever area. A second phase of this inversion involved the relation of spirit and nature in the Hegelian system. There nature (and matter as the principle of nature) was negation: the negative moment in the life history of the Idea as spirit. Spirit, by contrast, was seen as pure affirmation. Left-Hegelianism, especially in Feuerbach, inverted this relation too, placing the dialectic in nature, construing nature as primitive assertion or affirmation and Idea as negation. Matter is thus inverted into the positive principle. This process of inversion is basic to radical materialism and to historical and dialectical materialism as well. The writer who executes this inversion originally and most effectively and who most authoritatively represents radical humanistic materialism is Ludwig Feuerbach.

Feuerbach's thought has already been referred to in the consideration of the Hegelian left. Here, attention must be limited to one point: the character of his materialism. Answers to two fundamental questions must be sought: What is the concept of "matter" with which Feuerbach operates and how does he make this concept the unitary principle of the real?

Feuerbach's materialism is both subtle and complex. It may best be called *humanistic materialism* because it is a thesis, not in philosophy, but in his philosophical *anthropology*. The purpose of his anthropology is to vindicate the *integrity* and the *autonomy* of man. This integrity is violated, he feels, in two ways: by *naturalistic materialism,* which reduces man to a matter and a nature external to him, and by the sublimation of man to the status of pure spirit. Feuerbach is concerned with the second, rather than the first, of these possibilities. The form of this spiritual sublimation of man with which he takes issue is the form which, he believes, is to be found in the Hegelian philosophy.

This sublimation in turn takes two forms: the one ostensibly philosophical, the other religious. These forms are only speciously two, however; in reality there is only one. The ostensible philosophical form is represented most clearly and authoritatively by Hegel's "pure thought"; the religious, by Christianity—with its transcendent God and its notion of the human soul as endowed with a life and destiny in some way transcendent to its incarnate condition. Hegel's "pure thought" volatilizes human consciousness into a moment of the Absolute Idea, failing in the process to explain why or how the Absolute Idea should find itself entangled in the trammels of time and space, of the body, with its sensuous and passional life; consequently, it never adequately comprehends man but makes of him rather an aberration of the Absolute. Christianity seems to him a sheer movement of escape, an absolute asceticism, a mystical sublimation of human nature into transcendent spirit. His purpose, by contrast, is to exhibit the necessary integrity of man as matter and spirit, spirit which finds in matter its necessary locus and the necessary means of its self-realization.

Thus Feuerbach conceives matter as "incarnating" matter. It is matter which man discovers as the direct and immediate properties of his own existence, his own being-in-the-world. This matter is his own body—the concrete body of the existing man as he discovers his own existence in it. Enclosure in time and space is the first of these properties, the time and space *of the body.* It is the life of the senses, of emotion, of action, appetite, and passion. Corporeality, therefore, is Feuerbach's basic conception of matter.

This matter as corporeality and incarnation is not opposed to spirit; spirit is, rather, the constitutive essence of this matter. Spirit is what this matter reveals itself to be. Man does not experience his own existence in and through his body as a closed, mechanical system, but rather as a tension between the finite, immediate conditions of that existence and the infinite. (This orientation toward the infinite links Feuerbach clearly to the romantic tradition.) In all the operations of his body, man is made aware of the infinite; his body is the locus of the infinite. Consciousness, the generic form of man's presence to himself *in* and *through* the body is always consciousness of the infinite. Man's error is to have projected this infinite, which he discovers wholly within himself, beyond himself; to have conceived it as other to himself, as God, or pure idea, or as pure thought. This is the essence of his humanism: the immanence of the infinite in man's corporeal and finite existence. He says, "Absolute being, the God of man, is the very being of man. . . ." And again, "Do you think the infinite? The infinite which you think is the infinite power of thought, your own thought. Do you feel the infinite? You feel and affirm the infinite power of your own feeling." This yields the definition of spirit: the immanent infinity of man as existing body. Man is not, therefore, to escape into the worship of a transcendent God or to pursue an ideal of pure thought. He must realize the humanity within him, in both its dimensions: matter and spirit.

Upon reaching this exalted (and manifestly romantic) immanentistic humanism, Feuerbach seems baffled. How is this position to be translated into actionable terms? The limitation of the individual presents the first obstacle. How is the immanent infinity of man to be related to his finite individuality? This finitude is in the first instance numerical; Feuerbach tries to escape it by transferring the immanent infinity to the species (strategy, clearly, quite unworthy of western humanism, classical, Christian, or Renaissance). Death presents an even greater obstacle to this immanent infinity. Feuerbach struggles long and arduously with this problem of death. One of his most earnest works is his *Gedanken eines Denker über Tod und Unsterblichkeit* [Thoughts of a thinker on death and immortality], 1830. The only path which seems open to him is the development of this immanentistic humanism in utopian historicism. This position commits the existing individual, in the present, to work, with a sense of personal tragedy and of pride in the species, for ideal ends which only history, extended through an infinity of finite time, can realize. The tone of his writings does not lead us to believe that he embraces this prospect with the enthusiasm with which it will be embraced by a thinker whom he influenced extensively, Marx.

2. Psychophysical Materialism

This form of materialism is so dominant in the nineteenth century that some historians (cf. F. A. Lange: *Geschichte des Materialismus*, 1868; English trans. *History of Materialism*, 1950) reduce all other forms to it. Psychophysical materialism touches directly the very important problem of the status of the so-called "higher" or "spiritual" faculties or powers of man: thought, will, imagination, etc. In the course of western thought, these, and especially the first two enumerated, had been assigned a status and an operative capacity independent to a greater or lesser degree of the physical and physiological processes in which they are existentially involved. This independence had in turn become the basis for many of the propositions of the philosophy of man: the spirituality of the soul, the freedom of the will, the soul's immortality, etc. The thesis of psychophysical materialism seemed, consequently, to call many of these propositions of classical philosophical anthropology into question.

Psychophysical materialism is the attempt to establish, by a process of successive reduction, the total immanence of, dependence upon, and equation between all the psychic processes of man (and the analogous processes in other forms of organic life) and their physiological and physical conditions. All psychic phenomena could be described and explained in terms of physico-organic processes. No other principle, such as soul, spirit, etc., needed to be postulated. This process of reduction embraces a number of phases. The entire psychic life can be accounted for in terms of the functions of the brain and the central nervous system. All of the productive forces of life can be adequately described and accounted for in terms of the forces of matter. Atomic matter, as it is studied in the physical sciences, is the substratum of all organic and psychic forms. Culturally, many forces were at work in shaping this point of view. In the present context, only the purely speculative factors are of interest.

The immediate background for the development of psychophysical materialism was provided by the researches and investigations of such scientists as Hermann von Helmholtz and Heinrich Hertz. Helmholtz (1821–1894) was a physicist and physiologist, considered one of the founders of experimental and clinical psychology. His principal research lay in the areas of acoustics and optics, and he contributed basic findings in both these fields. Most important, however, was the schema within which he conducted his work. This was the total circuit between stimulus and the organism within which all the phenomena of sense life and psychic life could be exhaustively described and accounted for. Helmholtz leveled his criticism, in a special manner, at the Kantian *apriorism* of time and space; these, he held, could be exhaustively derived and accounted for in empirical terms within his schema. Heinrich Hertz (1857–1894), his pupil, continued his teacher's investigations, making contributions of especial value in the areas of the epistemology of science and the scientific method. These provide the theoretical bases for psychophysical materialism, because they outline the scientific validity of the reductive scheme on which it rested. Hertz stressed the function of symbols in scientific discourse, the symbolic character of concepts, and the importance of the principle of economy or simplicity in the explanatory scheme.

The salient features of psychophysical materialism may be illustrated by the thought of such men as Gustav Fechner (1801–1887), Ludwig Buchner (1824–1899), Jacob Moleschott (1822–1893) and Karl Vogt (1817–1895). Each of these men represents a particular aspect of this complex position, psychophysical materialism. If the reductive process mentioned above be taken as a continuum, each falls at some point along it, tending toward emphasis on either the physiological level or the more completely physical level.

Fechner may be considered the founder of psychophysical materialism. The name itself seems to come from the title of his fundamental work *Elemente der Psychophysik* [Elements of psychophysics], 1860. Trained in medicine, physics, and psychology, he was led to an intensive study of the problem of the soul by a religious crisis which he underwent in the years 1839–42. In the volume named above he defined psychophysics as "the exact science of the functional relations, or relations of dependence, between body and soul." He first proposes the hypothesis of *psychophysical parallelism* as a working basis. This hypothesis suggests that physical and psychical phenomena correspond reciprocally, as a text and its translation (his own arresting example). It should be possible, therefore, to measure psychical phenomena with mathematical exactness. The psychic fact may be considered the correlative of the nervous or physiological fact. The latter, in turn, could be considered in its relation to a physical stimulus, the magnitude of which could be measured exactly.

At this hypothetical level, Fechner's assumption proved fruitful. He is not content, however, to let it remain at this level. Through generalization he arrives at an "inductive metaphysics" in which he transfers experimental results to a realm beyond experience. In this "metaphysics" the material world and the corresponding "spiritual" world constitute a universe, an animated entity (principle of panpsychism), a single organism, whose ultimate animating principle is God. In this great organism, the material element, the cosmos, tends to define the range of the whole, just as, in the case of the living individual, the organism provides the basic context within which all transactions take place. Fechner recognizes no autonomy of the spiritual or psychic orders, whether in the individual or in the cosmos. Thus, he encounters great difficulties when he takes up the question of the relation between the psychic life of the individual and the animate life of the universe. If one is tempted to call him a panpsychist, the absolute immanence of the psychic principle in the material cosmos warns one to resist this temptation and to call his position a not unequivocal materialism.

The work of Jacob Moleschott falls into two areas. His work as a physiologist won him considerable repute. A Dutchman by birth, he was called to the chair of physiology, first at Turin and later at Rome. His influence from these posts was considerable: for example, on the criminal psychology of Cesare Lombroso. On the basis of these achievements in the field of physiology, he ventured metaphysical extrapolations. Because these metaphysical extrapolations seem to exceed their scientific bases by a considerable margin, he is commonly considered a dogmatic materialist. Placing great importance on mechanical models, he claims that all forms of reality, and especially those called "spiritual" and "transcendent" in the idealist tradition, can be explained in terms of the properties and transformations of a primitive matter, atomic in character, in response to the force which constitutes a primitive endowment of matter. This force "is not a God which gives impulse to matter, but is . . . an inseparable property of matter. There is no force without matter, nor matter without force. Life (organic and psychic) is not a product of any particular force, but is a state of matter based on its inalienable properties."

These, and other similar ideas, were advanced in such works as Moleschott's *Physiologie des Stoffwechsels in Pflanzen und Tiernen* [Physiologie of the transformations of matter in plants and animals], 1857, and the more celebrated *Der Kreislauf des Lebens* [The circulation of life], 1852. The latter work has a strong polemical flavor, directed against certain proposals for the reconciliation of theology and science; it was translated into Italian by Lombroso.

The position of Ludwig Buchner, expounded in his celebrated work *Kraft und Stoff* [Force and matter], 1855, is a popularized form of Moleschott's dogmatic materialism. The same assertions concerning matter and force are advanced in stronger and less conditional terms and with less pretense of scientific support. Karl Vogt is best remembered for a famous dispute with the physiologist Rudolf Wagner (1805–1864). The latter held that the doctrine of creation, in the Christian and biblical sense, could be reconciled with modern science. In the course of this dispute Vogt formulated the famous lemma of nineteenth-century materialism: "All is matter and nothing but matter." He is also credited with the most extreme formulation of dogmatic materialism with respect to psychic phenomena: "Thought is the secretion of the brain as bile is of the liver." In his less extreme expressions, Vogt leans toward a materialism of the monistic and evolutionary type best represented by Haeckel.

3. Monistic Materialism

The monistic tendency is already clearly present in psychophysical materialism. Nevertheless, a certain brake upon this tendency is also present there, because of its preoccupation with psychic phenomena. Monistic materialism, precisely so called, is more directly orientated toward the notion of matter itself. While it does seek to bring all phenomena, including those of the psychological order, within the range of matter, its main concern is to work out the implications of a certain concept of matter.

The scientific background of monistic materialism was provided by the electromagnetic theories of such scientists as W. Ostwald, J. C. Maxwell, and W. J. Rankins. These theories gave new prominence to the notion of energy. This energy was always conceived as one single energy, diffused through matter in atomic and molecular nuclei. This is a dynamic theory of matter, and its chief characteristic is that it conceives the all-embracing character of matter as the result of its inherent dynamism, the energy which it encloses and which really constitutes it. This materialism has not as yet felt the force of theories which would make it unnecessary to encapsulate energy in a material hull and would find it possible to account for "matter" itself in terms of energy, for example, as the density of a field. Representatives of monistic materialism include W. K. Clifford and J. C. Maxwell in England, and in France, the essayist Hippolyte Taine.

Taine (1828–1893) expounds his monistic materialism in his essay "De l'intelligence" [On the understanding], 1870. This essay purports to reduce the entire spiritual and psychological life of man, exhibited in the processes of thought, will and emotion, to a mechanical process of matter, conceived in terms suggested by the theories of electromagnetism, i.e., a matter which is the vehicle and locus of energy and hence capable of the dynamic transformations which the psychological processes represent. This mechanical process of matter is ruled by laws which, by reason of their rigorous necessity, are identical with the laws of nature. In order to understand the nature of psychological processes, Taine avers, it is necessary not to be deceived by certain words. Terms such as *reason, will, intelligence self,* etc., must be set aside; so too must such terms as *soul, vital force,* etc., which were excogitated to fill certain lacunae in our knowledge and comprehension. These are but literary metaphors which must be related to facts as established by observations.

Observation establishes that the psychic life of man is composed only of sensations and images; these possess a certain dynamism which involves them in movements of association and dissociation with other sensations and images. The reality of psychic life is constituted by the movement of images in relations of contiguity, contrast, opposition, or equilibrium. Metaphysically charged terms, such as *life* and *soul,* are invoked to express these movements. These images derive in turn from sensations.

Taine devotes the greatest amount of attention to the analysis of sensation. Sensation marks the limit of the psychic life, confronting it with another, contrasting world, the physical. An abyss, Taine avers, seems at first to separate these worlds. It is this abyss that his theory will bridge. Taine postulates that these two worlds are but the two faces of a common reality. The world of sensation is that reality as it is open to the observation of consciousness, especially introspection. The world of nature is that same reality as indirectly indicated to us by sensation, "inferred" in John Stuart Mill's sense. This situation is still unsatisfactory. The monistic tendency demands that one of these orders be brought under the other as its explanatory principle. The world of nature cannot be generated by the world of sensation. Taine rejects this possibility as one of the more genial delusions of idealism. The world of nature always appears a given to sensation. Therefore nature, of which matter is the principle, must support the monistic principle. Obviously, the concept of matter needed must embrace the dynamic possibilities of generating the world of sensation. This is precisely the concept of matter which the investigations of such scientists as Maxwell, in the field of electromagnetism, seem to provide. Taine adopts this concept of matter as the unifying principle of his synthesis of these two worlds, nature and consciousness.

The influence of Taine's views was large. The most prominent intellectual and literary figure to reflect them was Joseph-Ernest

Renan (1823–1892), a subtle, though basically unoriginal mind, who extended this materialism, as a critical instrument, into such varied fields as religious and literary criticism and the history of philosophy.

William Kingdon Clifford (1845–1879), during his short life, achieved distinction in a number of fields: mathematics, physics, and philosophy. In the context of the history of materialism, he is frequently placed among the evolutionary materialists. This would not seem to be correct. His materialism does not draw inspiration from evolutionary theory; rather, the latter found his materialism serviceable in its effort to find a principle to explain the dynamism of evolutionary process. His concept of matter was suggested to him by the theory of electromagnetism. This theory asserts that the ultimate particles of matter are not inert, but are endowed with a constitutive dynamism, with movement; every such movement is accompanied by an expulsive force, an ejection, which is fundamentally an electrical charge, which can become the object of consciousness. These expulsions are what we call sensations. Sensations, which in their "being-in-themselves" are expulsive electrical charges of matter, are also the "psychic atoms" of which conscious life is constituted. The monism implied is very clear. Nothing is necessary to account for sensations but the expulsive charge of the unit of matter; nothing is required for the complex world of consciousness save the psychic atoms, endowed with the capacity of combinatory movement. The germ of these ideas is contained in an essay in the journal *Mind* in 1878, the year before his death; it is entitled "On the Nature of Things in Themselves." His ideas are also presented in such works, published posthumously, as *Lectures and Essays* (2 vols., 1880) and *Seeing and Thinking* (2 vols., 1879).

James Clerk Maxwell (1831–1879), a physicist, is known best for his kinetic theory of gases, his theory of color, and the electromagnetic theory of light. Here interest centers on the philosophical extension he makes of these scientific ideas in his book *Matter and Motion,* 1872. This extension moves, albeit somewhat tentatively, toward an inclusive materialistic monism, on the basis of a concept of matter as dynamically charged that is implicit in his electromagnetic theory of light. It would be unjust to press this philosophical excursus farther than Maxwell did himself; issuing as it does, however, from a scientist of such stature, neither should it pass unnoted.

4. Evolutionary Monistic Materialism

While this form of materialism is closely identified with Ernst Haeckel, it is also expounded by other writers, for the most part deriva-

tive from Haeckel, such as J. G. Vogt in his works *Die Kraft* [Force],
1878, and *Der Absolute Monismus* [Absolute monism], 1908. The important work of Haeckel in this regard is *Der Monismus* [Monism],
1893, which belongs to his philosophical phase. Haeckel begins with a
notion of matter endowed with energy and moving in infinite space.
This matter possesses the capacity to form, through *concentration*
(pykosis), the whole range of natural objects, including all the species
of life. Through analogous processes, the species of life become capable of sensibility and consciousness. These elements are generated,
according to Haeckel, in the abysses of the oceans under the heat-
producing pressures of the ocean masses. Haeckel's ideas received a
fairly wide, but very transitory, currency; because many of his assertions, made with great assurance, lay beyond any form of verification,
his influence waned rather swiftly.

B. *Historical Materialism*

The inclusion of historical materialism in the general framework of
nineteenth-century materialism may demand some justification. Frequently it is dealt with as though it were a phenomenon of an entirely
different and independent order. Historical materialism is directly
related to the general current of materialism and was recognized as
being so related by its chief architect, Karl Marx.

This relationship is, in fact, two-pronged. On the one hand, historical materialism is related to the humanistic materialism of Feuerbach;
on the other, it is related—by way of Marx's conviction that he was
establishing the first genuinely *scientific* socialism—to those forms of
materialism which drew their notion of matter from the physical sciences. Marx, of course, reworked the derivative material of his system
in an original fashion; historical materialism, consequently, is no mechanical synthesis of alien elements. This dual relationship to the materialism of the period, nevertheless, provides its true historical context.

With what concept of matter was Marx working? This is the first
query which imposes itself. Immediately, a second, more restricted,
question must be added: What did he mean by calling his materialism
historical? Finally, it is necessary to ask: How did he use this notion of
matter as the unifying principle of his system?

The conception of matter with which Marx operates is man's productive capacity, work, as embodied in socially organized modes of
production. This conception is based on an analogy with the concept
of matter as extended in time-space and endowed with energy (or
reducible to energy) which is characteristic of contemporary materialism. Thus Marx's conception of man, as productive agent, links him

with the humanistic materialism of Feuerbach and the scientific forms of materialism.

This materialistic conception of man, as productive agent, and the work which is its identifying character can be interpreted either immanently or transitively—in terms, that is, of immanent transformations in the agent effected by the process, or in terms of its products. While the second interpretation is important in Marx's thought, it is the first upon which he lays greatest philosophical stress. Human work is immanent to man. What man produces by his labor is his own existence, his own nature. Man is what he makes himself through the social processes of work and production; the transitive products, goods or commodities, are relative to this and of lesser importance.

The historical character of this materialism follows from these features. The productive process as realized in terms of what man has made of himself can only be determined historically, in terms of man's own history viewed under the aspect of the kinds of social relations productive processes and their social organization have produced among men in history. There is no other way of saying what man is than by looking at what he has made of himself historically in terms of the social institutions in which the patterns of production have been fixed. Any other idea of "man" is an illusion, an abstraction, and eventually a distraction since it diverts our attention from man as he truly is. Marx establishes this point principally against Feuerbach. Feuerbach had indeed gone a long way toward bringing the idea of man down to earth from the heaven of Hegel's "pure thought." But man has to be brought down even further, in Marx's view. Feuerbach still thinks abstractly, in terms of the "essence," the "nature" of man. Marx insists that man be seen in his total concrete historical realization. But he does not make this point exclusively against Feuerbach; it is also the basis for his criticism of other anthropologies, for example, classical anthropology, the anthropology of Christianity, of Hegelianism, and of utilitarianism, as well as of all forms of "utopian" socialism. All deal with abstractions. Man can be found only in his concrete historical reality.

When he turns to history in quest of man, what is it then that Marx finds? Something quite other than we might have expected, something which reveals the romantic core of Marx's vision. Had he been consistent with his own materialism, Marx should have found only what man had inexorably produced by the social processes of work. He should then have given a phenomenology of this historical man. He could not, however, legitimately have conceived him as other than he found him. Like all the processes of matter and energy, those historical productive processes by which man generates or produces himself must have been entirely determined and could not have been other than they were,

either in their form or in their product. He would have been con-
strained logically to accept man as he found him.

Quite the opposite is the case. Marx rejects this man whom he discovers in history as a caricature of the "real" man, of man as he might
have been or might be, man as he must be in order to be truly man.
Marx spoke of the distance between man as he discovers him in history
and man as he could be, as he should be, in Hegelian terms. He calls
it *alienation*. Man in history is alienated man: man set over against
himself, man realized historically in a manner other than the ideal of
man, his potential, would demand. Consequently, Marx sets out to
give a phenomenology, not of historical man, but of alienated man, i.e.,
the characteristics of this alienation, its causes, and finally the norm by
which this alienation is measured and the ideal vision of man implied
in this norm.

The phenomenology of alienated man leads Marx to his critique of
bourgeois society and its economic system. The cardinal principle of
Marx's critique is that work is intransitive, or immanent. There is an
inalienable and infrangible bond between man as worker and the
product of his work, whether this product be something beyond himself which can become an object of commerce, a commodity, or a condition internal to man himself, his own mode of existence. Indeed, no
delimiting line can be drawn between these, because work and its
product, in any form, are one. The bourgeois economic system alienated man from himself because it broke this necessary bond between
man and his work. It expropriates the product of work, which naturally
belongs to the worker by whom it is produced. *Expropriation*, therefore, is the basic form of alienation. In the bourgeois or capitalist system of production, not only is the product of man's work alienated and
expropriated, but man himself, the worker, is turned into a commodity.
This constitutes the second characteristic of man's alienation from himself in bourgeois society. The worker's work, which is his inalienable
possession, both as activity and as product, is made into an object of
commerce, to be bought and sold like any other commodity, violating
the autonomous status of the worker as a person. This conversion into
a commodity is the polar opposite of Marx's conception of man's integral relation to himself. (At the basis of his view, very probably, is the
Kantian ideal of the person, who can never be used as a means but
must always be respected as a person, an end in himself.)

Bourgeois society, and in particular the economic system which is
its structural principle, is thus the cause of man's alienation. Alienation
could not be recognized as such, of course, were Marx not operating
with an ideal vision of man. The basic character of that ideal vision has
already been touched upon. Realizing that society, capitalist society, is

the cause of this alienation, Marx extends his ideal vision to include an ideal society in which all social relations and all institutions would be ordered to the respect, achievement, and maintenance of his ideal vision of man. His name for this society, for the human condition which it would bring into existence, is communism. These reflections reveal that Marx is, before all else, a moral thinker, even a moralist, the inheritor of a long line of secularist humanistic moralists, who places man's essential moral value in his own integrity and looks for a social condition in which this value will be realized and stabilized.

Marx's moralism is the source of the inspiration for Marx the revolutionary and utopian. There is a fundamental divison in his attitude toward history. He believes, on the one hand, that there are forces inherent in history as an objective process which will inevitably bring about the rectification of the alienation from which man suffers, by creating the ideal society in which his ideal vision of man will be realized. In this manner, he endows the objective forces of history with moral dynamism toward the ideal terms which he has defined. On the other hand, Marx is wary of moralizing the objective forces of history. This wary Marx feels that there must indeed be a force within history capable of bringing about a change in historical process which will advance the advent of communism, but he does not feel that this power resides in the objective forces of history. It resides rather in the moral will of men. And not, furthermore, in the moral will of all men, but only of certain elect men who perceive the gravity of this alienation and the injustice it involves and are willing to set themselves against the social and economic systems which generate and perpetuate this condition.

Thus historical materialism engenders both a deterministic-utopian and a revolutionary-utopian vision of history. According to the first, the intrinsic, constitutive forces of objective historical process alone will bring about the ideal social system; that process is freighted with a necessitarian dynamism toward the integral man as the supreme value and the communist social system in which that integrity will be realized. According to the second vision, history alone cannot be relied upon to generate this ideal condition. The moral will of man must intervene directly. The moral will of man is thus a revolutionary and utopian will, and it is this will which supplies the historical dynamism necessary to bring about the ideal social condition, communism.

Marx never resolved the tension between the deterministic and the revolutionary dynamisms of history. Nor did his successors. His contemporary and collaborator, Engels, laid emphasis upon the scientific character of Marxian socialism; he was thus led from historical to dialectical materialism. Lenin exacerbated, rather than mollified, this tension; his theoretical bent drew him toward an excessive evaluation of the necessitarian element; his practical, political bent drew him in the direction of the revolutionary element. At the highest level of his theoretical achievement he sought to show how dialectical material- ism provided the scientific basis for historical materialism, but it is questionable whether he achieved coherence in this effort. Stalin had but slight theoretical interest, and this was always at the service of his practical and revolutionary aims; nevertheless, in his essay "On Dialec- tical Materialism and Historical Materialism," he provides one of the clearest statements of the effort to incorporate dialectical materialism as the dynamic principle of historical materialism when he writes: "Historical materialism extends the principles of dialectical materialism to social life." This statement, however, remains a dogmatic assertion, because Stalin adduces no persuasive argument to sustain it, content- ing himself with the repetition of texts from his masters, Marx, Engels, and Lenin.

C. *Dialectical Materialism*

The germinal ideas of dialectical materialism are to be found in historical materialism. Dialectical materialism, however, develops a configuration proper to itself and exercises a historical and cultural influence distinct from that of historical materialism. This development exhibits four phases: 1) the germination of those ideas within historical materialism, 2) the fundamental formulation of dialectical materialism by Engels, 3) the modifications of Lenin, and 4) the dogmatization of the doctrine of Lenin in the form given it by Stalin.

1. The Germinal Ideas of Dialectical Materialism as Identifiable in Historical Materialism

The notion of the dialectic permeates the thought of Karl Marx in its more speculative phases; so too does the employment of the concept of materialism to designate certain aspects of the historical process. His historical materialism, consequently, is a first synthesis of these notions. His notion of the dialectic is fundamentally that of Hegel; however, he effects a revision of the inner economy of Hegel's dialectic similar to that which Engels was to effect within Marx's own. Marx expressed this revision by saying that Hegel had stood the dialectic on its head, while he intended to set it on its feet again. The positive ele- ment in Hegel's dialectic was mind or spirit (thought), while nature was simply the negative moment. Marx instead asserts anew the pri- macy of nature, the given (matter), making thought and mind the

mirror of nature and matter. Within this basic revision Marx continues
to use the Hegelian dialectical scheme to define the relations between
the various elements of his analysis. Thus, in the *Economic-Philosophical Manuscripts of 1844,* he asserts that the relation between social
man and nature (the sum of the material forces at man's disposal) is a
dialectical relation: Man is a part of nature, while nature is the means
of life for man. Society represents the synthesis of these in its economic
organization, in his terms: the *consubstantiality* of man and nature.
Society, as the dialectical synthesis of man and nature, represents the
perfect naturalization of man and the perfect humanization of nature.
Similarly, he employs the schema of the Hegelian dialectic in his analysis of social man: Social life consists essentially in work, the production of material things necessary for life, and man externalizes a part of
his inner being and power in this product. This externalization is the
same process by which, in Hegel's system, spirit posits nature by
exteriorization. It is a necessary but negative step. Just as, in the
Hegelian dialectic, this externalized nature must be taken up again
by spirit and its negative and external state overcome, so, for the
integrity of man, this moment of exteriorization in the process of work
and in the product must be reassimilated to the system of the inner
forces of man. This reassimilation takes the form of the vindication
of his right to the product, its inalienability. If this process of rein-
tegration is frustrated (as happens, Marx asserts, in capitalist society)
alienation ensues. This term, too, is Hegel's and the moment which it
designates for Marx is parallel to the moment in the life of spirit so
designated by Hegel. In Marx the term designates the condition of the
proletariat under capitalism—a condition not only of extreme material
exploitation and impoverishment but a state of spiritual oppression and
deprivation, which, on reaching the point of exasperation, must ignite
class warfare.

One point of ambiguity still persists, however: the exact meaning
of the term *matter.* This term does not signify for Marx the "given"
world of nature and natural process, "in itself," as transcendent to man.
It indicates the economic activities of man into which the elements of
nature enter instrumentally. This point is important, because the first
step in Engels' transformation of Marxian historical materialism into
dialectical materialism concerns the status of nature.

2. Friedrich Engels and the Formulation
of Dialectical Materialism

Because Marx considered nature only relative to human economic
action, his position is considered a *humanism.* (This is only one of the

reasons for assigning this character to his thought.) By contrast, the position developed by Engels is correctly recognized as a form of naturalism. The first revision which Engels effects within Marx's position is the assignment of an autonomous status to *nature*. Nature is no longer a negative moment, as it was in Hegel. Neither is it the merely *instrumental* nature of Marx, the nature which is "at hand," employable in the productive activity of man, and which reappears in its negative and alienated character as the *product*. Engels is more strongly influenced than Marx by the growth of the natural sciences. In response to this influence he posits nature as the absolute principle, to which man himself is relative. In doing so, he is carrying one step further that "setting Hegel on his feet" of which Marx boasted. He is also following the hints given by Marx in that passage of the *Economic-Philosophical Manuscripts* referred to earlier.

Having established nature as the positive moment, Engels transposes the dialectical movement to it, making of the dialectic the inner dynamic principle of matter itself. This is the basic sense in which he speaks of dialectical materialism: It is matter itself which exhibits and obeys the dialectical structure and movement. The spiritual dialectic, the dialectic of the Idea, is completely displaced. The humanistic dialectic of Marx is not denied but made a moment of the dialectic of matter. Stalin was later to say that this humanistic dialectic is the extension of the material dialectic into the social realm. It is more accurate to say that the humanistic dialectic is made entirely immanent to the dialectic of matter. Hence, Engels' thought is an example of a complete materialistic monism. Its peculiar feature is that, instead of conceiving the movement of matter mechanically, it conceives it dialectically, as exhibiting those features which Hegel had reserved for mind or spirit, the Idea, and Marx for the processes of history.

In the next stage of his thought, Engels set about determining the laws of the dialectical movement of matter. The dialectic of Hegel could serve him only as a remote model; its laws could not survive transference to matter. The same is true with regard to the humanistic and historical dialectic of Marx. Engels formulates three laws of the dialectical movement of matter: 1) the law of the passage from quantity to quality; 2) the law of the mutual compenetration of opposites; 3) the law of the negation of the negation. The doctrinal content of Engels' dialectical materialism consists in the development and exposition of these laws. He disclaims, however, the discovery of these laws. In a passage of *Dialektik der Natur* [The dialectic of nature], 1925, he protests that they are Hegel's laws and he points out the places where, he believes, Hegel had employed them in his works: the first law, in the first part of *Logik*; the second law, in the second part of the same book; while the third law provides the principle for the construction of the entire Hegelian system.

The basic significance of these laws may be indicated briefly. The first law is predicated on the fact that, while science demands the quantification of all material process, nature exhibits quantified and qualified characteristics. For a monistic system like his own, the closing of the gap between these two orders of characteristics in nature is a problem of basic importance. Unlike the antidialectician Kierkegaard, he could not admit any "leaps" from one order to the other. To meet this problem, the first law asserts that qualitative differences can be produced only by the addition or subtraction of matter or motion according to quantitative variations.

The second law deals with the same problem which, according to Engels, Hegel had faced in the second (and by far the more important) part of his *Logik:* the inner movement by which opposites divide and unite to generate the higher synthesis. On this law depends the continuity of the dialectical movement. If the law of the relation between opposites were simply that of contradiction, the process of the dialectic would be immobilized. Opposites are related by some nexus of affirmation and negation which obeys some other law than that of contradiction. Engels tries to express this relation by means of the notion of compenetration.

In another passage of the *Dialectics of Nature,* Engels tries to illustrate this idea by an example from science: the relation of attraction and repulsion between polar elements. Science, he says, has demonstrated that all polar opposites are conditioned by the alternate play of the two opposite poles upon each other, that the distinction and opposition between the poles can be made only within the context of their reciprocal union. Their union, in turn, can be grasped only through their mutual separation, the opposition between them. The force of this example seems dubious, however, for it does not provide for the step which he must anticipate: the higher synthesis toward which the dialectic moves.

The synthesis is brought into better focus by the third law, that of the negation of the negation. There are two possible meanings of this principle. The first ministers to the construction of the synthesis, the second to the continuity of the dialectical movement. In the first meaning, the field of the law's application lies within the triadic movement: thesis, antithesis, synthesis. Within this field, the negation of the negation is precisely that movement by which the force of the antithesis is overcome to open the way to the synthesis. In this case, the moment of the negation of the negation would be the precise moment of the "compenetration" of opposites. This sense of the law would make

Engels' illustration from polar movement irrelevant; in the polar movement, the precise moment of compenetration sends the constitutive movement back toward one of the poles and not upward toward the synthesis.

The second possible meaning of the law is that every synthesis becomes the thesis against which a new antithesis will be directed and from which the movement toward a fresh synthesis would be initiated. In this sense, the law of the negation of the negation serves the continuity of the dialectical movement. It is dubious, however, in what sense it can then be called a negation of the negation; it ought rather to be called the negation of the affirmation, i.e., the affirmation which is the heart of the synthesis.

Thus it also becomes clear that the illustration of the second and third of his three laws cannot be carried on independently; they involve each other so closely as to awaken the question whether they really are two.

Historical materialism, it was noted, is conceived as the inner constitutive part of dialectical materialism. It is important to understand how this relation is established by Engels. It involves, in the first place, the reduction, if not elimination, of the humanistic element in the formation of the relations of production which determine the ideological superstructure of culture in society. In Marx, that formation had, to a certain degree at least, involved man's self-determinative activity. In Engels, these relations, and with them the superstructure, become "natural products" of the materialistic dialectic. Engles is led to the formation of the rather strange notion of the "destruction of *praxis*." Marx has placed the utmost emphasis on *praxis*, human action. The improvement and correction of the social relations based on systems of production depended upon the intervention of human action in the processes of history. Engels, on the contrary, seems to interpret such intervention as an obstacle. The entire process of such improvement must be surrendered to the dialectic of matter. If this interpretation of his thought is correct, it is clear that within dialectical materialism Engels gives an interpretation of historical materialism which is significantly different from, and perhaps wholly destructive of, that originally offered by Marx.

3. Nikolai Lenin (1870–1924)

Lenin's contribution to speculative thought seems relatively slight. Nevertheless, it is of cultural concern for it still influences the basic thought of the Soviet Union. In the first phase of his thought, he had accepted dialectical materialism in the form it had been given by

Engels. He was not then aware of the philosophical speculations of Marx's youth on the problems of the dialectic. Engels had rested the case of dialectical materialism on science. It was this reliance on science which had induced the crisis in which Lenin discovered the doctrine. Science had undergone changes which made the science to which Engels confidently appealed seem outdated. The new physical theories of the atom held little promise of support for Engels' theories. The discovery of radioactivity, leading to a new understanding of the internal structure of the atom, brought about significant changes in the concept of matter. Some theorists even spoke of the disappearance of matter, of its "dematerialization." Philosophical criticism of scientific knowledge felt the attraction of "empirio-critical" or even idealistic theories of science, to Mach, Avenarius, Poincaré. Lenin, during his period of exile in western Europe, became aware of these changes and the consequences they involved for the philosophical basis of communism. His purpose became to engage these developments in order to defend the communist position and to restate that position in such a way that it could meet these new developments.

Lenin's first book: *Materialism and Empirio-criticism,* 1909, has been looked upon as one of the strangest in the literature of philosophy. Its strident tone, its strange use of political and revolutionary terms to characterize philosophical tendencies, its bizarre but perceptive modes of reasoning earned it the epithet "fantastic." Its purpose was to recover and save the scientific concept of matter in the face of the "anti-materialism" then emerging. To this end, Lenin thought it necessary to rehabilitate the realist epistemology upon which dialectical materialism, in the form given it by Engels, seemed to depend.

Lenin distinguished two concepts of "matter," the scientific and the philosophical. The first was orientated toward the ever more refined knowledge of the internal structure of matter (atomic, molecular, subatomic, etc.), and Lenin steered fairly clear of it. Under the philosophical notion of matter, however, he introduced the elements of realist epistemology: Matter is that which, acting upon our senses, produces sensation. A second formulation seems more precise: Matter is a philosophical category which designates the objective reality which is given to man in sensation, as that reality exists independently of sensation. All the changes which might occur in the natural sciences, he felt, could not call this concept into question. The objective basis of Marxist philosophical materialism, which was in turn the basis of his own revolutionary philosophy, was made secure.

To insure this situation still more, the problem of knowledge had to be attacked more directly. Against all modern epistemological theories, he sustained his own theory of "reflection." He seems to have firmly believed that this theory would meet all modern scientific and philosophical needs. This theory, in fact, proves to be nothing more than a heavy-handed revival of a point of view at least as ancient as the Epicureans: that our sensations are "copies" or "images" of an independent reality which lies behind them. As Gustav Wetter, an acute student of Lenin's ideas, has observed, the most he could have hoped to prove by this line of argument would be that some of men's theories are true. The theory of reflection itself, as Lenin states it, has no genuine theoretical force, for it explains neither why nor under what conditions knowledge is necessarily true.

To strengthen the position of dialectical materialism Lenin addresses Hegel directly. His immediate effort is to secure a mastery of the principles of the dialectic. The results of these studies were subsequently published as the *Philosophical Notebooks,* 1938. Here too, Lenin the philosopher is dominated by Lenin the polemicist. He is still in quest of the ground upon which to establish his rigid Marxism and from which to attack those "deviationists" within and without Russia who endangered Marxian orthodoxy by adopting mechanistic positions on matter. In this context he develops his notion of "spontaneous motion." This notion is intended to meet the problem of the initiation of the movement of matter, a problem which, in strictly materialist terms, need not be put. Spontaneous movement has its origin either in the unity or in the identity (Lenin does not decide this issue unambiguously) of opposites. As examples of this unity of opposites in matter he points out the *plus* and *minus* of mathematics, action and reaction in mechanics, the positive and the negative charge in electricity, examples of which he is not himself entirely confident.

In these notebooks Lenin also seeks to develop further his "theory of reflection" by assimilating it to the dialectical movement of thought in Hegel. This assimilation is intended to establish the essentially dialectical character of human thought. This dialectic of thought leads from non-science to science. Before non-science, the object stands as the "thing-in-itself." The dialectical task of science is to transform that "being-in-itself" into a "being-for-us," the object of knowledge. These speculations prove inconclusive. They throw no fresh light on Hegel and it is dubious whether they serve to clarify or strengthen the position which Lenin is seeking to define and defend. Even their service to his ideological and polemical purposes with respect to the dissident elements in Russian Marxism seem indirect and ultimately ineffective from a theoretical point of view. Practically, his views, however ambiguous, triumphed within the ranks of Russian Marxism. They served to define Marxist orthodoxy and offered the basis for the condemnation of all subsequent deviationists.

4. Joseph Stalin (1879–1953)

Stalin was an even less disinterested thinker than Lenin, if that is possible. He was above all the party disciplinarian. He sought to forge in dialectical materialism an instrument of party orthodoxy. His chief achievement in this effort is the formulation of the "seven theses" of Marxist thought. Of these, three expressed "Marxist philosophical materialism" and the remaining four "Marxist dialectical method." The classical passages for this formulation are to be found in his *Questions of Leninism* (sometimes rendered as *Problems of Leninism.*)

The three theses of "Marxist philosophical materialism" take the following form: 1) The world is material in nature and the diverse phenomena of the world are but different aspects of matter in motion; the elements of the world, consequently, which constitute and explain everything else, are matter and motion, matter endowed with motion (cf. the essay "On Dialectical Materialism and Historical Materialism" in the work cited above). 2) Nature (matter) is an objective reality, existing outside of and independently of consciousness; it is the *first given* because it is the source of sensations, of representations, and of consciousness; all the latter are secondary and derivative, the reflection of matter. Thought itself is nothing but a product of matter, when matter reaches a high level of perfection; this point of perfection is marked by the production of the brain. Thought is cerebral movement. 3) This world of matter in motion and the laws which control it are perfectly knowable, and our knowledge of the laws of nature as verified by experience and by action is a valid knowledge which has the value of objective truth.

At this point Stalin introduces certain important modifications into his position. The first is the thesis that, though thought is a product of matter, the essential difference between physical phenomena and psycho-spiritual phenomena is not to be denied or minimized. Stalin thus distinguishes his position from all vulgar, mechanistic forms of materialism. To trace the higher activities, moreover, *genetically* to matter and its movement is not to reduce those higher movements *formally* to the lower and more inclusive. Here lies the heart of dialectical materialism: the production of irreducible novelty, the genesis of the more perfect from the less perfect.

Stalin proceeds to analyze the laws of the dialectic of matter. The laws he identifies are a revision of the three laws which Engels had identified and had attributed to Hegel. In Stalin's hands they become "four essential traits" of the dialectic of matter, expressed as follows: 1) The world is not to be conceived as a casual agglomeration of objects or of phenomena, but as a unique, coherent whole, within which every element conditions every other and the whole, while the whole, in turn, conditions each. 2) The whole is to be considered in a state of perpetual movement and change, so that at every moment something new comes to be and develops and something dissolves and disappears. 3) The dialectical process is one which passes from hidden and insignificant quantitative changes to open and radical changes and finally to qualitative changes; all of this occurs rapidly, without prevision, by leaps from one state to another. Every change has two phases: first, a purely evolutionary change in which only nonessential transformations take place; and secondly, a revolutionary phase, in which, by way of an unforeseen leap, the thing in question changes qualitatively, ceases to be that which it was before, and becomes something else. Stalin thinks that he can thus explain novelty in the world, including the appearance of phenomena essentially superior to those preceding: life from inorganic matter, human spiritual consciousness from the animal psyche, and the latter from organic but unconscious forms. 4) The source of movement and development is determined without recourse to a first mover or cause of motion outside the world. Lenin had already indicated that the quest of such a mover was the consequence of a false concept of motion, that held by mechanism, which conceives matter as essentially at rest and hence must seek an initiating principle of motion outside that which is moved. Stalin avers that the source of motion is to be found within the objects which are moved and change. This source is the "contradictions" which are inherent in those things and the "oppositions" which characterize matter itself. He enunciates on this basis the "law of the unity and struggle of opposites" and formulates it thus: the phenomena of nature exhibit internal contradictions because they all have a positive and a negative side, a past and a future, elements which perish and elements which develop. The struggle between these elements constitutes the content of the process of development. As a consequence, the process of development in the world takes place, not according to a harmonious evolution, but rather through the manifestations of the contradictions inherent in things and through the struggle of opposing tendencies.

At this point, he believes, the relation between historical materialism and dialectical materialism becomes clear. This relation may be viewed in two ways. Dialectical materialism may be viewed as the extension of the dialectic, as Marx had discovered it in history, to the whole of reality; or, conversely, historical materialism may be seen as a specific process within the wider process of dialectical materialism. In either view, dialectical materialism is seen as the justifying principle of the struggle of classes which Marx had depicted; it also provides the basis for the entire theory of historical, revolutionary change and, specifically, for the revolution at whose head Stalin stood.

These traits, Stalin believes, make it possible to account for the appearance of spiritual phenomena from the material basis. Dialectical materialism can thus justify fully that order of phenomena, the spiritual, for which it was formerly thought necessary to deny materialism and characterize reality as spiritual. He identifies as spiritual values: liberty (which he conceives, in Spinozan fashion, as consciousness of necessity), finality in human activity (thus justifying that part of Marx's doctrine which had advocated human intervention in the determinate processes of history), and, finally, the category of "ought" or "duty," on the same plane as "being" and "necessity," which allows for the whole range of moral evaluations.

At a later stage Stalin modified this position in response to certain historical actualities. The Marxist revolution in Russia was definitive. The new task was the consolidation of the Soviet state. A new logic was required which would show that the process of dialectical materialism itself called for a limit to revolutionary change. This led, on the one hand, to the ideological war between Stalin and Trotsky; on the other, it led to the development of national communism. But these developments, so clearly ideological, really belong to the ideological history of Soviet communism rather than to the history of philosophy.

5. Some Further Developments
of Dialectical and Historical Materialism

Pierre Pascal sums up the situation in the Soviet Union after Stalin in the following manner: "Il n'y a plus, depuis 1930, de pensée vivant, même à l'intérieur du marxisme"; that is, "There is no longer, since 1930, any living thought, not even within Marxism" (*Les grandes courants de la philosophie mondial contemporaine*, Première Partie: "Panoramas Nationaux," Vol. II, p. 1172). Outside the Soviet Union, certain exponents of the official Soviet philosophy did bring to it a touch of living reflection. They reflect, not the official party line, but the effort to release dialectical materialism from the rigid ideological framework which had been imposed on it. Of these thinkers two deserve mention, Georg Lukacs and Antonio Gramsci.

The concern of Georg Lukacs (b. 1885) is to pierce the titanic complacency of the Soviet system and make room for that ontological anxiety which lies at the root of all human experience. He discovers the vulnerable point of that structure in art. The aesthetic theory of Marx and Engels, he demonstrates (*K. Marx und F. Engels als Literaturhistoriker:* [Karl Marx and Friedrich Engels as historians of literature] 1948), retained the idealist insight into artistic expression as an autonomous and creative act. The position of socialist realism which sought to bend this activity of the artist inexorably to the social and political purposes of the state is both contrary to the initial insights of Marxism and inimical to creative life within the Soviet system. Without negating any of the principal theses of Marxism, even in its Leninist form, Lukacs seeks to make a place within it for artistic and cultural life, both to insure the creative resources within Marxism and as a bond of coexistence at a spiritual level with the cultural world beyond the Soviet Union. (Cf. for Lukacs: Victor Zitta, *Georg Lukacs' Marxism: Alienation, Dialectics, Revolution,* 1964; the vast output of Lukacs' pen is listed in the bibliography pp. 253–295.)

Antonio Gramsci (1891–1937) founder of the Communist Party organ in Italy, "L' Unità," joined the Communist Party in 1924 and became its secretary. In 1926 he was condemned to twenty years imprisonment by the Italian Fascist government and died as a result of the rigors of his imprisonment. A moving document of his reflections during this period is his *Lettere dal carcere* [Letters from prison], 1947, which is reminiscent of the *Mie prigioni* [My imprisonments] of Silvio Pellico. His chief theoretical work is the group of studies published under the title: *Il materialismo storico e la filosofia di B. Croce* [Historical materialism and the philosophy of Benedetto Croce], 1948.

For the understanding of this work it is well to recall that Croce had, in an early phase of his career, engaged Marxism and had decided in favor of a historicism on spiritualistic principles, the center of which was the dynamic idea of liberty. Gramsci seeks, in this work, to regain the spiritual springs of Marxism by way of a fresh rapproachement with the thought of Croce. He wants to place the entire post-Marxian development of dialectical and historical materialism in parentheses and to make fresh contact with the Marxian *ethos* and its source in the Hegelian philosophy of spirit. If this could not be effected, he foresaw only the progressive rigidification of Marxism into soulless statism, having its theoretical basis in an illusory apotheosis of science. Some have called Gramsci a repentent Marxist, and this is perhaps true. What is also true, however, is that there is rekindled in his work something of the moral idealism of the original Marx.

Readings

I. Scientific Materialism

Buchner, L. *Force and Matter: Principles of the Natural Order of the Universe.* London: Asher, 1884.
Haldane, J. S. *Materialism.* New York: Harper & Brothers, 1932.
Hayes, J. A. *A Generation of Materialism (1871–1900).* New York: Harper & Brothers, 1941.
Sellars, R. W.; McGill, V. S.; and Farber, M., eds. *Philosophy for the Future: The Quest of Modern Materialism.* New York: Macmillan, 1949.

II. HISTORICAL MATERIALISM
Books
Bober, M. M. *Karl Marx's Interpretation of History.* New York: W. W. Norton, 1965.
Cornforth, M. C. *Historical Materialism.* New York: International Publishers, 1954.
Croce, B. *Historical Materialism and the Economics of Karl Marx.* Translated by C. E. Meredith. London: Allen & Unwin, 1914.
Federn, K. *Materialist Conception of History.* London: Macmillan, 1939.
Plekhanov, G. V. *Materialist Conception of History.* New York: International Publishers, 1940.
Witt-Hansen, J. S. *Historical Materialism: Method, Theories, Exposition and Critique.* Copenhagen: Munksgaard, 1960.

Essays and articles
Fleischer, H. "The Acting Subject in Historical Materialism." In *Philosophy in the Soviet Union,* edited by Ervin Laszlo, pp. 13–29. Dordrecht: D. Reidel, 1967.
Schiebel, Joseph. "Changing the Unchangeable Historical Materialism and Six Versions of Eternal Laws of Historical Development." *Studies in Soviet Thought,* VII (1967), 318–332.

III. DIALECTICAL MATERIALISM
Books
Acton, H. B. *The Illusion of the Epoch: Marxism-Leninism as a Philosophical Creed.* Boston: Beacon Press, 1957.
Bochenski, I. M. *Soviet Russian Dialectical Materialism (Diamat).* Translated by Sollohub-Blakeley. Dordrecht: D. Reidel, 1963.
Cornforth, M. C. *Marxism and Linguistic Philosophy.* New York: International Publishers, 1965.
Dutt, C., ed. *Fundamentals of Marxism-Leninism.* London: Lawrence & Wishart, 1961.
Joroavsky, D. *Soviet Marxism and Natural Science.* New York: Columbia University Press, 1961.
Monnerot, J. *Sociology and Psychology of Communism.* Translated by Jane Degras and Richard Rees. Boston: Beacon Press, 1953.
Planty-Bonjour, Guy. *The Categories of Dialectical Materialism.* Translated by T. J. Blakeley. Dordrecht: D. Reidel, 1967.
Sartre, J. P. *Search for a Method.* Translated by H. E. Barnes. New York: Knopf, 1963.
Somerville, J. M. *Soviet Philosophy: A Study of Theory and Practice.* New York Philosophical Library, 1946.
Wetter, G. *Dialectical Materialism.* Translated by P. Heath. London: Routledge & Kegan Paul, 1958.

Essays and articles
Bochenski, J. M. "Thomism and Marxism-Leninism." *Studies in Soviet Thought,* VII (1967), 154–168.
De George, R. T. "The Foundations of Marxist-Leninist Ethics." In *Philosophy in the Soviet Union,* edited by Ervin Laszlo, pp. 49–60. Dordrecht: D. Reidel, 1967.

CHAPTER V

Realism
and Naturalism

Introduction

The dominance which idealism exercised over European and American thought well into the first decades of the present century provoked two strong currents of reaction. The first of these, pragmatism, has already been considered. The second, naturalistic realism, is, in fact, a double reaction, first, against idealism and, second, against pragmatism and the manner in which pragmatism sought to refute idealism. Indeed, some of the most active critics of pragmatism in America, such as Arthur O. Lovejoy, are in the ranks of the new realists, and, while many of the naturalists, such as Woodward and Randall, show clear evidence of the impress of pragmatism, their own philosophical efforts are directed to the construction of a position which would sharply limit pragmatism's claims. The realist and naturalist reaction against idealism, like the pragmatic, is not limited to America, although some of its chief episodes took place there. It also extended to England, where it has very strong representatives, and to the European continent.

It is always dangerous to generalize a point of view, since the particular manner in which different philosophers develop common insights belongs to the essence of even the most coherent movement or school. However, some common characteristics of naturalistic realism may be established. These characteristics are present, though always with different intonations, in the various adherents of the position and may, consequently, be considered the basic elements to which all would assent, each in his own way. In the first place, realism and naturalism are linked by an intimate logic, for realism tends to assume the existence of nature as its point of departure and to take nature's mode of being as paradigmatic. Man and all his activities, including

90

those variously designated as "higher" and "spiritual," are considered parts or manifestations of nature and are to be understood through a knowledge of nature's principles. It is true that nonmetaphysical forms of realism are also found in the history of philosophy, but these represent not rejections of naturalistic bases but extrapolations upon them. When realistic naturalism defines itself (as in the present case) against idealism, certain other characteristics tend to take on greater importance. An example is the thesis that the object of knowledge is not a part, element, or creation of the subject of knowledge; that the object which comes to be known has a mode of being of its own, independent of the circumstance of its being known, and possesses properties which are not reducible to those which it possesses as known and that this mode of being is intrinsically knowable. Adequate knowledge is precisely knowledge of this proper mode of the being of objects. Finally, the most salient characteristics of realistic naturalism may be emphasized: The mode of being of all objects which can be known has its model in the mode of being possessed by natural objects.

In considering the manner in which these common characteristics are present in the individual representatives of this tendency, we will adhere to the following order: the English representatives of realism and naturalism; the neo-realist and critical-realist movements in America; George Santayana, who deserves monographic treatment because of the very individualistic manner in which he develops the common theses; and finally the naturalists of the "New York school," men such as Woodbridge and M. R. Cohen, who profited from the experience of the previous efforts. In this way we may come to a fairly comprehensive view of the current which will preserve some internal distribution of relevance and importance.

A. *English Realism and Naturalism*

George Edward Moore (1873–1958) must be accounted the dean of realistic naturalists in England, and his *Principia Ethica,* 1903, must be recognized as one of its fundamental documents. Even more fundamental, however, since it has been a charter and a program for this movement, is the essay "The Refutation of Idealism," which appeared in the English journal *Mind* in 1903. This essay established the basic lines along which realism and naturalism were to conduct the two-pronged campaign, principally against idealism and secondarily (and in a very minor way in England) against pragmatism. His other works —*Philosophical Studies,* 1922, *Some Main Problems of Philosophy,* 1953 (but dating originally from 1910–11), and the numerous articles he contributed to philosophical journals—developed the implications of that essay.

In "The Rufutation of Idealism," Moore compares idealism's concept of the *cognitive relation* with the realistic concept. For idealism the cognitive relation is *inclusive* and *internal:* to be an object means to be a part of consciousness or to be a quality of consciousness. Just as a part cannot exist outside the whole of which it is a part or a quality apart from that of which it is a quality, so objects can have no existence outside of or independently of the consciousness for which they are objects. Moore rejects this idealistic analysis. It fails to recognize that the cognitive relation is a unique relation. It is an external relation between two entities, mind and object. However, this relation does not change or modify the character of the terms between which it exists in such a way as to make them different than they would be independent of that relation. This point of view raises the question of the possibility and character of this kind of "external" relation. Moore takes up this problem in *Philosophical Studies,* where he criticizes the doctrine of "internal" relations and elaborates a doctrine of "external" relations. He maintains that, if an object possesses a relational property or characteristic, it may also not have it; thus, from a proposition which affirms that a term is what it is, there follows no proposition which affirms a relational property of that object. This theory of external relations, as proposed by Moore, is the most universal principle of all modern forms of realism.

Moore's refutation of idealism was associated with his defense of common sense. The realistic vision of the world in common sense is fundamentally true: physical reality is independent of facts of consciousness, that is, unaltered by them. Our knowledge is limited to such realities as the existence of material things and of other human subjects, while all metaphysical or theological propositions are without certitude or validity. Recent linguistic analysis has made use of Moore's thought in order to defend *common language* and even to give it a central philosophical value. Moore's ethics represents an application of these theories to the central concept of ethics, the notion of the *good;* and the testimony of common sense is given a place in its development. The idea of good is a simple, indefinable notion, which indicates a quality of objects. The same is true of its opposite. The work of ethics is to analyze the assertions which can be made about the qualities of things that are indicated by these terms. Such assertions may be of two kinds: assertions of the degree to which objects possess these qualities and assertions of causal relations between objects which possess these properties and other objects.

Moore has exerted great influence not only by reason of these doctrines but also through his method of conducting philosophical inquiry: the avoidance of systematic construction and an emphasis on linguistic analysis, especially of common, everyday language. For this reason, he may be considered one of the founders, not only of modern realism, but also of "analytic philosophy," the influence of which was to become widespread at a later date in both England and America.

C. D. Broad (b. 1887) enjoyed an influence which, though less than that of Moore, nevertheless justly places him among the most notable figures of the early phase of modern naturalistic realism. Among his important works are: *Perception, Physics and Reality*, 1914; *Scientific Thought*, 1923; *Mind and Its Place in Nature*, 1925; and *Five Types of Ethical Theory*, 1930.

Broad was weaned from an early devotion to idealism by Moore. From Moore he also derived his conception of the task of philosophy: the criticism of the concepts and language uncritically employed in science and common linguistic usage and the questioning of common fundamental beliefs. He was skeptical of speculative philosophy and in the construction of his own theories he employed, in addition to the critical techniques noted above, a comparative method in which he examined all the possible positions relative to a given problem before formulating that which seemed most nearly to meet it (most nearly, for no doctrine ever satisfied him completely). His realism and naturalism did not prevent him from entertaining a lively interest in psychic and spiritualistic phenomena. His constructive reflection centers about three main points or interests: the theory of perception, the value of scientific knowledge, and the body-soul dichotomy.

In treating perception (cf. *Perception, Physics and Reality*), he distinguished three elements, factors, or aspects, which had to be evaluated and related: *sensation* as a mental act or state, the objects of sensation (*sensa*), and physical objects. Of these, the second is the most important, and the problem is to relate it to the first and third. The *sensa*, the objective content of sensations, are the proper object of perception; they do not, however, form parts of physical objects. Nevertheless, Broad affirms the existence of physical bodies which persist in time and space and may be the correlatives of the proper objects of perception. Such objects, or our knowledge of them, is inferential.

In *Scientific Thought*, Broad takes up the problem of the value of scientific knowledge. He makes the value of this kind of knowledge rest on the fact that its objects are reducible to the status of perceptible objects and the relations between them are reducible to perceptible relations. Broad was much impressed by the revisions of traditional scientific concepts then taking place (e.g., formulation of the Einstein theory) and noted that the tendency of these revisions was to make the objects of science approach more and more closely to their sensible and perceptual bases. This, in his view, constituted an argument in favor of these revisions.

His comparative method is especially in evidence in the work *Mind and Its Place in Nature*. His preoccupation is the relation of matter and spirit, body and soul, and, to reach a reasonable and tenable position, he reconstructs and compares no less than seventeen possible positions. He is content finally with one which he calls "emergent materialism," which has affinities to the position called *epiphenomenalism*. In this view, every mental act is the product of a physiological process; but not vice versa. The higher level of consciousness emerges from the sustaining physiological processes. Consciousness exhibits a psychic dimension in addition to its organic processes, but that psychic factor does not constitute a substantial soul.

Finally, in *Five Types of Ethical Theory*, again employing his comparative method but with more limited scope, he treats ethics and its problems. Here a "regression" to his earlier idealism has been noted, for he affirms that moral qualities are not empirical but *a priori* and are the objects of a rational intuition.

Samuel Alexander (1859–1938) was the most systematic of the new realists in England. His chief work *Space, Time and Deity* (2 vols., 1920), originally the Gifford lectures for 1916–18, has been compared in its architectonic qualities to Spinoza's *Ethics*, and Alexander welcomed the comparison. The work is the result of a long period of reflection. Certain of its basic traits appear in articles which Alexander contributed to the *Proceedings of the Aristotelian Society* (1908–11) and to *Mind* (1912) during the years prior to his appointment to the Gifford lectures. His basic realism appears in an article ("The Method of Metaphysics and the Categories," *Mind*, n. s. XXI [1912]) in which he likens mental activity to the reactions of a plant to its environment; this relation is direct, and thus in the mind the objects are things and not representations. Again, in an important *Proceedings* article, after identifying consciousness as a quality of certain organic processes, he makes the distinction between *contemplation* and *fruition*. Mind knows external objects by contemplation; it knows itself, from within, so to say, by fruition. Finally, in an important article in *Mind* (1913, pp. 1–20), he undertakes a realistic reevaluation of the Kantian categories. These are, in his view, not forms of a transcendental subject but forms of reality itself.

The substance of Alexander's thought is to be found in *Space, Time and Deity*. This work opens with a sweeping affirmation of a realistic *monism*. Mind is one with the order of things; it is but the most highly endowed member of the democracy of things. We do not know our minds as we know other things, by contemplation, but by fruition; however, to an "angel" contemplating all things this status of our minds would be apparent.

As he has shown in his criticism of Kant's theory of the categories, mind cannot condition reality by means of *a priori* forms. But the problem of the categories still remains—that is, to explain how there can be characteristics which are necessarily found in all reality, in every thing. Taking certain hints from the Einstein theory, which he knew in its special form, Alexander asserts that space-time is the ultimate substratum of all things. The categories, or the categorical characteristics which are found in all things, are the fundamental characteristics of space-time. The most fundamental category is the relation between time and space. How is this relation, the root of all the categories, to be conceived? Alexander answers that it must be conceived on the analogy of the relation between mind and body in man. The essence of this relation has already been encountered in the epiphenomenalism subscribed to by Broad: mind and body are inseparable, but mind represents a higher manifestation within body. Alexander, however, employs his own terms, *fruition* and *contemplation*. The union is so close that, seen from without, contemplated, mind is a nervous process, but, seen from within, by fruition, mind is spiritual. But this is only an analogy, and Alexander does not fall into a panpsychism. The analogy, applied to space-time, reveals that time is, as it were, "the mind of space." Correctly understood, this means, not that time is a form of mind, but that mind is a form of time.

Time, as the "mind" of space, is the principle of the generation of all of the forms of existence. Since Alexander still conceives time as primarily succession, the form of this generation is successive or emergent. These forms of existence are generated along a line of continuous emergence in the order of mind and body, i.e., the higher emerging from the lower on the pattern of the epiphenomenalism already alluded to. Thus, life emerges from matter and mind from life, and the impulse of this process is time. Mind is the highest of the finite modes of existence known to us. But it cannot be the highest, strictly speaking, for time, as the principle of becoming, is infinite and contains no intrinsic limits within itself. (In this assertion Alexander seems to rely on the mathematics of the infinite contained in the writings of H. Minkowski.) Time must, therefore, carry this movement beyond the level known to us into a higher level of existence. At this point in Alexander's thought, we are assisting at the birth of God because this infinite, toward which the process of emergence is directed, is *deity*.

Deity is the empirical quality next superior to mind which the movement of time-space is orientated to generate or bring to birth. But that level of existence, deity, while knowable to us in the necessity of its becoming, rooted in time-space, is not knowable to us *in itself*. In his terms, we can neither contemplate the deity nor can we have fruition of it. Nevertheless, he makes some assertions about deity, somewhat in the manner of the classical negative theologies. God is not mind, though he supposes mind as mind supposes life, etc. Because deity is infinite, it is not actual but ideal and conceptual. There is no one, distinct actual being who would possess exclusively the quality of deity. However, there is the actual infinity of the world which, by reason of its very constitution as time-space, *tends* toward the deity. The reality of God is to be found in this *tendency* of the world of space-time toward a higher quality. God is that toward which the world tends, an aspiration rather than an achieved fact.

Alfred North Whitehead (1861–1947) in many ways eludes classification. His thought has a personal quality which sets it apart in a subtle way. Insofar as he can be categorized, he must be placed among the realists and naturalists, where he readily assumes a position of eminence.

Whitehead's earliest work was in mathematics and the philosophy of mathematics, culminating in his collaboration with Bertrand Russell on *Principia Mathematica*, 1910–13. But he passed very readily and quite early from that limited field to a broader field of philosophical speculation. In his investigations into the philosophy of nature, Whitehead employed a logical method or technique which he called "extensive abstraction." This method enabled him to construct a relativistic philosophy of time-space in which he was able to reject the notion of substance and all of the problems inherent in it. This phase is developed in his many writings on this topic between the publication of *Principia Mathematica* and the appearance of *An Enquiry Concerning the Principle of Natural Knowledge*, 1919.

From these early insights, Whitehead arrives at an "organistic" conception of nature. This theory conceives every fact as an event and every event as an *organism*. This organism represents the concretion, the bringing together into a complex whole, of elements which are objects of different "prehensions." This last term, of Whitehead's own coinage, is complex in meaning. It has a dualistic structure, for, on the one hand, it refers to the subjective aspect of apprehension and, on the other, to the constitution of the object or some element of it. But the "prehension" (which provides the sinews of the event as organism) is not a purely cognitive process. Whitehead says that it may or may not be cognitive. The realm of organic events and of prehensions constitutes the order of nature; but Whitehead's concern extends beyond this to the determination of the order of pure possibilities, of "eternal objects," of which the event-structure of the organic world represents the participating concretions. As he develops these ideas in his most important work, *Process and Reality*, 1929, Whitehead constructs a cosmology in which monistic substantialism is replaced by a dynamic pluralism. Organicism and relativity are brought into a complex synthesis.

Whitehead's relation with contemporary neo-realism rests, first of all, on his epistemological realism. This is established by his reference to the subject's direct experience of the causal efficacy, upon its own cognitive processes, of the surrounding environment. This external world does not seem to have any other purpose in Whitehead's thought than the generation of the subject and its states, but in this process those external forces follow principles and laws which are not dependent on the subject. The processes of "prehension" (one of which is the cognitive experience of the subject) from an independent ontological field. Within this ontological field, Whitehead distinguishes three orders of the real: The first is that of physical energy; the second, the *present* of human experience; the third, the *eternity* of divine experience. At this point Whitehead's cosmology passes over into a theology. He considers the attributes of God, who proves to be an emergent God reflecting the entire process of the universe. God carries the universe forward on the basis of physical energy to forms more complex than any given range of experience can project. Finally Whitehead proceeds to a theodicy in the course of which further light is thrown upon the divinity and its ways of acting.

The effective reality of evil proves that God is not omnipotent. This denial of omnipotence does not at the same time establish Whitehead's God as a finite God according to the pattern of some recent theologies. Rather it establishes God as the principle of the on-going dynamism of the universe, the principle according to which that universe is ever in a process of self-transcendence and self-affirmation. God is the name for the process of realization of the absolute possibilities of the real. Yet this God does not act through prepotence but by informing the cosmic processes with his own direction.

Whitehead's ideas, developed through a long series of publications (cf. *Bulletin of Bibliography*, XXIII [1961], 90–93, for a very inclusive, though not exhaustive, listing), have had considerable influence in America. His chief exponent is perhaps Charles Hartshorne, who has developed with special power the implications of Whitehead's thought for philosophical theology.

Bertrand Russell (1872–1970), far more than Whitehead, is a figure of such prominence in contemporary philosophy and of such prolific, complex, and brilliant achievement that adequate treatment of his thought must take monographic form. In a discursive account, only the most salient features can be touched on. Fortunately, however, his work as a whole is so lucid and clearly articulated that some brief account can be ventured without too much risk of creating a false impression.

Like so many other major figures of contemporary philosophy, Bertrand Russell was initiated into philosophy by way of the prevailing Hegelianism of the last quarter of the nineteenth century. At Cambridge he came under the influence of J. E. McTaggart and G. F. Stout, and their convinced Hegelianism proved contagious. As in many other cases, Russell's Hegelianism, though fervent, was fugitive. More penetrating study of the structures and methods of mathematics (his first and most enduring interest) led him to abandon Hegelian idealism for that kind of realism of common sense which was being defended by G. E. Moore. In the autobiographical essay "My Mental Development" (*The Philosophy of Bertrand Russell,* ed. P. A. Schilpp, 1946), Russell remarks that while Bradley argued that everything believed by common sense is pure appearance, he went to the other extreme and affirmed that everything supposed by common sense, uninfluenced by philosophy and theology, is real. His eventual realism would be of a far more sophisticated type, of course, but this remark is very significant. However, it would be a mistake to think that this transformation was purely academic; it was closely allied with Russell's concern for mathematics, as is proved by his remark that only on the basis of such a realism could mathematics come to be considered absolutely true and not merely a stage in the dialectic. Realism and logic as the basis of mathematics are closely related in his thought. And it will be his concern with logic which dominates his theory of language, of knowledge, and of ethical discourse.

Russell is said to have dated the origin of his logical program from the International Congress of Philosophy of 1900. There he heard the papers of Peano and his disciples and was struck by their precision. He was led to the study of Peano's works and gradually formed the conviction that the logical symbolism which Peano had developed could be extended with great profit to mathematics and other fields of investigation, which, he says, were infected with philosophical vagueness. More immediately, however, there took form in his mind the project later called *logicism.* Logicism as Russell developed it was really a two-pronged movement. On the one hand, it involved the reestablishment of the foundations of mathematics on the bases of logic; on the other, it involved a critique of the classical subject-predicate logic and its displacement by his logic of relations, which in turn included three elements: the calculus of propositions, the calculus of classes, and the calculus of relations.

With respect to the relation between logic and mathematics, the position of logicism is somewhat ambivalent. In one place Russell says that the two areas might be thought of as identical by way of the definition of the one and the other as the class of propositions which contain only logical constants and variables (cf. *Principles of Mathematics,* 1903, sec. 10). But in the same work he goes on to fix this relation more clearly. In this clarification, logic assumes a certain superiority to mathematics in the dual sense that the employment of logical symbolism assures a more rigorous language for mathematics and, more importantly, that every mathematical concept can be deduced from the fundamental concepts of logic, such as negation, identity, conjunction, disjunction, implication of propositions, etc., while every mathematical proposition can be derived from or discovered within the first enunciations of logic. This idea of the relation of logic and mathematics, stated in this fashion, was merely a program, as he states in *Principles of Mathematics,* and Russell recognizes that Frege sometime before had projected an analogous program. The realization of this program became the object of his joint enterprise with Whitehead, the three-volume work *Principia Mathematica,* published in the years 1910–13, a work which has taken its place with the great classics of logic and mathematics.

Russell went on to develop the logic of relations in the three directions mentioned above: the calculus of propositions, the calculus of classes, and the calculus of relations. These are highly technical developments, and only a very brief and general indication of the character of each can be ventured here. The calculus of propositions studies the relations of *material implication* between propositions. By *material* implication is meant that implication which is true if the conclusion at least is true. On this basis Russell established the proof of the laws of contradiction and the excluded middle as well as the formal properties of logical addition and multiplication. The calculus of classes studies implication between determined sets or classes. Here Russell distinguishes between the class and the class-concept by means of which the class is defined; the class-concept appears also as the *predicate.* The basic relation in the calculus of classes, according to Russell, is extension. The *class* is a unique term if it is considered as a totality or if it is that type of combination which is expressed by the copula *is* in all its varieties. Russell also introduces here the notion of propositional function, whereby, in any such proposition as "Socrates is a man," *Socrates* may be replaced by x. The proposition "x is a man" will be true for certain values of the variable, false for others.

In treating these two forms of calculus, Russell was following up the work of Peano. In developing the notion of the calculus of relations, he refers to certain ideas of Peirce. The logic of relations establishes the basic difference, in this view, between classical logic and the new logic; for, while classical logic considered only that form of proposition which results from the reference of a predicate to a subject, the new logic takes as its basis propositions which *express a relation.* There is a further difference, however: The classical subject-predicate logic assumed that in reality there are only things and qualities; the new logic denies that relations can be reduced to qualities of things. As a result, the ontological development of the new logic involves a criticism of the metaphysics of substance and accident or substance and quality.

In addition, Russell offers a philosophical interpretation of his technical construction of logic. In its first phase (the period of *Principia Mathematica*) this was an extreme realism; in this interpretation, logical entities (relations, classes, etc.) are endowed with a "subsistence" (though not a spatio-temporal *existence*) independent of the irrelevant problem of "minds." This realism is sometimes characterized as Platonic. With time, however, Russell modified this realism, first under the influence of Meinong's work on descriptive phrases and still later under the influence of Wittgenstein, when, abandoning the notion of mathematics as the discovery of a world of essences, he inclined toward treating it as a complex of tautologies. But he never came to a nominalistic position, as did the neo-positivists, for the concept of relation, absolutely fundamental in his thought, always retained an ontological value. In this context he reaffirms his initial attitude toward the realism of common sense.

A special acclaim attaches to Russell's contribution to the solution of the "antinomies" which, appearing first in mathematics, were subsequently found to be inherent in both the traditional logic and the new symbolic logic. The technical character of this problem precludes any detailed examination here, but its position in Russell's thought must be indicated. His contribution consists in his development of the theory of types: every propositional function must be of a logical type higher than the arguments in which it is involved, and every class must be of a higher logical type than its elements.

In "My Philosophical Development," Russell notes that he has always been extremely concerned with the problem of the theory of knowledge. He also asserts a point which will remain permanent for him in dealing with this problem, namely, that the theory of knowledge is concerned with the manner in which the individual knows and the manner in which his knowledge relates to that of science. This position is complex: While knowledge always begins with individual experience, the "egocentric" realm of immediate data, it attains to a status and range which entirely transcends this beginning and can never be reduced to that "egocentric" experience.

He conducts a lively polemic against the neo-empiricists or neo-positivists on the matter of verification. Their claim that the meaning of a proposition is its method of verification cannot be sustained, and the proof of this lies in perception which cannot be verified because it constitutes the verification of all other propositions which can be known. He gives a privileged place to private and immediate knowledge; in this knowledge we are aware of objects without any intermediary process of inference. The objects of this immediate and private experience are sense data, the reports of introspection, of memory, and also perhaps of the self or "I." Finally, we have such knowledge of universals, which knowledge constitutes the *concept.* He also recognizes knowledge by *description,* which is mediated knowledge but may eventually be reduced to its immediate bases. As a consequence of these views, solipsism has always been a temptation for Russell but one against which he has striven constantly, with inconclusive success. Russell has documented this concern for the problems of knowledge in a number of books, including: *Our Knowledge of the External World,* 1914; *The Analysis of Mind,* 1921; *An Inquiry into Meaning and Truth,* 1940; and *Human Knowledge: Its Scope and Limits,* 1948.

Also of considerable importance is Russell's theory of language, documented in such writings as the essay "On Denoting," 1905; *The Philosophy of Logical Atomism,* 1918; and the *Inquiry into Meaning and Truth,* mentioned above. Taken (at risk of considerable loss) out of the rich context in which he develops it, his theory may be brought down to the following points: Language is made up of propositions, the constituents of which are symbols; the symbols *mean* the constituents of the facts which render the propositions true or false, that is, the symbols correspond to those constituents; but knowledge of facts by direct acquaintance is necessary in order to interpret the symbols, although this last knowledge differs from subject to subject. This account indicates a rather serious fissure in the order of language. A perfect language would be constructable were it not for the fact that the direct and immediate knowledge which lies at the basis of all language differs from individual to individual. That perfect language would have a perfect one-to-one correlation between its basic terms and simple objects, and all other designations would be constituted of combinations of these. This was the kind of language he and Whitehead sought to construct in *Principia Mathematica.* But the condition of immediate acquaintance, which alone can give objective content to the language, renders such a language impracticable, and, strange as it may seem, language can become a medium of communication only by way of its imperfections, which will always reflect the diversity at the level of immediate acquaintance.

Of interest also, because quite influential, is Russell's theory of ethical discourse. He points out, as his previous statements would lead one to expect, that the immediate and private experience of individuals is the basis of ethical assertion. Statements such as "This thing is good," though they seem to be declarations of fact, are really simple expressions of desire. For this reason, it is not possible to adduce proofs for their truth or falsity. This is the case even when such statements seem to have transcendental form; the quasi-transcendentality is reducible to the projection of an individual desire. When these expressions are generalized—that is, expressed as desires in which all should participate—they become the elements of ethical discourse, which proceeds at a level apparently above that of individual desires but must eventually be reduced to that level. The very essence of the ethical would seem to lie in the desire that one's own desire should be shared by all subjects. But this desire, or any expression of it, can have no truth value or meet any of the logical conditions of truth or falsity.

In his own ethical judgments, Russell reflects a strong sense of liberty and an opposition to all moral and social dogmatism, but he has not formulated any truly coherent system of ethical statements. His utterances remain on the level Plato would have called "opinion."

B. *Realism and Naturalism in America*

1. Genesis and Polemical Phase of Realism in America

American realism may be said to have its origin in a controversy aroused by Royce's criticism, in *The World and the Individual*, of a position which he labeled "realism." Royce spoke of realism as asserting the absolute "independence" of subject and object, of object and idea, in the order of knowledge; i.e., the immunity of the object from any modification as a result of the process by which the subject constitutes the object as known. Consequently, no kind of relation can exist between the objects as known and the real object.

The force of Royce's remarks does not lie in their truth or falsity but, from the present point of view, in the responses they occasioned. In these responses are to be found the first manifestations of the movement eventually to mature, in its two major phases, as the "new realism" and as "critical realism." The first of these responses came from the pen of Ralph Barton Perry in an article in the *Monist* (XII, 1901–1902). Noting that realism in the form in which Royce had proposed it in order to attack it could hardly be defended, he offered his own formulation of that position—one which proves substantially indentifiable with that which the movement was more and more to embrace. Realist philosophy affirms, he wrote, that reality must be a *datum,* something given independently of any idea relating to or bearing upon it. The reply of C. A. Strong, published in the *Journal of Philosophy,* 1904, ran in a similar vein. For Strong, the purpose of knowledge is to enter into relation with reality. From the point of view of the knower, these relations must be purely external, and *a fortiori* they must be such from the point of view of the object known. E. G. Spaulding, in a series of articles in the *Journal of Philosophy,* 1904, develops the central point a bit more subtly. Studying the form of cognition, he asserts that within this form the object is always transcendent to the act of knowing, though present in it according to its own (the object's) reality, but in accord with the conditions of the activity of the knowing subject. Finally, W. P. Montague, in the *Philosophical Review* (XL, 1902), undertakes to defend a realistic notion of "independence" which would not appear naive. He proposes to consider consciousness as a relation in which both related terms retain their independence while the relation itself is both external and transitory.

2. The First Constructive Phase: Neo-Realism

It was apparent, however, that realism could not continue in this polemical phase. The only adequate reply to Royce's attack on realism would be a constructive exposition of that position which would make it clear that his attack lacked all solid basis. Thus, in reply to the challenge presented by the problem of realism in its purely speculative aspects, the constructive phase of the movement called "neo-realism" emerged. Two outstanding contributions to this phase came from men already engaged in the earlier polemical phase, Ralph Barton Perry and W. P. Montague.

· a. *Montague's "Monistic Realism."* Montague's contribution to this constructive phase of the new realism consisted in the formulation of a "monistic realism." Attacking what he called "dualistic realism," which he traced to Descartes, Montague points out that the task of knowledge is rendered impossible in that theory. Dualistic realism divides the universe into two orders of entities, one of objects directly perceived, "pure ideas," and another of natural objects, the world of nature and existence. The task of knowledge is to relate these worlds. Idealism does so by rejecting the world of nature; but it has amply proven that in doing so it solves nothing. The obvious alternative suggests itself: to eliminate the world of ideas as a special realm. What must be established is a monistic naturalism: an order in which all objects possess the same status, that of natural existents, each with properties of its own. This situation creates a pan-objectivism, a condition in which all the elements of the situation of knowledge have the same objective status. In this situation, the process of knowledge is not a transaction of the subject but an ensemble of relations between and among existents. The work of philosophy is to identify these relations, analyze them, and exhibit their causal basis.

b. *Ralph Barton Perry and the "Egocentric Predicament."* It was at this critical moment that Perry, in his celebrated article "The New Realism and Idealism" (*Philosophical Review*, 1908) posited, in the name of realism, a perplexing problem destined to evoke considerable discussion. It concerned the "egocentric predicament," which, according to Perry, was the source of the strength of idealism and hence should be avoided by the emergent realism. He depicts the "egocentric predicament" in the following manner: According to idealism, T (the thing) is necessarily based on the relation of Rc (consciousness) to E (the ego) in such a way that the relation $Rc(E)$ is indispensable for the constitution of T. In order to understand how T is transformed or modified by the relation $Rc(E)$, it is necessary to determine the case in which T would present itself outside that relation. But this is manifestly impossible, for such revelation would involve the very process of the relation Rc. Therefore, idealism concludes that the case cannot be given in which T is present as outside the relation Rc. Perry thinks this conclusion illegitimate, but he recognizes the difficulty of establishing this illegitimacy.

J. B. Pratt and A. O. Lovejoy, destined to be important figures in the new realism, leapt to the task which Perry indicated. Pratt pointed out the ambiguity of the "egocentric predicament" and claimed that Perry was assigning the new realism an impossible task and, at the same time, arbitrarily making its own persuasiveness dependent on resolving a conundrum which idealism had set. Lovejoy was more outspoken. He denounced Perry's depiction of the "egocentric predicament" as simply false. He refers the matter to the position of Montague, pointing out that Perry should appreciate the force of Montague's argument that only an unambiguous pan-objectivism would serve as the basis of the new realism.

3. The "Six"

In the year 1910, the cause of the new realism took a great stride forward with the publication in the *Journal of Philosophy* of the "Program and First Platform of Six Realists." The six realists were Perry,

Montague, and Spaulding (whose names have already been encountered), along with Holt, Marvin, and Pitkin (new to the movement). The platform and program consisted of the following points: 1) The entities (objects, facts, etc.) studied by logic, mathematics, and the physical sciences are not mental entities in the usual and proper sense of this term. 2) The being and nature of these entities are in no way conditioned by their being known. 3) There exists no logic or system of logic able in itself to discover an organic theory of knowledge or a conception of internal relations. 4) Certain logical principles logically precede every scientific and metaphysical system; one of these is what is habitually called the "external notion of relations." 5) The nature of reality cannot simply be deduced from the nature of knowledge. 6) For realism, things which are known continue to exist without being altered by the fact that they are known. 7) Cognition and its objects form part of the same universe; cognition has its place in the order of nature. 8) Realism, while admitting the tautological argument which holds that every known entity is in relation with knowledge, etc., holds that these relations are eliminable, so that the entity is known as it is, as though the process of knowledge had not taken place.

The publication of this platform and program aroused considerable comment and was followed by a more clear-cut assumption of position, pro or con, by many thinkers.

4. The New Realism: A Cooperative Philosophical Undertaking

A program and a platform are nothing if not implemented and realized. The implementation of the "Six" was quick in coming. It took the form of the publication of *The New Realism: Cooperative Studies in Philosophy,* 1912. The contributors were the same ones who had published the platform. This work, which constitutes the apogée of neo-realism, may be considered the expression of its fundamental doctrine. Some historians have noted how little cohesion the studies exhibit, but there can be no doubt of the basic unity of the point of view advanced. The introductory essay makes clear the large area of common assent among these writers. They take their point of departure in the criticism of idealism. In defining the task before them, the authors make it appear too much the concern of technicians, failing to note the relations of the movement with the social and cultural climate in America. M. T. Marvin, in the first of the essays, declares that metaphysics ought to free itself from epistemology. R. B. Perry reexamines the original problem out of which the movement sprang, the problem of "independence." Montague and Holt, in two of the best essays in the work, concentrate on the problem of error.

But if the "Six" imagined that their common work would establish a solid basis within the new realism from which further progress might be made, they were doomed to disillusionment. They had written, not the prologue, but the epitaph of the new realism. All of the criticism evoked by the work pointed in the same direction; the forces which would quickly transcend their position were already assembling. Before they could make themselves effectively felt, however, another document of the new realism was to appear: E. G. Spaulding's *The New Rationalism*, 1918. In this work the theory of external relations is strongly defended against the theory of internal relations upon which idealism rests. Spaulding employs the formula *xRy* to express the "simple relativity of terms in virtue of their relation." Applied to the case of knowledge, the theory of external relations assures a coherent realism which is prepared to defend its own ground.

5. Transition to the "Critical" Phase

The forces which would push the movement beyond the phase of the new realism soon began to make themselves felt, and the period of transition set in. One of its surer manifestations was the work of A. O. Lovejoy. First in a series of articles in the *Journal of Philosophy* and later in his masterful work *The Revolt Against Dualism*, 1930, Lovejoy made his critical position clear. In the articles Lovejoy develops his essential ideas until he reaches an independent position best characterized as an epistemological dualism. He attacks epistemological monism and the theory of external relations as the basis of an effective realism and suggests instead a theory of "mediation" which, in his view, better serves the ends which the realists share. At the same time D. C. Macintosh, in an article in the same review, sought to save epistemological monism by overcoming the inherent limitations under which it labored. At this point, one of the most impressive personalities of the realist movement, George Santayana, contributed an article to the *Journal of Philosophy* (XI [1914], 49–63) in which he criticizes the theory of knowledge proposed by Holt. Holt's was an extreme realism which held that things presented themselves in knowledge precisely as they were in reality, with no active mediation of consciousness. Santayana points out that this dangerously erases the line of demarcation between interior and exterior. He insists that the mind and consciousness must be assigned a much greater role in the knowledge process. These studies and the many others which might be mentioned are but indications of the direction in which the current was moving: toward a critical realism. The first complete affirmation of this critical realism was offered by Roy Wood Sellars.

6. The Critical Realism of Roy Wood Sellars

Sellars' *Critical Realism*, 1916, and his later work *The Philosophy of Physical Realism*, 1932, easily qualify him as one of the most penetrating and constructive members of the movement. Sellars begins by pointing out the difficulties inherent in the position which he calls "natural realism" and which is exemplified in the neo-realistic phase. Its difficulties rise, not from its realism, but from its acritical character. His "critical realism" is intended to meet these difficulties and to lay the groundwork for a realism which can both explicate itself clearly and meet objections launched at it from other positions. These difficulties are the following: 1) Perception demands conditions which are not present in what is perceived. 2) It is necessary to distinguish between the way a thing appears and its reality. 3) The absence of a concomitant variation and what is actually perceived of it must be reconciled. 4) The differences among the perceptions of each individual must be accounted for. 5) The image, dream, and memory must be differentiated. 6) The complex character of the object of perception and the presence in it of deduced elements must be related.

A consideration of Sellars' manner of meeting a number of these problems will suggest the character of critical realism as a whole. With respect to the first difficulty, Sellars is led to hold that things are truly what we perceive them to be but that we cannot perceive them directly. With respect to the differences among the perceptions of individuals, he notes that solipsism is impossible because of the social character of experience; this social character involves complex communicative relations among individuals, and the principle of mediation is the physical world. Much is suggested by his manner of dealing with the basic question: What is the status of consciousness in nature? He replies with a compromise that expresses the quintessence of critical realism: Consciousness is *in* the physical world but not *of* that world. To explicate this apparent enigma, Sellars has recourse to the concept of emergence, which will figure even more largely in his *Philosophy of Physical Realism*.

7. Essays in Critical Realism

A central event in the development of critical realism was the appearance of the cooperative work *Essays in Critical Realism*, 1920. The authors, who occupy the same position in critical realism which the "Six" occupied in neo-realism, included: Arthur Lovejoy, James B. Pratt, Arthur K. Rogers, Durant Drake, C. A. Strong, Roy Wood Sellars, and George Santayana. The inner structure of this work serves to place in a clear light both the solid bases of accord between these writers and neo-realism and the profound differences which separated them from it. The general characterization of critical realism is that it occupies a point between a realistic minimum and a maximum. Its essential feature may perhaps be its conviction that all knowledge is both "transitive" and "relevant." Knowledge is "transitive" to the degree to which things which exist in themselves can become objects of the mind which identifies and characterizes them; it is "relevant" to the degree that the object designated possesses at least some of the characteristics attributed to it by thought. Santayana's contribution brings the work to its culmination with his formulation of the "three proofs" for realism, which establish precisely these properties of "transitiveness" and "relevance."

8.   Lovejoy and *The Revolt Against Dualism*

Lovejoy's name had become more and more prominent among the realists. His contributions had always possessed great acumen resting on solid erudition and a strong critical talent. All of these came to focus in his major and highly original *The Revolt Against Dualism*, 1930, which defines a position distinctively his own.

The principal thesis of this work is clear. Lovejoy holds that the new realism and idealism have one thing in common: Both are forms of the revolt against dualism. But the fact that both end in an impasse suggests to him that this revolt is misguided, that a viable dualism is, after all, the most effective position. He develops this thesis both negatively and positively. The first part of the work is a long and minute analysis of this "revolt," which reveals Lovejoy's powers as a historical analyst. In the second part he expounds his own constructive point of view. After establishing carefully the difference between psychological or psycho-physical dualism and epistemological dualism, he sums up the dualistic epistemology of critical realism in the following three assertions: 1) There is an order of existing things and of events which persists independently of our perception of it. 2) This order is related to our sensations by a causal bond. 3) The particular elements belonging to this order cannot be identified without sensations. In a word, man has the power to act upon that order and to establish durable processes in its midst. Lovejoy maintains that only this dualism can support the view that the physical world has an existence proper to it.

9.   The Systematic Phase of Critical Realism

The appearance of Lovejoy's book brought to an end the formative phase of critical realism, the phase in which it was as much concerned to distinguish itself from neo-realism as it was to determine and develop its own principles. From this phase it passes into a period of systems, in which the latter effort becomes central while the polemical concern falls into the background.

Three of these systematic presentations are most representative: the "physical realism" of Roy Wood Sellars, the "realism of the person" of James Bissett Pratt and the "realms of being" of George Santayana.

The work in which Sellars presents his system of philosophy has already been mentioned, *The Philosophy of Physical Realism,* 1932. This system offers two prominent characteristics: It is a dogmatic materialism, and it is a form of "emergent evolution" in the pattern which has become familiar. Sellars first considers his system a form of *naturalism.* To appreciate this claim, it is necessary to take account of his definition of naturalism. Naturalism, he says, expresses belief in the self-sufficiency and intelligibility of the universe considered in time and space. His dogmatic materialism is supported by a view of matter which has been called elastic. Sellars has no intention of abandoning all of the qualitative richness of human experience in both form and content; rather, he tries to show that matter, in virtue of its components and its dynamic properties, is itself the source of this qualitative richness.

Sellars devotes a considerable portion of the work to the restatement and refinement of his epistemology, for he feels that this critical realism supports the entire structure of his system. The first systematic task is to revise some of the basic categories of classical naturalism. In this process he is led to replace the classical notions of substance and time by the synthetic notion of "event." This revised category is applied to the most diverse orders of reality, beginning with mind itself, which Sellars insists is a *brain-event.* In similar fashion, but with less success, he applies these categories to value and valuation. Valuation is an objective process in the same sense as thought. This large application of the categories of the new naturalism to the full range of phenomena generates Sellars' *humanism.* It is a thorough-going *naturalistic* humanism, for it shows man to be continuous with and integral to nature. Man is a product of nature, but within nature he is a central active element, the source of the highest forms of organization which nature achieves. From man's point of view, it is possible to grasp the perspective of the "emergent types" in which nature fulfills itself. Man is the culmination of these emergent types, and he will not be superceded in this movement, for it is only through him that nature may push on to higher forms, of which he will always prove to the active and central principle.

The presence of James Bissett Pratt (1875–1944) had made itself felt at various crucial moments in the career of critical realism. He perceived that the possibilities inherent in critical realism as the basis of systematic philosophical construction were multiple. As a consequence, the system he develops, to which the name "realism of the person" or "realistic personalism" has been assigned, presents a radically different configuration from the physical realism of Sellars.

There is no single text for Pratt's personalistic realism. It finds expression in a number of works, the most important of which are: *The Religious Consciousness,* 1921; *Matter and Spirit,* 1922; and *Adventures in Philosophy and Religion,* 1931. His first concern is to secure epistemological bases for his systematic construction by reaffirming the principles of critical realism. In doing so, however, he introduces a fresh dimension, consisting of theses on the nature of meaning and of the symbol. But the basis of Pratt's system is his manner of conceiving the self, the "I," or the subject. In this, his theory of meaning is brought into play. The notion of the self is suggested by the fact that all significant or meaningful situations are expressed in general and universal terms, but their ultimate reference, the concrete existent, lies outside the boundary of definition. He refuses to resolve these trans-significant unities into the processes of nature, holding them to be the ultimate principles and forms of existence. He identifies this concrete principle as a self, a presence, by reference to the continuity of thought which points clearly to such a subject as its sustaining principle. The transcendent ground of all experience is the person, whose existence is proven by procedures fully consonant with the principles of critical reason. The further developments of Pratt's thought are devoted to the exploration of this personal principle and the types of experience proper to it, namely, the religious, the ethical, and the aesthetical ranges.

The name of George Santayana (1863–1952) is associated with some of the most brilliant and penetrating contributions to critical realism. It would be a mistake, however, to confine Santayana within the ranks of the critical realists. As a philosopher, he achieves personal stature which places him beyond such categorization, and in strict justice he deserves separate treatment. When that treatment, as in the present circumstances, is not possible, however, his proper historical place is in the ranks of critical realism. He is the author of the most impressive systematic statement resting on the principles of that doctrine: *The Realms of Being,* 1927–40. This work marks a culmination in his personal career as well, in the progress which had produced *The Life of Reason, Plato and the Spiritual Life,* and many other works of singular beauty and penetration.

The epistemological bases of the *Realms of Being* are laid down in the work *Scepticism and Animal Faith,* 1923. While the position developed in this latter work had been presented previously by Santayana, this fresh statement is not without arresting new touches. Animal faith imposes a belief anterior to all the rest of man's beliefs. That faith does not proceed from the physical world but from a person, the substantial being which generates all experience. The belief in the material world is the initial expression of animal vitality exercising itself in the spiritual sphere. *Scepticism and Animal Faith* serves as a general introduction to the four component volumes of the system: *The Realm of Essence, The Realm of Matter, The Realm of Truth,* and *The Realm of Spirit.* A preliminary question is: What are these "realms of being"? Santayana denies them any *metaphysical* character in the sense which this term has had in the history of philosophy. Metaphysics, in his view, was a bastard concept, illegitimately uniting speculations on the physical universe, logical reflections, and purely rhetorical elements. The realms of being do not constitute a *cosmos* and are not parts of a *cosmos.* They are simply kinds of categories which apply to things which are manifestly different among themselves and which each possess a distinct value.

a. *The Realm of Essence.* Every essence, Santayana affirms, is perfectly individual. This character of individuality stems from the fact that the essence is an intuition given in a pure moment of consciousness and free from all the combinations which enter into the composition of existence. This individuality is precisely what endows the essence with its universality. Here, of course, *universality* means, not generality, but *plenitude* in its order. Every essence is absolute with respect to every other essence; it is also absolute and normative toward the order of existence in which it is manifested. Natural existence is incidental to essences; they may or may not find their way into the order of existence. But the order and kind of their *being* is superior and truer than that of existence or that of any substance, event, or experience. These latter may change, but the essence is immune to change; it *is.* The being of the essence is a *pure* being and Santayana undertakes the defense of this order of being against those who would immerse all being in existence.

b. *The Realm of Matter.* Santayana has defined himself, not only as a materialist, but as the last of the materialists. It follows, therefore, that matter must find its place among the realms of being. Matter is the matrix and the source of all things. Animal faith attests to the existence of matter and of the universe composed of it. The evidence furnished by this faith is stronger than the kind of criticism which would reduce matter to its appearances. Santayana finds a support for this affirmation of matter by animal faith in the analysis of experience.

Experience reveals matter as the condition for the appearance of essence and, hence, as the very substratum and precondition for the intuition of essence itself. But care must be taken not to give matter absolute properties and thus convert it into essence. The properties of matter are relative and functional. It prepares the ground for the appearance of the eternal essence in existence, in the flux of events. On the one hand, it has a quantitative character since it can be measured and its modifications are proportional. On the other hand, matter is atomic because existence is discontinuous. As a consequence of these properties, matter establishes nature as a determined and dynamic whole.

c. *The Realm of Truth.* In Santayana's scheme of things, the notion of truth constitutes the third realm of being. He understands truth as the sum of all possible assertions. Truth represents the sum of things and, at the same time, all things individual, seen in the mode of eternity. Truth establishes the identity of fact as we affirm it and as it exists, while the encounter with falsity provides us with a heightened sense of the nature and reality of truth. All truth and all particular facts are contingent, but the categories of truth and fact are essences. Like all other essences, they are demonstrated by examples consisting in particular assertions. Truth is subordinated to existence. It assures the success of one of the most important vital functions, the capacity of living things to adapt to the conditions in which they find themselves. An idea or a judgment is accounted true if it takes account of the truth, if it participates in it. Ideas and judgments may have empirical and accidental properties and relations. They prove useful to the degree to which they are compatible with other ideas and other judgments, but these properties remain marginal to truth itself. Finally, Santayana warns us against the dangers of panlogism, which is the identification of all truth with purely logical truth. He holds that there is also a truth which may be called "dramatic" and which is perhaps more profound than all other forms of truth because it characterizes existence and life.

d. *The Realm of Spirit.* Santayana's system reaches its culmination in the concept of spirit, which is at once within and beyond the natural universe. In this concept, the latent classicism of his thought is reaffirmed in a tone both diffident and imperious. Santayana is by temperament classical, but he is intimidated by the spirit of modern science, which he never really either comprehended or admired.

The first characteristic of spirit is its firm bond with nature, for he is above all else a materialist. Matter is but another name for being. Therefore, spirit does not pretend to envelop being as it has been basically defined. Spirit brings being and matter to a pitch of realization and refinement. It arises within nature and always remains immanent to it. It appears as the capacity for qualitative diversity within matter itself. Considered in its largest manifestation, spirit is that profound light which plays over reality or over our observation of it and which inundates all the life on earth in which man really participates. One can identify it approximatively with consciousness, sensibility, or thought, as long as one places emphasis only on its creative aspect. Spirit creates a world which is irreducible to that of the matter within whose bosom it arises, for that world is qualitatively different from the world of matter and of nature. For this reason spirit creates a world and a mode of being which nature can never destroy.

Nevertheless, there is an element of dualism in Santayana. He recognizes but one universe, that of matter or universal nature. Within that universe there is a possibility for the life of spirit, which does not, however, constitute a different world but realizes the beauty and the perfection which the natural universe suggests but which of itself it cannot bring into existence. Substance and power belong to the universe of matter. Although the universe of matter presupposes essence, creates spirit, and affirms truth, its dynamic élan takes no account of these realizations and excludes the moral and spiritual life-form implied in the concept of God. As a consequence, with respect to the great traditions which hold reality to be spiritual and the being and power of God sovereign, Santayana considers himself an atheist. He cannot be called a pantheist, if by that concept one understands that the whole of nature, or nature as a whole, exercises any spiritual activity. Although spirit represents the culminating point of life in its diverse manifestations, nature, in its totality, is not orientated toward spirit. Nevertheless, it is to spirit that one must assign the creation of those orders of value which man calls moral, aesthetic, and religious. Although one cannot discover their essential bases in existence, they nonetheless express the most profound views which man can form of the brilliant possibilities of life. That realm, immanent in nature, which spirit creates and constitutes is at the same time the fulfillment and the antithesis of nature. Nature is both realized and negated by spirit, while spirit, in its turn, both has its roots in nature and is destroyed by it.

C. *The Naturalism of Woodbridge and Cohen*

Two distinctive and distinguished statements of the viewpoint of realistic naturalism have issued from the pens of F. J. E. Woodbridge (1867–1940) and Morris Raphael Cohen (1880–1947). Woodbridge, for many years a professor at Columbia University and editor of the *Journal of Philosophy* during some of its most exciting days, wrote a number of books which attracted a small but select and responsive following. The most important of these are: *The Purpose of History,* 1916; *The Realm of Mind,* 1926; *The Son of Apollo: The Themes of Plato,* 1929; *Nature and Mind,* 1937; and *An Essay on Nature,* 1940.

Though he has sometimes mistakenly been assigned to the ranks of idealism, Woodbridge's realism seems firmly established. He conceives of mind, not as a thing in being, but as that realm of being in which the activity of thought arises. But thought is possible only in an intelligible world, a world which possesses an objective order. This order is neither physical nor ideal in a disjunctive sense but integrates both the physical and the ideal into the world of being. This order can be known to us by ideas which are not images or copies of that order but signs or characters which point to reality. These ideas permit us to predict and control reality, because the order of things and the order of ideas are the same. Thought, which is an entirely natural event and which takes place in the spatio-temporal world, is therefore symbolic in character and transitive. Woodbridge gives ample evidence of the influence both of Spinoza and of Santayana, but he is slavishly dependent on neither. He rejects the eternalism of Spinoza while accepting many of his other insights. Woodbridge's account of the relation of spirit and nature has greater precision than that of Santayana because he establishes this relation in the sign or symbolic function. A religious and quasi-mystical note inserts itself into Woodbridge's final reflection, for the ideal structure which thought discovers in reality argues, he feels, for a universal and supreme Good, which is the source and guarantor of human values.

Cohen thought of himself as primarily a logician, as his autobiographical contribution to *Contemporary American Philosophy* (eds. George P. Adams and Wm. P. Montague, 1930, I, 219–240) attests. The facts prove him more than this, though certainly his concern with logic and the method of science is central to his thought. He found empiricism theoretically inadequate and idealism scientifically untenable. He sought a middle way in his *logical realism.* He distinguished three levels or grades in reality: physical things, psychic states, and logical objects. The last alone constitute the data of knowledge and are essentially systems of relations. Psychic states are only vehicles, and things are but the indirect terms of reference of psychic states. Logical relations are necessary; relations of fact are contingent. A central role in knowledge is played by hypothesis, which, as he says, "guides us through the labyrinth of possibilities." Induction, central to scientific procedure, is a disjunctive process which determines which hypothesis, among those offered, is true in view of consequences. Concepts are signs of invariable relations, while probability resides in the relative frequency of an event. Cohen takes issue with Carnap and the school of logical positivism on the question of meaning and verifiability; that philosopher and school, at least in the early phases, held these to be in direct relation, but Cohen holds that meaning is independent of verification, and, hence, he demurs before Carnap's attack on metaphysics. These and related themes, developed with lucidity and relevance, occupy his influential *Preface to Logic,* 1944.

Scarcely less influential was his earlier *Reason and Nature,* 1931, in which, after defending the rights of reason against the claims of its surrogates (authority, intuition, etc.), he proceeds, on the basis of his interpretation of reason and its powers, to reaffirm many elements of traditional philosophy, among them the metaphysical task of philosophy, the concept of substance (redefined as the relation or structure which is the object of rational science), the rejection of mechanicism, etc. In the posthumous work *Studies in Philosophy and Science,* 1949, Cohen places emphasis on the self-corrigibility of science. Finally, his excellent work *Reason and Law,* 1950, defends a scinetifically sophisticated version of the theory of natural law against the juridical positivism of the school of Kelsen.

Readings

I. English Realism

G. E. Moore

Gellner, E. *Words and Things.* Introduction by B. Russell. London: Gollancz, 1959.

Schilpp, P. A., ed. *Philosophy of G. E. Moore.* Evanston, Ill.: Northwestern University Press, 1942.

White, Alan R. *G. E. Moore: A Critical Exposition.* Oxford: Blackwell, 1958.

C. D. Broad

Lean, M. *Sense-Perception and Matter: A Critical Analysis of C. D. Broad's Theory of Perception.* London: Routledge & K. Paul, 1953.

Mabbott, J. D. "Our Direct Experience of Time." *Mind,* LX (1951), 153–167.

Schilpp, P. A., ed. *The Philosophy of C. D. Broad.* New York: Tudor, 1959.

Samuel Alexander

McCarthy, J. W. *The Naturalism of Samuel Alexander.* New York: King's Crown Press, 1948.

Stiernotte, A. P. *God and Space-Time in the Philosophy of Samuel Alexander.* New York: Philosophical Library, 1954.

Alfred North Whitehead

Emmet, D. *Whitehead's Philosophy of Organism.* New York: St. Martin's Press, 1966.

————. "Alfred North Whitehead: The Last Phase." *Mind,* LVII (1948), 265–274.

Gentry, G., and Miller, D. L. *Philosophy of Alfred North Whitehead.* New York: Burgess, 1938.

Hammerschmidt, W. W. *Whitehead's Philosophy of Time.* New York: King's Crown Press, 1947.

Hintz, H. W. "A. N. Whitehead and the Philosophical Synthesis." *Journal of Philosophy,* LII (1955), 225–243.

Lawrence, N. *Whitehead's Philosophical Development: A Critical History of the Background of Process and Reality.* Berkeley: University of California, 1956.

Mays, W. "Determinism and Free Will in Whitehead." *Philosophy and Phenomenological Research,* XV (1955), 523–534.

Schilpp, P. A., ed. *The Philosophy of A. N. Whitehead.* New York: Tudor, 1951.

Shahan, E. P. *Whitehead's Theory of Experience.* New York: King's Crown Press, 1950.

Sherburne, D. W. *A Whiteheadian Aesthetic: Some Implications of Whitehead's Metaphysical Speculations.* New Haven: Yale University Press, 1961.

Bertrand Russell

Dorward, A. *Bertrand Russell: A Short Guide to His Philosophy.* London: Published for the British Council by Longmans, Green, 1951.

Fritz, C. A. *Bertrand Russell's Construction of the External World.* London: Routledge & K. Paul, 1952.

Jourdain, P. E., ed. *The Philosophy of Mr. Bertrand Russell.* Chicago: Open Court, 1918.

Santayana, G. "Philosophy of Bertrand Russell." In *Winds of Doctrine,* by the same author. New York: Scribner, 1926.

Schilpp, P. A., ed. The Philosophy of Bertrand Russell. Evanston, Ill.: Northwestern University Press, 1944.

II. AMERICAN CRITICAL AND NEO-REALISM

Only important books are listed; an exhaustive bibliography will be found in the work of Werkmeister listed below.

Adams, G. P., and Montague, W. P., eds. *Contemporary American Philosophy: Personal Statements.* New York: Russell & Russell, 1962.

Blau, J. L. *Men and Movements in American Philosophy.* New York: Prentice Hall, 1952.

Cohen, Morris R. *American Thought: A Critical Sketch.* Glencoe, Ill.: Free Press, 1954.

Evans, D. L. *New Realism and Old Reality.* Princeton, N. J.: Princeton University Press, 1952.

Farber, M., ed. *Philosophical Thought in France and the United States.* Albany: State University of New York, 1968.

Feibleman, James. *The Revival of Realism.* Chapel Hill: University of North Carolina, 1946.

Harlow, V. E. *Bibliography and Genetic Study of American Realism.* Oklahoma City: Harlow, 1931.

Santayana, G. *Winds of Doctrine.* New York: Scribner, 1926.
Schneider, H. W. *A History of American Philosophy.* New York: Columbia University Press, 1946.
_____. *Sources of Contemporary Philosophical Realism in America.* Indianapolis: Bobbs-Merrill, 1964.
Werkmeister, W. H. *History of Philosophical Ideas in America.* New York: Ronald Press, 1949.

John Herman Randall, Jr.
Anton, John P., ed. *Naturalism and Historical Understanding: Essays on the Philosophy of John Herman Randall, Jr.* New York: State University of New York Press, 1967.

George Santayana
Howgate, G. W. *George Santayana.* Philadelphia: University of Pennsylvania Press, 1938.
Schilpp, P. A., ed. *The Philosophy of George Santayana.* New York: Tudor, 1951.

The *Journal of Philosophy,* LI (1954), contains a number of articles on Santayana; among the authors are J. Buchler, R. Herman, Jr., C. I. Lewis, J. H. Randall, and D. C. Williams.

F. W. Woodbridge
Costello, H. T. "The Naturalism of F. W. Woodbridge." In *Naturalism and the Human Spirit,* edited by Y. Krikorian. New York: Columbia University Press, 1944.

Morris Raphael Cohen
Baron, S.; Nagel, E.; and Pinson, K., eds. *Freedom and Reason: Studies in Philosophy and Jewish Culture in Memory of Morris Raphael Cohen.* Glencoe, Ill.: Free Press, 1951.
Costello, H. T. "Logic and Reality." *Journal of Philosophy,* XLIII (1946).
Kuhn, Martin A. *Morris Raphael Cohen: A Bibliography.* New York: City College of New York Library, 1957.
Rosenfield, L. D. *Portrait of a Philosopher: Morris R. Cohen in Life and Letters.* New York: Harcourt, Brace & World, 1962.

CHAPTER VI

Neo-Scholasticism

Introduction: Scholasticism and Neo-Scholasticism

Scholasticism is the common name given to philosophy as it was taught in the medieval universities during the period of their greatest flowering, from the twelfth century to the fourteenth. This term, like so many others in intellectual history (e.g.: romanticism, classicism, humanism, etc.) has a double force. It designates a period in the history of philosophy which can be definitely located in time and which forms an indispensable link in that history; at the same time, it indicates a theoretical and doctrinal complex which, while entirely immanent to that historical period, exhibits a capacity to "migrate" beyond it and to reappear, in altered form, at other periods. In all discussions of scholasticism it is necessary to make clear to which of these designations reference is being made, and this necessity is felt with especial force in the discussion of the "neo-scholastic" movement of the nineteenth and twentieth centuries.

It would be easy to dismiss this "neo-scholastic" movement as an example of cultural atavism, as the effort to revive a method of philosophizing and a philosophical doctrine which are entirely comprehensible and even admirable in the context of their time and to transpose them to cultural clime to which they are essentially alien and which, in turn, must inevitably prove hostile to them. However, this would prove a grave error. Although the neo-scholastic revival to a considerable extent exudes the atmosphere of romantic medievalism which appeared in the nineteenth century, neo-scholastic philosophy is not directly attached to the historical reality of scholasticism and is not concerned to bring back a period in the history of philosophy. It attaches itself rather to the second denomination of the term scholasticism noted above: a body of doctrine and a method in philosophy. Even more radically, it attaches itself to the more subtle notion of a *"philosophia perennis"* and of the historical transcendence of philosophical truth.

118

"*Philosophia perennis*" is a theory of the movement of the history of philosophy which holds that, in the course of its historical progress and with no prejudice to the full recognition of the diversities, regressions, etc., which mark that course, philosophy has gradually built up a solid core of doctrine and an assured and tested method to which each successive period has in its own way contributed and which continues as the point of reference (sometimes unrecognized or at least unspoken) of all subsequent thought. The theory of the historical transcendence of philosophical truth holds that truth in its philosophical form is essentially transcendent to the historical conditions in which it is formulated and developed and must, therefore, be recognized by all subsequent effort. Both these theories influence the meaning of "neo-scholasticism." It is not a form of cultural primitivism seeking to transpose into the present a form of thought which has been historically transcended. It is rather, on the one hand, the effort to explicate the *philosophia perennis* and to extend it and, on the other, to testify to the essentially transhistorical character of philosophical truth. However one may evaluate the results of these efforts, the quality and relevance of what neo-scholasticism has to say, this must be recognized as its proper character.

Even this way of stating the matter is not, however, entirely satisfactory. Although scholastic philosophy is identified most closely with the Middle Ages and suffered severe reverses of fortune in subsequent centuries, it never completely disappeared from the history of philosophy. After the Middle Ages, it becomes a reduced and subdued but nevertheless persistent current, the presence of which is variously evidenced at different times. Some have suggested that this persistence has been galvanic, due to the support of the Catholic Church which had adopted scholasticism, especially in its Thomistic form, as an "official" philosophy. This allegation cannot be denied a certain truth. The fact remains, however, that thinkers quite outside the pale of that institution's influence have, at various periods and in various ways, reflected the ideas and the method of scholasticism.

The historian of philosophy is led, consequently, to view the neo-scholasticism of the modern period, not as something absolutely new, nor as a primitivistic revival, but as the latest in the succession of epiphanies which scholasticism has experienced from the time of its initial floruit to the present. He must also notice, however, that the present epiphany differs in important ways from earlier ones. While these others were for the most part casual—due, perhaps, to the interest of a single thinker or group of thinkers—the present one is much stronger, exhibiting traces of explicit organization and having the support of a vast educational system. While important, these differences are circumstantial from the philosophical point of view. The historian's main concern must continue to be the specifically philosophical character of neo-scholasticism, especially its effort to establish a bond of relevance between contemporary philosophy and the *philosophia perennis.*

Modern neo-scholasticism falls into two phases. These may be called the pre-Thomistic and the Thomistic. A third phase may also be distinguished, that of "transcendental Thomism." However, this last does not seem, to the present writer, to be on an equal level with the first two but must be considered a later development of the Thomistic phase. The dividing point between the two main phases is the publication of the papal encyclical *Aeterni Patris* on August 4, 1879. Prior to this event neo-scholasticism possessed the first character mentioned above: It was casual, sustained by the personal interest of individuals wherever it possessed a genuinely philosophical élan and sustained by theological necessity in other contexts. After that event, neo-scholasticism becomes a "movement" in the full sense of that term. It is acutely conscious of its social character and tends to generate centers of radiation, schools, even factions. Even in this phase, however, when the "official" character seems to mark it, the movement is sustained, in its purely philosophical dimension, by the efforts of outstanding individuals. Philosophy, it is again made clear, is never truly a corporate work; the individual is its true carrier.

A. *Pre-Thomistic Neo-Scholasticism*

The "Great Period" of scholasticism ended, not in the thirteenth or fourteenth century, as some would suppose, but in the seventeenth century, with the revival known as the "Second Scholasticism." This term designates the scholasticism which was contemporary with the Renaissance and the Counter-Reformation. The period of its greatest florescence followed the Council of Trent (1545–1563). Alongside the Dominican, Scotist, and Ockhamist schools, all deriving from the scholasticism of the great medieval religious orders, there arose the school of the philosophers and theologians of the newly founded Society of Jesus, who took as their mandate to carry into effect the reforms and proposals of the Council. In doing so, they displayed great versatility and speculative power, with an added emphasis on confronting the new problems of the day, which sprung principally from the Reformation. Among them the most outstanding figures were Francesco de Toledo (1533–1596), Benito Perera (1535–1610), and Pedro de Fonseca (1528–1599), who composed commentaries on the logic, the physics, and the metaphysics of Aristotle, respectively. They were followed by Luis de Molina (1535–1600), Roberto Bellarmino (1542–1621), Leonardus Lessius (Lenaert Lys) (1554–1623), Juan de Mariana (1535–1624), and above all by Francisco Suarez (1548–1617). The latter was particularly outstanding since he went far beyond the role he professed—that of "faithful commentator of Aristotle and St. Thomas"—to develop an original point of view based on direct concern with the exigencies of contemporary speculation. These men gave special attention to the concrete problems of human value, to the notion of the human person and the principles of the juridical and political, as well as the economic, orders. In this work they were equaled by the accomplishments of the Dominicans Domingo de Soto (1494–1560), Francesco Melchior Cano (1509–1560), Domingo Bañez (1528–1604), and John of St. Thomas (Juan de Poinsot) (1589–1644). The Spanish scholasticism of the period, especially the doctrine of Suarez, had wide influence, even in the Protestant universities of Germany. The movement declined, however, after the first impulse afforded by the Council of Trent. Perhaps the greatest achievement of the Second Scholasticism, as exemplified in the work of Suarez, was the disengagement of scholastic philosophical speculation from its theological matrix and its establishment as an independent discipline.

The florescence of the Second Scholasticism was followed by a period in which the modern currents in philosophy exercised a great attraction for the eccleciastical schools and universities. Abandoning the positions of traditional speculation, these tended to orientate themselves toward the new positions in philosophy, usually upon a highly eclectic basis. The Cartesian influence was especially notable. Nevertheless, though heavily muted, the traditional voice of philosophy could still be heard. To this period of its history belong such names as Antoine Goudin (1639–1695) and Salvatore Maria Roselli (?–1784). A special interest attaches, during this period, to the minuscule university called "Collegio Alberoni" in Piacenza in Italy. This school boasted an outstanding teacher, Francesco Grassi (1715–1773), whose teachings had a strong influence on a scholar of the next generation, Vincenzo Buzzetti (1777–1824). The latter set up in the seminary of Piacenza the first center consciously directed to a revival of Thomistic thought. His efforts were continued by a number of his students, most notably the brothers Serafino Sordi (1793–1865) and Domenico Sordi (1790–1880), both members of the Society of Jesus. They, in turn, influenced through their teaching and writings such figures of the scholastic revival as Luigi Taparelli d'Azeglio (1793–1862), Matteo Liberatore (1810–1892), Carlo Maria Curci (1810–1891), and Gaetano Sanseverino (1811–1865).

Sanseverino was professor of philosophy in the seminary at Naples.

By the foundation of the *Biblioteca cattolica,* the review *Scienza e fede,* and the Accademia di Filosofia Tomista, he promoted the serious and accurate study of the works of St. Thomas. His principal monument is his six-volume work entitled *Philosophia Christiana cum antiqua et nova comparata* [Christian philosophy compared with ancient and modern philosophy] . This work established itself as a model both of sound erudition in the scholastic sources and acute presentation of their doctrines and of the confrontation of these teachings with the most important modern movements of thought. Sanseverino showed himself remarkably well-versed in the latter area.

Chiefly, though not exclusively, through the efforts of Sanseverino, Naples became the center of interest in the renewal of scholasticism during this period. Sanseverino trained the very competent scholars and teachers Giuseppe Prisco (1836–1923), Nunzio Signoriello (1821–1889), and Salvatore Talamo (1844–1932). In the same period there had been founded in Naples the journal *Civiltà cattolica,* destined to become an organ with great influence; its founders included Carlo Curci, Luigi Taparelli d'Azeglio, and Matteo Liberatore, all Jesuits. While these men derived, as has been noted, from the movement initiated by the Sordi brothers rather than from the school of Sanseverino, the two groups shared the same interests and purposes. The review *Civiltà cattolica* proved to be particularly active, both in the publication of expository and analytic articles on the thought of St. Thomas and the other great scholastics and also in the task of establishing contact with modern currents of thought. Its single flaw was, perhaps, an over-polemical attitude in the latter effort. Soon after its foundation the journal was transferred to Rome and for a century and more has continued to exercise a substantial influence.

At the same time, a similar revival of interest in scholastic thought, especially that of St. Thomas, was taking place in other centers of Italy. In the Collegio di S. Tommaso alla Minerva, Tommaso Zigliara of the Order of Preachers, later cardinal, displayed an especially impressive talent for the presentation of St. Thomas' thought; his most important work was the *Summa philosophica in usum scholarum* [Summa of philosophy for the use of schools], 1876. The title of the work is too modest. It is not a textbook, but a well-thought-out exposition of the thought of St. Thomas with a sympathetic understanding of the conditions of modern thought to which it sought to relate the classical scholastic point of view. In Bologna, Francesco Battaglini (1823–1902) established the Accademia Tomistica, while a similar group was formed at Perugia which included among its most outstanding members Giusèppe Pecci (1807–1899), later cardinal, and his brother Vincenzo Gioachino Pecci (1810–1903), who reigned as Pope Leo XIII and was to promulgate the encyclical *Aeterni Patris,* which ushered in the second, neo-Thomist phase of neo-scholasticism.

In Spain the most important names of the movement are Ceferino González (1831–1892) and Jaime Balmes (1810–1848). The former, a Dominican, taught in the college of his order in Ocaña, near Madrid; while serious and ample, his work does not exhibit any particular originality or strength. Quite the opposite must be said of Balmes. Indeed, so genuine a speculative power did he display that it is doubtful whether he should be classed as the member of a school or movement, although his purposes were, in their widest scope, identical with those of neo-scholasticism. Though his basic intention was apologetic, his original genius shone through at every point in his work. His chief apologetic monument is his *El protestantismo comparado con el catolicismo en sus relaciones con la civilización* [Protestantism compared with Catholicism in respect to its relations with civilization]; this work, in four volumes, was published between 1842 and 1844. His more purely speculative works include *El Criterio* [The criterion], 1845, and the four-volume *Filosofía fundamental* [Fundamental philosophy], 1846. His philosophical formation had been eclectic; his apologetic interests had led him to seek support in the scholastic writers; of these, Roselli seems to have influenced him most. As his thought developed, the apologetic purpose receded, giving way to a purely speculative interest and revealing more clearly his speculative power. He exercised a very considerable influence, not in Spain alone, but in France, Germany, and Italy.

In France, the first phase of the neo-scholastic movement was one of erudition. New editions and translations of the works of St. Thomas heralded its coming. At the same time, very able expositors of the thought of the Angelic Doctor began to appear, such as Charles Jourdain (1817–1886). These men were but feeble harbingers of the future of neo-scholasticism in France, which was to become one of the strongest centers of the movement. Still it was they who prepared the way for that future achievement.

The beginnings of the revival of scholasticism in Germany were modest indeed. The true forerunner of all that was to develop was the work of the Jesuit Josef Kleutgen (1811–1883): *Die Philosophie der Vorzeit verteidigt* [The philosophy of antiquity defended], 1860–63. It was all the more outstanding when the preponderance of the Kantian and Hegelian philosophies, which had produced so much more disorientation among Catholic thinkers, is considered. Another signal achievement of the period is the *Philosophia Lacensis,* (1880–98). This was a cooperative effort of the Jesuits and its prime mover was Tilmann Pesch, S.J., (1839–1899). This "Cursus" included volumes on the philosophy of nature, on logic, on ontology, and on psychology. Pesch's chief concern was the vindication of the scholastic natural philosophy in an age of positivistic science. His volumes exhibit a creditable acquaintance with the science of his time.

The assessment of this phase of neo-scholasticism, to the issuance of *Aeterni Patris*, is difficult. One is arrested, first of all, by the body of solid erudition which its cultivators display; these early neo-scholastics were truly learned men. At the same time, they exhibit a peculiar relation to this learning. They seem not so much to be the master of it as to be mastered by it. No truly speculative motive penetrates their work to inform it with a purpose and to direct it. Their chief concern is to maintain scholastic philosophy as the organizing principle of speculative theology. This motive cedes place at times to apologetic and polemical aims. In their hands the scholastic ideas prove agile polemical and apologetic instruments, but this agility is rendered futile by the uncertainty of the aims it serves.

Beneath this overarching theological, apologetical, and polemical concern, however, a genuine philosophical concern shows itself. It is invariably accompanied by an attempt to establish a rapprochement with modern philosophy. Many neo-scholastic philosophers understood very well that much had transpired since the Second Scholasticism, and they were determined to establish a positive link between scholastic philosophy and modern thought. The radical character of the developments which had taken place since Descartes made this purpose very difficult to achieve. An entirely new conception of philosophy had emerged and the neo-scholastics did not always appreciate how radical this novelty was. They worked, consequently, with a conception of philosophy which was basically unrelated to what the moderns were doing. Even their most strenuous efforts toward a "synthesis," consequently, prove ineffective. Examples of this situation are to be found most clearly in the two fields to which practically every neo-scholastic philosopher devoted attention: logic and the "philosophy of nature."

When it is asked what positive achievement can be assigned to this body of thought, the answer must be given in historical terms. It served a purpose not unlike that of the culture of the great monastic establishments of the early Middle Ages. Those establishments kept alive a tradition of culture which they could not develop. Similarly, the persistent line of scholastic thought, running parallel to (often in counterpoint to) the development of modern thought, kept alive a speculative tradition which is integral to the whole pattern of western civilization. Thus historical ends were served by their activity, even while their immediate purposes were being frustrated. A culture can never afford to lose any portion of its spiritual patrimony; the preservation of any part of it must always be accounted a positive work. The neo-scholastic thinkers of this first phase achieved that positive work.

B. *Thomistic Neo-Scholasticism*

In its basic attitudes Thomistic neo-scholasticism, that stemming from the encyclical *Aeterni Patris,* offers a clear antithesis to that earlier phase. Thomistic neo-scholasticism is far more sophisticated historically, with a clearer conception of its relations both to its sources and to the world in which it is actually operative. It is also more sophisticated in a strictly philosophical sense, for it was prepared to appreciate, accept, and advance the conception of philosophy which had emerged in the modern period. Its work was neither preservative nor apologetic. It was conceived as a work of radical renewal, of re-creation. It is a modern movement with historical leverage; it is not an historical attitude persisting in an age fundamentally hostile to it. All of these traits are already present in the document which initiated this phase of the scholastic revival: the encyclical *Aeterni Patris.*

1. *Aeterni Patris:* Occasion and Character

The encyclical *Aeterni Patris* was not without antecedents. It had been preceded by two letters of Pius IX, which have been commented upon by Cardinal Mercier in his account of the origins of neo-Thomism. However, Mercier fails to note with complete clarity the difference in tone between these letters and the encyclical. The letters of Pius reflect his generally antimodern attitude, expressed elsewhere in his famous Syllabus of Errors; he sees in scholastic thought a refuge from, and an instrument against, modern thought. The tone of the *Aeterni Patris* cannot be characterized as antimodern. On the contrary, it is pro-modern, for it sees the work it projects as of the contemporary age, in accord with and responding to its spirit. This tonality has its own antecedent in the experience of the author, Leo XIII.

As priest and archbishop, Vincenzo Gioachino Pecci had already been active in the renewed study of scholastic philosophy and especially of St. Thomas. It was noted earlier that he was among the leaders of the group in Perugia. His approach to that study, even in that earlier period, reflected his own strong and progressive attitude and personality. He saw in the revival of scholastic thought, not a refuge from or an instrument against the modern world, but an avenue of approach to it. He set the dual aims which would control the entire Thomistic movement: first, the modernization of the thought of St. Thomas and, second, the exertion of a powerful leverage in the intellectual and cultural life of the modern world by bringing the principles of scholastic thought, as propounded by St. Thomas, to bear upon all the salient problems of the modern spirit. The thought of St. Thomas, as the highest expression of the great scholastic tradition, purged of all that was archaic and cumbersome in it, enriched by the subsequent advances of philosophy, would, in his view, secure an adequate intellectual formation of the clergy, develop an efficacious intellectual apostolate in the modern world, and contribute directly to the advancement of philosophy, the arts, and the sciences.

Aeterni Patris is not a legislating document. Thomistic neo-scholasticism is not the creation of eccleciastical authority. What the papal document did was reorientate the earlier neo-scholastic movement toward a creative and constructive goal, free it from all anachronistic elements, and project it into the modern world as a force for truth in its own right.

The encyclical *Aeterni Patris* was published on August 4, 1879. Leo XIII followed it immediately with other vitalizing provisions. The first of these was the creation of the Roman Academy of St. Thomas. Another important step was the provision for a new edition of all the works of St. Thomas, the celebrated Leonine Edition. The latter provision rested upon an appreciation of the handicaps under which the earliest neo-scholastic philosophers had worked and the desire to provide the new movement with a solid basis in erudition and a sure instrument of work. Succeeding documents such as the *Pascendi*, 1907, the *Studiorum Ducem*, 1923, and the *Humani Generis*, 1950, confirmed and advanced the basic positions delineated in the *Aeterni Patris*.

2. The Great Centers of Development

The impulse given to the neo-scholastic movement by the *Aeterni Patris* found its most immediate expression in the establishment of many centers for the study and diffusion of the thought of St. Thomas. These centers appeared in every country of importance in Europe as well as in the United States and Canada. Almost without exception, each of the centers founded a journal for the expression and diffusion of its own works. These journals became the lines of communication between the centers and with the modern world. The most striking characteristic of these centers and of their journals was the great diversity in spirit, method, and preoccupation, all within the ambit of the common purpose.

Without doubt, the most striking development was that of the Institut Supérieur de Philosophie at Louvain. It is the first important center organized as a direct consequence of the impulse given by the *Aeterni Patris*. Its origin dates from the suggestion of Leo XIII (who had served as papal nuncio in Belgium and had thus come to know the University of Louvain) to Cardinal Deschamps that he establish in that institution a center for the teaching and interpretation of St. Thomas along the lines which had been sketched in the encyclical. This task was assigned to Désiré Mercier, at that time a young priest (later bishop and cardinal and otherwise famous for his defense of Belgium's liberty and neutrality in the First World War). Mercier inaugurated the first course in the new program and institution in 1882. The language of the course was French, itself a significant innovation, for the customary language of scholastic philosophy had been Latin. Three years later, the Institute acquired the power to confer the licenciate and the doctorate "in the philosophy of St. Thomas"; the conferring of these degrees was still subject, however, to the regulations of the Faculty of Philosophy and Letters. The Institute took further shape in 1889 when Cardinal Rampolla suggested the establishment of two new chairs in philosophy. By 1895, under Mercier's constant guidance, the Institute finally achieved full stature and autonomy.

By this date the Institute already published a review with considerable prestige, the *Revue philosophique de Louvain*, and had begun the publication of the *Cours de philosophie*, which was to have considerable impact on philosophical culture. The principal contributors to this *Cours* were Mercier in logic, ontology, psychology, and general criteriology, Maurice De Wulf (1869–1947) in the history of medieval philosophy, and Désiré Nys (1859–1927) in cosmology. Mercier desired that his school should rest solidly on the scholastic achievement of the past, and St. Thomas always remained the primary authority for him. At the same time, he wanted the scientific spirit of the Institute to be open to every avenue of research and to all new discoveries. His motto became famous: "In philosophy the important thing is disinterested investigation of the truth, all the truth, without thought for the consequences."

Mercier's work has proved durable. His basic plan of the Institute has served as the model for many similar foundations. The Institute is today still strong and influential and trains a substantial number of the most prominent men in this field. The names of the chief figures of the school, such as Louis De Raeymaeker (1895–1970), Nicolas Balthasar (1882–1959), Ferdinand Renoirte (1894) and Joseph Dopp (b. 1901) are still among the most noted in the neo-scholastic world.

Little second to Louvain in historical and theoretical importance are the centers which were founded and still flourish in Italy. The oldest of these is the Aloisianum, located at Gallarate, in the vicinity of Milan. This institution in fact antedates the neo-Thomistic movement and is looked upon as the continuator of the neo-scholastic school of Piacenza, with which such names as Sordi, Cornoldi, and others are connected. Many of the best Jesuit representatives of the movement received their training at the Aloisianum. Today the most important center, because it is the training ground for an international student body from which issue many famous prelates and scholars, is the Pontifical Gregorian University in Rome. During the course of its long history many of the most illustrious names of the movement have appeared on its faculty, among them Juan José Urraburu (1844–1904), Louis Billot (1846–1931), Charles Boyer, S.J. (b. 1884), Petrus Hoenen, S.J. (1880–1961), and Paolo Dezza, S.J. (b. 1901), the historian of the neo-Thomistic movement. The Ateneo Angelico, known as the Angelicum, the continuator institution of the College of St. Thomas alla Minerva in Rome, previously mentioned in connection with Cardinal Zigliara, has become a center for intensive study of the Angelic Doctor under the direction of the Dominicans. The Pontifical Lateran University is a center more for canonical and juridical studies than for philosophical, but its interest in the general philosophical system on which its special studies rest has been given ample evidence.

Especially active has been the philosophical faculty of the Catholic University of Milan, founded by the well-known Franciscan, Agostino Gemelli (1878–1960). In many ways this is the most interesting of the more recent foundations, for it represents a point of view rather strongly in contrast to that of Louvain and broader and more flexible than that of the Gregorian (which has strong theological preoccupations in accordance with its chief function of preparation of the clergy). Its Thomism is considered more intransigent than that of the other schools, especially in the field of metaphysics. Thus, its founder Agostino Gemelli, wrote: "By neo-scholastic philosophy we properly understand the restoration of medieval thought within the scope of modern civilization; medieval thought is not considered as a transitory expression of a civilization but, in substance, as a definitive conquest by human reason in the field of metaphysics, a conquest brought to fruition through Greek speculation and Christianity and having realism and theism as its fundamental characteristics" (cf. *Il mio contributo alla filosofia neo-scolastico* [My contribution to neo-scholastic philosophy], Milan, 1932, p. 16 and passim).

About this rather inflexible metaphysical core, however, the Catholic University has constructed a vast network of interests touching on every aspect of modern thought and concerned with making direct contributions, in the most modern sense, to these fields. Metaphysical intransigence is balanced by a vital interest in the advance of every field of learning and a remarkable freedom in pursuit of this latter purpose. Among the names associated with the Catholic University in the area of philosophy, particularly the renewed study of St. Thomas, are Francesco Olgiati (1886–1963), Emilio Chiocchetti (1880–1951), Amato Masnovo (1880–1955), and Sophia Vanni Rovighi (b. 1908). Its important journal *Revista neo-scholastica* and its many publications have won it a considerable reputation.

Among other journals are the authoritative *Gregorianium,* published at the Gregorian University, the autonomous *Civiltà cattolica,* founded and edited since 1850 by the Jesuits, and *Divus Thomas,* published (with some interruption) since 1880 by the Alberoni College of Piacenza.

In Spain, the chief centers of the neo-Thomist revival have been the University of Salamanca and the Seminary of Comillas. The first has been conducted by the Dominicans, the latter by the Jesuits. But to speak of neo-scholastic thought only in terms of these centers would be incorrect, for many of the most important faculties in modern Spanish universities have representatives of this movement among their professors: Madrid, Valencia, Barcelona, Granada, and Valladolid. Especially promising for these studies may be the new University of Navarra, at Pamplona, for its orientation is strongly philosophical.

In France, strong centers for the study of the thought of St. Thomas are to be found in the Catholic Institutes of Paris, Lyon, and Lille. Antonin Sertillanges (1863–1948) and Jacques Maritain (b. 1882) both enjoyed periods of association with the Institute of Paris, and both made significant contributions to scholastic thought. The houses of study of the Dominican order at Le Saulchoir and St. Maximin and of the Jesuit order at Chantilly and Vals have fostered this work, while in Etienne Gilson (b. 1884) and Pierre Mandonnet (1858–1936) the movement found representation at the Sorbonne and in the Collége de France. Germany did not found any centers in the sense of those mentioned above, but it has been strongly represented in every branch of the neo-scholastic revival: by Cardinal Franz Ehrle (1845–1935), Clemens Baeumker (1853–1924), and Martin Grabmann (1875–1949) in the history and paleography of scholasticism, by Romano Guardini (1885–1968) and Josef Pieper (b. 1904) in the difficult fields of moral and cultural philosophy and in the treatment of the philosophical bases of theological problems.

On the North American continent, the Catholic Universitites of Montreal, Quebec, and Ottawa in Canada all fostered this study, but the most distinguished center is the Institute of Mediaeval Studies at the University of Toronto, founded by Etienne Gilson in 1929. Many of the best representatives of neo-Thomism in America were formed in its program, which combines sound historical erudition and speculative interests. In the United States, the Catholic University in Washington, which is the seat of the American Catholic Philosophical Association, and the Universities of Notre Dame and St. Louis constitute the strongest and most articulate representatives; though, in conformity with the basic pluralism of American culture, none of these institutions limits philosophical interest to this movement. On the South American continent, representatives of neo-Thomism are to be found in all the important universities, but special recognition is perhaps due the Catholic University of La Plata, represented by the work of Octavio Derisi, editor of the journal *Sapientia*.

3. Basic Characteristics and Present Tendencies in Neo-Thomist Philosophy

Centers of study and diffusion represent but the outer shell of the movement of neo-scholastic and neo-Thomist thought. They tell little or nothing of its inner character and quality as a movement of ideas and fail to indicate its place and influence in the intellectual life of our times. In order to appreciate this character and influence, it is necessary to consider what Thomism stands for in the order of ideas. We will consider these ideas as they identify neo-Thomistic thought and as they constitute a basic framework for the variety of points of view and lines of investigation and development carried out by individual thinkers. Two phases must be distinguished: 1) the basic framework of this movement and 2) its actual tendencies in the present period, both toward greater self-definition and clarification and toward rapprochement with other tendencies of modern thought.

The consideration of the basic ideas represented by neo-scholastic thought may best proceed in a historical framework, reflecting the exigencies of modern thought with which the movement sought to cope and the resources of its authors, St. Thomas and the other masters of the great period of scholasticism. This procedure will bring into view the historico-speculative physiognomy of neo-Thomistic thought and establish why its adherents thought that the ideas of the medievals were capable of resolving the demanding questions of modern thought. It will also reveal the inner character of the movement as an effort, not to reestablish a system from a period long past, but to draw upon the philosophy of the past to meet specifically modern problems.

The neo-scholastic movement makes its inception in the context of the critical problem; a problem, it should be noted, wholly modern in its origin and manner of formulation. The critical problem, as it presented itself historically, was defined by the opposition between the sensism of Locke and the *apriorism* of Kant. Both of these positions bear upon the same problem which has been the preoccupation of modern thought since Descartes: the justification, in the sense of establishing the origin, limits, and auto-criteria, of man's intellective knowledge. The specific point of departure of neo-scholastic thought was not the conflict of these points of view as stated by their respective authors as much as the efforts of the early nineteenth-century thinkers Antonio Rosmini (1797–1855) and Vincenzo Gioberti (1801–1852) to mediate the extreme attitudes to which they gave rise. Rosmini especially had sensed both the urgency of this problem and the inconclusiveness of its formulation and resolution in these extreme positions. The solutions Rosmini and Gioberti offered were based ultimately on the insight that in the history of western philosophy there existed resources for showing that this problem need not have taken this exasperated form and, indeed, could not be justly stated or adequately resolved in this form.

The proposed resolutions of Rosmini and Gioberti seemed to certain of the early neo-scholastic thinkers to be inadequate and marked by the same shortcomings which characterized the positions of Kant and Locke. An important document for establishing the complex of relations lying at the basis of the neo-scholastic reinstallation of the doctrine of the medieval thinkers is Serafino Sordi's *Lettere intorno al nuovo saggio sull'origine delle idee dell'ab. Antonio Rosmini-Serbati* [Letters concerning the new essay on the origin of ideas of the Abbé Antonio Rosmini-Serbati], 1843. Sordi seeks to establish, not only that Rosmini's resolution of the dilemma was inadequate, but also that the antinomies on which the whole critical problem rested had arisen through certain distortions within the tradition of western thought. He went on to suggest that the doctrine which might make clear the fallacious character of the critical problem as historically formulated and also indicate the more authentic form in which the problem of the validity of human intellective knowledge might be cast was already available in the texts of the masters of scholastic thought, especially St. Thomas. This is the doctrine of *abstraction*. Sordi proceeds to sketch his own interpretation of this doctrine and the manner in which it brings to light both the inadequacies of Rosmini's thought and the fundamental malformulation of the critical problem in modern thought. (Cf. also Dezza, *I neotomisti italiani del XIX secolo* [The Italian neo-Thomists of the nineteenth century], Milan, 1942, Vol. I., pp. 30–102, for documents bearing on many aspects of this same problem.)

The doctrine of abstraction became and remains a cardinal element in the whole structure of modern neo-scholastic thought. The doctrine has received exhaustive examination in its sources and varied interpretations by the succeeding generations of modern Thomists. (Cf.

Dezza, *I neotomisti italiani,* for the earlier treatments; and Georges
van Riet, *Thomistic Espistemology* [New York, 1963–64] for the
most complete study of the whole matter in both its historical and
speculative aspects.)

The consideration of the problem of the validity of man's knowledge
leads directly to the consideration of the second cardinal element of
the neo-Thomist synthesis: the Thomistic psychology. The Thomistic
theory of man is highly relevant because it provides the validating concepts for the theory of abstraction. Man thinks in the manner depicted
by the theory of abstraction because of his fundamental ontological
constitution. The doctrine of abstraction rests upon the psychological-
anthropological doctrine of the *soul as the form of the body,* a doctrine
to be traced to Aristotle which, as reformulated by St. Thomas, is the
fundamental thesis of Thomistic psychology and theory of man. This
doctrine, as brought to bear by the neo-scholastics upon the problems
of modern philosophy, strikes at that dualism or parallelism of body
and soul (the mind-body problem) as it had emerged with Descartes.
This dualism, through subsequent centuries, had dissolved the basic
unity of the human composite and made the union of body and soul,
as well as the processes dependent upon this union, something of a
mystery. The reformulation of the thesis of the soul as the form of
body, in this context, became the chief preoccupation of the early neo-
Thomist Matteo Liberatore, of Naples, in his works *Del composto
umano* [On the human composite], 1862, and *Del anima umana* [On
man]. (Cf. Dezza, p. 183ff.) Thereafter it becomes a basic thesis, and
indeed the foundation of the entire theory of man, and receives repeated elaboration at the hands of succeeding proponents of neo-
Thomism (cf. V. J. Bourke, *Thomistic Bibliography,* St. Louis, 1940).

By an inexorable movement, both historical and logical, the consideration of the structure of the human composite leads to the consideration of the much wider theory of the composition of matter and
form. To rest with the concept of the human composite as the basis for
the solution of the "critical" problem and the validation of the theory
of abstraction would be to offer a merely factual and scientific response
to these questions and not a speculative one. Matter and form and the
mode of their composition offer the general principles of which the
human composite is but a special case. Consequently, by the philosophical momentum of the inquiry, the consideration of the special
case leads to the general form. Hylomorphism, as this general doctrine
was and is still called, actually underlines the treatment of abstraction
and the human composite noted above and receives specific reference
at various points in those works.

The establishment of this theory, in its wider form, became the special preoccupation of another early neo-Thomist, Giovanni Cornoldi (1822–1892); (cf. his *La filosofia scolastica di S. Tommaso e di Dante* [The scholastic philosophy of St. Thomas and Dante], 1889; cf. further Dezza, p. 131ff.). The effort involved in the reformulation of this general theory was the more strenuous by reason of the greater difficulties which confronted it. In its historical formulation, this general theory seemed to be intrinsically dependent upon the physics, not only of St. Thomas, but of his source, Aristotle. To restate it and offer it as a meaningful thesis in the context of modern thought seemed to be flying in the face of the progress of the sciences, and Cornoldi found himself challenged even by the ecclesiastical authorities who were by no means inclined to sanction so ostensible an anachronism. Cornoldi had to make clear that this dependence, though indeed historical, was not intrinsic to the theory. He sought to do this by relating the hylomorphic theory, not to specific scientific theories, whether ancient or modern, but to the more basic problem of change, which was common to both and which could be formulated in a manner relevant to, but not dependent on, the specific sciences. This way of establishing the grounds of relevance for the hylomorphic theory has remained constant in neo-Thomism. (Cf. A. Maier, *An der Grenze von Scholastik und Naturwissenschaft* [On the contact between scholasticism and the sciences of nature], Rome, 1952; F. Selvaggi, *Problemi della fisica moderna* [Problems of modern physics], Brescia, 1953; E. Lowyck, *Substantiele verandering en hylemorphisme: Een critische studie over de neoscholastick* [Substantial change in hylomorphism: a critical study in neoscholasticism], Louvain, 1948.)

Hylomorphism, actually, represents a special case of a still more inclusive speculative theory, that of act and potency. By the same combination of historical and logical necessity, neo-Thomism, in its effort to achieve a living synthesis between the resources of the scholastic tradition and the exigencies of modern thought, was led to revive this metaphysical doctrine. Matter and form are but act and potency in the limited order of essence necessary to explain substantial change and numerical plurality. There are present in reality, however, other forms of change and other types of plurality. These involve other compositions of act and potency, leading eventually to the most immediate and indivisible union between them in the act of existence. It is here, in the analysis of existence, that the most intimate structure of act and potency is revealed. In its full range, this doctrine of act and potency constitutes, by general recognition, the master key to the whole of Thomistic metaphysics and indeed to the whole system of neo-Thomistic speculation.

A number of men are associated most closely with this effort to reestablish the doctrine of act and potency. Perhaps the central position belongs to Guido Mattiussi (1852–1925), the chief architect of the famous "twenty-four theses," which some have held to be a kind of manifesto of modern neo-Thomism, and of an elaborate and subtle commentary on these theses: Le XXIV tesi della filosofia di S. Tommaso [The twenty-four theses of the philosophy of St. Thomas], Rome, 1917, and many subsequent editions. In this remarkable work, considered by many a tremendous tour de force, Mattiussi makes the doctrine of act and potency the key to the entire structure of St. Thomas' thought. He distinguishes its place as first in the order of deduction and last in the order of invention. He then proceeds, by a kind of geometrical method reminiscent of Spinoza, to deduce the cardinal theses mentioned above (with many other more specific ones) from that first speculative ground. Like the ostensible structure of the Ethics, the system thus engendered is excessively rigid and tends to be so closed that it appears sterile and tautological. Other writers have tried, without in the least minimizing the central importance of the theory of act and potency in the structure of Thomistic metaphysics, to treat it in a more flexible and expansive manner both in itself and in relation to the other key concepts of the Thomistic speculative corpus. (Cf. L. Fuetscher, Akt und Potenz, [Act and potency], Innsbruck, 1933; C. Giacon, Atto e Potenza [Act and potency], Brescia, 1947, and Le grande tesi del tomismo [The principal theses of Thomism], 2nd ed., Como, 1948.)

These theses, as developed under the combined force of historical and logical necessity, provide the basic framework for neo-Thomistic speculation. They are generally held to represent both the fundamental lines of classical scholastic thought, as found in the text of St. Thomas, and the basis upon which a real dialogue can be established between that tradition and modern thought. Taken thus, however, in their bald structure, these theses must surely impart an appearance of over-rigidity to the whole Thomistic structure and to circumscribe excessively its range and movement. In fact, they do not do so. Within this structure there exists not only a wide range of interpretations and developments but a freedom of movement which is as essential to Thomistic thought and as characteristic of it as is subscription to these basic theses. This freedom may be illustrated in two ways: by noting the contemporary efforts and orientations of Thomism and, even more, by noting the work of selected individual thinkers whose thought has contributed significantly to the movement.

Though remaining constant to the basic orientation sketched above, neo-Thomism has shown itself very much open to all lines of philosophical research and, as a consequence, has developed a rather complex inner physiognomy. It has consistently sought to establish dialogue with the other currents of contemporary thought and to treat with philosophical rigor, in the light of the principles which define its own position, the most urgent and typical contemporary problems; for example, the problems of science, of aesthetics, of social and political thought, and of history.

Of the currents of modern philosophy with which neo-Thomism has established an effective dialogue, Kantianism comes to mind first. Indeed, a relationship with Kantianism had entered into the very origin of neo-scholasticism. The critical problem, as Kant had formulated it, could not fail to engage neo-scholastic thought immediately. In a certain sense this problem had always been indigenous to it, at least in the form of an attempt to determine the point of departure and the very possibility of metaphysics. All too frequently it is forgotten that Kant's ultimate purpose was not to destroy metaphysics but to determine the possibility and the starting point of authentic metaphysics. The basic metaphysical orientation of neo-scholasticism makes it particularly sensitive to this problem. On the whole, it does not take a complacent attitude toward the traditional manner of defining the character, possibility, and procedure of metaphysics; the latent intuitionism of Aristotle's manner of treating first principles has always aroused a certain inquietude. Kant has at least made neo-scholasticism aware that the authenticity of its metaphysics involved confrontation with the critical problem, which is precisely the problem of determining unequivocally the nature and procedures of that science. Consequently, its attitude toward Kantianism has not been negative; rather, it has sought to meet the demands of the Kantian question, insofar as these demands can be shown to be valid, and to refine its own point of departure and procedure to meet them. It has also launched solid and acute criticisms of the Kantian position, with special cogency against the shortcomings of the Kantian manner of formulating and resolving its own central problem. As an indication of the kind of dialogue which neo-scholasticism has conducted with the Kantian tradition from the very beginning one might consult Joseph Lotz, *Kant und die Neuscholastik heute* [Kant and neo-scholasticism today], 1955.

When it is recalled that the origins of modern phenomenology are to be traced eventually to the work of Franz Brentano (1838–1917), who had been formed, at least partially, in the scholastic tradition, the immediate sympathy and interest which this movement evoked in neo-scholastic philosophers may be understood. The links between these currents prove to be numerous and important. The anti-psychologism with which Husserl, in his *Logical Investigations*, prepared the groundwork for his restoration of philosophy (or its first advancement) to the status of a "strict science" was intrinsically congenial to scholasticism and seemed to echo many insights in the arguments of St. Thomas' *Summa*. This initial sympathy was vastly strengthened by the Husserlian doctrine of intentionality, which could be interpreted in the sense of Thomistic realism and which even suggested ways in which this realism could render itself more critical. Finally, the phenomenological theory of objects seemed to bear great resemblance and offer important parallels to the classical doctrine of substance. Perhaps the most illuminating pages illustrating the rapprochement between neoscholasticism and phenomenology on many basic points are to be found in the work of Edith Stein: *Husserl's Phenomenologie und die Philosophie des hl. Thomas von Aquin* [Husserl's phenomenology and the philosophy of St. Thomas Aquinas], 1929, in which she indicated three basic points of contact between the two currents. These are: 1) All knowledge begins with the senses; 2) all knowledge is an intellectual elaboration of sensible material; 3) intellectual knowledge has the character of vision and receptivity. Her last work, *Endliches und ewiges Sein* [Finite and eternal being], 1950, develops the same line of thought.

Perhaps the most extensive dialogue of all has been that of neoscholasticism with existentialism. At first glance there would seem to be little sympathy between them, whether in presupposition, methods, or problems. Such has not proved the case, however, in the view of many neo-Thomists. The point of contact between these two movements turns out to be one of great sensitivity, the relation between being and existence and essence and existence. Existentialism proded neo-Thomism to recall one of the strongest points of its metaphysics: namely, that it was a metaphysics of existence, in which existence is both the first form of the encounter of being and the ultimate status of being as act. Existentialism provided the occasion for scholasticism to purge itself of the last vestiges of the abstract rationalism and essentialism with which it had become somewhat confounded. It also suggested the reconsideration of the entire range of problems of the moral and situational life of man which had always attracted scholasticism but which the development of a rationalistic moralism had somewhat obscured. In the case of Kierkegaard—his critique of the Hegelian "system" and of the idea of system in general, his realistic ontology, and his emphasis on the idea of transcendence as established by the inner dimensions of concrete human existence in act—all provided points of similarity, though never of identity, between these currents and tended to strengthen and extend their dialogue. In addition to the work of Cornelio Fabro, the excellent book of Etienne Gilson *Being and Some Philosophers* (1949; 2nd ed. 1952) is most illuminating on this relationship. Without endeavoring to set up too positive an identity between them, this book shows, on historical and analytical grounds, how existentialism has acted as a spur to scholasticism to free itself from the rationalistic and essentialistic associations with which it had become encumbered.

The growth of modern science and the appearance of the philosophical problems which it entails are the true key to what philosophy is in our own day. The philosophical problems of science have also provided a direct challenge to neo-Thomist thought and established a firm relationship, at the level of the problematic, with modern thought. But there is not merely an occasional basis for this relationship; it has profound roots in scholasticism and in its own history. In the last analysis, scholasticism is a philosophy of nature, in the Aristotelian sense of that term. The world of time, space, and sensible experience is the world from which it takes its point of departure and within which it discerns its principles. Even its metaphysics is an extrapolation of the study of nature, formulated in function of the knowledge of physical nature. As early as Liberatore, neo-scholastic thinkers perceived that scholastic metaphysics, while developed in relation to natural science, was not restrictively related to the conditions of that science at any given moment of its history. It is not bound to the natural science of Aristotle or to that which was available in the days of Thomas Aquinas; it is related instead to the principles which underlie all investigation of nature, and, therefore, it has a functional relation to science. The growth of modern science did not constitute an obstacle to neo-Thomistic thought. It could accept the full range of findings of modern science and proceed to direct its attention to the philosophical problems which modern science engenders, confident that its principles could offer illumination for their solution. The notion that neo-scholastic thought would find itself encumbered by the untenable defense of an outmoded science proved a phantom.

A serious lack in classical scholastic philosophy had been the development of an authentic theory of art. It had been content to remain within the limits of the Aristotelian distinction between thought and action, and action and making, and to treat the problems of art within the terms of the last category, making. The richness of this category is not to be underestimated; nevertheless, western artistic experience since the Renaissance had raised problems and revealed aspects of art which could not be considered adequately in terms of this category alone. To this need for a philosophy of art which is responsive to the full range of this experience, neo-Thomism has shown itself especially sensitive. As evidence there may be cited such works as Maritain's early *Art and Scholasticism*, 1920, and his later supremely vital *Creative Intuition in Art and Poetry*, 1953, as well as the sober but perceptive work of Gilson, *Painting and Reality*, 2nd ed. 1957, and the acute reflections of F. Piemontese in his *L'intelligenza nell'arte* [Intelligence in art], 1955.

The problem of the history of philosophy, its nature and method, has also engaged the attention of the neo-Thomists with singular success. The name which stands out, perhaps above all others, is that of Gilson, who has not only written brilliantly on the principles of the historiography of philosophy, as in *The Unity of Philosophical Experience* (2nd ed., 1955), but has illustrated his method in a long series of works, general histories as well as monographs, in which solid erudition, controlled method, and brilliance of insight have been joined in rare fashion. Frederick Copleston's *A History of Philosophy*, which began to appear in 1946 and is still in process, and his incisive monographs on Nietzsche (1942) and Schopenhauer (1946) evidence the same qualities. Francesco Olgiati also has made an excellent contribution to the discussion of this problem in his essay "Il problema dell'interiorità e la storia della filosofia" [The problem of interiority and the history of philosophy] in *Revista de filosofia neo-scolastica*, 1932, no. 2.

The problem of history, seemingly so remote from the concerns of St. Thomas, has drawn the careful attention of some of the best of the neo-Thomists. A work on this theme, *Philosophy of History* (1957), is among those composed by Maritain; U. A. Padovani, perhaps the most consistently illuminating among recent Italian neo-Thomists, has contributed an excellent monograph to this discussion, *Filosofia e teologia della storia* [Philosophy and theology of history], 1955, while Charles Boyer, a professor at the Gregorian University and a representative of a Thomism more rigidly adherent to the thought of St. Thomas, has written *Il concetto di storia nell'idealismo e nel tomismo* [The concept of history in idealism and in Thomism], 1933.

The problem of man in all its aspects—anthropological, sociological, and political—has also preoccupied the neo-Thomists. They have shown, first of all, sensitivity to modern man's sense of his existential predicament. This sensitivity is traceable, of course, to the Christian basis of this philosophy; for Christianity is nothing if not a direct commentary on a salvific program for the predicament, and not even the highest speculative reaches of the Aristotelian tradition to which the neo-scholastics subscribe can distract them for long from this basis. On the whole, however, they have not succumbed to the dramatic urgencies of the existential analysis; they have been steadied by the classical elements of their tradition, grounded in universality, which makes the extreme fragmentation of being which the existentialists propose unpersuasive. Out of this tension has come a new humanism, which touches both the individual and the corporate status of man as the subject of being in existence. One of the best documents of this trend is without doubt, the *Humanisme intégrale (Integral Humanism)*, 1936, of Maritain; but it must be emphasized, that this is but one among many which might be cited, as any neo-scholastic bibliography will show. In the same manner, and with the same reservations, this author's *Man and the State*, 1951, may be taken as an example of the most alert neo-Thomistic response to the modern problems of politics from a humanistic point of view. With it should be ranked the fine reflections of John Courtney Murray, S. J., as exemplified in *We Hold These Truths*, 1960.

4. The Transcendental Method in Neo-Thomism

The truly remarkable resiliency of the scholastic philosophy has often been remarked. Again and again, in the course of history, when to all appearances it lay moribund, it has responded to the challenge and stimulus of new times and new cultural forces. An impressive instance of this resiliency is the recent current in neo-Thomism called "the transcendental method" (cf. O. Muck, *The Transcendental Method*, trans. W. D. Seidensticker [New York, 1968], and H. J. John, *The Thomist Spectrum* [New York, 1966], especially Chapters IV, IX, XII).

The epithet *transcendental*—taken, as it is intended, in the modern context—immediately reveals the Kantian filiation of the movement (if the term *filiation* is not too pretentious). The most general description of this current, consequently, identifies it as an effort to achieve a fresh affirmation of the insight into the primacy of being, so central to Thomism, by way of a development of the Kantian critical philosophy.

The neo-Thomist "transcendentalists," as a group, are convinced, first, that the Kantian criticism constitutes an absolute turning point in philosophy and that it is impossible to circumvent it by a return to any earlier position in the history of philosophy. They are equally convinced, however, that the Kantian agnosticism toward metaphysics is not warranted by the critical position which Kant himself developed. This agnosticism represents, rather, a failure on the part of Kant and the subsequent Kantians to press the critical inquiry and method to its furthest implications. When criticism is so pressed it yields not the Kantian agnosticism but the basis for a reaffirmation of the classical insight into being which is at once more sophisticated and more compelling than any which preceded it.

a. *Joseph Maréchal (1878–1944).* The writer who first advanced this conception of neo-Thomism vis-a-vis Kantian criticism was Joseph Maréchal. (It must be recognized at once, however, that a similar insight was advanced contemporaneously and independently by Pierre Rousselot in his work *L'intellectualisme de St. Thomas d'Aquin* [*The Intellectualism of St. Thomas Aquinas*], 1908, 3rd. ed. 1936; had he lived, his thought would no doubt have exercised even greater influence.) The work of Maréchal was so fundamental to this entire development of neo-Thomism that it has not infrequently been referred to as "Maréchalian Thomism." The chief work in which Maréchal developed his position is the five-volume *Le point de départ de la métaphysique: Leçons sur le dévelopment historique et théoretique du problème de la connaissance.* [The point of departure of metaphysics: essays on the historical and theoretical development of the problem of knowledge.] The volumes, and their various editions, appeared between 1922 and 1947. (For bibliographical details cf. *Mélanges Joseph Maréchal* [Paris, 1910], or Georges van Riet, *Thomistic Epistemology*, trans. Gabriel Franks, O.S.B. [St. Louis, 1963], pp. 236–271.) Though all are important, the volume which brings this series to its culmination is the fifth: *Le Thomisme devant la philosophie critique* [The confrontation of Thomism and the critical philosophy].

The strong influence of Kantian criticism is apparent at the very outset: Maréchal places himself, not *in medias res*, as had the classical Thomistic theory of being, but at the "point of departure" of metaphysics. His first concern is to establish the antecedent possibility and necessity of metaphysics and not to elaborate a metaphysical system. His assumption is that the metaphysics, whose possibility and necessity he is antecedently demonstrating, will prove to be, substantially, the classical Thomistic metaphysics.

The point which demands clarification at the outset is why Maréchal considered Kantian criticism the absolutely necessary starting point for the reaffirmation of metaphysics. The reason would seem to be Kant's own, namely, that otherwise metaphysics must remain, on the one hand, immedicably dogmatic, and, on the other, chimerical. Only criticism could plot a course between this Scylla and Charybdis by establishing, through its "retorsal" method, the possibility, even the absolute necessity, of metaphysics in such a way as at the same time to refute the scepticism of empiricism and indicate the reflectively developed ground for metaphysics as a science. But all this must *logically* precede the elaboration of a substantial metaphysics.

Since their task was clearly so much the same, why, it must be asked, did Kant's own effort fail to the degree that it had now to be done over again? Maréchal's reply is somewhat different than one would expect. Kant's failure resides, Maréchal says, in "his too complete separation of the areas of the theoretical and the practical, the 'formal' and the 'dynamic' " (cf. *Mélanges Maréchal*, I, 364). This observation contains his own doctrine in germ.

The new element in Maréchal's position is precisely the closer unification of the areas of the theoretical and the practical. This closer unity is revealed in the very structure of judgment in which the affirmation of being is achieved. In his analysis of the processes of pure reason Kant could bring this process no further than the phenomenal level. It was impossible by this path to reach the "noumenal" order, and hence to come to absolute being upon which the phenomenal order must be grounded. The same must be true, Maréchal thought, in the abstractive process typical of the Thomistic system. If the action of mind were to terminate at the point of contemplation of the finite essence abstracted from concrete existents in the acts of simple apprehension, it would come to rest, as does Kant's "pure reason," in a purely phenomenal order.

The fact is, however, that the mind does not, in the abstractive process, come to rest at this point. It is driven, rather, by an inner dynamic, the very principle of its reality as act, through and beyond this phenomenal level to the affirmation of noumenal being, indeed, the affirmation of the ultimate and absolute concrete *esse* which is God, as the ground of the whole structure of being. Kant's arresting of the critical process at the phenomenal level of being-for-another is abortive.

He is led to arrest the process in this way because of his failure to analyze the movement of mind itself. He remains at the level of a dualism between theoretical (purely contemplative) reason, or use of reason, and the practical. But the mind or spirit knows no such dualism, no such division. It is a seamless unity. It is the nature of mind as *act* (which Kant isolates from the theoretical dimension of mind) which provides the inner dynamism by which mind is carried through the phenomenal order to the affirmation of the noumenal, and finally to the affirmation of God as the concrete existent absolute which is the necessary ground of all that appears. The mind is driven or directed by its inner constitutive dynamism, by way of the phenomenal order, to the affirmation of absolute being as the antecedent ground of the necessity and possibility of all that appears or can appear in experience. To consider the "pure reason" as Kant does, independently of this dynamism and as though not moved by it, is to mutilate the unity of the act in which mind resides. (It is at this point that many historians recognize the affinity between Maréchal's position and Blondel's thought. A similar affinity, it is suggested, might with equal justice be detected between Maréchal and Bergson and Maréchal and Gentile.)

When the nature of mind as act is attained and its trajectory from the apprehension of the finite subject to the affirmation of absolute being as absolute *esse* (God) is understood, Maréchal believes, it is possible to recover and to restate with new assurance the entire content and structure of the classical metaphysics of finite being. This is true of the structure of the finite human subject (anthropology) as well as of the finite order of things in the world (philosophy of nature), although for him, as for Kant, the latter must be mediated by the former. To trace the stages of this reconstruction is to pass beyond the transcendental and critical phase to that of metaphysics proper. This is, naturally, the term toward which Maréchal's thought tends; to follow its course, however, is beyond the scope of this brief notice.

b. *Karl Rahner (b. 1904).* After that of Maréchal, the most celebrated figure associated with the "transcendental method" in neo-Thomism is Karl Rahner of the Society of Jesus. Rahner is best known for his theological writings, of course; but is is not difficult to ascertain how solidly these rest upon his philosophical work, especially his *Geist in Welt (Spirit in the World)*, 1937, 1957, 1964, and *Horer des Wortes (Hearers of the Word)*, 1941. (For further bibliographical information cf. *Gott in Welt: Festgabe für Karl Rahner*, ed. Johannes Metz, et al., 2 vols., 1964.)

The basic element of Rahner's formation is scholastic, the thought of St. Thomas, and this remains, throughout the transformations it has undergone, its solid framework. Hence, as has been noted, the constant strategy which Rahner has developed in addressing every problem: to take his point of departure in the classical scholastic and Thomistic position and to make every effort to "save" that position to the greatest possible extent. His formation also included contact with the work of Maréchal (which was first emerging during the years of Rahner's philosophical studies; in addition to following the regular scholastic courses, we are told, he also made generous notes from the *Point de départ*). But the most impressive influence was the thought of Heidegger, especially the later Heidegger, so that the basic tension of his thought appears to be between Thomas and Heidegger, touching obliquely, and in no merely dependent manner, the efforts of Maréchal. But the central point at which all these radii of influence meet is Kant. And the Kant in whom he is interested is precisely that Kant who undertook the critical enterprise in order to lay the foundations for a scientific metaphysics. In Rahner's case this interest in Kant served an ulterior purpose, for he realized that only such a scientific metaphysics could serve as the foundation of speculative theology.

No better summary of Rahner's thought from this point of view can be found, we believe, than the concluding chapter of his work *Spirit in the World,* in which he draws together the many threads of his thought as prelude to committing this position to the work of theology. The central question is the possibility of metaphysics, and Rahner perceives that this question is formulated in closely analogous terms by St. Thomas and Kant. Kant's agnosticism toward the possibility of metaphysics rests on the basis of his examination of pure reason and its operations. Human knowledge, he concludes from this analysis, is limited to objects of possible experience. The spontaneous dynamism of the human reason toward an absolute unity which transcends sense experience must, as a consequence, be merely logical and modal, not existential. Hence metaphysics, conceived as the realization of this absolute unity (i.e., the existence of God, the human soul, the world) at the existential and not merely the logical and modal level, is impossible and with it natural theology, rational psychology, and cosmology.

The point of linkage between Kant and Aquinas, Rahner perceives to lie at this point: namely, that the possibility of a metaphysics must be established on the premise of the basic reference of human knowledge to the sensible world. The form of this question in Thomistic terms must be: How is metaphysics possible if all human knowledge takes place through a *conversio intellectus ad phantasmata?* For this reason, Rahner's examination of the question and his engagement of Kant takes the form of an analysis and commentary on Part I, Q. 84, a. 1 of the *Summa Theologiae:* "Can the intellect actually know anything through the intelligible species which it possesses, without turning to the phantasms?" The strategy follows the classical lines of Rahner's thought: The "saving" interpretation of Thomas' text will meet the conditions of the question as stated in Kant's terms and consequently provide the fresh basis for the affirmation of the possibility of metaphysics in general and, in particular, of natural theology, "special metaphysics."

St. Thomas is aware, according to Rahner, that in asking about the conversion of the intellect to the phantasm he is simultaneously asking about the possibility of metaphysics. St. Thomas defined metaphysics, with respect to its "ultimate purpose" as the "divine science about first being" (cf. *In Meta. Proem, ad finem,* and *I Meta.* I, lect. 3, n. 64). With respect to its object (in Thomas' Latin "subjectum"), it is the science of being as such, science of "First Being" (God) and of common being, for "the science of first being and of common being are the same" (*I Meta.* VI, lect. 1, n. 1170). But this does not accurately represent the mind of St. Thomas as Rahner develops and interprets his thought, because the absolute or First Being (God) is not the "object" of this science at all. Metaphysics reaches God, First Being, only as ground, or principle, of the object of metaphysics, common being. The ground or principle cannot be in its turn an object; God is accessible to metaphysics only as the ground of its object, common being. In like manner, common being, the "object" of metaphysics, is accessible only as the ground of existents which it already presupposes. It too, like God, First Being, is not an object but a principle. God and common being are prior in human knowledge, not as objects, but rather as principles of the being and the knowledge of the first object of human science, which is the material *quiddity,* or, more accurately, the *quid-dity,* of material things. All knowledge of such *quiddity,* on the other hand, is knowable only in the "pre-apprehension" of absolute *esse,* not as object, but as principle. Hence the implicit affirmation of absolute *esse* (both as first being and as common being) is the condition of the possibility of any knowledge. It follows, then, not only that metaphysics is possible, given the *conversio ad phantasma,* but rather that such *conversio* is necessary. For the principles, God and common being, not being objects, can be known only by such reference to the *first object* of knowledge, namely, the material *quiddity.* The object can be known adequately only in the light of the principles, common being and first being.

Thus Rahner had established, by a circumambulatory and transcendental movement, both the possibility and the necessity of metaphysics on the very presupposition which St. Thomas and Kant share—namely, that the object of human knowledge belongs to sense experience; that the *conversio ad phantasmata,* of question 84, takes place necessarily and necessarily evidences the possibility of metaphysics.

This of course represents but a rude sketch of the fundamental lineaments of Rahner's thought. Its full development represents the effort of *Spirit in the World* and his numerous other writings, while in *Hearers of the Word* he has already begun to make use of this metaphysical reconstruction (displacing the traditional *preambula fidei* or establishing a new order of such *preambula*) in a fresh attack on numerous knotty problems of theology.

c. *Emerich Coreth (b. 1919).* The most important expression of the transcendental movement in modern Thomas may well be Coreth's *Metaphysik: Eine methodisch-systematische Grundlegung* (Innsbruck, Vienna, Munich, 1961); the condensed English version is entitled *Metaphysics,* ed. Rev. Joseph Donceel, S.J. (New York, 1968). In his fine appreciation of this work (*Gregorianum* 44 [1963], 309–318, reprinted in Donceel, op. cit., *ad finem*) Bernard Lonergan places it in a dual perspective. On the one hand he asserts that it represents a final liberation from the Wolffian conception of metaphysics as the science of the possible, for Coreth understands metaphysics as the understanding of actual existents; on the other, it is the implementation, along distinctive and original lines, of Maréchal's insights.

Metaphysics, according to Coreth, is the "Gesamt- und Grundwissenschaft"—the *total* and *basic* science. *Total* because it includes everything; *basic* because it accepts no suppositions save those which it itself justifies. This notion of metaphysics dictates its method: It must be a mediation of immediate knowledge; the phrase is Coreth's own (cf. *Metaphysik*, sec. 68, par. 233; Donceel, pp. 33–34). The immediacy involved is the metaphysical principle operative, but latent, in all knowledge. This must be mediated, i.e., rendered explicit and conceptualized. In this respect, metaphysics differs from science in the ordinary sense, for metaphysics moves, not to the unknown from the known, but from the latent and implicit state of the bases of all that is known to the explication of those bases. The latter point is important, for Coreth is in agreement with Rahner that the "being" with which metaphysics is concerned is not an object among or even beyond other objects, although it presupposes the objects of all the sciences as well as the objects of ordinary experience. For this reason, the procedure of metaphysics may be called "retorsal." Metaphysics is not concerned with substantive statements, for these may be in contradiction to the metaphysical principle which invests them and makes them possible. Metaphysics is rather concerned with the conditions of the possibility of statements, even when these may be in contradiction to the enabling principles. The linkage with the Kantian criticism and with the Maréchalian effort is apparent. With Maréchal, Coreth is concerned to correct the Kantian criticism by completing it; but he will attempt to do so by a procedure which, in his view, corrects the ambiguities of Maréchal's effort.

The retorsal procedure finds its first point of application in the *question*. Here the influence of Heidegger is apparent. Man is, above all, the questioner, the questioner of his own being and of being in the absolute sense. Metaphysics begins with the question—not with the concept of the question, but (to employ Lonergan's translation of Coreth's own term *Vollzug*) with its *performance*. The task of mediation is to link this "performance" of the question with the grounds of its possibility, thus achieving *explication* in Coreth's sense.

What is the ground of the possibility of the question as act, as performance? Not, obviously, the ground of the possibility of any particular question, but of questioning itself as realized in all particular questions and known basically from the fact of such particular questions? This ground is a quality or state of consciousness which is open, which looks beyond what is already known to what is unknown, what is to be made known. In its limited form this questioning is many and particular: many questions open to many objects; basically, as to its essence, all questioning is one and its object is one. That object is being. Being is thus the "horizon" of questioning as such, as limited forms of being form the limited horizons of specific ranges of questions.

The range between the question, in its basic form, and the horizon as being constitutes the field of metaphysics. Within it, all metaphysical problems arise and all metaphysical statements find their place. The substantial structure of the *Metaphysik* is constituted by the exploration of the problems and the statements which arise in this field. The actual program covers all of the problems of classical (Aristotelian-Thomistic) metaphysics: being and knowing, essence and existence, action and passion; the problem of the principles of being: identity, causality, the transcendentals. But all of these classical problems are now invested with a new light deriving from the plane on which they are projected. It is through the exploration of these problems that the meaning of being is established, including, most importantly, the being of the questioner. To follow out this pattern of inquiry is obviously not within the compass of the present treatment; but this brief note will at least indicate the sweep of Coreth's undertaking.

d. *Bernard J. F. Lonergan, S.J. (b. 1904).* Donceel demurs at the inclusion of Lonergan in the current of transcendental scholasticism, though recognizing that he employs the transcendental method with great skill and effectiveness (*Continuum,* Vol. VII, No. 1, p. 165). No direct linkage, he argues, can be established between Lonergan and Maréchal. He overlooks the fact that the very absense of such direct links strengthens the force of the transcendentalist position. For it now appears, not as the preoccupation and enterprise of one man, but as the response to a speculative need which many have felt simultaneously, a need imposed by the situation of philosophy at a certain moment in its development, *ipsis rebus dictantibus,* as Vico would say.

Despite what Donceel might allege, at least an ideal affinity between Maréchal and Lonergan is to be found in their common preoccupation with Kant. Like Maréchal, Lonergan recognizes that Kant's critical revolution was indeed effective; it imposes itself as the necessary point of departure for any relevant consideration of the problem of knowledge. He also recognizes that the real problems of knowledge is that which Kant indicates in the form of the transcendental deduction. It is the possibility of knowledge, its antecedent possibility, which is the true concern of epistemology. For this reason Lonergan does not hesitate to compare the result of his labors with what Kant imagined that he had achieved in the transcendental deduction of the *Critique of Pure Reason.* (Cf. Lonergan, *Insight: A Study of Human Understanding,* [London and New York, 1958], p. 339: "We have performed something similar to what a Kantian would name a transcendental deduction.")

Despite this common reference to Kant, which establishes at least an ideal affinity with Maréchal, Lonergan follows a different procedure, which exhibits no direct reliance upon either of these thinkers. His first concern is to identify the area of his concern. It is not the *known,* with which he is concerned, but *knowing.* The known, he agrees with Kant, is an infinite manifold, which is given to experience in a condition of flux. But as known, it belongs to an ordered system. The source of this order and system must be sought in the process of knowing, and the character of the known, as known, and not merely as given (which condition is exactly the converse of being known), must be determined from the ground of that process. Despite the vast concession to the principles of all idealism, Lonergan, again like Kant, remains a "realist"; for it is clear that the characteristics of the known, though determined through the process of knowing, will prove to be other than those of that process, will be "being-in-itself."

Knowing, taken in contradistinction to the known, exhibits a recurrent structure which can be educed from the actual processes of knowledge by a careful analysis (cf. *Insight,* Introduction, p. xvii-xviii). The two areas in which these recurrent structures can be traced are common sense and scientific knowledge. Thus he again shows an affinity with Kant, because he begins, as did Kant, *in medias res,* with the actual processes of knowing. It is not these in their substantive character, however, which interest him. Rather, it is the methodical moment which draws attention, i.e., that special effort by which knowing, by a critical and reflective effort, seeks to determine the *a priori* principles which control and make possible its positive and substantive achievement of knowledge. Common sense knowledge is less self-conscious than is science; that is, it is less prone to seek these *a priori* principles and to perform the necessary reflective and critical operations. For this reason, science, which has shown itself increasingly prone to becoming reflectively self-conscious, offers a readier field for such phenomenological examination. Nevertheless, Lonergan is insistent that the same patterns are to be observed in, and the same principles govern, common sense knowledge, which, under this aspect, exhibits a certain continuity with science.

When science is brought under phenomenological examination, from the point of view of determining these recurrent structures, it exhibits a dynamic character which immediately suggests an affinity (working against Donceel's restriction) with the finality of intellect which dominates Maréchal's work. This "striving" or dynamic principle appears in the first instance (an affinity with Rahner suggests itself at this point) as pure question. "This primordial drive, then, is pure question. It is prior to any insights, any concepts, any words, for insights, concepts, words have to do with answers; and before we look for answers, we want them; this wanting is pure question" (*Insight,* p. 9).

Like all dynamisms, however, this dynamism of the intellect is ordered, ultimately, to rest. This rest is *insight.* Insight constitutes the total relaxation of the tension of that dynamism and finality: the achievement in which that tension is resolved, that dynamism relaxed in its own *telos.* Lonergan has interesting things to say about this insight. "It is not any recondite intuition but the familiar event that occurs easily and frequently in the moderately intelligent" (*Insight,* Introduction, p. ix). Insight is not a function of external conditions, which can at best merely dispose to it, but of internal conditions. All inquiry moves toward insight as its goal; not, however, as a goal which it may consciously pursue or insure, but for the attainment of which, for the epiphany of which, it can prepare.

Between the question, in which the constitutive dynamism of intellect first appears, and insight, in which it finds final quiescence, lie the levels of knowledge. There is some doubt, however, whether the term *level* actually expresses what Lonergan has in mind. "Levels" suggests a forward movement of ascent for the dynamism of intellect. What actually seems to be intended, however, is a reflective movement backward, from substantive knowledge to its own conditions and determinants. This appears from the very way in which Lonergan characterizes these levels: "a level of presentations, a level of intelligence, a level of reflection. . . . Inquiry presupposes elements in knowledge about which inquiry is made. Understanding presupposes presentations. . . . Formulation expresses not only what is grasped by understanding but also what is essential to the understanding in [of?] the understood. . . . The level of intelligence, besides presupposing and complementing an initial level, is itself presupposed and complemented by a further level of reflection" (*Insight,* pp. 272–273). While not exactly pellucid, these animadversions sufficiently exhibit the drift of Lonergan's thought; they exhibit especially that regressive movement by which intelligence takes possession of its own principles, which constitutes the object of his own inquiry.

Insight thus appears to have a double role in his thought. In the first place, insight terminates the dynamic movement of inquiry at the substantive level. It appears thus as insight into a certain subject matter. However, insight also lies at the terminus of that other dynamism by which intelligence, moving reflectively over its own process, arrives at the antecedent and constitutive principles of its own operations and of the form of the world as known. The second of these would seem to be the more important, from the philosophical point of view, though the former has great importance in its own order.

In either position, however, insight exhibits identical characteristics. It is always "both *a priori* and synthetic. It is *a priori,* for it goes beyond what is merely given to sense or to empirical consciousness. It is synthetic, for it adds to the merely given an explanatory unification or organization" (*Insight,* Preface, p. x). This leads Lonergan to a universal principle of isomorphism between "the structure of knowing and the structure of the known. If the knowing consists of a related set of acts and the known is the related sets of contents of these acts, then the pattern of the relations between the acts is similar in form to the pattern of the relations between the contents of the acts" (*Insight,* p. 399). And again: "the pattern of relations immanent in the structure of cognitional acts also is to be found in the contents of anticipated acts and still will be found to obtain when the heuristic contents of anticipated acts give place to the actual contents of occurring acts" (*Insight,* p. 485).

This isomorphism culminates in a dual apex, so to say—the one in the order of knowing, the other in the order of the known. Insight, it has been noted, is synthetic, exhibiting unity and form. This it does in the order both of knowing and of content, the two orders governed by the isomorphism. In the order of knowing, this unity is exhibited most clearly in the unity of the knowing subject, the self. In the order of the "contents," this apex is reachèd in God, being-in-itself in the absolute sense. It is interesting that in this way, Lonergan is led to a position which would seem to bear striking resemblances to the position of Descartes, again offering evidence, perhaps, for the sway which that thinker still holds over all subsequent thought (cf. *Insight,* pp. 329–332, 668–731).

This mere sketch of Lonergan's position leaves unrecorded the rich concrete matrix within which he presents his ideas. It is sufficient, however, to evoke the overall structure and movement of his thought and, above all, to justify his inclusion in the current of transcendental scholasticism.

Readings

I. PRE-THOMISTIC PHASE

Bonansea, B. "Pioneers of the Nineteenth Century Scholastic Revival in Italy." *The New Scholasticism,* XXVIII (1954), 1–37.
Dezza, Paolo. *Alle origine del neotomismo.* Milan: Fratelli Bocca, 1940.
————. *I neotomisti italiani del XIX secolo.* 2 vols. Milan: Fratelli Bocca, 1942–44.
Perrier, J. L. *Revival of Scholastic Philosophy in the Nineteenth Century.* Reissue. New York: Columbia University Press, 1948.
Rossi, Giovanni. *La filosofia nel Collegio Alberoni e il neotomismo.* Piacenza: Collegio Alberoni, 1959.

Saitta, Giusèppe. *Le origini del neotomiso nel secolo XIX.* Bari: G. Laterza e Figli, 1912.

II. THOMISTIC PHASE

Ardley, Gauin. *Aquinas and Kant.* London & New York: Longmans, Green, 1950.
Bochenski, I. M. *Contemporary European Philosophy.* Translated by D. Nicoll and K. Aschenbrenner. (Pp. 237–252.) Berkeley: University of California Press, 1956.
Collins, J. "Toward a Philosophically Ordered Thomism." In the same author's *Three Paths in Philosophy,* pp. 280–300. Chicago: Regnery, 1962.
De Wulf, M. *Introduction to Scholastic Philosophy, Mediaeval and Modern.* Translated by P. Coffey. New York: Dover, 1956.
Fecher, C. A. *The Philosophy of Jacques Maritain.* Westminster, Md.: Newman Press, 1953.
Harvanek, B. F., S. J.: "Church and Scholasticism." *Proceedings of the American Catholic Philosophical Association,* XXXII (1958), 215–225.
_____. "Philosophical Pluralism and Catholic Orthodoxy." *Thought,* XXV (1950), 21–52.
Klocker, H. *Thomism and Modern Thought.* New York: Appleton-Century-Crofts, 1962.
Riet, Georges van. *Thomistic Epistemology.* Translated by Gabriel Franks. St. Louis: B. Herder, 1963.
Robbers, Joannes H. *Neo-Tomisme en Moderne Wijsbegeerte.* Utrecht: Het Spectrum, 1951.
Sciacca, M. F. "Neo-Thomistic Currents." In the same author's *Philosophical Trends in the Contemporary World,* pp. 517–551. Notre Dame, Ind.: University of Notre Dame Press, 1964.
Zybura, J. S., ed. *Present Day Thinkers and the New Scholasticism: An International Symposium.* St. Louis: B. Herder, 1926.

III. TRANSCENDENTAL THOMISM

Coreth, Emerich. *Metaphysics.* Edited by Joseph Donceel. New York: Herder & Herder, 1968.
Crowe, Frederick E., ed. "Spirit as Inquiry: Studies in Honor of Bernard Lonergan." *Continuum* II, No. 3 (1964), special issue.
Dewart, Leslie. "Appendix 2 On Transcendental Thomism." In the same author's *The Foundations of Belief,* pp. 499–522. New York: Herder & Herder, 1969.
Dirven, Édouard. *De la forme à l'acte: essai sur le Thomisme de Joseph Maréchal.* Paris: Desclée, Brower, 1965.
Donceel, Joseph, ed. *A Maréchal Reader.* New York: Herder & Herder, 1970.
_____. *The Philosophy of Karl Rahner.* Albany, N. Y.: Magi Books, 1969.
Gélinas, Jean Paul. *Summary of the Revival of Thomism and the New Philosophies: Blondel and Laberthonnière.* Thesis. Washington, D.C.: Catholic University of America, 1959.
Gelpi, Donald. *Life and Light: A Guide to the Theology of Karl Rahner.* New York: Sheed & Ward, 1966.

Isaye, Gaston. "Joseph Maréchal." In *Les grands courants de la pensée mondiale contemporaine: Portraits,* II, pp. 991–1032. Milan: Marzorati Editeur, 1964.

John, Helen James. *The Thomist Spectrum.* New York: Fordham University Press, 1966.

Muck, Otto. *The Transcendental Method.* Translated by William D. Seidensticker. New York: Herder & Herder, 1968.

Roberts, Louis. *The Achievement of Karl Rahner.* New York: Herder & Herder, 1967.

Rousselot, Pierre. *The Intellectualism of St. Thomas.* Translated by James E. O'Mahony. London: Sheed & Ward, 1935.

Shine, D. J. *An Interior Metaphysics: The Philosophical Synthesis of Pierre Scheuer.* Weston, Mass.: Weston College Press, 1966.

Tracy, David. *The Achievement of Bernard Lonergan.* New York: Herder & Herder, 1970.

CHAPTER VII

Phenomenology

A. *Preliminary Definition*

The term *phenomenology* has appeared earlier in the course of the history of philosophy in a variety of uses. Today it designates principally that movement of thought which, arising in Germany at the beginning of this century through the efforts of Edmund Husserl, has been continued through the work of his disciples: Max Scheler, Nicolai Hartmann, Martin Heidegger, Edith Stein, and others. This movement is a living force today and its influence on other movements is very extensive. Indeed, so pervasive is this influence, in the opinion of Van Breda, the director of the Husserl Archives at the University of Louvain, that it can be discerned "even when the author in question affirms the contrary and does not seem to be aware of it" (H. L. Van Breda, preface to *Cartesianische Meditationen und Pariser Vorträge,* 1950, p. vii).

In choosing to think of the movement he had initiated as "phenomenology," Husserl was quite aware of the earlier uses to which the word had been put by Lambert, by Kant, and, above all, by Hegel. He seemed to want both to relate to their uses and to differentiate his own employment. In its most inclusive sense, the term indicates the speculative theory of that which "appears" in experience. In its earlier employments, this meaning had been involved in the "phenomenon-noumenon" dichotomy, in which an opposition arose between that which *appears* and that which *is,* as though, in some way, that which is, *does not appear,* while what appears *is not.* Hegel had already seen the untenability of this dichotomy and had employed all the resources of his logic, not only to negate it, but to establish positively the contrary, namely, that what appears *must be,* and what is *must appear.* And it is to this positive note in Hegel's phenomenology that the meaning of the term in Husserl attaches (as the later French students of Hegel and Husserl, such as Ricouer, will note). For his phenomenology, wholly a speculative concern with what appears, is at the same time an inquiry into what *is*. Husserl's phenomenology is the speculative effort to determine what is, wholly on the basis of the examination and analysis of what appears. This statement, while both valid and concise, demands clarification which can come only from the consideration of Husserl's own work.

B. *Edmund Husserl: Life and Works*

Born in 1859, Husserl began his career as a student of mathematics under the celebrated Karl T. H. Weierstrass (1815–1897) and received his degree with the presentation of a thesis on the calculus of variations. During the years 1884–86, he attended the philosophical lectures of Franz Brentano. This was a decisive experience, for it fostered his decision to devote himself entirely to philosophy. What seemed to attract Husserl was the rigorously "scientific" conception of philosophy presented by Brentano. His first chair in philosophy was at the University of Halle, whence he moved to Göttingen and later to Freiburg im Breisgau, where he remained until 1929. His was a life devoted entirely to study and teaching; he enjoyed almost exclusively the company of men of similar intellectual interests and above all that of his students. His last years were darkened by an intense isolation, which was due in part to that "war of philosophical schools" which has always been a part of European intellectual and university life and in greater part perhaps to the anti-Semitism of the National Socialist regime.

Husserl's work must be divided into two great parts: that which saw publication during his life and that which he left in manuscript. While the published works constitute the core and basis of the documentation of phenomenology, it is the measured conclusion of the best students of Husserl that it is impossible to come to a complete understanding of his thought unless the works he left unpublished are consulted. Of the published works the most important are: *Philosophie der Arithmetik* [Philosophy of arithmetic], 1891; *Logische Untersuchungen* [Logical investigations], 2 vols., 1900–1901; *Ideen zu einer reinen Phänomenologie und phänomenologischen Philosophie (Ideas: General Introduction to Phenomenology)*, 1913; *Volesungen zur Phänomenologie der inneren Zeitbewusstseins (Phenomenology of Internal Time-consciousness)*, 1928; *Formale und transzendentale Logik (Formal and Transcendental Logic)*, 1929; *Meditations Cartésiennes (Cartesian Meditations)*, 1931. Also important is the article "Philosophie als strenge Wissenschaft" ("Philosophy as a Rigorous Science"), published in the review *Logos* (Vol. I, 1910–11, pp. 289–341). In 1913, with a group of his students and followers which included Moritz Geiger, Adolf Reinach, Max Scheler, and (later) Martin Heidegger, Husserl founded the *Jahrbuch für Philosophie und phänomenologische For-schung* [Yearbook for philosophy and phenomenological research] of which eleven volumes appeared, containing documents of primary importance for the movement.

On his death Husserl left nearly 40,000 pages of unpublished manuscripts, practically all of which treat problems of phenomenology. In 1938–39 these manuscripts, together with his personal library, were evacuated from Germany and were brought together in the Husserl Archives, an institution founded specifically for their conservation, editing, and publishing at the University of Louvain, in Belgium.

C. Antecedents of Phenomenology

To attempt to determine the antecedents of a doctrine as original as that of Husserl is perilous. Nevertheless, this ought to be done, for Husserl himself was quite free in recognizing and acknowledging his indebtedness. It was always his contention that phenomenology is in the mainstream of classical modern thought and that its links with what has gone before it must be understood in order to appreciate phenomenology itself. The most important of his predecessors with whom Husserl sustains clearly defined relations are Descartes, Kant, Lotze, Leibnitz, Bolzano and, above all, the man whom Husserl habitually called "my teacher," Franz Brentano.

The relation to Descartes is clearly established by Husserl in the *Cartesian Meditations;* he both follows and goes beyond the Cartesian doubt in his determination to reach the purely evidential ultimate of thought. Husserl accepts Kant's distinction between "pure" and "applied" logic; he rejects, however, the Kantian definition of "reason" and "understanding" as mental faculties. All faculties of "normal" thought, he holds, presuppose "pure logic," because pure logic defines the normal. Herbart seems closer to Husserl's own position, because Herbart essays a sharp distinction between "pure logic" and "psychology" by means of his doctrine of the "objectivity" of the concept, i.e., the fact of logical presentation of a content as distinct from mere empirical presentation. Husserl acknowledges a like affinity to Lotze, who continues Herbart's influence in his logical works, though he never dissolves the admixture of logic and psychology. The relation to Leibnitz seems much closer than to any of the foregoing. Husserl finds in Leibnitz an idea of pure logic to which he can subscribe. The *mathesis universalis* of Leibnitz envisages an *a priori* organon of knowledge independent of all psychological processes, mathematical in form and regulatory of all science. For Bolzano in turn, Husserl has little but praise; although he made no attempt to define "pure logic," Bolzano,

Husserl feels, actually constructed such a logic along correct, though inconclusive, lines.

The relation to Brentano deserves special note. The first point of affinity between them was Brentano's conception of philosophy. Following Kant, Brentano insisted that it be conceived as a "rigorous science." This idea exercised a strong attraction on Husserl, and he takes up the theme in the essay "Philosophy as a Rigorous Science." This is but a superficial affinity, however, in comparison with that invoked by Brentano's doctrine of "intentionality." Brentano's basic concern is to differentiate "psychic" phenomena. The character of the psychic, he holds, is determined by its representational function. Representation means or signifies the presentation of an object. All of the psychic states of man have this in common, that they present an object. Brentano defines representation as "relation to a content" or "orientation toward an object" (which need not, in his sense, be a "real" object). The phrase he especially favored was "immanent objectivity," which in turn defines "intentionality." Brentano's definition of the psychic brings together all of these reflections; psychic phenomena are those which "contain within themselves an object, constitutively and intentionally." Brentano's notion of intentionality, as will be noted further, constitutes the positive point of departure of Husserl's elaboration of the phenomenological doctrine.

D. *The Phenomenological Doctrine*

1. Disengagement from Brentano

We have noted that Husserl always spoke of Brentano as "my teacher." As in so many important instances in the history of philosophy, the sense of indebtedness remained long after Husserl had gone his own way. This indebtedness has both a negative and a positive aspect. Negatively Husserl owes to Brentano the inception of the struggle against psychologism in logic. Psychologism was the position of Brentano in his chief work; *Psychologie vom empirischen Standpunkt* [Psychology from an empirical standpoint]. The science of psychology provides the basis for the science of logic. Husserl agreed with this point of view and adopted it in his early work *Philosophie der Arithmetik*. Thus, he holds that the concept of multiplicity, which lies at the basis of the concept of number, is provided by the act of relating (*verbinden*), a psychological operation; similarly the notions of "one" and of a being, something (*Etwas*), which in their turn lie at the basis of the notion of multiplicity, are reduced to the "content of a representation" and are born of "reflection of the psychic act of representing" (cf. *Philosophie der Arithmetik*, Halle, 1887, p. 86). This is the portion of Brentano's thought which Husserl will abandon, perhaps at first under the influence of Bolzano, then as a result of Frege's criticism of *Philosophie der Arithmetik.*

He will, however, retain another element of Brentano's doctrine which will become central to his own positive thought: the concept of "intentionality." Its meaning and role in Husserl's thought go far beyond anything found in Brentano, from whom he derived the seminal element of it. In a certain sense it may be said that the entire elaboration of the position of phenomenology is the development of this concept. Further, it is the development of the notion of intentionality which, to a great degree, makes it possible for Husserl to disengage himself from his first commitment to Brentano's psychologism.

2. The Rejection of Psychologism
and the Intuition of Pure Phenomenology

The composition of the two volumes of *Logische Untersuchungen* marks Husserl's initial "breakthrough" to the position he will eventually occupy and develop, pure phenomenology. The first volume develops the critique of psychologism, demonstrating the impossibility of reducing logical laws, which are rigorously necessary, to psychological laws, which are always inductive and hence contingent. The conclusion of this volume is relatively negative; aside from excluding the possibility that the "logical" is the expression of a psychic fact, Husserl leaves the intrinsic character of the logical unexplicated. In the second volume Husserl begins to formulate more positive solutions to the radical problem which preoccupies him, namely, what is the character of logical being? He holds that the "logical" belongs to the order of "what is signified" and not to the order of the act of signifying; nevertheless, he goes on, "what is signified" is not to be confused with the "thing known." His concern, consequently, becomes the analysis of the specific character of "what is signified." The course of the argument, in both its negative and its positive phases, may be indicated briefly.

A mistaken identification of the "signified" with the "thing known" has, in Husserl's view, led empiricism to deny the existence of universal concepts. Since all things are individual things, empiricism concludes that the universal does not exist. Husserl undertakes the review, and eventually the refutation, of this position in the second of the "logical investigations" (*logische Untersuchungen*). It is possible, he maintains, for individual objects, such as this thing or this redness, to be present, but universal meaning, such as "red" or the number "two" can also be present. Between these, there is not merely a difference of degree, as though the second might merely be a confused image of the first.

There is a specific difference. The individual object is *this* object speci-
fied *here* and *now,* while the universal meaning is undetermined under
either of these notes and is completely a "something" (*Was*). Husserl
calls this "something," this *Was,* an *eidos,* the original Greek term
from which "idea" derives. Husserl then asks the nature of the act by
which we reach this *eidos.* In this context he still calls it by the ancient
and revered name "abstraction," but he immediately goes on to distinguish it from the act usually indicated by that term in the past. This act
does not consist in separating from an object a quality which it might
have "in common" with other objects. All the qualities of an individual
object, he notes, are themselves individual. To talk of a quality being
"common" assumes that it has already been "universalized," considered
specifically in its "essence" (*Wesen*) and not in its individuality. Therefore, that process (which he still calls "abstraction") by which we
reach the universal, the *Was,* or the *eidos,* is not an act of confrontation or of mediation, but a fresh and original act of direct vision (a
fact which later, in the *Ideas,* etc., will persuade Husserl to speak of it
as "intuition"). Husserl is concerned to avoid the impression that the
eidos, though reached by "abstraction," is itself abstract. The "essence"
or *Was* is always the essence of an individual thing and is always
reached in a given of experience. The apprehension of the "essence,"
whether the process of that apprehension be called abstraction or intuition, is the basis of the *a priori* order of propositions. The case may be
put in this way: There can be universal and necessary (i.e., *a priori*)
propositions only insofar as the terms upon which such propositions are
based are *essences* and not *facts.* What is true of an essence is always
and everywhere true; it is true of any individual thing in which the
essence is realized. Propositions which have the essence as their subject
are specifically different from those which are inductive, or generaliza-
tions on experimental fact, like the laws of natural science. Logic and
mathematics are formed of *a priori* propositions, for they express relations between essences. Husserl thinks that a philosophical ethics
would have the same form; so too would the propositions of his projected "regional ontologies," of which more will be said.

The fifth of the logical investigations also constitutes an important
phase in the formation of the phenomenological doctrine, for it takes
up the notion of the "intentionality of consciousness." This notion, to
which some reference has already been made, was drawn by Husserl
from the teaching of Brentano; but it underwent, at Husserl's hands,
significant refinement. Husserl proceeds by making several careful
distinctions. "What is signified"—the *Was* or "essence" or *eidos*—indeed
appears in consciousness, but it does not belong to consciousness as
one of its constituting parts, but rather as its "intentional correlate," as

that which is understood (*gemeint*) by consciousness. Therefore, Husserl reasons, two dimensions must be distinguished in consciousness: first, one by which consciousness is established as a reality, a fact or an event, a complex of psychic facts (called by Husserl *Erlebnisse* or *Ereignisse*); the latter constitute a real becoming or a kind of stream of consciousness (which Husserl calls *Erlebnisstrom*). (Cf. *Logische Untersuchungen* V, secs. 1 and 3.) But within these facts of consciousness *something appears to consciousness,* an *object* is *present;* herein resides the other dimension of consciousness. Husserl complains that the psychology of his time used a common term, "contents of consciousness," to refer indifferently to these two distinct dimensions of consciousness, thus giving rise to notorious confusions.

The confusion of the intentional order and the constitutive order of consciousness involves the risk, on the one hand, of reducing logic to psychology and, on the other, of destroying all possibility of objective discourse, that is, discourse about objects and not about the constitutive elements of consciousness. There is a clear difference, however, between the way in which a color or a sound appears to and in consciousness and the way in which a feeling or a sentiment belongs to consciousness. They are both integral to consciousness but the relation of each to consciousness, the manner in which they enter into the integrity of consciousness, differs vastly. Feelings and sensations are constitutive parts of consciousness; they are among its *Erlebnisse.* Color and sound, however, are not constitutive parts of consciousness; they are its "intentional correlates." Consciousness is constituted of sensations in which things, sounds and colors, appear. "We see the process of appearing as belonging to consciousness," Husserl writes, "while things appear to us as belonging to the phenomenal world. The appearing itself does not appear to us; we *live* it" (*Logische Untersuchungen* V, sec. 2).

In the *Ideas,* Husserl gives this distinction a terminological form by calling the act of consciousness in its real aspect *noesis* and that which appears in consciousness *noema;* and he will speak of consciousness as being open to the *noema.* Intentionality designates this distention of consciousness between its real constitutive elements and its intentional correlates. It should be clear that for Husserl there is no question of separating these two dimensions since both are integral to consciousness.

Though the logical investigations marked a great step forward in the development of Husserl's thought, they left many questions unanswered and raised others which demanded careful consideration. These problems preoccupied Husserl between the publication of *Logische Untersuchungen,* in which the "breakthrough" to phenomenology is achieved, and that of the *Ideas,* in which phenomenology received a definitive formulation. Two important works document this period and Husserl's concern with these "intermediate" problems: *Die Idee der Phänomenologie (The Idea of Phenomenology)*, and "Philosophy as a Rigorous Science." The first comprises five lectures delivered in 1907 at the University of Göttingen; the second is an article which appeared in the journal *Logos* in 1911. Each deserves consideration in an integral view of the growth of Husserl's thought.

The Idea of Phenomenology marks the transition from the tentative and exploratory phenomenology of the logical investigations (whose procedure Husserl still thinks of as a descriptive psychology) to the mature phenomenology of the *Ideas*. From the point of view of the internal development of phenomenology, this work is illuminating because Husserl for the first time introduces many of the major themes and much of the characteristic terminology of the mature phenomenology. He fixes the term *phenomenology* more clearly and introduces the notions of "phenomenological reduction," the *epoché* or phenomenological "bracketing" of the natural attitude, "eidetic abstraction," the "pure phenomenon," the different modes of transcendence and immanence, and the problem of the "constitution" of the objects of knowledge.

On the eve of the presentation of these lectures, Husserl composed, for his own use, a short statement of the "train of thought" in the lectures. While this cannot stand in place of the lectures themselves, it is filled with illuminating lapidary statements which show the direction of Husserl's thought. Of chief interest are his distinction of the three levels of phenomenological orientation, which have their point of departure in the criticism of the "natural attitude" in cognition. At the first of these levels he speaks of the necessity of accomplishing the "phenomenological reduction, the exclusion of all that is transcendently posited." At the second level, "eidetic" abstraction emerges as the central point, for it yields "inspectable universals, essences, species" and "gives a new objectivity as absolutely given, i.e., the *objectivity of essences.*" The third level is that of the "constitution of objects of all sorts within cognition." In this précis Husserl was obviously trying to fix the fundamental direction of the thought which proceeds more formally in the lectures. The progression is clear: from the natural attitude, in which everything about cognition and its validity is taken for granted, to the constitution of the objects of cognition of every kind, that is, their grounding, the explication of their necessary coming to be as objects.

The basic program for the lectures is the same. The first lecture treats the "natural attitude" in thinking and "science of the natural kind," i.e., ostensible science resting on the natural method. The natural attitude of mind is "as yet unconcerned with the critique of cognition." In the natural mode of reflection we are turned to *the objects* as they are given to us each time and as a matter of course, even though they are given in different ways and in different modes of being. Natural knowledge gives rise to sciences of the natural kind, whether these be sciences of nature, like physics and psychology, the sciences of culture or the mathematical sciences.

In contrast to the natural attitude and the sciences founded on it, Husserl delineates the philosophical mode of reflection. This has its origin in the "abyssmal" difficulties which arise when we reflect about the relation of cognition to its objects. Philosophical reflection is concerned with this problem in all of its aspects. But when the problem of the critique of cognition is presented in its purity, free from any metaphysical purpose, there emerges the idea of a "phenomenology of cognition," which has the task of "clarifying the essence of cognition and of being an object of cognition." Philosophical reflection leads to the pure phenomenology of cognition.

The program of the second lecture is more ambitious. Operating on the phenomenological plane, as identified in the preceding lecture, it initiates the critique of cognition, treating as questionable every claim to knowledge, reaching the ground of absolute certainty in pursuance of Descartes' method of doubt, and defining the sphere of the things which are absolutely given. There is a pause in the direct line of argument so that Husserl may refute certain arguments against the possibility of the critique of cognition. Then the argument is resumed by analyzing further the "riddle" of nature which centers about the notion of transcendence; and a distinction between the concepts of immanence and transcendence is established. The "initial" problem of the critique of cognition is then addressed: the possibility of transcendent cognition and the introduction of the notion of "epistemological reduction."

The third lecture seeks to carry out the "epistemological reduction," i.e., "the bracketing of everything transcendent." The theme of investigation then becomes the "pure" or "absolute" phenomenon and its "objective validity." Husserl next discusses phenomenological cognition as the cognition of essences and the two senses of the concept of the *a priori*. The fourth lecture extends the range of the investigation to the consideration of intentionality, the self-givenness of the universal, then to the philosophical method of the analysis of essence and the theme of evidence; it concludes with the assertion that no limitation can be assigned to the sphere of real immanence and with the projection of the theme of the "all-givenness."

The fifth lecture draws the process to a climax by introducing the idea of constitution, first of "time-consciousness" and then of the order of essences as objects of cognition, both in their individuality and in their universal aspect. It terminates in a projection of the trajectory of phenomenological investigation, embracing the constitution of the different modes of objectivity in cognition and the problem of the correlation of cognition and the object of cognition. This survey of the content of the lectures included in *The Idea of Phenomenology* serves very usefully to deploy before us the architecture of Husserl's phenomenology in all of its fundamental dimensions.

In the essay on "Philosophy as a Rigorous Science" Husserl returns to another point he had received from Brentano, the conviction that philosophy should acquire the character of a strict science. He investigates the reasons why this has remained an aspiration rather than an accomplished fact of philosophy. He notes that all efforts of modern thought to establish philosophy on the theory of knowledge have this as their ultimate purpose. They have failed because they have not rendered philosophical thought completely presuppositionless but have, instead, tended to make it rest upon the presupposition of a natural entity, such as the existence of a knowing subject with its representation. In presupposing the existence of that which needs to be justified these efforts have involved themselves in a circle. In order to become a strict science, philosophy must become free of all presuppositions. It must admit nothing in its process of the constitution of the world of cognition which is not apodictically evident. Therefore, it must "place in parentheses" everything which has not yet been justified.

Husserl's phenomenology reaches its mature formulation in the *Ideas*. This is not to say that it did not proceed beyond the position there established but all its subsequent development remains within the scope of this work, within the trajectory of the thematic and methodological development which it delineates.

In a certain sense, the *Ideas* undertakes anew the whole work of phenomenology, retracing the steps already traversed in order to clarify the position gained with the new force and to extend its range of vision. In this work, Husserl exhibits a very clear sense of the value of phenomenology to philosophy. Phenomenology, he feels, is destined to open a new path in philosophy; it looks to a radical transformation of philosophy by means of a return to the original sources of intuition. By this process of *clarification*, phenomenology would open a vast field of strictly scientific research which would prove useful not only for philosophy but also for the other sciences, whenever their principles were questioned. All of this is implied quite clearly in the first book of the *Ideas*, published in 1913 in *Jahrbuch für Philosophie und phänomenologische Forschung*, the yearbook Husserl had founded.

Consonant with the "new-beginning" of the whole phenomenological task undertaken in the *Ideas*, Husserl stresses again that what chiefly characterizes phenomenology is its distinction from the "natural attitude" (*natürliche Einstellung*). It does not take as the object of its inquiry phenomena as they are conceived in the various natural sciences. It is a "new science," a "science of essences." The basic procedure of this new science, by which it delivers itself from the encumbrance of all previous scientific methods and reaches the world of essence proper to pure phenomenology, is "phenomenological reduction." Husserl cites an example from psychology to stress the effect of phenomenological reduction. Psychology is an experiential science, a science of "facts," which are assumed to be "real." These "facts," in their given existence, are intimately related to living beings, in whom they manifest themselves and in whom they may be determined, according to relations of time and space, subject and object, cause and effect, interiority and exteriority. But phenomenology is not a science of "facts." It is by contrast a "science of essences" (*Wesenserkenntnisse*).

Through this example Husserl attempts to do two things: 1) to identify the essence as the object of phenomenological research and 2) to define the autonomy and range of phenomenological consciousness. He does both by disputing the presumptive claims to reality of the world given in psychological experience. This reality is presumptive, since beyond the facts of psychological experience lies the world of universals, which is in no way dependent for its reality upon that world of "fact"; further, since meaningful discourse about the world of facts can only be carried on through relation to the world of essences, the reality of that world of fact is seen to be "accidental" and "ungrounded," demanding to be explained and justified. Just as the world of empirical reality is presumptively real, so is the claim that consciousness is in some way dependent upon that world. Consciousness itself enjoys the same kind of transcendental status with respect to empirical experience that the essences enjoy with respect to psychologically manifested facts. The purpose of the "phenomenological reduction" is to release both the realm of essences and the pure transcendental phenomenological consciousness from this incarnation, on the one hand, in the realm of natural fact and, on the other hand, in the natural process of psychological experience and to bring them face to face.

When this is done, the range of phenomenological research is defined; it is the exploration of the realm of essences at the level of transcendental phenomenological consciousness. Included in this range is the essence of that transcendental phenomenological consciousness itself, for it cannot be presupposed as a fact. The realm of essences and the transcendental phenomenological consciousness are the two poles which bracket the entire "natural" world, both from the point of view of the subject (the empirical and natural subject) and from the point of view of the world of objects (the natural facts which preoccupy the sciences resting on the natural attitude). This "bracketing" means two things: 1) that this natural world is not, in its givenness, the object of phenomenological inquiry, and 2) that its claim to reality is called into question because, as bracketed, it appears to be ungrounded and in need of being established by a dialectic with the phenomenological world.

Ultimately, however, it is not merely the natural world of appearances which will have to be "grounded," i.e., established in its logical necessity, but also the world of essences and phenomological consciousness. It is a strange quirk of the history of western philosophy, Husserl seems to be saying, that the world of essences and of phenomenological transcendental consciousness has been accused of "irreality" with respect to that natural world (the empirical attitude) while the case would seem actually to be that it is this natural world which is infected with accidentality and presumptive reality. Nevertheless, it would be erroneous to think that Husserl is transferring a "natural" reality to the world of essences and transcendental phenomenological consciousness. From a truly philosophical point of view, the reality of both orders is presumptive, for each in turn demands to be "grounded" in logical necessity, to have its presence rendered logically necessary both as to its content and as to its mode of being present.

Another point, however, is of great importance, and Husserl labors to bring it clearly to the fore in the *Ideas*. The establishment of the realm of essences and that of transcendental phenomenological consciousness is not the result of speculative thought in the sense, for example, in which Hegel might have defined it, and the propositions defining those areas are not philosophical truths. It is the result rather of a purely scientific process, even a transcendentally empirical process, which renders the realm of essence and the transcendental phenomenological consciousness reflectively present and presents them in their autonomous actuality. For this reason, Husserl will eventually protest that philosophy can become a strict science; because its bases are phenomenologically present. The path of this transcendental experience, which terminates in the presence of the realm of essences and the autonomous phenomenological consciousness, takes its point of departure in the multiple contradictions of the world and of thought, when it confronts itself and the world. Reflection upon any such contradiction and the doubt it engenders is, at the same time a *conversion,* a turning of the act of reflection inward upon consciousness itself, making it aware of the distance (cognitional) between itself and the world. In this conversion the presence of pure consciousness is established. The term of the phenomenological or transcendental reduction is reached in this positive establishment of pure or phenomenological consciousness.

This establishment of the presence of the phenomenological realm is one phase of the process of *epoché* the placing in parentheses or bracketing of the natural world. But the other phase also needs to be considered. What is the status of the natural world and, for that matter, of all the sciences which deal with it and with the natural attitude? Are they simply denied? Obviously not. The process of *epoché* in no wise involves the negation of the world or even of the natural attitude of the subject of experience and knowledge. The entire natural realm is placed in parentheses, not to deny it, but to reestablish it on other grounds than those spurious claims to reality which it exhibited in its merely natural state. The old adage of philosophy "distinguish to unite" is replaced in Husserl by the maxim "deny to affirm," bracket to reestablish on the basis of logical necessity what, in the first place, is presented on purely presumptive and accidental or contingent grounds. Husserl's own way of saying this is that "what is placed in parentheses is not wiped out from the phenomenological table or range, but is simply symbolized by an index, which is precisely the parenthesis itself. By this index, the content placed in suspension and at the same time characterized by the parentheses truly presents the principal subject of phenomenological research" (*Ideas* I, sec. 32–33).

This may be summarized by saying that the path of phenomenology describes a wide ellipsis. Taking its point of departure in doubts about the natural world, the natural attitude, and the sciences based on the natural attitude, it moves by phenomenological conversion to the plane of phenomenological or pure consciousness, placing in the brackets (suspending assent to) that natural world. Having gained the phenomenological world, however, and established its nature and constitution and its relation vis-a-vis that natural world which has been placed in parentheses, it then seeks to reestablish that natural world on its constitutive bases, explaining now in apodictic terms of logical necessity the existence and appearance of that world, which before had been present simply as presumptively real, without justification or basis in logical necessity. This would complete the elliptical movement. Knowledge would be completely *founded*.

It may be observed that this was essentially Hegel's task; but there is a difference between the way in which each philosopher thought that it could be carried out. This difference is significant to Husserl. Hegel's method of speculative thought would, in Husserl's view, still belong to the natural attitude because its bases would not have that positive transcendental givenness which Husserl demands of principles. His own method, not speculative but phenomenological, terminates in the positive presence of his principles and hence imparts a scientific character to the philosophical process itself. Students of Husserl's later thought, such as Ricoeur, will return to this relation between Husserl and Hegel.

The *Ideas,* in the first book, come to a climax by establishing the problem of *constitution*. The generic notion of constitution in Husserl may be grasped if we recall that he is engaged, as was Hegel, in converting reality as *given* into reality as *established* with logical necessity. Constitution is passage from empirical givenness to presence in logical necessity. And this passage, it may be added, defines the path of science, in the classical sense of the term. This passage does not involve any alteration in the character of the world or of reality as immediately given; it doesn't change the world at all. But it does work an internal revolution in the constitution of the world. What before was given groundlessly, simply as fact, and contingently, is now constituted in logical necessity.

Within this generic notion of constitution, the concept takes on special configurations in Husserl's thought. The distinction between the two meanings of constitution in Husserl is important for the battle which later raged over whether Husserl was an "idealist" or a "realist." The first meaning of constitution in Husserl, developed principally in the first book of the *Ideas,* involves the dependence of the world upon consciousness—needless to say, upon phenomenological and not empirical consciousness. This dependence seems to imply that the world is established *by* phenomenological consciousness. The second meaning of *constitution* concerns the way in which an object of any order is constituted or constitutes itself *for* consciousness, which is by no means the same as being constituted *by* consciousness. In either case, however, there is an effort to meet the conditions indicated in the generic notion of constitution, and the decision between the two latter meanings rests ultimately upon the degree to which they meet the condition enunciated in the first or generic meaning.

In his handling of this problem, Husserl is trying to avoid the horns of the dilemma on which, he believes, western speculation has been suspended during much of its course. This is the opposition between naturalistic objectivism and transcendental subjectivism; the view, on the one hand, that reality is entirely given to the subject as being-in-itself, in no wise dependent on the subject (including the subject itself, which is treated as immanent to that objectivistic system of the given), and, on the other hand, the view that reality is established by the transcendental subject and that its being is, therefore, entirely being-for that subject (the being of the subject itself here being treated as immanent to that subjective process which constitutes the world). Husserl holds that this dilemma is unwarranted, that a truly rational theory of the world cannot rest content with this dilemma, and even less with acquiescence to one or the other of its members but must press on to the determination of the common root of the one and the other, nature and subject, and the way in which each is constituted in itself and for the other.

While struggling to undercut, as it were, the opposition between the two subgeneric meanings of constitution, Husserl actually seems to continue to be suspended between the horns of that dilemma. He offers two different treatments of constitution without, in the final analysis, reconciling them in what an unregenerate Hegelian would be tempted to call "a higher synthesis." At this point two things should be noted with care.

The first is that no confusion should be permitted between logical and existential constitution. Husserl's inquiry is entirely in the cognitive, not in the natural, order. For him, the existence of the natural world and of the subject in the world of nature is a given, a pre-given which he called *Lebenswelt*. There is no question of the constitution of the existential order, therefore, in its existentiality. The whole problem is that of the logical constitution of all objects, including the natural world, as objects of cognition, ultimately of apodictic cognition, i.e., cognition in the pure mode of necessity from which every vestige of contingency has been purged. The second point is that the problem of constitution opens up for phenomenological investigation the whole range of problems which have traditionally preoccupied both the natural sciences and philosophy but which can now be approached from a specific point of view, the phenomenological. Husserl ventures into this range of inquiry when he takes up the problem of our relation to our own bodies. It is his followers, however, such as Scheler, who carry the task of phenomenology more clearly into this area. It may finally be noted that the existentialists, employing Husserl's own procedures, questioned his exclusion of the realm of existence from the field of phenomenological constitution and demanded to know the phenomenological constitution of existence itself.

Husserl develops the first of the two subgeneric modes of constitution in the first two sections of the first book of the *Ideas*. In the latter sections of this book and in the second and the third books of the *Ideas*, published posthumously, he treats the problem of constitution from the second subgeneric meaning. His effort to find some mediation between them appears in his effort to move from phenomenological constitution to genetic phenomenology.

In developing the first sense of constitution Husserl lines up with those thinkers who in the past have been called "idealists." This position may be summarized by saying that, because everything given is given to consciousness, therefore, everything given is constituted *by* consciousness. The problem then becomes: What are the constitutive processes by which the subject constitutes its order of objects? The whole of reality resides, from the point of view of its logical necessity, in these constituting operations, which are not natural but logical and cognitive processes.

In developing this aspect of his thought, Husserl moves on a line of advance from Descartes. Even as far back as the *Idea of Phenomenology*, 1907, he had presented his doctrine as a deeper and more coherent development of the Cartesian insights. Important at this point is Husserl's distinction between *immanent* and *transcendent* perceptions, a distinction which has a Cartesian basis. Immanent perceptions are those which consciousness has of itself and of its own proper experiences; transcendent perceptions are those which consciousness has of things. In the immanent order, perception itself and what is perceived form an immediate unity and establish a unique concrete *cogitatio;* in transcendent perception, objects or things are given under multiple appearances which can never be finally unified, even though the thing is immediately present. In the later case, doubt about the reality of those things is always possible; in the former case, doubt cannot enter. The subject, grasping itself in that seamless unity as the pure subject of its life, necessarily says: I am, my life is, I live, I think.

Since not only the reality of things but the existence of other consciousnesses (which we entertain in that particular kind of experience which Husserl calls *Einfühlung* and which may be translated "empathy") can be called into doubt, the affirmation of the existence and reality of the pure subject of self is necessary and indubitable. The self is left, by this process, in what Husserl calls "a singular philosophical solitude." But the crucial point has been established. If the reality of the world and of other selves is to be established with certainty, they must be established on the basis of that certainty which the self has of its own reality. Any other basis would leave the world and other selves in that same dubious condition. The basis and assurance of their reality must be found by phenomenological inspection by the self; no other way is possible. Husserl speaks of this process as consisting in "the autoexposition of my ego in so far as it is the subject of possible cognitions, conducted in the form of a systematic ecological science, taking account of all the existential meanings possible for me as a subject."

This same process of "self-exposition" would at the same time constitute the exposition of the meaning of every type of being which I, the self, can think, especially of the transcendence of nature (which experience gives me as real), of culture, and of the world in general; in other terms, it is the systematic revelation of *constitutive intentionality* itself. The explication of the meanings of being is identified with the explication of the pure possibilities of the self. Husserl writes, in the *Cartesian Meditations* (sec. 41), that the fact that nature—a world of men and culture with its forms of social life, etc.—exists for me, means that certain corresponding experiences are possible for me. Independently of my real experience of objects, I can at any instant realize them and develop them in a certain synthetic style. But only the self is sufficient to itself insofar as there "pertains to its essence the possibility of a self-seizure, of a self-perception." The self "has its own surrounding world constituted as a non-self, as an *ensemble* of pure objects which are only constituted by a self but which are not, as such, constituted in themselves, as a self." Thus, from the phenomenological point of view, "the other is a modification of myself"; and it is the self which "with a motivated and constitutive operation" brings about an intentional modification of itself and of its primordial reality which achieves validity under the title of a perception of otherness, "perception of the other." In this manner the world is constituted on the indubitable reality of the self.

The self as constituting the world by discovering its own range of possible experience was denoted by Husserl as transcendental idealism. This is in obvious contrast to all other forms of idealism, which, in his view, never achieved truly transcendental status. The basis of transcendentalism in Husserl's thought is intentionality. But transcendental idealism is not the unambiguous implication of intentionality. Intentionality also seems to support another view of the object, which has been called by some of Husserl's commentators his "realistic" aspect. What this realism means fundamentally has already been mentioned. The alternative to the constitution of the world of objects by the subject is the constitution of the object *for* consciousness but not *by* consciousness. Husserl's phenomenology also develops this possibility.

It is characteristic of intentionality, Husserl notes, that the relation which it induces between consciousness and its object does not establish that object as a part of consciousness in the sense that one reality or thing can form a part or element of another. As Husserl says in the *Cartesian Meditations* (sec. 11) and again in the *Ideas* (I, sec. 36), while the self which has achieved the *epoché* is not part of the world, neither are the world and the objects in the world part of my self; they are not to be found really present in my psychic life as its parts, as complexes of sensible data or psychic acts, or as events. The world and the objects in it remain "transcendent" to the self, even though the only evident existence which can be attributed to the world rests on the evidence of our selves and our acts. This characteristic relationship may be called the "essence" of intentionality, in Husserl's own meaning of "essence," and is the basis of his so-called "realism."

Consciousness is, for Husserl, a flow of lived experiences (*Erleb-*

nisse), each of which has its own essence (i.e., perception, recollection, emotion, velleity, etc.) To these experiences and at the level of their essence, the transcendent objects in the world present themselves in a more or less adequate manner. But such presentation does not cancel out the transcendence of the object. As Husserl says (*Ideas* I, sec. 35), the object may be said to be a "pole of identity," always endowed with a preconceived meaning which is to be realized in actual knowing. In every act of consciousness, the object is the *index* of a noetic intentionality which is the meaning or significance of the object. (Cf. also *Cartesian Mediations*, sec. 19.) For this reason, the object does not form part of the lived experience, but constitutes itself *for* that experience. This is the reason for Husserl's distinction between *noesis* and *noema*. The former may be called the subjective, the latter the *objective*, dimension of the cognitive process. There may be reason to think, however, that Husserl, in making this distinction, is trying to avoid rather than repeat this subjective-objective dichotomy. As he goes on to explain, the *noema* is not the object itself; the object is rather the pole about which are grouped the *noemata* of lived experience. Not every *noema* or complex of *noemata* has an objective pole which is really present. The sense of a *noema* may remain empty and unrealized, in the sense that it may have no corresponding object—for example: *an image*, as in poetry or the figurative arts.

The process by which the object establishes itself or constitutes itself as present for the subject, without, however, being constituted by the subject, is the objective constitution of the object. The subject must recognize that nothing can be said of the object or of the complex structure of a *noema* without an object (though it should be noted that everything in the objectless *noema* is still referred to the absent object and not to the *noema* itself) save that which comes from the subject's experience or is found in it. What is thus said or predicted does not come from the determination of the subject, but from the object presenting itself or constituting itself as object for the subject. This realism, consequently, must be present. It should be noted with what care Husserl avoids the pitfall of the "thing-in-itself," whether of Kant or of the metaphysical realism of the scholastic tradition.

But the balance between objective realism and transcendental idealism is not struck. They are obviously alternatives which need to be related to each other in some more basic fashion. Husserl came to realize that the full significance of his thought should, in some fashion, carry him and western philosophy beyond the old subjective-objective, idealistic-realistic dichotomies and dualisms. His attempt to formulate this further implication of his doctrine and analysis has been given the name "genetic phenomenology."

In genetic phenomenology Husserl is addressing the absolutely ultimate problem of the constitution of the entire process which in his earlier analyses he had structured according to the schema of transcendentalism and then according to that of his so-called realism. He is now trying to render phenomenologically present the entire process within which subject and object, and all the other distinctions he has labored to establish, constitute themselves. This may be called the self-constitution of reality as such. Husserl's fundamental insight into genetic phenomenology is given in a line from one of Husserl's manuscript remains, edited by G. Brand: "The being of the world is always constantly *en chemin,* in process of becoming" (*Welt, Ich und Zeit nach unveröffentlichen Manuskripten E. H.* [World, self and time, from the unedited manuscripts of E. H.], 1955, pp. 17–18). This constant becoming explains why what seems at one moment so "familiar" to us may seem in a succeeding moment quite strange and alien. The danger of earlier phenomenological analysis was that it tended to present the world of essences as entirely static, as eternally given. This tendency seemed to deny the dimensions of reality and made it impossible to understand the structure of reality as given in phenomenological analysis itself: why, that is to say, subject and object should appear in the world; why the subject should be incarnated, so to say, in the world: why the object must constitute itself for the subject in order to possess its own being for itself; and, finally, why the world of essences can be discovered in the world of existence, the *Lebenswelt,* and why the latter is entirely without meaning until the presence of essence has been discerned within it.

The earlier emphasis had been altogether too structural. It needed now to be complimented by a genetic phenomenology which would discern the eternal coming-to-be of the world, the coming into existence of essence, and the achievement of meaning in existence through the dialectic with essence. The concept under which this genetic phenomenology can best be captured is that of *history,* or historicity. For this reason, time (which had always preoccupied Husserl to a great degree) assumes a central importance in the perspective of phenomenology. Time is the medium of genetic phenomenology; it is the medium of incarnation, whereby the world of essence enters the world of existence or the one is generated by the other. What must now be rendered phenomenologically present is this time process of the dialectic of essence and existence, of necessity and contingency. The time-ideal process of history itself, it must be noted, must be rendered present under the same conditions which Husserl imposed for his earlier structural analysis. In this discussion Husserl evokes an unmistakable recall to an earlier thinker, Vico, the essence of whose theory of history, as developed in the *Scienza Nuova,* is precisely the mediation

of "ideal and eternal history and the passage of the nations in time."
Thus, phenomenology brings us, by no forced passage, to the central
philosophical problem of the modern world, history.

The foregoing account of the phenomenological doctrine of Husserl
cannot, of course, lay any claim to completeness. However, it does not
seem to leave out of account the fundamental points which go to make
up Husserl's basic effort and achievement. It may serve as a point of
departure for a more adequate and comprehensive acquaintance with
Husserl's thought, the richness of which can only be suggested. Much
of this wealth lies in the concrete analysis which Husserl undertook in
specific areas, for example, the analysis of inner time, mentioned above.
His technique in phenomenological analysis was followed by some of
his earliest disciples with gratifying results. We may complete our
account of phenomenology by noting some of the developments of
Husserl's insights by these men and by indicating briefly, through
examples of very recent scholarship, the influence and fascination
which Husserl's thought continues to exercise.

E. *Developments of Phenomenology*

1. Alexius Meinong (1853–1920) and the Theory of Objects

Meinong cannot be called a direct follower of Husserl; he must
rather be considered, as Abbagnano aptly suggests, an *analogous*
thinker, and his theory of objects an analogue of phenomenology. Like
Husserl, Meinong was a student of Brentano; thus, he underwent the
same formative influences. He became professor of psychology at Graz
in Austria and exercised an influence there not unlike that which Husserl was to exercise in Germany. Of his many works the *Untersuchungen zur Gegenstandstheorie und Psychologie* [Researches on the
theory of objects and on psychology], 1904, containing the essay "The
Theory of Objects," and the work entitled *Uber die Stellung der
Gegenstandstheorie im System der Wissenschaften* [The place of the
theory of objects in the system of the sciences], 1907, are perhaps
most deserving of attention.

Meinong takes his point of departure in the observation that there
can be no knowledge which is not "knowledge of something." Every
representation or judgment necessarily has an object. This object is
not a part of the representation or judgment, but there is something in
these acts which directs us to the object. This directive force is intentionality, which Meinong, like Husserl, considered the essence of lived
experience. The presence of intentionality makes every act of knowl-

edge an act of *transcendence* toward the object. Following Brentano's suggestion, Meinong adopts the view that an act of cognition is implicit even in noncognitive acts, such as volition, desire, etc.; therefore, he conceives that it is possible to erect a theory of *objects as objects,* a theory which would take for its province the totality of objects. This theory of objects cannot, he insists, be identified with metaphysics in the classical or traditional sense; for while it may be true that metaphysics takes for its concern the totality of existing objects, it must also be recognized that existent objects form but a small part of the objects of knowledge in the inclusive sense indicated. There are also, for example, ideal objects which *subsist* but cannot be said to *exist.* Instances of such ideal objects are: relations like similarity and differences, and number.

Pursuing this line of thought, Meinong divides objects in general into two great classes: *Objekten,* real objects and *Objektiven,* objectives. He seems to owe this distinction to the one which Frege had established between what is signified and meaning. The "real object" constitutes the signification of a word; the truth or falsity of a proposition referring to the object depends on the existence of the object. The "objective" constitutes the content of a word or a judgment. Therefore, every judgment, in his view, has an "objective" as its internal element but also possesses an "object," which is the transcendent entity to which the judgment refers. The objective, therefore, is the immediate element of the judgment, while the object is given it only indirectly, as that to which it refers.

Meinong goes on to subdivide the "objectives" into two classes, *Seinobjektiven* and *Soseinobjektiven.* An example of the first is such an assertion as "there is water" or "water exists"; of the second, such an assertion as "water is wet." The difference comes out in the predicate which, in the first instance, is simply "existence" but which, in the second instance, is "existence in such or such a way." Thus, every objective is either the simple existence, or the existence in a certain way, of an entity; but the character of the objective is that it does not exist. It would be meaningless to assert the existence of the existence of water, for this would involve discourse in an infinite regression.

The objective subsists and cannot be referred to a thing. A *fact* is an objective. But not all objectives constitute facts. Objectives which constitute facts are true; and truth and falsity are exclusive properties of objectives and not of the objects of experience. Objectives, according to Meinong, are timeless or transcendent to time even when they are ingredients of facts; objectives may also be negative when, for example, they carry a privative sense with reference to objects, e.g., blindness. The same obviously cannot be said of objects, which are entirely positive, for they are existent and a privative sense cannot involve existence in itself. Objectives also include the range of impossible objects. The non-being of a centaur is an objective in the same sense as the being of a real object. Therefore, the truth of a judgment, and of all discourse, depends, not on the existence or nonexistence of its objects, but on the subsistence of the objectives in virtue of which discourse is constructed about the object. Thus, two propositions may be equally true or false though one concerns an existing, the other a nonexisting, object. The truth of those propositions   depends on the being of their objective which, in the second instance noted, is the nonexistence of an object.

While not all knowledge must be about existing objects, nevertheless, all knowledge must eventually be about *facts*. Fact, as has been noted, is the objective of the judgment; and every judgment is evident to the degree that it has the objective as its ingredient. The evidence may be *a priori* or *empirical;* there may also be purely presumptive evidence. While judgments concern objectives, representations concern objects. The object is the basis of the representation. But the production of representation is a purely empirical situation; the fact that the representation rests on the object is, however, *a priori*.

Some indication of the influence of Meinong's theory of objects may be gathered from the fact that Russell employs it in the elaboration of his doctrine of denotation with special reference to the notion of negative objectives. Santayana and American neo- and critical realism also have recourse to certain aspects of this doctrine.

2. Nicolai Hartmann (1882–1950)

The most impressive speculative structure erected on the basis of phenomenology would seem, without doubt, to be that of Nicolai Hartmann. This structure rests squarely on that dimension of phenomenological analysis which has earned the epithet "realistic." Of Hartmann's many works, all of them impressive for their erudition and their analytic and constructive power, the two most important would seem to be: *Möglichkeit und Wirklichkeit* [Possibility and actuality], 1938, and *Der Aufbau der realen Welt* [The structure of the real world], 1940. Hartmann's thought is rich in themes and analyses which relate it vitally to all contemporary thought and which can only be suggested in a brief summary.

For Hartmann, phenomenology is only the first stage of philosophical reflection. It is extended and completed first by *aporetics,* that is, the enucleation of the problems which emerge from phenomenological analysis itself, and by theory, which would project the solutions of the problems presented by aporetics.

Hartmann draws from phenomenology the cardinal principle of his theory of knowledge, namely, the notion of *knowledge as transcendence*. Knowledge is not merely a phenomenon of consciousness; it is a transcendent relation between the representations which the subject has of the object and the object itself as it exists independently of such representation. This leads directly to his realism: the conception that the being of an object is not exhausted in its *being an object*. This would seem to lead to a return of the notion of the thing-in-itself, which Hartmann calls the sphere of the "transobjective residuum" since it includes that dimension of reality which is not projected to the consciousness of the subject as its object. This "transobjective residuum" is unknowable in its basic character; it is elastic in the sense that, while knowledge always seeks to comprehend it more inclusively, it always remains beyond the competence of consciousness.

Hartmann's notion of the "new" ontology is based on this conception of the transobjective residuum. This ontology involves the fundamental schematization of being into three projective dimensions: "transobjective residuum," "ideal being," and "subjective being." Subjective being is that dimension of being which belongs to the subject and depends on it. Ideal being is that dimension of being which is presented to the subject but does not arise from the subject; it is clearly the field of scientific and philosophical analysis in the strict cognitive sense. Ideal being is said by Hartmann to be *independent* or *adherent*. As examples of *independent* ideal being he adduces the entities of logic, mathematics, and value judgments. As examples of *adherent* ideal being he adduces the ideal forms, such as essences, laws of being, and the essential relations of real beings. Hartmann's attitude toward ideal being is opposed to that of Platonic idealism. Real being is, for him, superior, and not inferior, to ideal being. The latter never reaches the concreteness and effectuality of individual, existent reality. In this sense, all ideal being is unreal being; nevertheless, while all ideal forms are unreal, not all unreal forms are ideal. Hartmann enumerates also the order of the "pure unreals," in which he includes thought, imagination, the dream, etc. He does not, however, deny that these forms of "pure unreals" possess a transcendent dimension toward objects.

At this point Hartmann's particular notion of reality emerges. Reality is distinguished from the being of the ideal sphere and appears as the object of the noncognitive acts of the subject. These acts place the subject in contact with that aspect of reality which arouses fear, hope, and the other emotive reactions and which demands of the subject decision, struggle, and commitment or engagement. These emotive transcendent acts are divided, in Hartmann's analysis, into three classes: receptive, prospective, and spontaneous. The surprises which life always has in reserve, the stress of lived experience, the subjection to circumstances and to other persons which man must endure are examples of *receptive acts*. Prospective acts anticipate the future in various modes, such as hope, fear, etc. Spontaneous acts, such as desire and love, are those which seek to seize a transcendently real object.

In *Möglichkeit und Wirklichkeit* Hartmann develops his ontology with greatest clarity and force. The cardinal principle of this ontology would seem to be that necessity is the ultimate modality of reality. This means the systematic elimination from reality of all indetermination and problematicity, as well as all the other modes of being which classical metaphysics had sought to distinguish. Hartmann achieves this reduction of all modality of being to necessity by the rigid application of what he calls the "fundamental modal law." This law indicates that both necessity and possibility, as modes of being, are merely relative. Their meaning can be determined only with reference to a more fundamental concept: *effectuality*. This is the fundamental mode of being in the sense that from it alone all other ostensible modes can be denominated. This all-inclusive determinism of being, which makes the effectively real the measure of all being and all *right* to being, immediately places in a problematic light the status of the "ought" *(Sollen)*.

Hartmann seeks to bring the realm of the ought, which classically has been the realm of man's freedom, into the ambit of his determinism by referring to it as the necessity of something which in itself is possible because it finds its basis in a concatenation of effective conditions. This concatenation must be brought to its full effectuality. The "ought," therefore, prescribes nothing else than that which can and must be realized. It concerns that possibility which is already real and already effectual in itself, although it may not appear so and may even appear otherwise. Viewed in this manner, the "ought" becomes identified with the "must" of effectual reality.

Der Aufbau der realen Welt develops Hartmann's ontology further. Hartmann conceives this as a general theory of the categories, because, for him, the categories are in reality and are not structures of the subject, as he thought they were conceived in Hegelianism. In this work Hartmann projects a theory of the planes or levels of being. To him, such stratification of being is an evident fact, illustrated by the discontinuity between organic and inorganic nature, between organic and psychic nature, and between psychic nature and spiritual being.

This stratification of being does not, however, offer the model for his categorization of being. The categories of being cut across these planes or strata. In the first place, they include the modal categories, which he distinguished in *Möglichkeit und Wirklichkeit;* the bipolar categories: quantity-quality, continuity-discontinuity, etc.; and, finally, those which express the fundamental laws of real being. The last, clearly, are the most important. He divides them into four groups which are governed, respectively, by the laws or principles of value, coherence, stratification, and dependence. The principle of value indicates that the value as a category lies in the fact that it is a determining necessity of effective, real being. The principle of coherence indicates that the categories are principles of real order, of unity and diversity, in the realm of effective being. The principle of stratification makes it possible to express the relation between the different levels of real being which he had previously indicated as evident from observation; this principle, Hartmann holds, indicates that the categories of the lower strata return in the higher, not vice-versa; thus, every higher level of being implies a new categorial moment that is not reducible to the elements of a lower stratum. He calls this the "law of the novum." There is, consequently, between the different strata of real being an irreducible distance governed by the law of the *distance of strata.*

Hartmann excludes the notion of liberty in all of its possible senses from all the realms of effective or effectual being. He would seem to be especially clear in excluding it from those two particularly human areas: will and history. He indicates that the form of determination of the will cannot be presented in terms of causal necessity; therefore, he speaks of "extracausal determinants." These may or may not be known and recognized as such in the analysis of human action; nevertheless, they effectively exclude the so-called freedom of the will. The exclusion of freedom from history rests on a further distinction between subjective and objective spirit. History is the work of objective spirit, which, while it does not exist outside of finite and personal spirits, operates in and through them in a universal, impersonal, and wholly determined manner. The objective spirit, with respect to the level of personal consciousness, is a *novum* in the sense mentioned and therefore cannot be reduced to the order of personal consciousness. All the productions, actions, and events of history must be referred to the objective spirit. Consequently, they carry the mark of its determined and effective reality, necessity.

3. Max Scheler (1874–1928)

Scheler's relation to the phenomenology of Husserl lies in his attempt to develop and extend the phenomenological analysis of the practical and emotive aspects of consciousness. Such analysis, as has already been noted, fell well within the purview of Husserl's program, though he gave it relatively little attention. Scheler's work was cut short by his premature death in 1928, at the age of fifty-three. During his active career, however, he produced works which place him at the forefront of modern personalistic, ethical, and social thought. Chief among these must be considered *Der Formalismus in der Ethik und die materiale Wertethik* [Formalism in ethics and the material ethics of value], published in Husserl's *Jahrbuch* during the years 1913–16, and *Wesen und Formen der Sympathie (The Nature of Sympathy)*, 1923. His many other books have also exercised an increasing influence in many areas of modern thought. Our brief presentation will be limited to the consideration of four of his basic concepts: value, person, sympathy and love, and community.

Scheler commits himself quite unconditionally to Husserl's notion of phenomenology when he defines it as the "quest of a knowledge in which objects are no longer related existentially to life and vital values" and goes on to say that "phenomenological philosophy represents empiricism and positivism under their most radical forms." He meant to indicate by the latter statement that the values claimed by these philosophies are more fully realized in phenomenological philosophy.

The special mark of Scheler's thought is that he takes *emotive* experience as the object of his phenomenological inspection. The objects which are present to that type of experience "in person," in Husserl's phrase, are *values*. Thus, Scheler conceives his *ethics* as the phenomenology of emotive experience and defines its scope or purpose as the clarification of the specific objects of that experience, *values*. Scheler opens his analysis of values by making a sharp distinction between values and both *ends* and *goods*. The good is that which a value embodies; the end is the term of an aspiration or a tendency which may or may not have value. However, value, as given directly in emotive experience, is indifferent to being the embodiment of anything or to being the term of a tendency or aspiration. On the other hand, the emotional experience to which value is present is not a simple emotion such as pleasure or pain; it is the *intentional* emotive experience which Scheler also names *emotive intuition*. He then draws a parallel between emotive intuition and value, and the representation or concept and its object: value is to emotive intuition as the object is to representation or concept. Therefore, the world of value is objective, that is, independent of the act by which values are apprehended.

As an objective order, the world of value has its own *a priori* laws. These *a priori* laws determine the *hierarachy of values,* which is objective in the same sense in which values themselves are objective. Within this hierarchy Scheler distinguishes the levels of *pleasing* or *unpleasing,* of *vital* values, of *spiritual* values, and finally of *religious* values. Just as values in their objective character are present to *emotive intuition,* so the hierarchy of values is present to a specific act which

Scheler calls *preference*. This preference is to be distinguished from aspiration, choice, or volition; it is an *a priori* preference to which the standing of any order of values in the hierarchy is objectively present. Finally, Scheler places love and hate at the apex of our intentional emotive life. He introduces an order among these three levels of the revelation and presence of value: emotive intuition, preference, and love and hate. The first is the simple apprehension of values; the second is a more originative act than emotive intuition because the preferential evidence of value is more immediate and superior. Love and hate constitute the highest mode of the presence of values; they discover values even before these are present to preference or to emotive intuition. In calling his theory of value and the ethics based on it a *material* ethics, Scheler is distinguishing his position from Kant's ethical *formalism*. In Scheler's view, the latter rested on Kant's confusion of values and ends. Values are objective in a way that ends cannot be, as Scheler has pointed out, and this objectivity guarantees their universality and autonomy.

Scheler constructs his theory of values as a preparation for his phenomenology of the human person. He is at pains to call into question the classical conception of person as the pure subject of rational activity; this would imply, he argues, that the person is one and identical in all men. He prefers to think of the person as the essential concrete unity of a complex of acts which are essentially different in each case. It is the one person who is the subject of both rational and emotive acts, for example, and to whom the objects corresponding to these acts are present. Similarly, the whole person acts in every action; but the person is not exhausted in the series of its acts, however extended, but essentially transcends them. Scheler establishes a distinction between person and consciousness and between person and *self*, or *ego*. The *self* or *ego* is defined in relation to the *thou* and the *world;* but the person is anterior and indifferent to these oppositions. The correlate of the person is the *world,* and an individual world corresponds to every individual person. It follows that metaphysical truth, while it is truth without qualification, has a different content for each individual person. This does not imply any relativity of truth, however, since this relation depends entirely on the essential relation between the person and the world. As a consequence, the idea of a unique, identical real world implies the idea of an infinite, perfect, concrete spiritual person. Therefore, Scheler holds, the idea of God is given at the same time with the identity and the unity of the world. The unity of the real world cannot be affirmed without the affirmation of God. But this unity is an affirmation of the ideal order and does not imply the reality of God. This last can be established, not by philosophy, but only by God's revelation of himself in a concrete person.

The relationship to the organic body constitutes an essential element of the person; the body is the *property* of the person. This relation provides the basis for the general notion of property. The slave was not considered a person but was given both to himself and to others simply as a thing. Still, the slave was recognized as having consciousness and this serves as proof to Scheler that the person is not constituted by such determinations as consciousness or character. While every person is a single individuality, diverse and distinct from every other, the person is never shut up within himself. Every person is present to himself as a member of a community of persons. Thus, the idea of community is directly involved in the notion of the person itself. The finite person is essentially a member of a social unity. Therefore, every finite person has a singular *person* and a communal *person* (or personality in either case) which are in reciprocal relation to each other. The theory of all the possible forms of social unity constitutes for Scheler *philosophical sociology*. His efforts to construct such a science constitute the apogee of his thought.

The results of these efforts are presented in *The Nature of Sympathy*. In this work, *sympathy*, understood in its phenomenological and hence objective sense, is considered to be the only authentic form of relation between persons. This alone protects the autonomy of the person and explains the possibility of intercommunication among persons. The effort to characterize sympathy is central to this work. Scheler first distinguishes sympathy from the kind of emotional contagion which is found in gregarious masses. Sympathy is not an affective state but an affective *function*. Scheler illustrates this point by noting that pity for another's suffering does not imply that the affective state of the other is assumed by the subject of pity. Sympathy, on the other hand, implies and establishes the diversity of persons and does not fuse them. The real function of sympathy is the creation of community by destroying the illusion of solipsism and by revealing the other person to us as endowed with a value equal to our own. Sympathy has certain limits, however, in exercising this function because in all its forms it is passive, and not spontaneous and active. Only love can go beyond the limits exhibited by sympathy and substitute a relation in depth for the contactual or peripheral relations of sympathy. But Scheler insists that love, even more than sympathy, demands the diversity and the autonomy of the person; the profoundest meaning of love resides precisely in not considering and not treating the other as though he were identical with myself. Love directs itself to the valid center of things, to their *value*. It tends to realize the highest possible value.

F. *Continued Influence of Phenomenology*

Phenomenology by no means came to an end with the work of Husserl and his immediate followers like Scheler and Hartmann. Its influence has continued and indeed, in certain contexts, has been decisive. The most extensive development, as will be seen in a subsequent chapter, was in the complex movement called *existentialism*. Neo-scholasticism was also strongly attracted by the realistic dimensions of Husserl's thought and sought to construct some relation between his notion of intentionality and that proper to scholastic realism. In the direct line of phenomenology, there has been a constant interest in the work of Husserl himself. The first form of this interest has already been noted, the work of the Husserl Archives of Louvain. This work is most erudite, involving the editing not only of Husserl's published works but of the mass of manuscripts he left. The second form is a constant effort to penetrate more deeply the implications and reaches of Husserl's thought in an extensive body of interpretative work.

This interpretative current may be said to have begun with the work of E. Fink published in *Kantstudien* for the year 1933, (pp. 319–383). Fink's work had great influence, especially among the historians of the phenomenological movement. An important indication of this influence was the essay contributed by Ludwig Landgrebe to the *Revue Internationale de Philosophie* of the same year, devoted to Husserl's phenomenology and the motive of its development. In 1939 an Italian scholar, S. Vanni-Rovighi brought out an important study, *La filosofia di E. Husserl* [The philosophy of E. Husserl], which emphasized the systematic aspect of phenomenology and its relation to neo-scholasticism. The year 1940 saw the collective work, edited in the United States by Marvin Farber, *Philosophical Essays in Memory of Edmund Husserl*. In 1941 the French scholar Gaston Berger published two works, one concerning the place of the Cartesian *cogito* in Husserl's thought (*Le 'cogito' dans la philosphie de Husserl*) and a more constructive one on the conditions of knowledge (*Recherches sur les conditions de la connaissance*) in which Husserl's influence was very clear. Marvin Farber published the most important work in English to that date, *The Foundation of Phenomenology*, in 1943. A. Brunner's penetrating study of phenomenology and existentialism, entitled *La personne incarnée*, appeared in 1947. In 1950 Paul Ricoeur published his French translation of the *Ideas* with a very important introductory essay. (He had already published the first volume of his *Philosophie de la volonté* [Philosophy of the will] in 1949.) In 1953 came a dense and penetrating work, *Phénoménologie de l'expérience esthétique* [Phenomenology of aesthetic experience], by Mikel Dufrenne. The important work of Maurice Merleau-Ponty will be mentioned more extensively in the chapter devoted to existentialism. These brief indications do no more than point out the continuing attraction of Husserl's thought and the fruitfulness of his phenomenological method in a variety of fields.

Readings

I. GENERAL WORKS

Chisholm, R. M., ed. *Realism and the Background of Phenomenology.* Glencoe, Ill.: Free Press, 1960.
Farber, Marvin. *The Aims of Phenomenology.* New York: Harper & Row, Harper Torchbooks, 1966.
Lauer, Quintin. *Phenomenology: Its Genesis and Prospects.* New York: Harper & Row, Harper Torchbooks, 1958.
Spiegelberg, Herbert. *The Phenomenological Movement. (Phaenomenologica V.)* 2nd ed. The Hague: Martinus Nijhoff, 1965.

II. INDIVIDUAL PHILOSOPHERS

Edmund Husserl
Books
Bachelard, Suzanne. *A Study of Husserl's Formal and Transcendental Logic.* Translated by L. E. Embree. Evanston, Ill.: Northwestern University Press, 1968.
Osborn, A. D. *Edmund Husserl and His Logical Investigations.* Cambridge, Mass.: Harvard University Press, 1967.
Ricoeur, Paul: *Husserl: An Analysis of His Phenomenology.* Translated by E. G. Ballard and L. E. Embree. Evanston, Ill.: Northwestern University Press, 1967.

Essays and articles
Farber, Marvin, ed. *Philosopical Essays in Honor of Edmund Husserl.* Cambridge, Mass.: Harvard University Press, 1948.
Ricoeur, Paul. "Kant and Husserl." *Philosophy Today,* X (1966).
Tillman, Frank. "Transcendental Phenomenology and Analytic Philosophy." *International Philosophic Quarterly,* VII (1967).

Alexis Meinong
Books
Bergmann, Gustav. *Realism: A Critique of Brentano and Meinong.* Madison, Wisc.: University of Wisconsin Press, 1967.
Findlay, John N. *Meinong's Theory of Objects and Values.* 2nd ed. Oxford: Clarendon Press, 1963.
Linsky, Leonard. *Referring.* London: Routledge & Kegan Paul; New York: Humanities Press, 1967.

Essays and articles
Russell, B. "On Denoting." *Mind,* n.s. XIV (1905).
Suter, Ronald. "Russell's Refutation of Meinong in On Denoting." *Philosophy and Phenomenological Research,* XXVII (1967).

Nicolai Hartmann

Books

Mohanty, G. N. *Nicolai Hartmann and Alfred North Whitehead: A Study in Platonism.* Mystic, Conn.: Verry Press, 1957.
Samuel, O. *A Foundation of Ontology: A Critical Analysis of Nicolai Hartmann.* Translated by Frank Gaynor. New York: Philosophical Library, 1954.

Essays and articles

Collins, James. "The Neo-scholastic Critique of Nicolai Hartmann." *Philosophy and Phenomenological Research,* VI (1954).

Max Scheler

Books

Frings, Manfred S. *Max Scheler.* Pittsburgh: Duquesne University Press, 1965.
Ranley, Earnest. *Scheler's Phenomenology of Community.* Thesis: St. Louis University. The Hague: Martinus Nijhoff, 1966.
Staude, John R. *Max Scheler: An Intellectual Portrait.* New York: The Free Press, 1967.

Essays and articles

Scheler Symposium. *Philosophy and Phenomenological Research,* II (1942). Theme: "Significance of Scheler for Philosophy and the Social Sciences."

Other Figures

Collins, James. "Edith Stein as a Phenomenologist." In the same author's *Three Paths in Philosophy,* pp. 527–547. Chicago: Henry Regnery, 1962.
Stewart, David. "Paul Ricoeur and the Phenomenological Movement." *Philosophy Today,* XII (1968).
Symposium. *For Roman Ingarden: Nine Essays in Phenomenology.* Gravenhagen: Martinus Nijhoff, 1959.

CHAPTER VIII

Bergson

Introduction

The name of Henri Bergson (1859–1941) has already attracted notice in these pages. In our discussion of evolutionary philosophy, it was suggested that the doctrine most closely associated with his name, "creative" evolution, marks the culminating point in that philosophy. It was noted at the same time that so distinctive was the manner in which Bergson developed the evolutionary insight that his position demands separate consideration. What is it that makes this development so distinctive? Bergson's unique contribution might be stated succinctly in the following way: by a vigorous reexamination of the premises, principles, and implications of evolutionary philosophy, he effected its complete transformation from within. From materialistic and mechanical evolution it becomes, in his hands, spiritualistic evolution in which the principle of liberty achieves fresh expression and supreme value. Moreover, at the same time, and by the same process, Bergson effected an equally distinctive transformation of the spiritualistic tradition, into which he was led by desire to penetrate the principles of evolution to their utmost implications.

In *Evolution créatrice (Creative Evolution)*, 1907, Bergson protested that the great error of spiritualist doctrines had been the belief that if the spirit were completely isolated from the world of matter it would be rendered immune to attack. In fact, this had simply placed spirit in danger of appearing a mirage. His achievement was the establishment of a new relation, a relation of immanence, between matter and spirit, the body and the material universe and the life of consciousness. In the following pages we shall trace briefly the chief stages by which Bergson, beginning with his initial acceptance of the evolutionary insight, developed the philosophical position, so completely his own, which has had such a wide and persistent influence.

A. *Bergson and Positivistic Evolution*

The basic tension between positivistic evolution and spiritualism within Bergson's thought was established very early in his formation. Among the teachers at the Ecole Normale Supérieur were such representatives of spiritualism as Boutroux and Ollé-Laprune. Nevertheless, Bergson, by his own admission, preferred the study of the English philosophers, especially Spencer. He explains that the basic attraction those philosophers held for him was their espousal of a philosophy which sought to draw its impulse from things and to model itself on facts. Nevertheless, he was aware of the difficulties which beset the doctrine of evolution and evolutionary philosophy as Spencer, for example, presented it. His earliest formulation of his speculative purpose expressed the determination to deliver evolutionary philosophy from these weaknesses and difficulties. He clearly felt the weakness of Spencer's *First Principles,* Bergson wrote in his work *Pensée et mouvant* (trans. as *The Creative Mind*), but this weakness seemed to him to stem from the fact that its author, insufficiently prepared, had not penetrated to the "ultimate ideas" of mechanics. Therefore, he proposed to take up this part of the work anew, completing and consolidating it.

In carrying out this resolution, he suffered that "surprise" (the term is his own) which really placed him on the path of original speculation. The concept of time was obviously central to the doctrine of evolution and to the principle of mechanics by which Spencer had sought to explain it. It was assumed by Spencer that the time at stake here was *real time.* The surprise lay in Bergson's perception that this was an illusion. The time with which mechanics worked was an abstract, a fictitious time. *Real time* could not be formulated and expressed in the mathematical and mensurational terms proper to mechanics. It presented itself rather as the immediate datum of consciousness, the form under which consciousness is given to itself for direct observation. Its structure is entirely different from the structure of mensurable and successive time with which mechanics works. Real time presents itself as duration (*durée*), which is the pure form of consciousness when it is relieved of all intellectual or symbolic transformations.

This surprising discovery about the locus of real time and its true form convinced Bergson that his initial purpose of completing and consolidating the Spencerian position was futile. A much more profound task now presented itself to him: the total reconstruction of the evolutionary philosophy upon this new insight into real time as duration and duration as the pure form of consciousness to itself. Thus, it is entirely true, as many historians and critics have pointed out, that the Bergsonnian philosophy begins with this discovery of real time as duration and duration as the pure form of consciousness, the form under which it is given to itself.

B. *Time and Freedom*

The first results of Bergson's attempt to work out, even in a limited way, the implications of this insight are found in the impressive thesis which he submitted for his doctor's degree and which was published in 1889 as *Essai sur les donées immédiates de la conscience* [Essay on the immediate data of consciousness]. Its original title, however, *Temps et liberté* (English ed.: *Time and Free Will*), is far more striking and reveals far better the problem with which it is concerned. Bergson attempts to show that, from the discovery of real time as duration, the path to the discovery of spirit as liberty is direct and without detour. At this point, however, it is only a *via negativa*. Bergson's immediate task is to show as unfounded positivism's contention that the phenomena of consciousness are subject to and comprehensible in terms of quantitative measurement. He does this by showing the untenability of the modes under which it was maintained, in psychophysical dualism, that it was possible to measure the intensity of a psychic state, time, and freedom.

In each case there is the question of a dialectic between interior and exterior. The psychic state is interior, i.e., sensed by the subject as his own but subject to quantitative measurement deriving from extension, divisibility, and multiplicity in space. Bergson's procedure is to show that, in each instance, the interior is not subject to exterior quantitative measurement, but must be accepted in its own terms and developed in them. In the first instance, intensity of psychic state, he shows that what is experienced interiorly is a pure quality, which thus differs from all other qualities, and not by any quantitative diversity. In the second, he shows that the multiplicity of duration is a multiplicity of pure quality and not the multiplicity which is mediated by space and is therefore quantitatively distinguishable. Duration, real lived time, is a realm of pure qualities, which does not demand exteriority and does not need space in which to develop.

Finally, Bergson makes no attempt to demonstrate human freedom (which is a datum of immediate consciousness) but does attempt to disprove determinism in all its forms. His argument is that the very reasonings employed to establish determinism are those which disprove it most clearly. Thus, it is possible to speak of an "action" being determined by a "motive." This statement is clearly patterned on the analysis of external nature, where all is mediated by space. But, in the interior of consciousness, all is interpenetrating on the qualitative plane, unmediated and in need of no mediation by space. Therefore, to say that an action is determined by a motive or representation is identical with saying that it is determined by itself, or is free. In this work Bergson has established his spiritualism in principle, though only by way of a negative dialectic. The task which lies before him is to determine the character of this interior life of spirit, the autonomy of which he has established against the claims of positivism.

C. *Matter and Memory*

The first positive step toward the determination of the character of this interiority is taken in Bergson's work *Matière et mémoire (Matter ter and Memory)*, published in 1896. As in all his writings, Bergson here attacks a particular problem, but he places that problem in a perspective which reveals its broad implications. Having laid bare the unconvincing character of the contentions of psycho-physical parallelism, he is now embarking upon a reconstruction of the relationship between spirit and matter in line with his earlier contention that while spirit can never be identified with matter, neither can it ever be isolated from matter. He tries to reconstruct the concept of matter with regard for the autonomy of spirit in order to determine the real relation between them. Rejecting both the idealist and the realist theories of matter, he takes his stand upon the common sense view, which holds (as he interprets it) that the affirmations of both have meaning but, taken in isolation, are unilateral. For common sense, the material object is an image, but an image which exists in itself, even while that very "in-itselfness" of the image is present to consciousness in the sense datum (though not identical with it). The world of matter is the system of these images and the most immediate evidence of this is our own bodies, which are not present to us as "objects" but precisely as such image systems upon and through which we act immediately. Awareness of body, and of ourselves in and through our bodies, is therefore the first form of perception; and this act in its larger sense is the act by which we gain entrance into the entire system of existent images which is the world in its complexity of being-in-itself and being-for-another in consciousness.

Perception, however, is an act of the living body in the immediacy of the present. Perception does not reflect the full range of man's awareness, the range of consciousness. This is the function rather of memory. Unlike the English empiricists, from whom he drew much, Bergson does not place the full weight of his analysis on perception and make memory only a less intense form of it. Memory, as the continued vigency of past images, generates a matrix for perception itself, which it sharpens and guides. Perception inserts us into the world, but memory integrates us with the world and gives to our immediate perceptions and actions a range far beyond that possible in their pure immediacy. The world, as the integrated locus for action and perception, is the creation of memory, through its power to retain and to recall past perceptions and past images. Thus, it also follows that memory is real and actual only in the present and immediate act of perception, to which it gives orientation, context, and direction (not, for example, in reverie, idyllic recall, etc., where memory is, as it were, free-wheeling and functionless). This character and function of memory is again evidenced in the perception of the self, which is wholly and always an immediate act, but one in which the entire past is resumed and rendered present; one which is given substance precisely by being the locus of that summation. Memory thus also relates the self, the body, with the whole process of becoming and makes the self and its body one with the larger process of the world in its act of becoming.

From this it is clear that the spiritualism of Bergson is not a form of antimaterialism. Matter is integral to spirit as spirit is integral to matter, even the ground of matter. Bergson can speak of man as body and spirit in much more authentic terms than could other forms of spiritualism. Here he has succeeded to a high degree in dissolving that isolation in which spiritualism had historically tended to immure itself. Finally, this analysis completes the refutation of psycho-physical parallelism which he had undertaken earlier, by showing the manner in which spirit necessarily spatializes itself from within, so that the world of matter exists for it, not as something other and alien by which it is unauthentically measured, but as an authentic and necessary dimension of its own interior being.

By his investigation of the relation of matter and memory, Bergson is able to clarify the basic concept of the spirit as interiority. This clarification rests upon his distinction between pure recall, image memory and perception, and the relation he establishes between these terms. This relation explains the passage from real duration, as the purest form of the process of the interior life of spirit, to that moment in which duration becomes action and reaction within the world. Bergson describes the entire process of the interior life in the following fashion: Ideas, pure recollections, which are called forth from the depths of memory, develop into memory-images which are ever more capable of inserting themselves into the motor scheme. To the degree that these memory-images take the form of a more complete representation, one that is more concrete and more conscious, they tend to become identical with perception, for which they provide the authentic orientation.

This is a continuous flowing process, the very stuff and reality of the life of spirit. In this process, the function of the body, which is always orientated toward action, is to interrupt the pure flow of consciousness in order to direct it toward action. This conclusion makes it possible for Bergson to give a definition of perception which covers all its various discrete dimensions: Perception is the possible action of our bodies on other bodies, guided by the pattern supplied by memory. This analysis also makes clear, however, that spirit, in its very union with the body, is still transcendent to and unlimited by any part of the body. Its locus is the body as a whole, in which it is present, according to its own character, which is *totum in omni parte, omnis pars in toto*. This analysis leaves Bergson with a dualism which demands resolution. He had dissolved the old dualism of body and spirit and created a new form of their unity. Here, however, he seems merely to have replaced that dualism by another, that of action and memory. This new dualism, which is, in fact, merely the recurrence of the earlier one on a higher plane of analysis, provides Bergson with the task which he takes up in his most famous work, *Creative Evolution*.

D. Elan Vital *and* Creative Evolution

In *Creative Evolution* Bergson achieves two purposes. First, he completes the picture of the interior life of spirit which had begun with the *Essay* and, second, he proceeds to apply the principle which he had formulated in this area to the whole wide range of evolution as it embraced all forms of life. Indeed, these two achievements are really one when we consider that he applies to the entire process of evolution the same principle which rules the interior life of spirit. This principle, as it reveals itself first in the interior life of the individual and then as the principle of the entire process of evolution, is the *élan vital*.

The notion of *élan vital* is not a new discovery. It had already been present in virtually all that he said. He is now compelled, however, to give it a fresh and clearer formulation in order to resolve the dualism which appears in the analysis of *Matter and Memory*. That dualism between action and memory had resulted from Bergson's concern to emphasize that spirit is transcendent to body as well as to action and perception, which are bound up with body. This concern reflected another, that of refuting those psycho-physical parallelists who had sought, in pursuit of their doctrine, to assign specific "spiritual" functions to certain parts and actions of the body, for example, memory to certain portions of the brain. Bergson refuted this, but, in doing so, he interrupted the flow of his own developing ideas. This line of development moved toward the synthesis of the spiritual life and the life of the body, memory and action or perception. The doctrine of the *élan vital* closes this dualism as effectively as his earlier analysis had first sharply distinguished, and then reintegrated, the life of body and spirit. Consciousness has revealed the authentic character of the life of spirit to be the pure movement of lived time which, recovering and conserving the past through the activity of memory, provides the orientation for action and perception in the present. This is the *élan vital* in its pure form. But now it becomes clear that the passage of the spiritual life into the specific forms of perception and activity through a process of auto-limitation is not accidental or contingent but necessary and forms an integral part of the movement of *élan vital*. However, this necessity is a form of liberty and freedom; for there is no necessity outside the *élan* which compels its incarnation in one or another of the forms of action or moments of perception, but every such incarnation represents a movement of auto-determination or freedom. Again, therefore, Bergson achieves a type of synthesis which preserves, in a new and free unity, elements which before had been either sharply contradistinguished or subordinated one to another.

What is at stake here may be illustrated by the life career of an individual. In its essence this life is a pure movement of real time, duration, *time lived through*. This duration is not a transitive time, but one which, through the power of memory, grows upon itself and carries with it, in its flow, its entire past. Therefore, in a qualitative sense, it is an incremental time, one which expands qualitatively from within. But this temporal life is forever pinpointed into the present where, in and through the body, it takes the form of action and perception. At the same time, it is clear that the configuration of the life which is thus in process of continuous self-creation and self-determination is at once free and limited.

The conjunction of pure duration and the moment of present action and perception creates a dialectic of possibility and actuality, which, working upon itself, generates the positive configuration of that life; nevertheless, until death, it remains an open configuration, capable of further modification from within. Life as pure temporal flow and impetus is a realm of pure possibility; this possibility, however, is reduced to concrete actuality, through the mediation of perception and action. Thus, the true picture of a life emerges: the pure thrust of life through temporal duration as pure possibility, constantly mediated through action and perception, generating a concrete, limited and free form. More importantly, life is revealed as intimately constituted by a dialectic of pure possibility and mediated actuality. Thus, every life, in its concrete form, is a configured actuality on the plane of pure possibility.

There is clearly no dualism here but a dialectical unity, for the mediated actuality is the ground of the possible, just as the possibility implicit in life as pure temporal thrust is the ground of the freely determined actuality. Every life is a concretion of the pure possibility of life through the free self-limitation of that possibility. The dualism of action and memory is closed in the *élan vital*.

But the effort of *Creative Evolution* goes a step beyond the closing of this dualism on the level of the individual life. This work takes Bergson back to his original intention of revising, refining, and consolidating the doctrine of evolution in its widest scope, as he had first discovered it in Spencer and, more importantly, as he had retained it after rejecting the limited and crippled form in which Spencer proposed it. The doctrine of the *élan vital* gives Bergson the seminal principle for the revision of the doctrine of evolution in spiritualistic terms. This revision is the doctrine of creative evolution.

Bergson has already noted that evolutionary process cannot be explained mechanically; his observation, indeed, had been his basic point of departure. He also denies, however, that it can be explained finalistically, i.e., that it is presided over by an ultimate plan which can give unity to its multiplicity and explain the emergence of that multiplicity from its basic unity. The vast complexity of life, with its limitless diversity of forms which concretize the basic reality of life, can be the result only of the act which produced it, and its explanation must be found in the character of that act. That vast complexity is the manifestation of the *élan vital* which Bergson had discovered in the movement of individual life. What he has seen taking place in the production of the individual life configuration he now sees taking place on an almost limitless scale in life itself. The *élan vital*, which is simple and unitary in itself and which is pure thrust through duration, divides and multiplies through the concrete conditions of matter to produce the vast variety of the forms of life. In the case of the individual life, the *élan vital* encountered certain inherent limitations of possibility due to the essential finitude of the individual. Among possibilities open to the individual, the election of some excludes the realization of others, so that every life, in presenting its positive configuration, also presents a system of limitations, of "might have beens," which end finally in the annihilation of possibility, which is death. But life itself, the *élan vital* as cosmic principle, is subject to no such limitations since its medium is pure duration without intrinsic limit. Its possibility remains absolute, and if thwarted in one direction, it has the capacity to secure and generate other avenues.

At any given instant, this process of cosmic *élan vital* will find itself expressed in a concrete and limited number of forms, even though, absolutely speaking, the cosmic *élan vital* transcends these forms. This limitation in the cosmic process of evolution must also be accounted for. Bergson ascribes this limitation to matter, as he had done in accounting for the determinate form of the individual life; not to matter as an alien principle, but to matter as the realization of an inherent exigency of the *élan* itself. In certain instances matter presents an obstacle to *élan vital* and arrests its thrust and movement in relatively fixed forms; along other lines, matter offers no such obstacles but, instead, fresh possibilities of concretion which allow the evolutionary process to continue and grow, increasing differentiation and realizing its inherent possibilities over a wider range.

Hence, the pattern of evolution is not unilinear progress but many contemporary divergent lines of development. One such line of divergency passes between the vegetal and the animal realms. Within the animal realm, two principal lines of divergent development emerge, the one leading toward the arthropodes, etc., the other toward the vertebrates, particularly toward man. On this first line of animal development, *instinct* achieves dominance—that is, the faculty of utilizing organic instruments immediately. On the second, intelligence appears, which is the faculty of creating inorganic instruments for more or less conscious ends. Instinct thus appears as a principle of fixation, set against change and hence imposing rather rigid limits, while intelligence appears as a principle of liberation because it dominates the objects at its command. Instinct possesses greater immediate contact with the primordial flow of life; but intelligence exhibits greater adaptability, which enables it to press on indefinitely in the movement of evolution.

It is clear that Bergson assigns an instrumental role and character to intelligence, which gives him some affinity (rather tenuous, however) with the pragmatic movements. The scope of intelligence is the utilization of the inorganic order for practical ends. This accounts for the fact that it tends toward patterns of exteriorization, toward mathematical space and toward matter. Hence, Bergson does not see intelligence as the true instrument of philosophy; intelligence, being turned of its own weight not toward interiority but toward exteriority, is not apt to reveal the inner principles of reality and of life, but only its exterior, patternized forms. It is removed from the basic and immediate flow of the primordial *élan vital*. This strongly influences his reflection in its quest for the authentic instrument of philosophical reflection and truth; he finds this, not in instinct or in intelligence, but in another faculty of movement, *intuition*.

E. *Intuition*

Intuition has affinities with both intelligence and instinct, but it transcends both in its power to lay bare the true lineaments of the real. With instinct, it shares immediacy of relation to life; with intelligence, it shares reflective power. Thus, it is in reflective immediacy with the source of life and attains to that source in a purity and intensity greater than either instinct or intelligence since it possesses the most valuable element of each. For this reason it is not only the preferred but the sole instrument for the philosophical comprehension of reality and of life itself. Indeed, it is the most intense moment of life itself, the moment in which life comes into reflective possession of itself.

Bergson discovers the first evidence for the existence of intuition and its availability to man in art. Aesthetic intuition makes it possible for man to glimpse that individual reality of things which eludes perception; because perception, directed to action, is sensitive only to those impressions which serve action. While the aesthetic intuition is immediate, it is not blind, for in the expressive process the highest degree of reflection is evidenced. Art lifts the veil which the uses of action, language, custom, cast over the essence of things. But it does so only for the individual; hence it is not the instrument of philosophy, but only the indication of the reality of intuition and its availability to man.

Philosophical intuition, or pure intuition, retains all of the characteristics and capacities of aesthetic intuition but raises them to a higher power. Philosophical intuition has the power to grasp reflectively, not merely the reality of individual things, but the reality of life itself, that is, the *élan vital* in its pure form, as it transcends and invests all particular and individual manifestations of reality. Thus, intuition reveals duration as the pure form of consciousness and frees us from the spatialization and quantitative measurement which intelligence imposes. Intuition enables us to grasp that *élan vital* which is the creative principle of all life, both in the individual and in the realm of life in all its forms. Finally, intuition makes it possible to grasp man as interiority, as spirit, thus revealing his true essence. In Bergson's words, intuition is the direct vision which spirit has of itself. The basic sign of intuition is that it perceives always in terms of duration, of spirituality, or of pure consciousness.

These reflections lead Bergson to set up a kind of hierarchy of sciences. At the summit stands "metaphysics," whose organ is intuition and whose object, as has been noted, is spirit. At the second level is science, whose proper object is matter in both its theoretical and its practical aspects. But these levels are not rigidly exclusive of each other. Just as spirit and matter are in intimate relation to each other, so too are science and metaphysics. They have a common area of experience from which each selects a distinct aspect for relief, but neither can ever be separated absolutely from the other. It is clear, however, that the superior position of philosophy in this hierarchy cannot be challenged, for philosophy provides the basic orientation within which all other modes of experience and reflection find their place.

F. *Morality and Religion*

Bergson had found the highest point of development of cosmic evolution in man. In man he had discovered the capacity to extend, consciously and reflectively, the movement of evolution. He was therefore led to ask: In what way does man take up and extend the creative action of life? This question provides the theme of his very impressive work *Les deux sources de la morale et de la religion (The Two Sources of Morality and Religion)*, published in 1932.

Morality and religion, even more than art, are the means by which man draws closest to the creative force or thrust of life, and even becomes capable of advancing its creative movement. In order to understand this, it is necessary to distinguish, first, between open and closed morality, and similarly, between open and closed religion. Closed morality is that which society instills in its members for the purpose of its own conservation; it is a morality of *habit*, difficult to acquire but, like all habit, difficult to lose and practiced more or less automatically. Such morality has force only among the members of a given community. By contrast, open morality is the thrust of pure love or charity; it knows no limits and, by inherent tendency, extends to all mankind, even more, to the whole of creation. In this way Bergson has isolated the two sources of morality: social control and the *élan* of charity or love. Bergson rejects the idea that it is possible to move from the one to the other, from the closed to the open morality, by a gradual process. There is a qualitative difference between them which no such gradual process can bridge. The passage can be effected only by a leap. Nevertheless, in the individual the two can coexist, and a relation of mutual support may emerge between them. When this happens, the pure thrust of charity illuminates and warms the morality of social control, imparting to it a new qualitative tone, while some of the obligatoriness of the closed morality may pass over into the movement of charity.

A similar contrast and dialectical unity exists between closed and open religion. Closed religion is static. It arises from man's desire or need to protect himself from the imagined destructive effects of the employment of intelligence. In order to avoid facing the profoundest problems of life with open intelligence, man surrounds himself with a complex of myths or fables which he takes to be answers to those problems: death, failure, confrontation of the future and the unknown, etc. The source of this form of religion is fear, self-deception, and ignorance. In contrast to this closed and static religion is open or dynamic religion. Bergson calls this religion *mysticism;* however, he gives this term an *active* meaning which sharply distinguishes it from earlier, *contemplative* attitudes to which the same term has been applied. Mysticism resides in a supreme effort of the human spirit by which it places itself consciously in the very mainstream of the creative movement of the world, the constitutive *élan vital.* At any time throughout the course of human history, only a few privileged individuals can, by their own effort, achieve this vital identification; but such is the force of these few that they draw the mass of humanity, however inert it may be in itself, along with them, so that the whole moves closer to that vital force. The source of religion in this sense is again that *élan vital* which sustains all reality.

Bergson concludes his considerations on the two forms and the two sources of morality and religion by noting that mysticism, in his sense of the term, has reached its full expression and activity only in Christianity. He finds, too, that a revival of the mystical sense of religion may prove the power which can redeem man from the materialism and hedonism to which technology has enslaved him. The latter, he holds, is by nature an instrument and ought to be treated as such for the improvement of man's material lot. It should not become an end in itself but should release man from material necessity in order to free him for the higher forms of activity: those of the morality of love and the religion of mysticism. In this perspective the universe would come to be seen for what it is in essence, a "machine for the creation of Gods," for, by releasing man from the economic necessities of existence, it would endow him with a life close to that which the divine principle has ever been thought to exercise, a life of wisdom, love, and creative action.

Readings

Books

Alexander, Ian Welsh. *Bergson, Philosopher of Reflection.* London: Bowes & Bowes, 1957.

Carr, H. Wildon. *The Philosopher of Change: Henri Bergson.* New York: F. W. Dodge, 1912.

Chevalier, Jacques. *Henri Bergson.* Translated by L. A. Clare. New York: Macmillan, 1928.

Flewelling, Ralph T. *Bergson and Personal Realism.* New York: Abingdon Press, 1920.

Gunter, P. A. Y., ed. *Bergson and the Evolution of Physics.* Knoxville: University of Tennessee Press, 1969.

Hanna, Thomas, ed. *The Bergsonian Heritage.* New York: Columbia University Press, 1962.

Kuman, Shiv. *Bergson and the Stream of Consciousness Novel.* New York: New York University Press, 1963.

Le Roy, Edouard. *The New Philosophy of Henri Bergson.* Translated by Vincent Benson. New York: Henry Holt, 1913.

Maritain, Jacques. *Bergsonian Philosophy and Thomism.* Translated by M. L. and J. G. Andison. New York: Philosophical Library, 1955.

_____. *Redeeming the Time.* Translated by H. Binsse. London: G. Bles, 1946.

Roberts, J. D. *Faith and Reason: Pascal, Bergson, William James.* Boston: Christopher Publishing House, 1962.

Tymieniecka, Anna T. *Why Is There Something Rather Than Nothing?* Assen: Van Gorcum; New York: Humanities Press, 1966.

Essays and articles

Anderson, James. "Bergson, Aquinas and Heidegger on the Notion of Nothingness." *Proceedings of the Catholic Philosophical Association,* XLI (1967).

Capek, Milic. "Time and Eternity in Royce and Bergson." *Revue Internationale de Philosophie,* XXI (1967).

Gallagher, Idella. "Bergson on Open and Closed Morality." *The New Scholasticism,* XLII (1968).

Hart, Thomas N. "God in the Ethico-Religious Thought of Henri Bergson." *The Thomist,* XXXII (1968).

Lovejoy, Arthur O. "Some Antecedents of the Philosophy of Bergson." *Mind,* n.s. XXII (1913).

Meissner, W. W. "Spirit and Matter: The Psychological Paradox." *Journal of Existentialism,* VIII (1967–68).

_____. "The Temporal Dimension in the Understanding of Human Experience." *Journal of Existentialism,* VII (1966–67).

Riccaboni, Joseph J. "Bergson's Metaphysical Intuition and Science." *Journal of the History of Philosophy,* V (1967).

Schouborg, Gary. "Bergson's Intuitional Approach to Free Will." *The Modern Schoolman,* XLV (1968).

Singerman, Ora. "The Relation Between Philosophy and Science: Bergson and Whitehead." *Iyyun: A Hebrew Philosophical Quarterly,* XIX (1968).

PART II
THE POST-COLONIAL AGE

Introduction

Croce, speaking of the Baroque Age, complained that its philosophy was the "philosophy of an unphilosophic age"; it has been suggested that the same complaint might, perhaps with even greater justice, be lodged against our own. The evidence for such a complaint, however, would not be readily forthcoming. Quite the contrary, surveying the period, one must conclude that however the quality of its performance in this area be appraised, ours is an age hungry for philosophy, deeply in need of it, and conscious of this need.

The first item of evidence in support of this opinion is the very plethora of philosophical positions advanced and defended. These could surely arise only in response to a need very deeply felt, though its character might not be clearly apprehended. One is reminded of the Hellenic age, when so many opinions competed for the adherence of men's minds. If it be agreed, as indeed it must, that the mark of a philosophical age is precisely this need for philosophy, this hunger for it, even while its true nature be only dimly perceived, then it must be agreed as well that ours will eventually come to be known, not as a period of great philosophical achievement perhaps, but as an age genuinely philosophical in its quality.

What persuades men that the age is unphilosophical is the difficulty of fixing the character of its philosophical spirit in any easy formula. It has been called the age of analysis. But this can only be a limited and perhaps even superficial characteristic. It is true that the spirit of system in philosophy is frequently declared to be dead, just as one of the more facile shibboleths avers the death of God. But both allegations prove to be most premature. The allegation of the death of God has been shown to be but the masked form of the hunger for God in a self-consciously secular age. Just so, it has been shown that the spirit of system underlies even the most assertively asystematic positions, such as that of Wittgenstein. Analysis would seem to be too restricted an operation fully to reflect the quality of the philosophical life of the age. And the same might be said for the philosophy of science, which some

hail as *the* philosophical concern of the period. In fact, it is the preoccupation of specialists which has little or no impact on the ethos of
the culture.

To gain a deeper insight into the quality of the philosophical culture of the age, one must turn a more penetrating glance on some of
those currents which are neglected in Britain but which are dominant
in western Europe and have appealed very strongly in America, especially to those most sensitive to the humanly unrewarding character of
analytic philosophy and the philosophy of science. Most notable among
these movements, of course, is existentialism. But existentialism, it has
been suggested, is already a thing of the past. It is too negative in its
innermost claims to excite, much less sustain, adherence or assent. Of
greater interest and promise are the strong movements of modern
spiritualism, especially Christian spiritualism.

The appeal of spiritualism for man is as strong and profound as
that of its opposite (in the banal antinomy), materialism, is superficial
and tenuous. Spiritualism speaks to the deepest, though inarticulate,
convictions which man entertains about himself; those which he feels
are most cavalierly set aside and denigrated by materialism, positivism, and scientism. The more strongly man feels this denigration, the
more forcefully he asserts the countervailing persuasions and the more
closely probes their origins and validity. It might well be argued that
personalism, whose metaphysical basis is spiritualism, is a strong can-
didate for the characterizing persuasion of contemporary thought.
Even logical positivism, which initially granted little status to such
empirically elusive concepts as the person, has come to appreciate the
central position this notion holds in contemporary thought. For this
reason, in the following chapters the effort has been made, without
detriment to the treatment of other currents, to sketch a stronger pro-
file and to create a more vital sense of the spiritualist currents than is
usually attained, or even striven for, in other histories. The paradox is
even suggested that the institutions most cherished by the western,
and especially English-speaking, world rest squarely on speculative
positions which that world has been inclined to denigrate. While it is
dangerous to characterize any age by a single trait, the least risk of all,
it might be ventured, would be to characterize the philosophic temper
of the West as gradually awakening to this paradox and the dangers
it conceals.

CHAPTER I

The Philosophy of Action

Introduction: Intrinsic Character of the Philosophy of Action

The movement of the "philosophy of action" must be considered one of the most misprized in contemporary philosophy. It has suffered from a number of confusions and mistaken associations which have surrounded it with a cloud of ambiguities, obscuring its true sense and character. Yet it is a movement which stimulates considerable interest, both cultural and philosophical. Culturally, it is the sensitive expression of one of the most profound spiritual exigencies of its time (which continues to be an exigency of our own), that of exploring anew the basis for an intellectual commitment to the Christian faith; philosophically, this inquiry was carried on by men of profound philosophical culture and acumen and was productive of insights whose philosophical quality is authentic and arresting.

The ambiguities begin with the very name. Its origin is traced, on the one hand, to the title of the chief work of its most representative figure, *L'action* (1893) of Maurice Blondel and, on the other, to the intervention of Emile Boutroux, who first employed the phrase "philosophy of action" at the International Congress of Philosophy in 1900. Boutroux might have averted to the fact that Blondel had employed the phrase only to reject its application to his own thought (cf. *L'action,* 1893 ed., p. 27). The term which has subsequently suggested itself as expressing more truly the intrinsic character of the movement, both as Christian and as philosophical, is "Christian Integralism"; but this term has never gained currency.

The ambiguity in the term reveals itself in the implications and associations which have erroneously been assigned the movement. Seizing on the imprecise suggestion of the term "action," some historians have included in the movement all those doctrines which in any way subordinate knowledge to action or which recognize the principle of action, the will, as the basis of truth and certitude. In this way, Sorel, who shares none of the inner religious anxiety out of which this movement grows, is sometimes brought under its rubric. The term also invited an association with pragmatism, which Blondel, in the remarks on pragmatism which he contributed to the *Bulletin de la société de philosophie* (May 7, 1908), rejects. Similarly, the philosophy of action has been confused with a form of fideism, with forms of religious empiricism, and with forms of intuitionism. Culturally, of course, such associations are not to be repudiated absolutely; the movement arose in an atmosphere in which all of these were present. Nevertheless, in its intrinsic character it differs from all of them and is, in fact, a direct effort to correct some of them. Consequently it becomes all the more imperative that any treatment of the philosophy of action begin with some effort to identify its intrinsic character.

The most important feature of the philosophy of action is that it is a *Christian* philosophy, in the most radical sense of term. Unlike the great syntheses of the past, those of Thomas Aquinas and of Malebranche, it is not an effort to achieve some unity between the Christian faith and a historical philosophical system such as that of Aristotle or Descartes. Nor is it concerned with synthesizing, in more generic terms, the counter-dynamism of faith and philosophy within the human spirit. It is concerned directly with the philosophical exigency inherent in Christianity itself. It rests on the insight and the conviction, first, that Christianity, as a faith, must be intellectually and philosophically explicated in order to reach its full status as faith; and, secondly, that contained within Christianity are philosophical insights which illuminate, not only faith itself, but the entire philosophical enterprise as it has arisen and developed in western culture. The philosophy of action is, therefore, a Christian philosophy in a sense in which this term can be applied to no other movement. The phrase "Christian philosophy" here signifies, not a synthesis of elements which have some autonomous status, but a unitary movement toward philosophical articulation within the Christian experience. Its quest for philosophical truth is a living and organic movement within the life of faith.

The philosophy of action may be said to revolve elliptically around two poles. The first of these is faith itself, as a human act, with all of its presuppositions, implications, and consequences. In a somewhat Kantian way (though Blondel specifically rejects any affinity to Kant's "practical reason" and its imperatives [cf. *L'action*, 1893, p. 28]), the philosophy of action is concerned to establish the possibility of faith as an authentic human attitude and act. Faith here is not a generic term; it is specifically the faith which establishes the believer as a Christian, which assuredly resides not merely in the *what* but in the *how*, the *act* of that faith. The second pole of the philosophy of action is the exploration and elaboration of the philosophical world which is latent in faith both as an act and as the object of that act. It would seem clear, once the authenticity and the character of faith as a human act and attitude have been established, that it must be the center of an entire view of reality which can only be expressed in ideas. The act of faith cannot be an isolated or eccentric transaction. It is real, it is in the world, and it is vitally related to every dimension of reality. Lines of ontological affiliation with the entire system of the real must radiate from it. These affiliations can be expressed only in philosophical terms and are the object of genuine philosophical inquiry. The thought of the philosophy of action moves around these two poles in an elliptical pattern, with a constant enrichment and increment of knowledge about either locus and with strong lines of mutual implication binding all into an integral system.

From this review of its intrinsic character, it can readily be seen why the appellation "Christian integralism" more fully and fittingly reflects the movement. This integralism, in its turn, may be said to have two aspects—the relevance of faith to the whole of what is and the relevance of all that is to faith. Under the first, it is the act of faith which exhibits the integral character: It is an act of man, possible and necessary to the degree to which the human subject achieves the integrity of his own being and existence and it is the act through which, as an existential process, that integral character is achieved. Under the second aspect, it is the entire system of the real which exhibits the character of integrality. The integrality of the entire system of the real is both the projection of, and the ground of, the integrality of the human person as achieved through the act of faith and the substance of faith. It can be said that the philosophy of action is seeking to fulfill, in terms which meet the conditions of the modern world, the primitive exigency of the Christian faith for intellectual fulfillment. This must surely be taken as the final mark of its integrality.

What we have been trying to present here as the intrinsic character of the philosophy of action must necessarily appear very generic. As in all other "movements" in the history of philosophy, the concrete realization of this character must be sought and can be found only in the work of the representative figures of the movement. Here again, it is the diversity of ways in which the individual representatives realize the common effort of the movement that possesses the greatest interest. No massive unanimity unites them, but a common urgency impels the thought of all and a common purpose inspires it. The philosophy of action will therefore have to be sought in the particular works of its most representative figures. These are not many, for it was never a large or even influential movement; indeed, it was forced to struggle to maintain its identity in the world of ideas, to resist inclusion within stronger currents and associations which might embarrass and confound it. We shall confine our attention to four of the most imposing of these representatives, who speak with both charm and authority for the values it represents: John Henry Cardinal Newman (1801–1890), Léon Ollé-Laprune (1839–1898), Maurice Blondel (1861–1949), and Lucien Laberthonnière (1860–1932).

A. *John Henry Cardinal Newman*

The rich and subtle literary expression of the great English Cardinal, who passed from his Anglican adherence to the Roman Catholic profession, was devoted to a dual concern: first, to the discovery of the faith which truly commanded the assent of the believer, and, once this was found, to its explication and defense. The first concern dominated his thought to the time of his conversion and the second from his conversion to the end of his life. In an age of apologetics, he towered among apologetes. Of his works, the two which are of most interest to philosophy, and specifically to the explication of the philosophy of action, belong one to the first and the other to the second phase of his activity.

The *Essay on the Development of Christian Doctrine* was the product of the first phase. Published in 1845, the year after his conversion, it was composed during his last and most trying years as an Anglican. The argument was not academic for him, for it vitally involved his own religious life. When he reached the culminating point of its argument, he found himself not only convinced of logical and historical conclusions, but inwardly altered in his basic religious orientation. Thus, the true conclusion of the book was not a proposition but his act of conversion. For this reason it was left unfinished and was not given definitive form until the edition of 1878. The *Essay in Aid of a Grammar of Assent*, published in 1875, was the work of Newman's full maturity in every aspect of his personal and intellectual endowment. Apologetic in its original intention to demonstrate the reasonableness of religious assent as an act of the human spirit, it rises swiftly to the truly speculative plane to become a major contribution to the cognitive self-penetration of the human spirit, not merely in the tradition of Hume, as has been asserted, but in that far greater tradition of Augustine. The stature of Newman cannot be measured by identifying him as an exponent of the philosophy of action in the sense in which that position has been indicated above; it far exceeds that measure. But, incidentally to his larger purposes and in the course of their pursuit, he is one of the major contributors to that point of view. The works in which this contribution is made are precisely the two mentioned.

The argument of the *Essay on the Development of Christian Doctrine* may be said to proceed at two levels. On the first level Newman defines and defends the notion that Christian doctrine and belief has necessarily undergone a process of historical development. His argument is directed against two opposing points of view. The first was the Protestant viewpoint, which tended to hold to a kind of doctrinal primitivism in which it was asserted that the faith of the primitive church (including its self-understanding of its own character and the meaning of its beliefs) was normative. The second was Catholic traditionalism, which tended to see Christian doctrine as a fixed deposit of faith to which the historical experience of the Church could add nothing essential, and the scholasticism of classical Catholic theology, which seemed to believe that Christian faith had reached the culminating point of intellectual self-penetration and expression in the theology of the high Middle Ages, which, therefore, was also taken as normative.

Newman argues with disarming simplicity and directness that truth, considered in itself—that is, as it is in God—is certainly eternal and unchanging. Man, however, can only live this truth as it is revealed to him on a historical plane, for such is his very nature. There is, then, a historical development of truth, related to man's nature and historical experience; only in terms of this nature and experience does man truly apprehend and live the truth. What is the case for truth in general, is even more directly the case for the beliefs of Christianity. Their truth can only become apparent, can only be apprehended and lived, through the function of man's historical nature. Consequently, they have a history, just as man, to whom they are addressed, has a history.

Newman is not content to let the argument rest at this level. He is concerned to fix the character of the development involved. To this end, he worked out his theory of development, which embraces the celebrated signs of development: conservation of the primitive type, continuity, force of assimilation, logical consequentiality, anticipation of the future, preservation of the past, and enduring vigor. Newman sees this developmental process as providential in character and argues that Providence must of necessity have established an immutable authority which would guide and control the process. This principle is the Church.

It is not this argument, however, which is of direct interest in the exposition of the philosophy of action. We are most immediately concerned with the presupposition upon which this argument, more or less explicitly, rests. This presupposition anticipates the argument of the *Grammar of Assent* and directly involves the integrality of the spirit in its relationship to truth and the notion of *real* truth as the integrating principle of the human spirit itself. Discussing the conditions which govern the career of ideas among men and in history, Newman makes a basic affirmation. When an idea, be it real or not, he says, is of such a nature as to arrest and possess the mind, it may be said to be living; it is alive in the mind which receives it. To illustrate this point, he says that the ideas of mathematics, while real, can never be properly said to live, at least not in the ordinary course of thought. They do not solicit man's living assent. But when some great idea about human nature, the good, government, duty, or religion is diffused among men and commands their attention, it is not received in merely passive fashion but becomes a vital principle within their minds, a principle which reorders their own inner, living awareness of themselves and draws them to comtemplate that idea as a living principle. This living character of truth is the true principle of its development in history, and the signs which Newman specifies are mere indices. At this point, Newman's affinity to the philosophy of action becomes abundantly apparent, as does the precise character of his contribution to it. An idea, in the fullness of its nature, is living and vital; it engages not just the intellect of man but his entire nature; it becomes a principle of integration and actualization both within man and between man and the universe of being, which, in its highest principle, is God.

It is this idea which constitutes the living link between the *Essay on Development* and the *Grammar of Assent*. The latter may be rightly conceived as the development of the former through the intense explication of this germinal idea. The *Grammar* presents a certain aspect of paradox (an aspect hardly absent from any major speculative work): it develops *intellectually* the notion of the integration of the human spirit in a total act which *transcends* intellect. But the paradox must be accounted superficial. More profoundly considered, this very operation illustrates the thesis of integrality with great power. The basic motive of the *Grammar* is to determine man's standing before God; not man in the abstract, but the concrete human subject. This aim has led some to establish an affinity between Newman and existentialism, especially the existentialism of Kierkegaard. But this affinity would seem to be weak for a reason which places in relief the essentially classical and intellectual character of Newman's philosophy of religion. Newman's assent, the establishing act of man's integral religious character and the fundamental principle of his relation to God, differs profoundly from the "standing before God" of Kierkegaard. The one is an act of man in his integrity, the other an act of his brokenness; and the principle of that integrity is precisely a man's capacity to give an intellectual foundation to his act of recognition and submission to God. The structure of this act is Newman's concern in the *Grammar of Assent*. Its integrality emerges from this keen and, at times, not wholly unscholastic analysis.

Newman initiates his inquiry with a distinction among types of propositions. These, he believes, are three: interrogative, conditional, and categorical. With respect to these, man assumes three correlative attitudes: doubt, inference, and assent. Of doubt, little need be said, though Newman's analysis of this (which was, for him, no mere idea but a vivid personal experience) is subtle and penetrating. Inference is conditional and conditioned because the conclusion of the inference involves the acceptance of premises and can have no other degree of probability than that possessed by the premises. This is the attitude of the philosopher, Newman suggests; he is committed to conclusions which are always corrigible in view of the probable character of their premises, and he lives in a constant state of self-criticism and self-rectification. Newman is at pains to emphasize that this is an integral attitude; it reflects fully man's actual status in reality and involves his entire and integral being at this level.

The third attitude is *assent*. Newman's concern is directed above all to this attitude. Assent is immediate, unconditioned, and unconditional acceptance, without justification of premises or of logical procedures. Assent is the attitude of the believer. While assent lends itself to analysis, Newman's chief point is that assent is always an act of the whole, existing man, involving, not one of his faculties dominating the others, but his entire being as an existing subject seeking reality and truth. Newman's analysis must be interpreted against the background of this integralism.

The first stage of his analysis yields the distinction between *notional* and *real* assent. Assent is notional if its object is an *idea;* it is real if the object is a fact, a *res*. Real assent always resides in the direct experience of the particular, existing subject, involving his entire moral being. Its characteristic procedure is the *illative sense,* an implicit process of reason into which the whole of the subject's life enters not merely abstract premises. Through it he reaches a conclusion which intellect alone cannot explicate. The supreme object of assent is God. When assent to that object is notional, what is reached is theology, a doctrine *about* God. When that assent is real, *God himself* is attained as a real object, and the moment realized is *religion*.

Newman then comes to the crucial moment of his analysis: the relation between inference and assent. Are they two completely diverse moments with no passage between them, or is it possible to pass from inference to assent? Much misunderstanding has arisen on the point of his answer to this question. Newman affirms that such passage is possible and emphasizes the part played in it by will. As a result, charges of voluntarism and fideism have been lodged against him. A consideration of his entire thought on the point makes it clear that these charges are unfounded. Again the crucial consideration is that faith is an integral act of the integral man. Newman assigns no dominant force to the will in the passage from inference to assent or from notional to real assent the object of which is God. His insistence on the will is simply an effort to counteract the overemphasis on the intellect which characterized earlier analyses. Equal emphasis is placed on the agency of the cognitive and the affective faculties. To lose sight of this integralism is to miss the whole force of Newman's thought, namely, that real assent to God as reality, even as *res,* is the integral act of the integral person. He had the custom of referring to this integrality as *moral.* The term is justified since he is considering the involvement of the total person as opposed to the abstract operation of one faculty over another, for the status of the integral person is certainly that of a moral entity. However, it might be better to refer to that integral act as ontological and existential rather than moral, for in this way the real character of the integrity is placed in relief.

Newman, as has been noted, cannot really be placed within the ambit of any school or current. It is at the same time, however, clear that his highly personal reflections on these problems place him in a direct line with the current of the philosophy of action or Christian integralism.

B. *Léon Ollé-Laprune*

Ollé-Laprune must be accounted the initiator in France of the philosophy of action as a self-conscious current, aware of its own inner character and of its attitude toward other points of view which contested the field. In a more specific manner, Ollé-Laprune established the two central points which his pupil Blondel would develop: 1) the deepening of the current of French spiritualism, which had its origin in Maine de Biran, into humanistic integralism, and 2) the deep religious and Christian conviction which, wedded to that integralism, created the synthesis of "Christian integralism."

The first of these themes already appears in one of Ollé-Laprune's earliest and most substantial works, his essay *La philosophie de Malebranche* [The philosophy of Malebranche], 1870. To the rigid rationalism of Malebranche, he opposed a spiritualistic-dynamic view of the universe in which emphasis is placed upon the initiative and co-creative activity of single spiritual entities and upon the harmonic development of reality in a dependence upon the First Cause and Creator that is not rigidly mathematical but providential and paternalistic. But this view of the universe is not merely a contemplative one. Man's involvement in being has a direction which is indicated by Christianity: an ascent to God by the engagement of man's integral being in harmony with the whole of creation. The universe is the theater of the Christian's vocation and destiny to reach this harmonious relation with the providential First Cause—not through a negative ascetic, but through a positive and total engagement of his nature.

This concept of total Christian engagement—not merely the engagement of the Christian in the whole, the universe, but his engagement *as* a whole, in his integral nature—bears directly upon Ollé-Laprune's vision of truth. Against the background of the abstract and purely objective truth of rationalism in the Cartesian tradition, he places emphasis on the *moral* nature of truth. It is necessary for an understanding of his thought to see clearly the meaning of *moral* in this context. It obviously is not related to abstract juridical morality. It is directly involved in the notion of total engagement. Truth is the apprehension of being in its concreteness and fullness. This apprehension does not come to man through the isolated operation of one of his faculties, such as the intellect or reason. It can be apprehended only through the coordinated effort of his entire being in its integral character. When so apprehended, it constitutes, not an external acquisition, but a possession of being from within which at the same time is the real completion and final integration of man's own inner being. For Ollé-Laprune, all of the great theses of philosophy—God, liberty, the moral law, the future life—are of this order. They are moral theorems, engaging the whole man.

As a consequence, the primary concern of philosophy, in its methodological aspect, is the problem of *moral certitude*. Again, the view of morality as total engagement of the human person must be emphasized. Ollé-Laprune does not use the phrase "moral certitude" in the context of that trinity of certitudes—moral, logical, and ontological—which had appeared before in western thought. Such a fragmentation of truth and certitude is repugnant to him. Moral certitude is that apprehension of truth which man achieves through the total engagement of his being and total truth, which brings completion to his being by placing it in contact with the inner reality of the being of the universe, which is God. The problem of philosophy is the acquisition of moral truth and certitude in this total sense.

These reflections lead Ollé-Laprune to the consideration of the meaning of "integral" with respect to the nature of man. This integralism may be said to have three levels or aspects. The first is the constitutive integrity of man's nature as that nature is possessed and exercised by every individual. It is in the development of this aspect that he seems to call most directly on the resources of French spiritualism. The second is man's operative integrity, his action in the world as it may be called. The third and final level is his access to the total being of the universe, not merely in its diffused state in nature, but in its concrete creative principle and center, God.

The insight into the integral character of the nature of man in its concrete existent principle, the person, demands a total revision, in Ollé-Laprune's view, of the dynamic structure of the human existent. In this reconstruction, it has been alleged, Ollé-Laprune shows himself to be a voluntarist; that is, against the intellectualists, he makes the will the central integrating principle of man as concrete existent. A reasonably careful reading of such texts as *De la certitude morale* [On moral certitude], 1880, *La raison et le rationalisme* [Reason and rationalism], 1906, and others, would seem to prove this incorrect. Ollé-Laprune is not concerned with a contest of the constitutive faculties for supremacy; it is the central constituting reality of which all of these faculties are radiations that he seeks. He finds this in the *act*. The *act* is the constituting unitary and integrating principle of man. The existing concrete man is *act*. This act is not something distinct from action or from *acting*. It is wholly immanent to the concrete process of life, to acting, in all its forms. At the same time, it is transcendent even to the process of action in all its varieties. It unifies, relates, integrates all the diversity of action, which deploys itself into the constitutive faculties of man. This deployment is the necessary expression of the inward fecundity of the act, which cannot be exhausted in any one direction but demands the full range of the active potentialities of man—sensation, reason, will, appetite—to fulfill itself.

The basic insight of integralism is to grasp this act in its unity and multiplicity, its immanence and its transcendence, its permanence in being and its dynamism in the whole range of life. The integrity of man is in the *act* and in the reference of all action to the *act*. Man's truth is in the fulfillment of the act, in the creation and reassimilation of the totality of action into one complex but integral center.

The act in the world finds a corresponding expression and realization in the multitude of forms of cultural life which man's dynamism generates. In the very perceptive essay *La philosophie et le temps présent* [Philosophy and the present age], 1890, Ollé-Laprune presents a veritable philosophy of culture. Culture is precisely man's creative integration *of* the world and *with* the world. The work of culture is everywhere the same, the bringing together of the diffused being of mundane existence into significant spiritual forms. This central activity of culture reflects the central principle of man's inward existence, the act. But, like the act, culture is self-diffusive and dynamic. It is essentially pluralistic. Art, science, morality, and social life are all forms of creative activity emerging from the centrality of the act. There is no imbalance in his vision; no sector of the cultural life of man holds dominion over any other, just as no faculty of man's inward life holds dominion over the others. All are radiations from, and are in turn mediated by, the act, which, in this process of culturalization, enriches the world as it enriches itself.

Nevertheless, the true complement and fulfillment of the act does not lie, ultimately, in the generation of the world of culture in its unity and complexity. It lies rather in the transcendent principle of that universe of concrete being which appears in the world and, more intimately, in the unity of man's integrating principle, the act. The principle is God. At this point the Christian principle enters dynamically into Ollé-Laprune's thought. He considers the possibility of the passage from the center of human existence to the center of universal concrete being, God. Can this passage be direct—for example, by way of nature? Ollé-Laprune believes not. The way has been indicated by a transcendent act of God, namely, his self-revelation in Christ. The appearance of Christ is crucial, because it creates a historical center for the apprehension of the divine center of the universe of being. The center of integration now passes both from the centrality of the act in man and from the transcendent creative center of the universe of concrete being in God to the historical center in Christ.

Christ's appearance imposes a new form upon the whole philosophy of the act. The central problem now becomes that of the relation of the individual existent to Christ. What is the nature of the act by which the reality and meaning of Christ are assimilated into the integrity of the person? This is the act of faith, the final integrating act of human existence. Faith has Christ as its direct object and the universe of Being—in its center, God—as its ultimate concern. Ollé-Laprune's analysis of this act remains fragmentary, however, except for some master lines which Blondel will take up. Among these the most important are Christ as the concreteness of truth and the act of faith as an integral act: an act of the total personality of the individual, existing man directed toward the total assimilation of the integral principle of reality as manifested in Christ. The act of faith is taken by Ollé-Laprune from the shadowy and somewhat ambiguous area in which it has remained so long, to be made the central act of the human existent as act. This achieves the integration of all of the levels of existence which he has distinguished. What is lacking in Ollé-Laprune's thought is an analysis of the act of faith itself, a lack which Blondel seeks to supply. But from Ollé-Laprune's thought the outlines of Christian integralism emerge both full and firm, providing a frame of reference which will not alter substantially in its further developments.

C. *Maurice Blondel*

The philosophy of action or Christian integralism finds its most complete and coherent expression in the thought of Maurice Blondel. Blondel, a modest and retiring professor who spent the greater part of his career in the provincial university of Aix-en-Provence, possessed a depth of insight and a power of speculative thought which have revealed themselves only slowly with time. It may confidently be said that his influence has only begun to make itself felt.

In its broadest perspective, Blondel's thought, like that of Newman, was apologetic. He was concerned to establish and vindicate the philosophical validity of the teachings of Christianity and, more specifically, of Catholic Christianity. It is important to note at once the exact meaning of his apologetic enterprise. In Blondel, apologetics has none of that external and polemical character which has come to be associated with the term. It is not concerned to defend the beliefs of Christianity against an external attack in an atmosphere of controversy. Apologetics, in the Blondelian spirit, responds to an inner need of the faith and of the believer, and the atmosphere in which it is conducted is that of pure reflective thought. The inward need in both faith and believer to which his apologetics responds is the need of integrality, wholeness. In the believer this wholeness is the integrity of his human nature. He seeks to know in what way that nature is fulfilled in the faith, in what way the faith forms an integral element in the potential life of his spirit. In the faith itself, taken in the broadest sense as the invitation to the supernatural life, this wholeness involves its power to respond to the need of the human spirit to fulfill itself completely and, at the same time, to the need of the absolute spirit of God to fulfill its own nature and decrees in the salvation of the individual man, that is, the fulfillment of the supernatural potential of his existence. Only when this wide context and prospective is kept in mind can the full sweep of Blondel's thought be appreciated.

Within this broad context, the work of philosophy occupies a clearly defined place. Philosophy is the wholeness of life. It is not the actual living of life, and even less is it the actuality of the life it contemplates and guides. The life of the human spirit ranges from the simplest movement and impulse of physical life to the sacramental life which grace opens to it. It lives this life at every point and stage in the concreteness of its existence. Within that concrete life, philosophy constitutes a moment of primary importance. It is the moment in which the human spirit achieves integrity and integrality in principle and idea, that is, in which it comes to possess in thought the fullness of its life. The integrality imparted by the act of philosophical reflection to the concrete life of the human spirit is the basis of unity and wholeness. Unless it is unified in this moment, the life of the human spirit, no matter how it seeks to achieve a material integrality, must always remain diffused and inorganic, without center and, hence, with neither limits, form, nor integrity.

The access of faith does not displace this center in reflective thought. Blondel does not think of faith as an alternative center of integrity for the human spirit. On the contrary, it is through philosophy that faith enters into the human spirit as an integral and integrating power. But again, this is not to be taken as a shallow rationalism. It is not the abstract doctrine of religion which must be justified before philosophy. It is the moment of faith itself as an integrating force in man's spirit with which philosophy is concerned. Blondel's thought belongs to the central philosophical tradition of the West, for man's reason always remains the true integrating point of his life; but it is entirely free from the abortive rationalism which would make abstract reason the measure of the possible. It is clear from these reflections that in Blondel the apologetic concern does not in any way cripple the autonomy of philosophy. The appearance of the faith, of Christian revelation, upon the horizons of man's life does not impose limits upon or question the autonomy of reason. On the contrary, it extends the range and authority of reason and philosophical inquiry, for the faith itself now enters into the range of its necessary and autonomous inquiry. According to the most unambiguous norms of philosophy in western culture, Blondel's is a thoroughly philosophical enterprise.

These reflections also make it possible to state Blondel's view of philosophy in terms of its actual object, its method, and its competence. In its object, Blondel's view of philosophy is of transparent Augustinian and Pascalian inspiration. It is nothing less than that *possessio sui* in a contemplative and reflective act of which both the great saint and the sage of Port Royal speak. The task of philosophy is to convey to man the possession of his own being in idea: his nature, his potentialities, his origin, and his destiny. In its method, Blondel's philosophy is again Augustinian, Cartesian, and Pascalian. His is the method of immanence, in the sense that man reaches the truth by the inward penetration of his own existence and not by any outward inspection of the "objective" world. He might have taken as his own the oft-quoted words of Augustine in the *Liber de vera religione:* "Noli foras ire, in te ipsum redi, in interiore hominis habitat veritas." Blondel's interpretation of the method of immanence has become the object of considerable criticism—much of it, we may suggest, resting on a single point of misunderstanding. Many have thought that the purpose of his method of immanence was to set up a rationalistic criterion for the intrinsic verity of religious truths and, thus, to bring the transcendent truth of revelation under the scrutiny of an abstractive reason. A careful reading of Blondel proves that nothing could be further from his intention. His true intention was, on the basis of the immanent self-reflection of the human spirit, to determine its openness to the invitation of the supernatural life rather than to prejudge the truth value of revelation, which, as revelation, must have a truth value that transcends the truth values formally determinable on the basis of reason.

These last remarks point out the competence of philosophy for Blondel. It is not a substitute for life, but life's inward guide. It is an inward light, present in every moment of life but not displacing or usurping life in its concrete forms and moments. Without philosophy the integral life of man is not possible; but philosophy is not itself that integral life. The integral life resides in the concrete fulfillment of every actual possibility of life, the possibility of the supernatural life included.

During his long active life, Blondel composed and published many works. However, his entire literary creation centers about two poles, *L'action* and what is known as the "Tetralogy." According to its full title, the former is: *L'action, essai d'une critique de la vie et d'une science de la pratique* [Action: an essay toward a critique of life and a science of praxis]. It was offered by Blondel as his doctoral thesis in 1893. It immediately aroused great interest and, at the same time, considerable opposition. While the recognition of its brilliance was universal, fear was expressed in some quarters that it constituted a danger for the very values (those of religion and, specifically, Catholicism) which he sought to serve. The "Tetralogy" is composed of four works which were elaborated by Blondel during his years of teaching and were published between 1934 and 1946. These are *La pensée* [Thought], *L'être et les êtres* [Being and beings], *L'action* [Action], which was an elaboration on the original work of this title and finally *La philosophie et l'ésprit chrétien* [Philosophy and the Christian spirit]. His numerous other writings may be considered as ministering to these central works—clarifying a point, preparing the ground for a discussion, refuting an erroneous interpretation of his views, or indicating the application of a principle.

A considerable discussion has grown up about which of these major expressions of his thought is more representative of his authentic ideas. This question can be approached from many points of view, but in the present context only one point of view is relevant: to which must Blondel's importance in the history of philosophy be traced? Which defines his particular place in that history? When the question is put in this form, the answer seems beyond doubt. *L'action* is Blondel's fundamental work. By way of this essay his thought enters the great stream of western philosophy. The seminal ideas which it develops define his own position in that history and in turn determine the position assumed by a number of contemporary philosophers. For this reason the limited space available here will serve the reader best if devoted to an analysis of *L'action*.

This is not a denial of the philosophical power of the works included in the "Tetralogy." Indeed, these works alone would serve to establish a lesser man in history, and within the economy of Blondel's own thought, the development of the seminal ideas of *L'action* throughout the works of the "Tetralogy" constitutes an intellectual phenomenon of the highest order. In *L'action*, the argument proceeds primarily on the moral, religious, and psychological levels. In the volumes of the "Tetralogy" it is transported to the ontological plane, which is the only level on which it can develop fully. In making this transfer, Blondel is responding to an internal exigency of the earlier work. In chapter three of the fifth part of *L'action* it becomes clear that only an inclusive ontology of the act could reveal the nature of human action in the moral and religious spheres. He seeks to supply this ontology in the pages of the "Tetralogy." Nevertheless, this later development is always a function of the original problems and theses of *L'action* and cannot be understood except by reference to them. Consequently, for the history of philosophy Blondel and *L'action* are one and the same.

To secure a clear view of the principal doctrinal aspects of *L'action*, we may propose a number of questions. What, in the most inclusive sense, does Blondel understand by action? What is the method for the study of action in this work? What are the chief concrete ideas he offers about human action?

To avoid any confusion with discussions about the relation of thought and action, it may be useful to compare Blondel's conception of action and Descartes's notion of thought (as given in the *Discourse on Method*). Blondel subjects the notion of action to the same kind of revision to which Descartes subjected the notion of thought. In each case the notion is first rendered more *inclusive*, only to be defined thereafter with greater rigor and assigned the decisive role in human existence. Descartes, in his well-known definition, extends thought to include sensation, willing, desiring, etc. He immediately makes it clear, however, that thought for him is the purest form of man's concrete being and presence, that which he *is* and not something which

simply transpires within him. In like manner, Blondel extends the
notion of *action* to include every vital movement of the human subject
of existence; for him thought is action, just as for Descartes action must
be defined by way of thought. But immediately Blondel proceeds to
intensify the notion of action. Action is not what man *does;* it is what
man *is*. He *is* action because it is in action that his concrete being
resides; his *to be* is to be in action. His being is entirely dynamic, and
his nature can only be defined by action.

At this point two clarifications are in order, or better perhaps, a
clarification in two directions. First, it is necessary to note that Blondel says that man is *action* and not *act*. A scholastic and Aristotelian
reminiscence is alive here. *Act* implies the perfection of being, which
excludes any further becoming because its order of potentiality has
been realized. Action, by contrast, is the pure act of becoming, the dynamic movement toward a state of being which it does not, as action,
possess. Thus, the term *action* is chosen with great care. On the other
hand, Blondel's use of the term is to be distinguished from the notion
of action which underlies most pragmatic analyses. Unfortunately, a
positive comparison has sometimes been introduced between the two
points of view, but it would seem to be ultimately illusory. For pragmatism, man is ultimately reducible to the sum of his *actions,* his
operations, his *transactions*. For Blondel, this can never be the case.
Indeed, it is precisely because man *cannot* be identified with the sum
of his operations that it becomes clear in what sense he is truly *action*.
Pragmatism and the philosophy of action have but an apparent and
superficial similarity; actually, they differ profoundly, as their differing
conclusions about man clearly demonstrate.

Although the term *"phenomenology of action"* is not his, Blondel's
first intention has justly been described by this phrase. The phrase is
justified since his account of action is neither phenomenal nor ontological. He is not primarily concerned with the phenomenal description of
human actions but with rendering present, through that phenomenal
veil, the essence of human action; he is, at this point, content simply to
identify that essence as it appears, without determining its ontological
status. His phenomenological inspection of the structure of human
action proceeds on a hypothesis which is never allowed to reach the
stage of assertion. His hypothesis is that human action represents a
closed or "determined" system. This is to say, action is a system in
which the available forces or powers are always sufficient, without the
invocation of external forces, to realize the end of the action, which is,
by any description, simply the *act* of that action. This is not an arbitrary hypothesis; it is suggested by the conception of action both in
physics and in psychology. However, the purpose of the phenomeno-

logical inspection is not to validate or invalidate this hypothesis. It is to render the essence of human action present and apparent.

Every human action appears under the form of *will*. The notion of will in Blondel must be carefully distinguished from the meaning of that term in some of the other contexts in which it appears; in a faculty psychology, for instance. His notion of will is rather close to that of Spinoza and shares many of the characteristics of the Spinozan *conatus*. Will is nothing but life itself apprehended as *action* in the sense noted above; it is the apprehension of that constitutive dynamism in its élan toward its own act. Therefore, the will is wholly immanent to action, and action is in no sense the product of will.

Within will, phenomenological inspection reveals a fundamental dualism. This is the dualism between the *willing will* and the *willed will*. The form of this dualism is similar to that which the Italian philosopher Gentile will establish in the *act of thought* between *pensiero pensante* and *pensiero pensato*, *thinking thought* and *thought thought*. It is important not to be caught in the play of words but to fix the meaning Blondel has in mind. By *willed will* Blondel means the individual transactions of the human subject as these are distinguishable in the life-flow. These are the individual decisions by which specific, limited, and identifiable objects are pursued, usually with some degree of awareness but almost always, he notes, with an awareness that is not wholly free from deception or illusion. The most noteworthy characteristic of these transactions, which are frequently conceived (by Croce, for example, with his positivism of the act) as constituting the total concreteness of the human will and action, is that they can be denominated only externally; i.e., they can only be fixed in their determinable and identifiable character by elements extrinsic to the action of willing itself. All the determinants of a specific decision derive from its circumstances; as Ortega y Gasset would presently say, from the object willed (whether immanent or transcendent). Blondel notes that the entire world of culture is in this sense the creation of will. It is the product and expression of man's creative will within the world, that is, under circumstances. Similarly, a life, in terms of its concrete identifiable decisions and options is the work and the expression of the creative will of the individual as circumstanced.

Seen from within, the configuration of the specific acts of will, and their content, the realm of the *willed will*, alters profoundly. All of those determining and identifying lineaments, which impart plurality and an illusory firmness of outline to these acts of will, dissolve. The world of the *willed will* dissolves into the world of the *willing will*. This is the will, action, in the pure state in which it reveals itself, not as action to this or that end, not as will which has a determinate and finite end or content, but as pure will, infinite both in itself and in its object. With this dissolution of the world of the *willed will* into the infinity of the *willing will*, the notion of action as a closed system, the hypothesis under which his phenomenological inspection of action has been conducted, also disappears. The sum of the concrete, determined acts of will and the world of values which it creates is never adequate to realize or fulfill the infinity of the willing will, its essential boundlessness, its fundamental orientation to the infinite. Not only are these two orders of willing incommensurate and incommensurable, but the order of concrete and finite acts of will, taken together or in the singularity of the constituting acts, must be recognized as a deviation from the infinity of the willing will, an attempt to pour off that infinity into the cup of finite satisfaction. In and through the world of the willed will, life as action, as willing will, is ever reaching for something beyond, for something which responds to the infinity within itself. The economy of will and its objects as a determined system is shattered and revealed to be but the surface fragmentation of the seamless will to the infinite which is the purity of human life as action.

The discovery of this disequilibrium within his life as action, the discovery of the incommensurability between the world of the willed will and the pure élan of the willing will, confronts man with the decisive choice of his life as will. The choice is deceptively simple. He may enclose himself within the world of the willed will, and shutting out the perspective of infinity, elect an absolute immanence, as Croce bids him do. (In justice to Croce, since his name has entered the discussion, it should be noted that he introduced the notion of intensive infinity, an idea hardly novel in the context of philosophical romanticism, i.e., the idea that infinity is sought in the concrete and individual act or transaction, as the poet seeks absolute beauty in every line.) Or man may open himself to that infinity, to the transcendent and unknowable which beckons with the promise of an infinite object, God himself. It is clear in what direction the decisive weight in this option must, in Blondel's view, fall. To enclose oneself in finitude, in absolute immanence, is to truncate one's life, which is constitutively orientated toward the infinite. It is to doom oneself to incompleteness, to stop short of integrity. It is to surrender to the world which is one's own creature and which, in its essence, is the sign and index of one's unfulfilled will. In Blondel's view, the option must be for the infinite. Must man, he complains, will infinitely but never will the infinite?

Yet a peril is inherent in this option of the infinite. This peril lies in the delusion that, since the infinite or transcendent is the only commensurate object of the infinity of man's will, the infinite can be willed as such. It cannot be, and here lies the deepest paradox of man's nature. Here also is the point which differentiates Blondel's doctrine from classical romanticism—that sickness with the infinite, as it has been called—as well as from Croce's neo-romanticism of the absolute immanent or of the intensive infinite. Blondel sees neither of these doctrines as consonant with the full phenomenological essence of man. What is proper to man is neither the vain willing of the formless infinite nor enclosure within the endless finite. Man's essence is openness or, in a sense, *waiting*. Thus, action itself must take the form of openness and waiting.

It is at this point that the relevance of these reflections for his apologetic purpose becomes apparent. Openness to the infinite, waiting for the word of the infinite, is the essential disposition of the human spirit in its primal integrity. Openness or waiting is the form of that integrity when the essence of man is grasped phenomenologically. It can go to the infinite by no act of its own, but, by its own act, it can open itself to the infinite. This is the basic attitude of faith and of religion. This attitude is what Blondel calls "transnaturality of human nature." Transnaturality is the justification, within the very structure of the human essence, for the acceptance of supernatural revelation and for the order of grace; for revelation and grace are the coming of the infinite to man and the completion of man through his union with the infinite under the form and the economy of grace. The religious life, not in the vague sense of natural religion or of the romantic world-longing, but in the concrete sense of the acceptance of God's manifestation of himself to man, is the fulfilling and integrating act of human nature.

These few indications do little more than suggest the direction and hint at the richness of Blondel's insight. Despite the opposition which his ideas have aroused from many, many quarters, their force has progressively made itself felt and has perceptibly altered the tone of the philosophy of religion in many ambients.

D. *Lucien Laberthonnière*

For a considerable time, the thought of Laberthonnière lay under the shadow of his alleged affiliation with the vague movement of modernism. But the period of the terror of modernism having definitively abated, his thought is being reconsidered. Seen in its own right, it is readily recognized as a weighty, though by no means decisive, contribution to the effort to construct a philosophy of Christian integralism. His fundamental ideas are to be found in the following works, a number of them published after his death in 1932: *Essais de philosophie religieuse* [Essays in religious philosophy], 1903; *Réalisme chrétien et idéalisme grec* [Christian realism and Greek idealism], 1904; *Critique de la conception aristotélicienne du christianisme* [Criticism of the Aristotelian conception of Christianity], 1933; *Esquisse d'une philosophie personnaliste* [Essay toward a personalist philosophy], 1942.

A priest of the Oratory, Laberthonnière takes his basic inspiration from the Augustian tradition of that congregation. (It will be remembered that Newman was also a member of the Oratory.) His chief concern in philosophy is to provide the instrument for a new apologetic for the Christian and Catholic faith. In this effort he takes a firm stand against the traditional Thomism (firmer than that of Blondel, who, as his thought advanced, made many concessions to it). Laberthonnière felt that a more vital basis must be found for the presentation of the Catholic faith to the world and for the penetration of Catholic teaching.

The basic idea of modern philosophy, he holds, is that there is no truth which man must "suffer," which he must passively accept. Such truth would be slavery and not liberty, death and not life, hence, not truth, which, as Christ himself has said, is both freedom and life. Philosophy is not an abstract discipline before which man is contemplative. It is a force which pierces to the ideal and living sources of life; it expresses itself in a way of life. Every metaphysics involves a way of life, and every way of life a metaphysics. Ideas, to be understood, must be lived, must be forms of lived experience; and the only true and full manner of possessing ourselves in our experience and not being passive before it or possessed by it is through ideas. Man seeks certainty of being, but this certainty must always have the character of lived experience, not abstract assent to an abstract proposition (cf. *Essais de philosophie religieuse,* pp. xvi, 4–5, 8–9, 14–15, 45–47, 103–105). The echoes of Newman's distinction between notional and real assent are strong.

The consequences of this view are drawn in the essay *Réalisme chrétien et idéalisme grec,* with direct application to the problem of a Christian philosophy and of apologetics. By idealism Laberthonnière understands the intellectualistic heritage of Greek, and especially Aristotelian, thought. He considers the notion of truth inherent in this tradition erroneous. Even more erroneous is the effort made by classical theology to constrict the living truth of Christianity into the conceptual molds of Aristotelian intellectualism (cf. *Réalisme,* pp. 74–80; *Critique de la conception aristotélicienne du christianisme, passim*). That effort made Christian truth an imposed truth, not a lived or experienced truth. It thus destroyed man as a person, for personality is living possession of truth. To reach truth as living, we must take our point of departure from within ourselves, for no true knowledge comes from without. (cf. *Réalisme, passim; Essais,* pp. 125, 37–40). The inward possession and affirmation of being is the end of philosophy. But to affirm being means to recognize the *One* who *Is,* that is, God. Only in the affirmation of God do we affirm ourselves by positing that assent to truth in which our own actuality as persons consists.

These, Laberthonnière affirms, must be the philosophical presuppositions of any apologetic of the faith which hopes, on the one hand, to penetrate to the nature of faith itself and, on the other, to defend the faith before the bar of modern critical opinion. In nature itself, our nature as living vehicles of truth, are to be found the exigencies of the supernatural order which Christianity offers. Those exigencies do not belong to nature simply as nature; they belong to the free gift of God, who offers them to man from the superabundance of his love. However, they do complete possibilities and aspirations which correspond fully to man's nature. Without the realization of the supernatural life, man's nature would not cease to be nature, but it would fall short of all that is possible for it under this disposition and dispensation of God's grace. The gift of the possibility of supernatural life is made to mankind through Christ and the Church, which is brotherhood in the truth that Christ brings. Planted in the heart of man and in his midst in the Church, this truth is not an inert thing but a principle of life and growth. Faith, the Church, and man as an individual must live this truth, follow it, and grow in it; every man, every age, and the Church in every age must experience it and fulfill it in the concrete forms of life. In this way the faith must appear to modern man, not as a dead weight from the past imposed upon his spirit, but as an invitation and a challenge to rise, in terms of the conditions of his own life, to the level of supernatural faith and grace which God offers him through Christ and the Church.

Readings

Very little material on this movement of thought is available in English. The best account is to be found in M. F. Sciacca's *Contemporary Trends in Philosophy,* translated by A. Salerno (Notre Dame, Ind.: University of Notre Dame Press, 1965), pp. 36–41.

I. General

Vidler, Alec. *A Variety of Catholic Modernists.* The Sarum Lectures in the University of Oxford for the year 1968–69. Cambridge: Cambridge University Press, 1970.

II. Particular Figures

John Henry Cardinal Newman
Boekraad, A. J. *The Personal Conquest of Truth According to John Henry Newman.* Louvain: Editions Nauwelaerts, 1955.

Bouyer, Louis. *Newman: His Life and Spirituality.* New York: Kenedy, 1958.
Culler, A. D. *The Imperial Intellect.* New Haven: Yale University Press, 1955.
Flanagan, Philip. *Newman, Faith and the Believer.* Westminster, Md.: Newman Press, 1946.
Kenny, Terence. *Newman's Political Thought.* New York: Longmans, Green, 1957.
Walgrave, J. H. *Newman the Theologian.* New York: Sheed & Ward, 1960.

Maurice Blondel

Berger, Gaston. "The Different Trends in Contemporary French Philosophy." *Philosophy and Phenomenological Research,* VII (1946), 1–21.
Bouillard, Henri. "The Thought of Maurice Blondel." *International Philosophical Quarterly,* III (1963), 392–402.
McNeill, J. J. *The Blondelian Synthesis.* Leiden: E. J. Brill, 1966.
Poncelot, Albert. "The Christian Philosophy of Maurice Blondel." *International Philosophical Quarterly,* V (1965), 564–593.
Somerville, James M. "Maurice Blondel: 1861–1945." *Thought,* XXXVI (1961), 371–410.
_____. *Total Commitment: Blondel's L'Action.* Washington, D. C.: Corpus Books, 1968.
Trethowan, Illtyd, O.S.B. "Blondel's Le Sens Chretien." *Downside Review,* LXXXV (1967), 367–384.
Valensin, Auguste. "Maurice Blondel: A Study of His Achievement." *Dublin Review,* CXIV (1950), 90–101.

Lucien Laberthonnière

Ratté, John. *Three Modernists.* New York: Sheed & Ward, 1967.
Vidler, A. *The Modernist Movement in the Roman Church: Its Origins and Outcome.* Cambridge, England: Cambridge University Press, 1934.

CHAPTER II

Absolute Historicism and Actual Idealism

Introduction: The Revival of Idealism in Italy

The apogée of positivism in the mid-nineteenth century had barely been reached when a strong reaction against it appeared. This reaction took the form of a revival of idealism in a multitude of forms. This reaction, widespread in European and American culture, possesses a special interest in its Italian form. Here it was eventually to inspire two of the most impressive speculative constructions of the first half of the twentieth century: the *absolute historicism* of Benedetto Croce and the *actual idealism* of Giovanni Gentile.

These philosophical positions, though Italian in origin, are really European in inspiration and in ultimate influence. Croce, in two important documents—his autobiography, *Contributo alla critica di me stesso (Benedetto Croce: An Autobiography)*, last edition 1931, and the concluding chapter of his *Storia d'Italia 1871–1915 (History of Italy 1871–1915)*, 1929—gave a firsthand account of this revival. Its center was the University of Naples, where a tradition of idealism had long existed. Its three most representative figures were Augusto Vera (1813–1885), Bertrando Spaventa (1817–1883), and Piero Martinetti (1872–1943). Vera attached himself directly to the classic Hegelian center. Martinetti, a more original thinker, was to prove a chief inspiration of the movement of Christian spiritualism. Spaventa, though not the most speculative interpreter of Hegel, was the most important figure in this revival, for he exercised direct influence on Croce and even stronger influence on Gentile.

A. *Benedetto Croce* (1866–1952)

Benedetto Croce, the dominant figure in Italian philosophy for half a century, was born on February 25, 1866. His long life was dominated

223

by a single purpose: the qualitative transformation of Italian culture and the restoration of the Italian cultural influence to its once-commanding international position. To this end he created, as his organ, the review *La critica,* which during his lifetime, remained one of the most authoritative and influential in Europe.

Croce always repudiated the status of philosopher *ex-professo.* He was, as Santayana called himself, the eternal student. His life was devoted to learning and inquiry. His philosophical activity arose as a natural movement within this career of study: on the one hand, as the effort to clarify the methodological principles of inquiry and, on the other, as the effort to reach first principles in whatever area of inquiry engaged his attention. The Crocean philosophy resides more in this inner movement of the life of inquiry than in any set of doctrines. Always responsive to the demands of philosophy as ultimate inquiry, Croce never hesitated to reexamine, revise, and refine any doctrinal position he might have assumed. A doctrinal exposition of Croce's thought would, therefore, clearly be a distortion. An effort must be made to follow the living movement of inquiry through the various orders of problems which engaged it and its successive efforts at inward clarification in terms of methods and principles.

Taking the founding of *La critica* as the crucial event in Croce's intellectual life, we shall first review his speculations prior to that event. All of the basic themes of Croce's thought receive their first formulation during this period. We shall then consider Croce's sole, and admittedly not wholly successful, effort to formulate a *system* of philosophy, the "Philosophy of Spirit." Finally, we shall follow the later reflections through which he arrived at a characterization of his position as "absolute historicism." The number of Croce's published works makes any review of them here impossible. For bibliographical information the reader is referred to *L'opera di Benedetto Croce: Bibliografia a cura di Silvano Borsari,* Naples, 1964.

1. The Seminal Phase: To 1902

Croce initiated his intellectual activity with works of historical research in literary and art history, the history of customs and of political thought and events. Three basic themes of philosophical reflection were suggested by his scholarly investigations: the aesthetic theme, involving the nature of art and the conditions of literary and artistic criticism; the historiographic theme, involving the nature of history and the conditions of historiographical inquiry; and finally, the ethico-political theme, involving the nature of political action and its conjunction with ethical principles. These themes of philosophical reflection find expression in a number of fundamental documents. These are: *La storia ridotto sotto il concetto generale dell'arte* [History subsumed under the general concept of art] (now in *Primi Passi*, 1919, pp. 3–72); *Tesi fondamentali di un'estetica come scienza dell'espressione e linguistica generale* [Fundamental theses of an aesthetics conceived as the science of expression and general linguistic], 1900 (cf. Croce: *La prima forma dell' "Estetica" e della "Logica,"* 1924, pp. 1–118); and, finally, *Materialismo storico ed economia marxistica* [*Historical Materialism and the Economics of Karl Marx*], 1900).

The first of these documents is an ambivalent attempt to bring the notion of history under the general concept of art. Here the two most fundamental ideas of his thought—art and history—are encountered in an unresolved, even paradoxical relation to each other. The essay is a first effort to clarify this relation by one of the simplest processes available, that of the reduction, without residue, of one concept to the other. The concept of art is dominant, and it is to art that he seeks to reduce history. Eventually, it will become clear that this reduction is invalid. While the form of historical expression must always meet artistic or aesthetic conditions, the inner spiritual reality of history appears to be autonomous. (However, it might be remarked that the reduction to art seems more plausible than the contrasting efforts of positivism to reduce history to science.) In the reduction process, certain elements of both concepts, art and history, emerge which are to remain constant in his thought. The first is the lyrical character of art. It is the emphasis on the lyrical character of art which places the autonomy of history most in evidence. History resists lyricism and demands another principle to define its relation to reality. Croce will eventually find this other principle in his ethico-political view of history.

No such ambivalence or ambiguity attaches to the second of his fundamental works, the *Tesi Fondamentali*. This document contains all of the basic insights which will later structure his first important book, the *Estetica*. These insights include: the notion of art as intuition; the first form of the idea of the lyrical character of art, of the concreteness of the image, and of the substantive principle of sentiment and its human resonances. Though continually reexamining and revising them, Croce remains faithful to these insights throughout his writings on aesthetics, from the *Estetica* to *La poesia* of 1936.

The essays on historical materialism are important for a number of reasons. The first is their value as a criticism of the themes they discuss. Croce's criticism of the Marxian theory of the falling rate of interest has become classic. The second lies in the fact that they introduce, though only remotely, Croce's ethico-political conception of history and his ethical liberalism, both firm bulwarks against Marxism and cred-

ited with damming the influence of theoretical Marxism in Italy for
many decades, until Antonio Gramsci reformulated the Marxian position. Most important, however, is the strong humanistic spirit which
animates them. Against Marxian determinism, Croce emphasizes the
primacy of the human spirit, its creative power, and its ethical character. The economic structure of society is recognized as possessing laws
proper to itself; but it is also seen as subject to man's freedom of action
to his ethical conscience, and his concepts of justice and charity, for its
ultimate form. History is conceived as the field for the creative energies of man in the generation of values, not as the theater for the play
of blind and deterministic forces. Thus, there are two levels of significance in the essays: the precise and technical criticism which Croce
advances against Marxism and the doctrines of Engels, and his own
emerging spiritual vision of man in history as creative and responsible
consciousness and the generator of values. The gap between these
levels will widen. Marxism will prove a passing object of Croce's interest; the spiritualistic vision will deepen and broaden into a conclusive
historical humanism.

2. The Philosophy of Spirit

Between 1902 and 1917 Croce published four volumes which together constitute a philosophical "system" to which he assigns the title
"philosophy of spirit." The formulation of this systematic statement
constitutes an important phase of Croce's philosophical development.
Later he is to assume a complex attitude toward the achievement,
never wholly committing himself to this system and never wholly dis-
owning it. The present treatment will propose the following points for
brief comment: a) The character of the works which constitute the
system; b) Croce and the spirit of system in philosophy; c) The meaning of spirit and the distinction and dialectic of its moments; d) The
moments of spirit and their internal relation; e) The role of the philosophy of spirit in Croce's subsequent philosophical development.

a. *The Works Comprising the Philosophy of Spirit.* The first work
of the "system" is the *Estetica come scienza dell'espressione e linguistica generale* [Aesthetics as the science of expression and general lin-
guistic]. It is considered the most fundamental of Croce's works and
the foundation of the system of spirit. It has its roots in the *Tesi fondamentali*, mentioned above, and will prove the constant point of reference of all Croce's subsequent treatments of the problem of art. Within
the system of spirit, it considers art as expression and intuition. Art in
this sense is both a fundamental moment and the pervasive form of
presence of spirit both to itself and to the other. Art is a moment of

spirit in dialectical relation to the other moments; but it is also the form of all the other moments and of spirit itself as a dialectical system, for it is only through expression, which is always artistic, i.e., subject to aesthetic principles, that spirit is actualized.

The *Logica* (*Logic*) of 1909 clearly has its roots in the *Lineamenti di una logica come scienza del concetto puro* [Outlines of a logic as the science of the pure concept] of 1905. It finds its prolongation in Croce's subsequent preoccupation with problems of method, culminating in his theory of philosophy as the methodology of historiography, which is in turn the prologue to the conception of philosophy as absolute historicism.

The *Filosofia della pratica* (*Philosophy of the Practical*), constituting the third part of the system of spirit, has its antecedent in Croce's early and constant preoccupation with ethics and social action; it contains the principles of both his moral stoicism and his ethico-political view of history.

The fourth and concluding volume of the series, *Teoria e storia della storiografia* (*The Theory and History of Historiography*), looks backward, on the one hand, to the reduction of history to the concept of art and forward, on the other hand, to the later, classical statement of his view of history in *La storia come pensiero e come azione* [History as thought and action] and the synthesizing essay on the concept of philosophy as absolute historicism. Between these points, it touches on Croce's many other statements on history, such as those to be found in the *Logic* on the nature and universality of the historical judgment.

b. *Croce and the Spirit of System.* The bibliographical notes given above illustrate one point: Croce's genius is essentially critical; his form of thought, progressive and problematic. Moving from concrete problems, his thought describes a spiral, returning always to those problems in order to pass beyond them. His thought has no basic affinity to the spirit of system. It is especially alien to that conception which finds in system the ground from which a deductive and anticipatory movement toward the actual can begin. The unity in his thought is the vital and dynamic unity of the critical play between problems and principles. Nevertheless, in the "Philosophy of Spirit," Croce did undertake the construction of a system of sorts. This fact demands some comment.

Any explanation must be circumstantial. The circumstances which make this systematic construction comprehensible are two. The first is intrinsic to Croce's thought; the other is provided by his historical orientation. Immanent to his thought was the need for unity and coherence, even for aesthetic symmetry. The first image of that unity was presented historically by the Hegelian system and by the romantic conception of system in general, as well as by the logical rigor of Herbart. Croce's first philosophical effort, consequently, took the form of a systematic construction on this model. However, he lived to appreciate the fact that the unity native to his own thought was not a unity of system but a critical unity. He nevertheless was not tempted to abandon the system he had constructed. Instead he turned it to his own uses, making it the matrix within which his critical thought moved. It became a methodological schema rather than a metaphysical construct. The real meaning of the philosophy of spirit, consequently, is the use Croce made of it. It is not an "iron parenthesis" in his thought but a metaphysical enterprise which survived as a methodological tool.

c. *The Meaning of Spirit.* Croce's "system" is a philosophy of "spirit." What then is "spirit"?

Spirit is the concrete, existing human person. The concept has no other content; it refers to nothing transcendent to the person. But spirit is the human person seen from a particular angle: as the creator of values. The generation of value not only characterizes the human person; it defines him. The activity for the generation of value is his entire human reality.

The human existent person achieves the status of spirit only in his effort to realize and express *universal* values. In this act he transcends himself, creating that realm of expressed and communicated human values which, in its totality, we call culture. The human spirit is completely immanent in its works, in culture, though at no given moment in history is it exhausted by the immense collectivity of the works of culture. As a consequence, there is but one path to the concrete knowledge of the human spirit—by way of its works. The quest of spirit in and through its works is, finally, a work of spirit itself. It is the essence of what Croce means by "history," the key to what he means by "absolute historicism."

The purpose of the self-knowledge of spirit in history is not narcissism, sterile self-contemplation. It is critical knowledge, by which spirit reaches its own *principles.* Historical knowledge is thus the supreme reflective moment of the self-creation of spirit. In history, spirit discovers the abiding springs of its creative and expressive life.

These reflections define the relation between the individual and the universality of spirit. Some critics have said that Croce annihilates the individual, submerging him completely in the universal spirit. This would not seem to be the case. The universal values of the human spirit are always the creation, not of an abstract or transcendent absolute spirit, but of historical human individuals. And the full value of the universal insights of the human spirit is realized only in the individual consciousness. But it is the presence of the universal, as term of achievement and as principle of human communication and solidarity, that defines the humanity and the spirituality of the individual. Outside this circle, he remains an abstraction. Thus, individual and universal are completely reciprocal and immanent in each other in the order of spirit; each can exist only on the basis of the reality of the other.

The philosophy of spirit as system undertakes to identify and relate the forms of spirit in their specific characters and in their mutual relations through the concrete historical unity of spirit. The first question Croce proposes is the following: Why does the unity of spirit pass through the process of self-distinction into a diversity of forms or moments? The reply is clear: Spirit enters into the dialectical process of self-distinction in order to achieve the plenitude of its presence to itself. Before such distinction, its unity can only be the unity of indetermination. Plenitude of presence demands the explication of the inherent distinctions and their reunification as explicated.

The fundamental distinction within spirit is that between thought and action, theory and practice. Thought is the moment of inner clarification of action. The human spirit is entirely action, for it is wholly movement and life. Without the inner illumination of thought, action is casual and spastic; thought renders it reflective, self-possessed and directed. Croce is not sympathetic with the notion of thought as contemplation; the natural terminus of thought is action, just as the source of form in action is thought.

Within each of these moments, thought and action, Croce distinguishes two further moments. Within theory he distinguishes poetry (art) and logic; within action, the economic and the ethical moments.

Poetry or art is intuition, the first form of knowledge. It is knowledge of singulars, of the individual. Perception of an individual is intuition. But intuition, unlike perception, need not be intuition of a real object; it embraces real and unreal alike in a pure undifferentiated unity of presence. Intuition is *expression*. The intuitive activity is actual only to the degree that it expresses. It is an illusion to think that there can be intuition without expression. Art is not intuitive expression of a particular sort; the difference between "common intuition" and "artistic intuition" is one of degree, not of kind. The difference concerns the purity of presence in each. Poetry is the name assigned to the pure expressive moment of artistic intuition. Finally, Croce asserts that poetry is the source of language; aesthetics and linguistics are, in their philosophical form, one.

Logic is the realm of the pure concept. The "purity" of the pure concept is established against empiricism and also against mysticism. The first reduces the concept to a form of the practical; the latter denies that reality can be expressed conceptually. The essential character of the pure concept, as it was of the moment of poetry, is expressivity. Thus, the aesthetic moment pervades the whole life of spirit. To expressivity are added other characteristics proper to the pure concept: universality, omnirepresentativeness, concreteness. These proper characteristics serve to contradistinguish the pure concept from the image, on the one hand, and from the "pseudo-concept," on the other. The latter belongs properly, not to the theoretical, but to the practical moment. Pseudo-concepts are practical fictions with a practical end; they provide the structure of the natural sciences. Finally, the concept is expressed in laugnage as the definitive judgment in which the unity of subject and object as well as that of essence and existence is realized. The latter unity establishes the unity of logical thought and historical thought. The definitive judgment and the historical judgment are one. History, therefore, is philosophical knowledge of the real, while philosophy can be born only historically and is historically conditioned. The unity of philosophy and history is, therefore, a logical principle.

The practical moments of spirit are two: economic and ethical. Their common principle is volition. Between volition and action there exists the same kind of identity that exists between intuition and expression in the aesthetic moment. There is no real intention without effective volition or action, just as there is no real intuition without expression. Volition is volition either of the individual or of the universal. In the first case volition is economic, in the second ethical. Economic volition is autonomous with respect to the ethical; there are actions devoid of morality and hence perfectly economic. Ethical action, by contrast, transpires always with respect to the economic moment. There is no pure moral action, no volition of the universal as such. Ethical action always has its center in an economic value, a particular and concrete good. It seeks to transpose this value to the universal plane, the plane of principle. Thus, for example, no statesman can will peace, for peace is a contentless universal; he must will all of the concrete elements which constitute the situation called peace. The ethical life is a constant inward transformation of the concrete economic actions of life. The ethical life has no content distinct from the economic but represents the qualitative transformation of the economic life in its content and principle. The specific ethical principle, in view of which the ethical transformation of the economic takes place, is for Croce liberty. Liberty is the principle governing both the morality of the individual life and the ethico-political character of collective life. His ethical point of view reaches full expression in his view of history as the history of liberty, the theory of ethico-political history.

Each of the moments of spirit mentioned above is taken up by Croce in one volume of the series constituting the "Philosophy of Spirit": art in the *Estetica,* the theory of the pure concept in the *Logica,* the economic and ethical moments of will in the *Filosofia della pratica.* In the fourth volume, *Teoria e storia della storiografia,* Croce addresses a more basic problem: What is the ultimate category of spirit, i.e., the category in which spirit must think itself, be present to itself, in its totality? The answer he provides is *history.* History, as the supreme and ultimate category of spirit, is not the abstract becoming of idealist metaphysics. It is the concrete becoming of spirit in the unity and diversity of its *a priori* forms. Even more concretely, it is the self-positing of spirit in the unity and multiplicity of its concrete historical expressions and in the unity of the reflective act by which it discerns its own movement and presence in those expressions. Here we encounter, for the first time, an explicit formulation of the thesis of philosophy as "absolute historicism."

d. *The Internal Relations of the Moments of Spirit and the Ultimate Unity of Spirit.* The distinction of the moments of spirit has been undertaken for one purpose: the preparation for the concrete unity of spirit. Antecedent to such distinction, the unity of spirit is abstract: the unity of indifferentiation. The concrete unity can be established only after its specific moments have been clearly distinguished from one another and then related or synthesized into a unity which includes and is based upon that distinction. What is this relation, and what is the quality of the unity to which it leads?

Croce's reply to this question can be found in his doctrine of the *circularity* of spirit. Spirit achieves its ultimate unity neither by obliterating all distinctions between its moments, nor by reducing one of its moments to another, nor finally by making one of its moments supreme, as Hegel had done to the logical. This unity is achieved by way of the dynamic process by which the distinct moments of spirit engender each other in a circular movement. Thus, the distinction of theory and practice is seen to demand their synthesis in the concreteness of spirit. This synthesis is not, however, the reduction or subordination of one to the other, but it is the reciprocal demand (logical and existential) that the positing of the one creates for the other. Action generates the demand for thought as its inner moment of clarification; thought demands action as its terminus, short of which it lacks all actuality and degenerates into mere contemplation or speculation. The same relation exists between the moments which Croce has distinguished within each of these larger moments: between the moment of art and the logical moment, between the economic and the ethical moments of *praxis.* The moment of art or poetry demands the universalization and necessitation which presence achieves in the pure concept; equally, the pure concept demands concretion in the image, in the individual, lest it become an abstraction, an empty form. The economic moment, basically orientated toward the immediacy of the environment and conditions of concrete action, demands the reflective universalization of the ethical moment for its elevation to principle; but the latter equally demands a return to the concreteness of the economic moment, for here alone, through its transforming power, does the ethical principle gain significance. Thus, the inner relation of the distinct moments of spirit is reciprocity, and the law of the movement of spirit among them is the law of circularity. The circular, self-generating movement of spirit through its reciprocally related moments constitutes the concrete process of spirit in history.

e. *The Role of the Philosophy of Spirit in Croce's Thought.* The "philosophy of spirit" is neither the whole of Croce's philosophy nor an "iron parenthesis" within his thought. The philosophy of spirit performed a specific and complex function in his intellectual development. In the first place, it served to create an all-inclusive framework within which Croce might conduct the basic critical work to which he was devoted. Criticism demanded an inner clarification in terms of apodictic principles related to each other. This is what Croce sought to construct in the philosophy of spirit. No sooner had it been completed, however, than he perceived that, as system, it now presented itself as an obstacle to be overcome. A return to the concreteness of experience and expression had to be achieved. If not, the absoluteness of the system of spirit would become a procrustean bed on which all concrete expression would be stretched to be tortured and mutilated. The function of the philosophy of spirit as an obstacle then became to define the limit against which the concrete movement of spirit in history must be discerned. In a word, it had to be converted from a quasi-metaphysical structure into a methodological process.

This is the origin of Croce's view that philosophy is the methodological moment of historiography. This formula was not framed to denigrate philosophy. It was framed to achieve the return from the abstract point of the philosophy of spirit as system to its concrete immanence in historical process as the clarifying principle of the work of criticism, the act by which spirit renders itself reflectively present to itself in the concrete order of its works. For this reason Croce never was attached to the philosophy of spirit simply as a speculative construction. Nor did he ever abandon it. His constant aim was to render it available for the concrete and specific work of criticism.

3. Development Subsequent to the Philosophy of Spirit

Subsequent to the philosophy of spirit, Croce's thought enters a period of development and achievement substantially richer than that which preceded its composition. This increased richness lies not only in the range of themes and problems addressed and the forms of expression essayed but in the marked elevation of insight which characterizes the treatment in each area. Freed from the systematic incubus, yet having profited from that effort, Croce is able to give freer play to his greatest native gift, his critical powers. To this period belong his most mature works in the areas of his constant concern: aesthetics, moral and political philosophy, and historiography and the theory of history.

a. *Aesthetic Development.* The problem of art always remains the Crocean problem *par excellence.* In the period subsequent to the philosophy of spirit, his concern with this problem becomes more intense in every way and his reflection presses far beyond the position taken in the first *Estetica.* The documentation for this intensified concern is to be found in such works as the *Nuovi saggi di estetica* [New essays in aesthetics], 1920, and *Ultimi saggi* [Recent essays], 1935. The culmination of this development is to be found in *La poesia* [Poetry], 1936. The process of development turns about two concepts: the *lyricism* and the *humanity* of art and poetry.

The development of these concepts represents a dual movement in Croce's thought: the concept of lyricism, the movement toward an intensification of the aesthetic experience in its purity and autonomy; the concept of the humanity of art, the movement toward the extension and broadening of that experience in its relevance to the whole range of possible spiritual experience. The medium for the extension of the aesthetic experience implied in the concept of the humanity of art is the further concept of *sentiment.*

In western culture, the lyric poem has always represented the moment of purest distillation and expression of experience; first, experience *of*—of the world, of love, of sorrow—but, ultimately, the pure sense of the human *to be* as it reveals itself in the concrete subject. This traditional evaluation of lyricism is Croce's point of departure. Art is the moment of pure experience in its most intense and expressive form. To this classical conception, however, he adds a new dimension by associating lyricism with intuition, which had already played a fundamental role in his aesthetic theory. At that point intuition and expression were identified. Now the further note of lyricism is added; art becomes the pure lyric expression, expression untrammeled by any of the countless conditions and restrictions which surround and qualify experience of the direct and immediate sentiment of being in the human subject. Above all, lyricism releases art from the limitations of the personal. All genuine art has been restless within the limits of the personal experience of the artist and has striven to transcend those limits in order to reach the heart of existence in itself, in its universality. The lyric expression is the *personal leap* beyond the personal to the universally human. It is their lyric quality which makes the words of Shakespeare forever indelibly his own but forever resonant in the heart of every man.

The humanity of art is intimately related to this idea of art as lyric intuition and expression. The humanity of art extends the human range of art, as lyricism had deepened its intensity. The non-differentiation of real and unreal, which had been present in the notion of intuition and lyricism, is transcended. By the humanity of art Croce means a number of things. He means, first of all, that all human experience, actual and possible, is contained, in essence, in every work of art. He means that there is no human mind and heart which the poem, the authentic work of artistic expression, cannot touch, cannot awaken to a sense of the condition in which every human mind and heart lives intimately and which, at the same time, it shares with all men, living and dead, past, present, and to come. He means, finally, that the poem represents the true transcendental principle of human life, the principle which is given in all experience of life but which is beyond that experience in that it lays bare what that experience *means,* what makes it possible and necessary; and in so doing it lifts the weight of darkness and doubt from the human spirit. The true community of men, in their direct and immediate humanity, is established by the aesthetic moment through this lyric character of art. Here, in the concrete moment of the poem, far more than in the abstract unity of the pure concept, mankind lives.

b. *Ethical Liberalism.* Croce's political theory is more closely bound up with the structure of the philosophy of spirit than any other dimension of his thought. At the same time, it is very closely related to the historical drama of the times through which he lived. This historical period was marked by 1) the decline of the pre-First World War Italy, which had witnessed the *Risorgimento* of modern Italy and which Croce, to the end, considered the age of heroes; 2) the "iron parenthesis" of Fascism; and 3) the second *Risorgimento,* the rebirth of a free Italy after the cataclysm of the Second World War. The historical experience of his time convinced Croce of the transcendence of the ethical moment in the order of political values. It gave birth to his *ethical liberalism.*

Classical liberalism, the liberalism which had assisted at the birth of the modern world was not an *ethical* liberalism. The moment of force and the form of utility were dominant in it. These lurked in the idea of free competition and in the theory of state protectionism. They guided the formation of the great national unities of modern Europe. (The formation of the modern Italian nation seemed an exception to this: Cf. Croce, *History of Europe in the Nineteenth Century* [New York, 1963]; also, Caponigri, *History and Liberty*, [London, 1955].) The idea of liberty which inspired this liberalism was an external liberty, only with difficulty to be distinguished from the free or uninhibited play of force against force. In the structure of the philosophy of spirit, this historical fact corresponded to the autonomy which Croce ascribed to the economic moment of spirit: the moment of force, impulse, and utility.

The First World War was the crisis of the world which that classical liberalism had built. In one sweeping gesture that war unmasked the force and violence which lay concealed beneath the official irenic rhetoric of classical liberalism and ushered in the century of violence, the century in which we live. In Italian historical experience, it ushered in Fascism, which revealed the violence and tyranny that lurked beneath the civil and free Italy which the *Risorgimento* has ostensibly created. This historical crisis precipitated a crisis within Croce's thought which involved the relative status of the ethical and the economic moments in the life of the spirit. Out of this crisis emerges his ethical liberalism, in which all Machiavellianism is overcome, and the normativeness and transcendence of the ethical over the economic and political moment is categorically asserted.

The keystone of the doctrine of ethical liberalism is the notion of liberty. The progressive formation of Croce's concept of liberty is still to be told, but its trajectory lies along the path of the interiorization of the seat of freedom. The character of liberty in classical liberalism had involved, on the one hand, freedom of action without interference and, on the other, moral unaccountability for action. The economic order (in Croce's sense of this term) is autonomous. This liberty of action readily becomes a thin mask for force, and that moral unaccountability becomes the seed of modern tyranny. At first, Croce's theory, resting on the autonomy of the economic order, had rather uncritically fostered this attitude. Law and politics, he had held, belonged to the economic order; they were thus essentially amoral. Now, however, he begins to apprehend that there can be no liberty resting on the amorality of action. The only liberty consonant with man and truly creative in history is liberty resting on the *a priori* justification of action in an ethical principle. The greatest manifestation of liberty is the self-limitation of power (the economic moment) by a universal moral principle. Only the person, the nation, the state which exercises this kind of self-limitation of power according to a universal ethical principle is free. Liberty is identical with this transcendence and normativeness of the ethical within the order of the economic. The myth of the autonomy of the economic order is exploded. Liberty and ethicalness are equated.

These reflections on liberty, force, power, and their actualization in the social and political order find expression first of all in Croce's celebrated historical writings: *The History of Europe in the Nineteenth Century, The History of Italy 1871–1915,* etc.; also in such analytic works as *Elementi di politica* [Elements of politics], 1925; *Etica e politica (Politics and Morals),* 1931; *Pagine politiche* [Pages on politics], 1945, and *Pensiero politico e politica attuale* [Political thought and contemporary politics], 1946. The culmination of these reflections was the famous address before the Congress of Bari at the war's close (in *Due anni di vita politica* [Two years of political life], 1948). They found their practical expression, at an ever-accelerating pace, in Croce's opposition to the Fascist regime and in his service as the rallying point of the liberal and civil forces in Italy after the cessation of conflict and during the difficult years of the formation of the present Italian Republic.

c. *Philosophy as "Absolute Historicism."* A recent historian of philosophy has noted that Croce's historicism must be differentiated from all other forms of modern historicism precisely by virtue of its claim to be "absolute historicism" (cf. Abbagnano, *Storia della filosofia,* 1963, III, 503). Our concern is to find the seat of this difference by asking what it is that Croce meant to convey by this definitive characterization of his thought.

In the simplest and most direct terms, he means that philosophy is possible only when it takes the form of history, that history is the supreme transcendental principle and the ultimate category of spirit, which renders present both the *a priori* conditions of spirit's intelligibility and the concrete synthesis of the infinite manifold of thought and action.

When it is formulated in this way, one readily sees that Croce had been moving toward this position from the beginning of his critical work. His insight into the concreteness of spirit as immanent in its works had led him to history in the most literal sense, i.e., the documents: the work of art, the work of literature, etc. These became, first, the objects of his critical analyses; eventually, however, under pressure of the need to comprehend his own operations, he was led to perform the critical operation in the Kantian sense, to determine the antecedent and inherent conditions of the type of expression he was addressing. This critical operation led him, by way of the polemic with naturalism, positivism, etc., to the concept of spirit. The discovery of spirit confronted him with the most fundamental question of all: that of the constitutive *a priori* principles and forms of spirit itself. The answer presently emerged: The principle of the life of spirit was history. Outside history there can be no reality, and all discourse about the real must eventually assume historical form. Philosophy itself, i.e., the self-establishing act of spirit, must be historiographic. History emerges as the supreme category of the real, and historical discourse, resting on the philosophical formulation of its own principles, as the normative form of significant expression.

B. *Giovanni Gentile* (1875–1944)

Giovanni Gentile, the most important Italian philosopher of this century, was born in Sicily in 1875. He attended the lectures of the Hegelian philosopher Jaja from 1893 to 1897 and through his influence came to know the works of Bertrando Spaventa, who was to become Gentile's intellectual mentor. The project of a "reformation" of the thought of Hegel, which Spaventa had envisaged, became Gentile's objective. In 1907 he succeeded to the chair of the history of philosophy at the University of Palermo, and in 1914 he was appointed to Jaja's chair at the University of Pisa. He went to Rome in 1917 as professor of theoretical philosophy, a post he left only to engage in the wider activities of political life as minister of education. He early became associated with Benedetto Croce in the work of *La critica* and in 1920 founded a personal organ of high scholarly quality, the Critical Journal of Italian Philosophy, and retained its direction until 1943.

In his *Introduzione alla filosofia* [Introduction to philosophy], Gentile wrote that "historically, actualist philosophy [the name he assigned his own position] is related to German philosophy from Kant to Hegel both directly and by way of the partisans, commentators, and critics which the German thinkers of that period found in Italy during the last century. But it is also related to Italian philosophy of the Renaissance (Telesius, Campanella, Bruno), to the great Neapolitan philosopher Giambattista Vico and to the restorers of Italian speculative thought during the age of the national *Risorgimento:* Galluppi, Rosmini and Giobert." While not rejecting this account of his derivation, students of Gentile's thought also see the influence of Fichte and of Spaventa; moreover, they tend to qualify Gentile's claim to descent from the thought of the Italian Renaissance by pointing out that this relationship rests more on the immanentistic interpretation which Gentile tended to impose on these thinkers than on any direct reading of their texts. The evident elements of transcendence in Campanella, Vico, and Rosmini make this genealogy less evident than Gentile would suggest.

The constant point of historical reference is Hegel. The project of the reformation of the Hegelian dialectic remains basic. Gentile's purpose is to "establish the equation between Hegelian becoming and the act of thought as the unique concrete logical category" (*Riforma della dialectica hegeliana*, pref.). Hegel, in Gentile's view, had taken being and non-being as abstract presuppositions of becoming. But being and non-being are not presuppositions of thought; they are the products of or abstractions from the concrete act of thought. Hegel's logic is only the apparent movement of "ideas which have been thought"; it is not the real becoming of "*pensiero pensante*," thought in its concrete actuality. This would seem to constitute Gentile's fundamental insight: the object of thought is the "act" of thought itself; in his own words, "thought which thought begins to think as other to itself" (*Riforma*, p. 25). What is thought is the act of thinking itself, as it objectifies itself. Outside of the act of thinking in its concrete actuality, there is no concrete object. The subject has consciousness of an object only to the degree to which it is aware of itself in the act of thinking; it posits the object in the moment of its becoming self-conscious. Gentile calls the method proper to this philosophy the method of "immanence." This method rests on the concept of the absolute concreteness of the real within the act of thought. It excludes transcendence of any order: God, nature, logic, law, historical reality as event. Even the "I" of thought, the subject, is absolutely immanent in this act and can in no wise be presupposed or substantialized.

Gentile develops the implications of this insight in a series of works, only the most important of which can be named here: *Sommario di pedagogia come scienza filosofica* [Summary of educational theory as a philosophical science], 2 vols., 1913–14; *La riforma della dialectica hegeliana* [The reformation of the Hegelian dialectic], 1913; *Teoria generale della spirito come atto puro (General Theory of the Spirit as Pure Act)*, 1916; *I fondamenti della filosofia del diritto* [Foundations of the philosophy of law], 1916; *Sistema di logica come teoria del conoscere* [System of logic as the theory of knowledge], 1917–24; *Discorsi di religione* [Discourses on religion], 1920; *La riforma dell'educazione (The Reform of Education)*, 1920; *Filosofia dell'arte* [Philosophy of art], 1931; *Introduzione alla filosofia* [Introduction to philosophy], 1933; and *Genesi e struttura della società (Genesis and Structure of Society)*, 1946, posthumous.

The originality of Gentile's thought lies in the concept of the spirit as pure *act*. It is the statement, in terms which reflect the sophistication of two thousand years and more, of the principle which constitutes the culmination of Aristotle's speculation: *noesis noeseos,* the inward-ness of all being, including that of thought itself, to the act of thought, to the concrete thinking of the subject. Gentile, establishing yet an-other historical link, often quotes the famous dictum of St. Augustine: "Noli foras ire, in te ipsum redi: in interiore hominis habitat veritas": go not outside yourself; look inward upon yourself; in the inwardness of man does truth abide. The mark of Gentile's originality is the literal-ness with which he interprets this classical insight and the rigor with which he carries it to its ultimate conclusions.

Gentile's first speculative efforts center about the theoretical prob-lems of education. These problems occupy his earliest major philosoph-ical work the *Sommario di pedagogia.* This work already contains, in seminal form, the philosophical position which he was to develop as "actual idealism." Gentile takes up the classical theme of *paideia:* the formation of the whole man. The theme of *interiority* is announced immediately and gives continuity and structure to the whole work. The dual enemy is ancient sophism and modern positivism. The formation of man is not accomplished from without, as both these positions sug-gest. Education is wholly from within. It is the quest and the discovery of the truth, which is within and which is constitutive of man, and the gradual effoliation and expression of this inward truth in the forms of the spirit: ethos, culture, beauty, and worship. The process of educa-tion is the "in te ipsum redi" of Augustine. This conception opens the problem of the human person. Gentile discovers the person to be essentially *interiority;* not substance, but *act,* a pure becoming, the limits of which cannot be defined from without by nature but which opens within to eternity, to the eternity of the ideas, of the *archai* of being, to God himself.

This idea of the educative process defines the relation of the sub-ject of education to the "content" of education, on the one hand, and to the teacher, on the other. The content of education, the material to be mastered, becomes authentically educative and formative only when its interiority is discerned. If such discernment is not attained, that work remains alien and dead and its mastery a sterile process. However, when the inward spirituality of any work of human culture is grasped, it can become the spark which awakens the corresponding inwardness of the subject of education; between work and subject a living dialogue ensues. Between the teacher and the subject of educa-tion only one relation is possible: that which St. Augustine delineated in the *De magistro.* That relation is a true dialogue in which, in the words which Newman chose as his own motto, *cor ad cor loquitur,* interpreting "heart" as the whole inward man of two human subjects, at differing levels of spiritual maturity but in the same order of interiority. The work of education is entirely a work of the liberation of the subject, the inward flowering of his being.

From the *Sommario di pedagogia* to the *Riforma della dialectica hegeliana* seems a far leap, marked by a certain inconsequentiality. In fact, however, there is a very close relation between them, which may be expressed by saying that the *Riforma* is the first attempt to translate into theoretical terms the insights about the human spirit which had been achieved in the *Sommario*. The work comprises a number of essays composed at different times, some prior to the *Sommario*. Nevertheless, the work possesses a genuine unity, much deeper than its structural diversity. Gentile is seeking to free his direct insight into the inwardness of the human spirit from the weight of the traditional interpretation of Hegelianism, while retaining a link to the vital center of Hegel's thought.

Gentile's critique of Hegel comes down to one central point: Hegel's is a *retrospective* dialectic, a dialectic of the past and not of the living present, the actual life of the spirit. The dialectic of Hegel belongs really to the realm of nature, not that of spirit and mind. The "phenomenology" of mind as Hegel depicts it is the "march-past" of the empty and alienated forms of spirit, abstract and ghostlike. They are the forms through which spirit has lived, not the forms of living spirit. For Gentile there is only one dialectic, that of the living and actual moment of the spirit in which it lives through, in unity and distinction, its actual becoming. The "reformation" of the Hegelian dialectic is, therefore, the transformation of these alienated moments or forms of spirit into the interior dialectic of the eternal present and becoming of the concrete and actual act of thought. Hegel had emptied spirit out into nature; he had depicted spirit and mind under the guise of the *other*. Gentile's purpose is to return spirit to its own inwardness and self-dominion, to render it present to itself, not as other, but in the interior identity of its living act.

While the movement from the *Sommario* to the *Riforma* may seem oblique, that from the *Riforma* to the *General Theory of the Spirit as Pure Act* is direct and uncomplicated. The latter represents the positive development and elaboration of the program of the former. The background of this development is a polemic against the adversaries of the philosophy of spirit in general and those of actualism in particular. These include every form of empiricism, positivism, materialism, and naturalism. "Nature" appears in Gentile's thought as the essential and eternal antagonist of the "spirit." Spirit, indeed, becomes spirit through the negation of nature. Nature is the realm of beings, of entities, of things; for this reason spirit can never be a "being," an "entity." It appears rather as the eternal "ought to be" or pure becoming; the act which must be actualized but which is never fully so.

Yet Gentile recognizes that nature could not have been admitted into the order of reality without reason. Nature represents the necessary negative moment of the life of spirit. It represents the immobilized, actualized, and transacted moment of spirit's own life, which spirit must forever transcend in its life-course. Nature is identified with the past; Gentile calls it "the eternal past of our eternal present." Here he clearly recognizes the limit of the spiritual life of man, its undeniable link with material conditions, including its own material life. Gentile uses this limit as the basis from which to affirm and emphasize the creativity—in his term, the *autoctisis*—or self-positing of spirit. This recognition does not stand in contradiction to his other constant affirmation that the philosophy of spirit has no presuppositions. Nature, as the past of spirit, constitutes only a negative presupposition based, as has been seen, on the negation which spirit as act carries out in order to become itself. Nature is a moment in the self-positing and liberating act of spirit.

The disengagement of spirit from nature places in relief its most positive characteristic: historicity. The historicity of spirit (not its appearance as an event in history as transacted among the *res gestae* with which the historian deals) has two aspects. On the one hand, historicity is the dialectical development of the spirit through time; on the other hand, it is the self-transcending leap of spirit from time to eternity. Thus, it is the dialectical movement through time which prepares the way for the transcendental passage to eternity.

Gentile attempts to resolve the dualism between temporal history and the "ideal eternal" history of which Vico had spoken. He does so by a bold and daring stroke: He identifies spirit with that eternal moment. Spirit is the ideal eternal moment of history, what history must always seek to become but cannot be in any of its temporal discrete moments. Yet the eternal moment which is spirit is under the necessity of negating itself and diffusing itself through the forms of spirit and the discrete moments of temporal history in order to project its own inexhaustible fecundity under the conditions of concrete existence. There is, consequently, a great movement of circularity between temporal and "ideal eternal" history, between the forms of spirit and its absolute unity.

At this point, the profound ethicity of the notion of spirit in Gentile becomes apparent. The process of the dialectic of spirit transpires, not on the level of mere being or existence (where it would be a meaningless gyration), but on the level of value. The forms of spirit are denominations of value. The whole meaning of spirit is the denial of the reality of evil, not in the sense of a vulgar optimism, but in the sense of the life of spirit as the generation of value at every level.

Gentile identifies the locus of spirit unequivocally. It is the existent individual person. He retains nothing of the Hegelian tendency to make spirit a transcendent impersonal force and idea in which the concrete individual is lost. The entire process of spirit in all its dimensions is entirely immanent in the concrete individual.

At the other extreme stands that tendency in Gentile's thought which Croce characterizes as "theologizing." This charge implies that against the principle of absolute immanence Gentile is raising that of transcendence. This is both true and untrue. It is *not* true if interpreted to mean that there is a recurrence of a "natural" theology, a restatement of the transcendence of God in terms of the otherness of nature. It *is* true according to the interpretation of Armando Carlini, who holds that actualism rediscovered God, not in the "outward" world of nature, but in the innermost subjectivity of the person. Here God reveals himself as the highest implication of the infinity of the act which constitutes the subjectivity of the person.

Some insights into the concrete implications of the position advanced in the *General Theory* are provided by the brief work *I fondamenti della filosofia del diritto*. The problem which dominates this work is the ostensible transcendence of the law to the legislating will and the subject will alike. Gentile seeks to reduce this transcendence by the force of the concept of the spirit as pure act. He shows that the law cannot be other than the selfsame will of the subject of the law when the consciousness of that subject is directed to the universality of the good. He goes on to show that the legislating will which enunciates the law is only the objectified form of the universality of the ethical will of the subject of the law. The absolute immanence of law is affirmed.

These reflections give rise to the problem of the status of will in the life of spirit. Gentile applies to this problem the dialectic which he has already applied to the relation between spirit and nature. Reality is nature or will when the act which realizes it is considered as completed. In thinking of an act of will as already completed, thought oppose itself to will as *theory* to *practice,* as understanding to will. This opposition is, at the same time, a synthesis, since spirit as thought understands itself as the constitutive principle of will as the completed act. Law, therefore, as an act of will, is an immanent dimension of spirit as thought, the rule which spirit gives to itself as liberty.

Gentile's most ambitious work is the *Sistema di logica*. In the introduction to this book, Gentile again seeks to place his thought in the total perspective of western speculation. His is a *new logic,* but only in the sense that it continues and advances the aims of this discipline from its inception.

The salient point of the work is the distinction established between *abstract* logic and *concrete* logic, the *abstract logos* and *concrete logos*. The abstract *logos* is thought "which has been thought," (*pensiero pensato*); the concrete *logos* is the living act of thought, as it transpires in the existent subject whose reality it constitutes (*pensiero pensante*). There exist a logic of the first form of thought and a logic of the second, but these do not possess equal value. They are both moments, and necessary moments, of logic as a philosophical science, but there is an order of value, both scientific and vital, between them. The mistake, as Gentile says (*Sistema di logica,* II, 10), lies not in the construction of a logic of *pensiero pensato,* but in the illusion that such a logic is self-sufficient and constitutes the whole of logic. This logic constitutes the logic of the *objects of thought.* But the object of thought (*il pensabile*) presupposes the act of thought (*il pensare*); therefore, the logic of the possible objects of thought postulates another, which passes from the objects of thought to the act of thinking itself. The order of the *pensiero pensato* is a closed *logos,* the result in which a living dynamic process terminates and hence becomes other to itself; it is the "concept" as governed by the principle of identity. The act of thinking is an open *logos,* becoming, in its rationality. Logic as a philosophical science aims at the synthesis of these moments. In historical terms, its object is a synthesis of classical (Aristotelian) logic and the romantic (Hegelian) dialectical logic. Both are really abstract logic in that each projects only one aspect of the dual movement of thought. Actualistic logic is concrete logic which meets both of these exigencies and passes beyond them to establish the logic of *pensiero pensato* in the logic of *pensiero pensante.* In this logic, the partialities of both Aristotelian and Hegelian logic are overcome while the intention of each is realized. Within the Hegelian system itself, actualism resolves the ostensible contrast between the "absolute idealism" of the Hegelian right and the materialistic immanentism (historical and dialectical materialism) of the left.

The *Filosofia dell'arte,* which Gentile published in 1931, and the *Introduzione alla filosofia* of 1933 are both penetrating excursions into the presuppositions and implications of actualism. The former reveals a more profound dimension or field of human existence, in which even the logical processes originate and are nourished, the world of *sentiment.* Sentiment, which finds expression in art, is the pure envelop of immediacy in which spirit encounters itself. What is achieved in art is the pure *quality* of human existence, anterior to and conditioning the mediations which thought introduces. Thus, art is the pure matrix of the life of the spirit, within which all other processes transpire and without which they lack reference and substance.

The *Introduzione alla filosofia* extends the inquiry of the *Sistema di logica.* It tries to establish what the *Sistema* had only asserted, the concreteness of thought as true. This concreteness consists in the reduction of possibility to necessity. As long as being is conceived in the primal mode of possibility and existence as a *casual* reduction of one of these possibilities to actuality, by a free choice which is essentially absurd, the world, the self, etc., remain abstractions, infected with a radical contingency which excludes truth. Concreteness involves the rationality of the actual and the elimination of its contingency at the dual levels of fact and principle. The source of this concreteness is *autoctisis,* the self-positing and the self-determination of the existent. *Autoctisis* dissolves contingency by the radical process of projection and negation. The range of possibilities abstractly open to existence is reduced by self-determination. This self-determination is the very opposite of determinism; its essence is liberty. The openness of possibility, contingency, always implies the possibility of the act of another as the source of existence (nature, God), leaving the radical contingency untouched. In *autoctisis* contingency is reduced radically; the subject is both completely determined (alternative possibilities are not real) and completely free (grounded in its own act).

The Genesis and Structure of Society was published posthumously. In this work, Gentile applies his conception of the concreteness of spirit to a domain of basic importance, society and the state. Two problems preoccupy Gentile in this work: the origin and nature of society and the origin and nature of the particular institution of the state. The first is discovered in the person. Society is an interpersonal transaction, based on the fundamental perception of the other as self and spirit. This perception has a double effect. On the one hand, it places an unbridgeable gulf, an infinite spiritual "space," between self and self. Every self is established in inviolable subjectivity and solitude. There is no principle or power which can resolve the self. On the other hand, there emerges, with the recognition of the other as *self* or *spirit,* an intimacy, a need and a communion which can never exist between self and other simply as other or object. The other self, even while it is completely other, is immediately *socius,* one bound to me, one with whom I possess a radical unity. Gentile relates this to his concept of *autoctisis.* The basis of the social bond is the fact that in recognizing the other as self, as subject, I recognize my own self. The *autoctisis* includes the positing of the other self as a projection of the infinity of the positing self. Society thus has its origin in the self-determination of the subject at its most profound level, that at which it posits other selves as integral to its own self-constitutive act of *autoctisis.*

The theory of the state has traditionally been caught between two extremes, each of which places the rationality of that institution in peril. On the one hand, it has been conceived as the free (in the sense of casual, conventional, or utilitarian) creation of individuals; on the other hand, it has been elevated into the overarching and all-consuming principle of value and ethicalness, into the totalitarian state which leaves the individual without ethical status or stature. Both conceptions violate the intimate nature of the person on which Gentile has placed such stress. The only possible justification of the state, the only rational conception of its nature, must be founded on the free and necessary act of the person.

The state, like society, is the creation of the *autoctisis* which lies at the basis of the ontological reality of the person. The state is the formal and public structure within which the reciprocal inviolability of persons and their reciprocal mutuality is guaranteed. It is, therefore, an ethical structure. Its mark is publicity, in contrast to the more intimate but also less stable forms, such as friendship, the family, etc., in which the mutuality and reciprocal inviolability of persons is affirmed. It becomes, by reason of its publicity, the guarantor of these less stable forms. It is not the negation but the ultimate affirmation and creation of man's ethical will.

Readings

I. CROCE

Books

Caponigri, A. R. *History and Liberty: The Historical Writings of Benedetto Croce.* London: Routledge & Kegan Paul, 1955.

Carr, H. W. *The Philosophy of Benedetto Croce.* London: Macmillan, 1917.

Collingwood, R. *The Idea of History.* Oxford: Clarendon Press, 1946.

_____. *Philosophy of History.* London: G. Bell, 1930.

Mandelbaum, M. *The Problem of Historical Knowledge.* New York: Liveright, 1938.

Orsini, G. N. *Benedetto Croce: Philosopher of Art and Literary Critic.* Carbondale, Ill.: Southern Illinois University Press, 1961.

Sprigge, C. *Benedetto Croce.* Cambridge, England: Bowes & Bowes, 1952.

Essays and articles

Bramstedt, E. K. "Croce and the Philosophy of Liberty." *Contemporary Review*, CLXVIII (1945), 293-297.

Brown, Merle E. "Croce's Early Aesthetics: 1894–1912." *Journal of Aesthetics and Art Criticism*, XXII (1963), 29–41.

Caponigri, A. R. "Ethical and Sociological Bases of Italian Politics." *Ethics*, LIX (1948).

Gilbert, K. "Vital Disequilibrium in Croce's Historicism." In *Essays in Political Theory*, edited by M. Konvitz and A. Murphy. Ithaca: Cornell University Press, 1948.

Harris, H. S. "What is Living and What is Dead in the Philosophy of Croce?" *Dialogue*, VI (1967), 399–405.

Romanell, Patrick. "Romanticism and Croce's Conception of Science." *Review of Metaphysics*, IX (1956), 505–514.

Schapiro, J. S. "Croce's History as the Story of Liberty." *Journal of the History of Ideas*, II (1941), 505–508.

Pubblicazioni dell'Istituto Italiano di Cultura di Londra; Benedetto Croce: A Commemoration. Gilbert Murray, Manlio Brosio, Guido Calogero, contributors. London: 1953.

II. Gentile

Books

Crespi, Angelo. *Contemporary Thought in Italy*. New York: Knopf, 1926.

Harris, H. S. *The Social Philosophy of Giovanni Gentile*. Urbana, Ill.: University of Illinois Press, 1960.

Holmes, R. W. *The Idealism of Giovanni Gentile*. New York: Macmillan, 1937.

Lion, Aline A. *The Idealistic Conception of Religion: Vico, Hegel, Gentile*. Oxford: Clarendon Press, 1932.

Romanell, Patrick. *Croce versus Gentile*. New York: S. F. Vanni, 1946.

_____. *The Philosophy of Gentile*. New York: S. F. Vanni, 1946.

Ruggiero, G. de. *Modern Philosophy*. Translated by A. H. Annay and R. G. Collingwood. London: Allen & Unwin, 1921.

Essays and articles

Ascoli, Max. "The Press and the Universities in Italy." *Annals of the American Academy of Political and Social Science*, CC (1938), 235–254.

Burgh, W. G. de. "Gentile's Philosophy of the Spirit." *Philosophy*, IV (1929).

_____. "On Historical Greatness." *Aristotelian Society*, Supplementary Vol. XI, (1932), 1–22.

_____. "Philosophy and History." *Hibbert Journal*, XXXV (1936–37), 40–52.

Caponigri, A. R. "The Status of the Person in the Humanism of Giovanni Gentile." *Journal of the History of Philosophy*, II (1964), 63–70.

Crespi, Angelo. "Actual Idealism: An Exposition of Gentile's Philosophy and of its Practical Effects." *Hibbert Journal*, XXIV (1925–26), 250–263.

Duckworth, F. R. G. "Gentile on the Teaching of Literature and Language." *Church Quarterly Review*, CIII (1927), 201–215.

Evans, Valmai B. "Education in the Philosophy of Giovanni Gentile." *Ethics*, XLIII (1932–33), 210–217.

_____. "The Ethics of Giovanni Gentile," *Ethics*, XXXIX (1928–29), 205–216.

_____. "The Philosophy of Giovanni Gentile." *Personalist*, II (1930), 185–192.

Garnett, A. C. "Giovanni Gentile." *Australasian Journal of Psychology and Philosophy*, IV (1926), 8–17.

Holmes, Roger W. "Gentile's Sistema di Logica." *Philosophical Review*, XLVI (1937), 393–401.

Horowitz, I. L. "On the Social Theories of Giovanni Gentile." *Philosophy and Phenomenological Research*, XXIII (1962).

Murri, Romolo. "Religion and Idealism as Presented by Giovanni Gentile." *Hibbert Journal*, XIX (1920–21), 249–262.

Pellizzi, Camillo. "The Problems of Religion for the Modern Italian Idealists." *Proceedings of the Aristotelian Society*, XXIV (1923–24), 153–168.

Prezzolini, Giuseppe. "School and Church under Fascism." *Survey*, LVII (1927), 710–711, 756–757.

Ruggiero, G. de. "Main Currents of Contemporary Philosophy in Italy." *Philosophy*, I (1926), 320–332.

CHAPTER III

Existentialism

Introduction: Inception and Distribution

It is difficult to assign a definite date or event as the beginning of a movement of thought. The fluid current to which the name "existentialism" is assigned seems least likely of all movements to offer the historian such a fixed point. Yet existentialism is one movement which offers dates, events, and documents which invite wide consensus as to its inception. The date is 1919. The event is the appearance of two documents of primary importance for any account of existentialism: the *Römerbrief* [Commentary on St. Paul's Letter to the Romans] of Karl Barth and the *Psychologie der Weltanschauungen* [Psychology of world intuitions] of Karl Jaspers. These documents share two characteristics: First, each is a recall to the thought of Kierkegaard, which was to have a continuing influence on existentialism in all its forms, and, second, each is an exemplar, though in very diverse areas, of existential analysis.

The authors and works singled out are German. It would be a mistake, however, to conclude that existentialism is exclusively, or even chiefly, a German movement. In a few decades existentialism established itself as a truly European phenomenon. It took root spontaneously in every major country of Europe and in each assumed a character reflective of the specific culture of that nation while losing nothing of that element which made it truly European.

In Germany, existentialism takes up with renewed force Kierkegaard's single-handed challenge to Hegelian transcendentalism and panlogism, and extends and deepens the criticism of traditional cultural and spiritual values initiated by Nietzsche. In these areas Karl Jaspers is its chief spokesman. Existentialism has also, however, in the work of Martin Heidegger, revived the historicism and psychological typological analysis of Dilthey and employed with new force, in areas and ways not originally foreseen, the phenomenological doctrine and method of Edmund Husserl. In the case of the rich theological thought of Karl Barth, it also reaches back to the more distant and profound sources of German spirituality, medieval mysticism, and Reformation theology.

The development of existentialism in France has been, if anything, more extensive and daring than in the country of its ostensible origin. This development has in many respects been independent of the German sources and has characteristically sought its own origins in French antecedents. Thus it takes up anew the tradition of French spiritualism which, originating in Cartesianism, finds its best representation in Pascal and Malebranche and which was given fresh expression by Maine de Biran and later by Hamelin and Bergson. The strain of French existentialism which has close affinity to the German and the Kierkegaardian is represented by Jean Wahl and the contributors to the journal *Recherches philosophiques.* The strain most directly related to classical French spiritualism is represented in the program of the review *Esprit* and the collection of publications called *Philosophie de l'esprit;* among the names associated with this review and collection are those of Le Senne, Lavelle, and Mounier. Gabriel Marcel, always an independent, but not unrelated, thinker, reflects both of these strains in his very original elaboration of the themes of existentialism. A later development, directly related to German phenomenology and especially to the thought of Martin Heidegger, is the philosophy of Jean Paul Sartre, who directed the important review *Le temps moderne,* through which he influenced such thinkers as Merleau-Ponty, Mikel Dufrenne, and Paul Ricoeur. France has also seen the development of a powerfully expressive literary existentialism, especially in the drama and novel, to which Sartre, Marcel, and Camus have contributed.

The Russian expression of existentialism finds native roots in the spiritualistic philosophy of such writers as Dostoevski and Soloviëv; it finds its chief representatives in that circle of emigrés in Paris in which the names of Shestov and Berdyaev are prominent. Italian existentialism appears under the aegis of German thought but finds many sources of inspiration and direction within the Italian tradition. The existentialist revolt in Italy against idealistic actualism, the position of Giovanni Gentile, has been compared to the revolt against Hegelianism initiated by Kierkegaard; this reaction found particular expression in the thought of Nicola Abbagnano. These thinkers have been spoken of as representing the "left wing" of actualism. Another strain, which had its origin in the "right wing" of actualism and which remained basically faithful to the thought of Gentile, developed a very inclusive and highly articulated form of spiritualism and personalism which displays many affinities with its French counterpart, the work of Le Senne, Lavelle, and others. The names of Guzzo, Carlini, Stefanini, and Sciacca are associated with this movement. Existentialism has also had powerful influence in Hispanic countries. In Spain it is very evident in the thought of such men as Unamuno, Ortega y Gasset, Julián Marías, and Pedro Laín Entralgo.

Those writers who have tried to identify the features which characterize existentialism through all its variations frequently emphasize *method*. Perhaps it is incorrect to speak of an existentialist method in a rigid sense. Existentialism does, however, possess a manner of proceeding proper to itself, which embraces a diversity of attitudes and styles. Its initial aversion to the dialectical method of Hegelianism, expressed by Kierkegaard, gives rise to its criticism of reason as *abstract* and thus unable to reach through the concept to the concrete individuality of the single existent thing. Shestov impugns the absolutist and necessitarian pretensions of reason, which falsify the constitutive finitude and contingency of things and make it impossible to formulate an authentic philosophical problematic reflecting these characteristics of what exists. Reason is accused of having an incurable tendency to *objectify*. This tendency leads it, on the one hand, to consider the existent as *an object*, a *thing*, thus alienating it from what establishes it intimately, its *act* of existing; on the other, it leads it to detach being from the act of reflection on being as though this being might be "in-itself," while, in fact, it *is* only *for* that act of reflection. Philosophy is concerned with the being of existence, not with that pale shadow, "objective" being, produced by the abstractive reflection of reason. All the important existentialists in one way or another subscribe to these strictures on the classical notion of reason; theirs is not the procedure of classical rationalism and transcendentalism.

The procedure of existentialism, characterized positively, has been called the way of *immediacy* in obvious contradistinction to *mediation*, so basic to dialectical reason. The quest for immediacy explains the choice of expressive forms: the diary, the journal, the novel, the play; the existentialists try to give philosophy the immediacy of art. Berdyaev speaks of a personal philosophy which would be one with the life of the person. Likewise, Jaspers gives considerable direct attention to methodological considerations. An early section of Heidegger's *Sein und Zeit (Being and Time)* is especially notable. There he holds as premise that the meaning of being can be reached only by an investigation exercised here and now by a specific subject (*Dasein*). He considers two possible ways of conducting such an investigation. The first would be "existensive" (*existenziell*) or "ontic"; it would consist in a concrete description of the single existing thing. It would be achieved through introspection and would find expression in such forms as the diary. The second would be an "existential" (*existenzial*) and "ontological" analysis. This would prescind from the single existent subject and consider *in abstracto* its possible structures and determinations. The description of the *existent* subject is *ontic;* that of *existence* is *ontological*. Heidegger chooses the second, drawing directly on his understanding of the procedures of Husserl's phenomenology. This second way gives the investigator a phenomenological description of being here and now (*Dasein*), a direct vision of the "how" of that *act* of existing in which the concrete reality of being resides. "Ontology," Heidegger writes, "is possible only as phenomenology."

Jaspers prefers something which is more akin to what Heidegger has called the "existensive" procedure. Philosophical inquiry does not investigate the abstract conditions of being. It is the concrete subject reflecting on itself. This is true, he says, in *Von der Wahrheit* [On truth], even of logical reflection and investigation. Sartre unabashedly takes the "phenomenological" method from Husserl and Heidegger; he calls his chief work, *L'être et le néant (Being and Nothingness)*, an "essay in phenomenological ontology." Similar reflections on method are to be found among the Italian existentialists and those of the French spiritualist school.

The renovation of the language of philosophy is characteristic of existentialism. Its purpose, the description of concrete experiences, "states of soul," etc., leads existentialism to employ a language which renders the object of description vividly present. Its language frequently has the freshness of the immediately engaged imagination; it is filled with metaphors which spring from a direct contemplation of the root meanings of terms. This language has sometimes been accused (as in Carnap's famous satire on the language of Heidegger on non-being, nothing) of inaccuracy and ineptitude. This accusation would seem unjust. The language of existentialism is remarkable because it renders present aspects which the older language of philosophy, worn thin and smooth with centuries of use, has tended to obscure.

A second unifying principle of existentialism is to be found in its thematic and problematic, shared by all existentialists despite wide diversity in manner of treatment. Four basic themes with their adjunct problematic formulations may be identified: the theme of being, the moral theme, that of society and history, and, finally, that of art.

Heidegger assigns the principal place to the problem of being. His intention is to reopen the basic theme of classical ontology in opposition to the disordered preoccupation of modern thought with the problem of knowledge. He adds immediately, however, that it is impossible to speculate about being as the ancients did, from a point ostensibly *outside* being, as though we were spectators of being. On the contrary, the only revelation of being which we possess lies in that concrete being which we ourselves *are* (Dasein), the being *here and now* of being. The fundamental characteristic of being viewed in this way, as we actually *live* it and *are* it, is *finiteness,* defined as being in time and space, *here* and *now*. This is what existentialism calls *situation*.

We do not create situation but are flung down into it and, as it were find ourselves suddenly there. Finiteness insures that being is always concretely individuated. In Kierkegaard's words, I am *singularity;* in Heidegger's phrase, I always recognize being as *my* being; or, as Jaspers says, I am an exception, I cannot be brought under any generality (such as the Kantian consciousness-in-general); or, finally, as Marcel writes, I am being *incarnated*.

The finiteness of being is *contingency*. To exist means to come into being from nothingness; it is, therefore, essentially the possibility of not being, of nothingness. Thus, the problem of the relationship of existence to being emerges. This relation is dynamic. With respect to being, existence cannot be said to be but only to be posited. It *posits* itself. But this it cannot do absolutely. It can only posit itself within the terms of its situation; i.e., it cannot transcend its situation. Nevertheless, the intimate character of existence is precisely transcendence, the effort to give itself being outside situation, as its essence. This is the sense in which existence is said to precede essence, in a phrase which has been widely repeated. It is not essence which takes on existence, as classical ontology seemed to imply, but existence which strives to achieve essence through transcendence of situation.

The moral theme in existentialism is not an interest added to the ontological. It is inherent in all speculation about being and its conditions. Once it is affirmed that being is only in the concrete existent, in the existence of the human subject, it becomes clear that inquiry into being is not a matter of pure speculation but rather the very act by which man comes to question himself with his life in the balance. In existential ethics, three concepts previously developed in ontological inquiry are fundamental: liberty, choice, and situation. The existent subject, finding itself placed in a determinate situation, realizes moral values to the degree to which he is successful in transcending that situation. By this effort human existence becomes *authentic*. It becomes authentic by freeing itself from that inauthenticity which resides in abandoning oneself to situation, thus renouncing one's proper *personality* and falling back into impersonality, the anonymity of "daily" life.

For existentialist ethics, the distinction between theistic and atheistic existentialism, both founded on the ontological analysis of existence, is of great importance. For atheistic existentialism, a contradiction arises. The ethical life resides in transcending situation through liberty; but the atheistic existentialists, such as Sartre and Heidegger, tend to identify liberty and situation. As a consequence, liberty can generate no values for them; the existent cannot, in fact, transcend situation; he can only recognize and accept it. Liberty and necessity are one, and the moral life takes on the quality of an illusion. The theistic existentialist finds it possible to vindicate the original existential analysis precisely through the fact of God's existence and availability. God calls man and human existence to *participation* in being, the absolute being of God, and hence guarantees a value and meaning to human life.

Existentialism shows itself particularly sensitive to the problem of communication, of colloquy and society. It does so because it is so much concerned with the person. What it fears most is loss of personality, personal identity, and authenticity, through merging with, and submergence in, the common or the anonymous. This sensitivity expresses itself in a strong condemnation of those aspects of modern society which threaten the individual with loss of identity, with anonymity, and with banality. It also expresses itself in various proposals for the solution of the problem of social communication. In others, it issues a condemnation of society without appeal and a recommendation of solitude. For Kierkegaard, the only possible society is that between God and the singular individual, between the Alone and the alone. Sartre sees society as a situation in which the existent confronts other existents but cannot communicate with them. Each one, just as he tends to appropriate things for his use, tends to appropriate the personality of others and submit it to his own advantage. Society, he says in his famous play, *No Exit*, is the true definition of hell. This position was softened somewhat as a result of Sartre's experiences in the resistance during the Second World War; this situation of heroic resistance, he found, did make authentic communication possible.

Heidegger fears that every attempt to achieve the basis of authentic communication with others must inevitably decline into mere *chit-chat*, into commonplaces which conceal rather than reveal the person to the other and end in concealing him from himself. Jaspers holds that communication and coexistence are necessary for the achievement of authentic existence; but that achievement is always highly problematical. Marcel's theism makes it possible for him to give a central place to society, because the self can achieve authentic communication with itself only through communication with the other—above all, with and through God. Communication with God is the pattern of all communication and participation between men.

Their discovery that time is present in the very structure of human existence leads the existentialists to the development of various subtle theories of time as well as to a preoccupation with the correlative problem of history. On this point, the distinction between theistic and atheistic existentialism is important. On the whole, atheistic existentialism sees in history but the temporal prolongation of situation: a meaningless succession of events, from which no value which might justify facts and events can emerge. Theistic existentialism shares this dark view of immanentistic history; however, it finds it possible to view history, not only from within, but from a transcendent point of view, as resting on the presence of God; thus, they are able to discern eschatological and soteriological values in it. Heidegger and Abbagnano offer examples of skepticism toward history as the vehicle of value. Jaspers, while not rising to theistic optimism, finds value in history because it creates a tension between time and eternity which enables the subject of existence to touch the profoundest sources of his being. Barth illustrates the more optimistic view which theism makes possible. He holds that *Historie*, the succession of natural facts, must give way to *Geschichte*, which is the divine meaning in history. God, not man, gives meaning to history by his election of facts to a significant place in his intentions. The Russian Berdyaev further accentuates this divine sense of history, while for Lavelle history is the basis of man's participation in eternity.

Because of the emphasis upon immediacy, art has a special value for existentialism. Its interest has been to discover the existential meaning of the human attitude involved in art. Its evaluation of this attitude has ranged from espoused aestheticism to a stern condemnation of the aesthetic attitude. The outstanding example of the latter is to be found in Kierkegaard. Heidegger, on the other hand, finds in poetry, as exemplified in the poetic experience of Hölderlin and Rilke, a new power to reveal the meaning of existence. Poetry halts for a moment the precipitous movement of existence toward death. The poets understand human destiny better than the philosophers. For Sartre, art, like philosophy, reveals to us the nothingness which lies at the heart of existence; it is significant that art depends on the imagination, which he defines as the power to posit the object as nothing.

A. *Existentialism in Germany: Jaspers and Heidegger*

1. Karl Jaspers (1883–1969)

Karl Jaspers came to existential analysis by a long and circuitous route of intellectual preparation. Originally trained in jurisprudence, he passed thence to medicine. The latter discipline contributed basically to his *forma mentis* and determined, to a considerable extent, his ultimate approach to philosophical problems. From medicine he passed to psychology, whence he drew much of his technique in the analysis of human existence. His philosophical interests gradually overshadowed, though they never displaced, his psychological interests, and in 1921 he obtained the chair of philosophy at Heidelburg. Throughout, however, Jaspers remained the physician, the healer; he has been called the *physician* of existence, as Barth has been called its *pastor*.

In philosophy, he sought with customary thoroughness to understand the thought of the masters: from Plato to Plotinus, and on through Cusa, Bruno, Spinoza, Kant, and Hegel. His true teachers, however, those to whom he acknowledged the greatest debt, are Kierkegaard and Nietzsche. He had direct contact with the phenomenological analysis of Husserl, but its impress on him was less than decisive. While appreciating Husserl's ideal of philosophy as a rigorous science, he was repelled by Husserl's indifference toward, if not disdain for, the vital problems of life and reality. He recognized a considerable intellectual debt to the German sociologist Max Weber.

In addition to his *Psychologie der Weltanschauungen* [Psychology of world intuitions] (the importance of which has been noted), Jaspers published extensively. The titles most important for an understanding of his thought are the following: *Die geistige Situation der Zeit* (*Man in the Modern Age*), 1931; *Philosophie* (3 vols.), 1932; the monographs on Max Weber, 1932, on Nietzsche, 1936, and on Descartes, 1937; two others on Nietzsche called *Nietzsche und das Christentum* (*Nietzsche and Christianity*), 1946, and *Nietzsche*, 1950; the series of conferences published as *Der Philosophische Glaube* (*The Perennial Scope of Philosophy*); and finally the synthesis to be called *Logik* on which he embarked with a first volume called *Von der Wahrheit* [On truth] in 1948. He has also published other lesser philosophical essays and works on psychology that are of scientific rather than philosophical interest. Jaspers was relieved of his professorship for political reasons in 1937; but he took up university work again in 1945 as professor of philosophy at Basel.

The influence of Jaspers' early training in medicine, psychology, and psychiatry on his approach to philosophy has been mentioned, but it deserves clarification. His work in these fields, as expressed in his *Allgemeine Psychopathologie* (*General Psychopathology*) of 1913, constitutes the first expression of a *phenomenological* psychiatry. Jaspers seeks to understand mental illness, not, as the mechanists had done, as a series of defaults due to the failure of organic factors, but as the expression of a *form of life* possessing a meaning in itself. The mentally ill subject is not merely a deviation from an organically determined normal pattern. He is working out a life intuition and pattern which, while it does indeed depart from the "normal," nevertheless, has a positive principle of its own. Phenomenological psychiatry seeks to isolate and identify this pattern as the basis of diagnosis and treatment. This insight will remain constant in his existential analysis. The interior life pattern of the subject in its concreteness remains central to his interest, both in itself and as involving intersubjective relations. His analysis has been called "phenomenological," but his meaning of this term must be clarified since it is fundamentally different from that of Husserl. He makes no reference to the "reduction" that is so important to Husserl's method. He understands *phenomenology* as the effort to reach the meaning of the interior life pattern insofar as this meaning eludes the objective method of science. This does not mean that he returns to the method of "introspection." Rather, phenomenology constitutes for him a third way, falling between introspection and the "objective" method of science. This third way turns about the doctrine of *Erscheinung*, which may be translated "expression." The interior life of the subject realizes itself in the effort to generate *expressions* of that life which will manifest it to others. An understanding of this interior life, not merely as it appears to another but as it is lived out by the subject, is to be secured by the interpretation, the hermeneutic, of these expressions.

The work *Psychologie der Weltanschauungen* makes the definite transition from psychological and psychiatric to philosophical preoccupations. Jaspers' intention here is not to establish a causal relation between a certain psychological and characterological pattern and certain philosophical doctrines and attitudes. He undertakes the more subtle task of determining how a certain manner of viewing the world may also be a manner of living the world in terms of the subject's own life. In doing this, Jaspers rejects any attempt to decide in favor of the *truth* of one philosophy emerging from a given world-intuition, over that of another emerging from an alternate intuition. He neither poses nor resolves this problem but is concerned solely with the derivation of intuitional patterns from psychological patterns and the reciprocal influence of the one on the other. In later works this question of the truth of philosophy will not remain bracketed.

Man in the Modern Age is frequently considered an introduction to Jaspers' first extensive philosophical work: *Philosophie*. The problems treated are not philosophical in themselves, but they are treated philosophically. Jaspers is concerned with the pseudo-universalization of man through technology. Philosophy has always sought the universal principle in man, he avers, but this universality has always been understood in an interior and spiritual sense. Technology makes it possible to impose an abstract, exterior, and superficial universality, which eventually alienates the subject from himself and from others. A technological culture imposes certain "objective" conditions of behavior, feeling, and even thought. The individual seeks himself, not in his own authentic interiority, but in that external universalized image which the culture imposes. Similarly he establishes relations with others, not on the basis of a mutual interiority, but on that same externalized basis. The spiritual problem of our time is the reconquest of interiority in the face of the externalizing and superficializing influence of technical culture.

These works are all introductory. Jaspers' philosophical thought proper begins to emerge with the work *Philosophie* and is developed in the subsequent works. These works do not, however, constitute a progressive movement toward a systematic position. Jaspers' thought is thematic, not systematic. The basic themes of his thought are three: 1) science and its relation to man's understanding of himself, 2) existence, and 3) transcendence. The most fruitful approach to Jaspers' thought lies in the exploration of his meditative enrichment of these themes.

Jaspers has been called a philosopher of crisis. By this is meant that his philosophical reflection begins on a negative note; he conceives his work, not as the fulfillment of, but as a reaction against, what has preceded. The ostensible object of this reaction is the Hegelian system. The form which this reaction takes in Jaspers in the twentieth century is very different from the form it took in Kierkegaard in the nineteenth. The great intervening fact is science. Jaspers reacts against the Hegelian system because he believes that it ministers to the pretensions of modern scientific knowledge. These pretensions are two: exclusivity and totality. Science entertains the notion that it can construct a knowledge which is universally valid and absolutely compelling or "demonstrative"; and it claims to be the sole way of erecting such knowledge. Finally, it thinks of such knowledge as being the only true knowledge. In these pretensions Jaspers sees modern science taking as its own the claims of the Hegelian system. The first or crisis phase of his thought involves the exposé of these pretensions in the name of a more authentic knowledge, above all of man.

For science, the totality of empirical entities constitutes and exhausts our idea of reality and defines the range of experience. An object is real only if it can be the term of experience, only if it can be fitted into the empirically determined system of such objects. This world or totality rests wholly on itself, is entirely immanent to itself, and is potentially transparent. Is the world self-contained in this manner, Jaspers demands? Or is there not always something beyond the empirical which cannot be brought under the conditions of *object* and fitted into the system of objects as science demands? His reply to the first question is negative, to the second positive. By establishing these replies he defines philosophy.

The notion of world and totality upon which science bases its claims, Jaspers submits, is equivocal and ambiguous. The scientific notion of world and totality is the sublimation and refinement of the common sense notion of world. Common sense thinks of the world as everything but the proper subjectivity of the subject. Will this notion tolerate analysis? He believes not. The distinction between self and what-is-not-the-self cannot be made, as he says, "effective." These terms are strictly relative to each other. The self grasps the world, not as the simple other, but as the condition, prolongation and effectuation of itself. As there is an indeterminable variety among subjects, the world is never an abstract totality but always a positive perspective related to the actual subject. By contrast, the abstractly universal world of science is present to no concrete and existing subject. It is pure spectacle, present to an impersonal and abstract "self," a *spurious* self.

Further, science misprises its own procedures. The "pure spectacle" world is the excogitation of the theorizer, not the actual world in which the scientist works. A laboratory experiment, for example, always involves trust in the powers of an actual concrete man who can understand and communicate the results only as a man working among other men. Finally, he holds, even granting the order which science postulates, i.e., a completely objectified order of entities present as spectacle to an impersonal self, one could not conceive that order as a unity or totality. Rather, that order is formed of four spheres of reality, each of which supposes that which precedes but none of which necessarily implies that which follows: matter, life, sensible consciousness, objective spirit. In the order of objective spirit (the notion is Hegelian) this situation repeats itself: between science, religion, art, action, and philosophy, there is no order or progression which would justify the application of the notion of totality to the realm of objective spirit.

The criticism and dissolution of the scientific notion of world and totality involves a similar dissolution of its claim to exclusivity. Yet Jaspers' intention is not to discredit science. His criticism now makes it possible to establish the authentic place and claims of science in the life of spirit and to relate science to other forms of knowledge, particularly philosophy. Science is knowledge of the objective empirical world. The movement of the spirit which leads to the creation of science is integral to the movement of all human effort, the aspiration of being to being. Science errs in offering itself as the only, full realization of that aspiration to the exclusion of the other movements of spirit, including philosophy. Each of these others has its own autonomy and authenticity. In the past, in idealism, philosophy seems to Jaspers to have conspired with the claims of science to the diminution of philosophy. But philosophy has its own authentic and specific work in the life of spirit. The critique of the spurious claims of science point to this work in a negative way by making clear that philosophy is not merely the prolongation of the work of science. Before the area of philosophy appears in its positive outline, however, a fundamental distinction must be established: that between *Dasein* and *Existenz*.

Dasein as a state of being is closely correlated with the claims of science and its notion of world. *Dasein* is the self as a bodily reality that is universally perceptible as the other objects of science are. As *Dasein*, the self is present to itself and to others under the conditions defined by science and perceives and understands itself in and through the explicative system of science. The self, as *Dasein*, tends to identify itself with the abstract subject of scientific knowledge, consciousness in general. As such, the self is subject to all the inauthenticities which Jaspers has laid at the door of science. As it was necessary to pass from science to philosophy, so it is necessary to pass from being as *Dasein* to *Existenz*. *Existenz* is the subject as authentically present to itself: as entirely singular (and not a cipher in an abstract totality or universality), as liberty, as the power of generating and choosing possibilities which are entirely its own and not the possibilities-in-general of science. This passage involves a radical transformation of the mode of presence of the subject to itself and of the mode of its relation to being.

The movement from *Dasein* to *Existenz* is not a continuous development. It is an act of transcendence. By this Jaspers means that this movement involves a break and a leap. He also means that no process of "reason" (no act of the pure speculative faculty) can effect this passage. Still, *Existenz* is not the negation of *Dasein*. On the contrary, it *presupposes Dasein*. The act of transcending which establishes the subject as *Existenz* is the act of a subject already existing, albeit inauthentically. *Existenz* is, therefore, self-grounded in the act of an existing subject which is the subject of both modes of being. Transcendence is the free and liberating act of a subject already in *Dasein* by which it is established in authentic existence. It is self-grounded because it is its own act which so establishes it. The function of philosophy is the comprehension and illumination of *Existenz*.

Philosophy proceeds in a manner and with purposes proper to itself. First, it has no scientific pretensions with respect to existence; i.e., it will not try to erect the *system* of existence. Philosophy is not a science; it is an invocation and an engagement. It may employ a general language to enucleate the general structure of *Existenz*, but it has no pretension of determining what *Existenz* is, of determining its essence. Its task is more subtle: to suggest or invoke, beyond that universal language, the possibilities of concrete *Existenz* in the immediate subject. The philosopher speaks to his auditor through the universal language, but in order to awaken him to the sense of the concrete possibilities which are present in him concretely and uniquely. The process of philosophy ultimately is interpersonal dialogue. *Existenz speaks to Existenz.*

Employing the universal language, but with the intention noted, it is possible to speak of general properties of *Existenz.* Among the first of these is *liberty.* Liberty is not so much a *property* of *Existenz* as identical with it. The act of self-establishment in authentic *Existenz* is concrete liberty. Such liberty cannot be *proven,* as older psychologies thought they could prove the freedom of the will. It is lived through and appears in the clarification of *Existenz.* It is not absolute, i.e., without conditions. Paradoxically, it is liberty founded on necessity. On every hand it encounters limits. These limits do not negate freedom but place its authenticity in greater relief. The limits make liberty possible, for they trace the path by which man comes to himself, i.e., to *Existenz.* Man cannot choose himself directly. He must do so by way of the world and intramundane choices. These limit his freedom, but they also define the conditions under which he can authentically choose himself.

Communication is equally important among the fundamental properties of *Existenz.* Communication implies the presence of others. Jaspers does not envisage the problem of the possibility of the other; for him, the other is already present at the level of *Dasein.* He is more concerned to clarify the kinds of relations possible between the self and the other, that is, communication. He develops this notion by a series of paradoxes. Communication is a process, in the phrase of Paul Ricoeur, of "reciprocal creation"; in communication the self creates the other in the same process by which the other creates the self. This process is illustrated by friendship. In communication, the independence of the self and the other is established through the recognition of their mutual dependence. Communication does not lead to the fusion of persons; it establishes each in its fullness through the acceptance of the other. Communication does not exclude solitude but makes authentic solitude possible. Neither is it irenic; it does not exclude conflict, which is one of its forms. Communication leads each person to *his* truth, the truth of his own existence. Here Jaspers is not speaking of truth as the content of an affirmation or assertion; he is speaking of adherence to truth and its fulfillment or realization. Every *Existenz* realizes truth, his truth, in a fashion uniquely his own; but this realization does not exclude, but demands, the like realization of other truths. Finally, communication is always precarious and full of risk. It can be lost in silence; it can die. Worst of all, it may lose its interpersonal character and take on a deceptive form at the level of *Dasein*, becoming pseudo-communication, conventional, deceptive, false.

Existence as liberty and communication is bound to the world; therefore, it is subject to "limit-situations." This concept is essential to Jaspers' thought. Every empirical subject, as *Dasein*, is defined as being in "situation." Passing to the condition of *Existenz*, through transcendence, the subject is not freed from situation but finds itself in a new form of situation. Situation is inevitable. Moreover, it is constantly changing. No situation is definitive, though being in situation is inevitable and constitutive of the subject. The notion of limit-situation emerges from this circumstance. The limit-situation is a dimension of existence which opens it to transcendence, which reveals to it something beyond itself. Examples of limit-situations are to be found in death, suffering, guilt. Death places the subject directly in the presence of the possibility of his own annihilation and forces him to decide, in his uniqueness, what death will be for him. Death awakens both despair and hope, depending on the quality of the existent. For the subject for whom existence is identified wholly with the empirical self, there would seem to be only annihilation. Death may also generate hope, which is the substance of transcendence, the promise of being, immortality. Suffering seems but a foretaste of death. It may be approached in different ways. The physician Jaspers speaks when he says that the only objective can be its elimination; but he is aware of the path of transcendence which suffering can open to the subject, as St. Teresa of Avila witnesses. Guilt offers what is perhaps the most striking example of limit-situation. For Jaspers, guilt is the weight of existence itself, confronted by its impotence to become effectively what it feels itself to be, that is, absolute. This sense of impotence may also open the subject to the transcendent.

From the consideration of *Existenz* Jaspers passes to a phase of his thought which he calls *metaphysics*. The term has a specific content for him. Metaphysics directly concerns transcendence. Existence possesses a constitutive relation to transcendence. In the first instance, this relation is felt as a privation. Existence becomes aware of transcendence through the fact that all its efforts to become effectively itself end in a kind of shock, a "being thrown back" upon itself. The meaning of this shock, this "being thrown back" or "down" is not fixed but depends to a great extent on the existent. In all its forms and degrees, however, shock involves a relation to an *other*, the veiled other of the transcendent. The problem of metaphysics as the philosophy of transcendence is the character of that other. The other appears under three diverse incarnations: the world, other selves, God. The nature of these and the relation of the existent to them through transcendence preoccupies Jaspers in that part of his philosophy which he calls metaphysics, the philosophy of transcendence.

Metaphysics, the philosophy of transcendence, falls into two phases. The first is concerned with the movements of transcendence, the second with its nature. In the first, Jaspers takes a position against all prior metaphysics, which have been rationalistic in character. These held that transcendence or the transcendent can be proven or demonstrated. The conspicuous example is the classical effort to demonstrate God and his existence. For Jaspers, the movement of transcendence and the manner in which it offers itself to *Existenz* is the object, not of demonstration, but of *philosophical faith*. Jaspers is concerned to distinguish philosophical from religious faith. The latter rests upon the direct self-revelation to man of an Absolute Being under the form of the Word of God; it is faith in an Absolute Being who speaks directly to man. The object of philosophical faith is a transcendence which does not speak, which does not reveal itself, which is silence and mystery.

Metaphysics in its second phase is reflection upon the transcendence which is the term or object of philosophical faith. This reflection is not *thought* in the sense of conceptualization and affirmation. Reflection upon transcendence encounters the problem of language which had appeared in *Existenz:* It must employ language in a way which goes counter to the normal movements of language; it must compel language to reveal indirectly what it cannot directly express.

Reflection upon transcendence has two chief tasks. The first resembles the task of the "negative" theology of the older tradition; it undertakes to show that transcendence has no determinations and that none of the categories can be applied to it, save at the risk of turning into their opposites. The second task is the *reading of ciphers.*

The notion of cipher is important for Jaspers' thought and peculiar to it. He has said that transcendence does not speak or reveal itself; nor can one reach transcendence by discursive argument, from premise to conclusion. At this point the notion of cipher enters. Certain objects, under the metaphysician's reflection, dissolve, lose their opacity as objects, and point to an ineffable beyond themselves which they cannot be said to express but which they evoke. It has been noted that Jaspers' account of this transaction has many points in common with Rilke's account of the poetic transaction (cf. Rilke's *Letters to a Young Poet*).

What are the ciphers of transcendence? *Nature*, especially as approached by romantic poetry; the great *myths* evoked by the human imagination and incarnated in a thousand ways in language, institutions, and behavior; the great *religions* and the *Ways* which they inculcate; the great *philosophical systems,* when understood in their expressive, and not merely material, totality; and *history,* which is perhaps the greatest cipher of all. Finally, *Existenz* itself may be interpreted as cipher, for all its movements terminate in shock and send it beyond to transcendence.

The reading of ciphers is attended by risk, however. The danger lies in thinking that ciphers bear a direct relation to transcendence and that in them, therefore, transcendence may be revealed definitively and delivered to existence. The cipher does not reveal the transcendence toward which it orientates existence. The transcendence remains ultimately veiled. Thus, the reading of ciphers is also a shock, for it sends the subject back upon itself, back upon philosophical faith. Jaspers' last word is the omnipresence of shock, the fact that in all its effort to reach beyond to being, the existent is thrown back upon itself. There remains but one way, which is, in the last analysis, Jaspers' way: to find in shock itself the ultimate witness to Being.

2. Martin Heidegger (b. 1889)

The most representative figure of existentialism in Germany is Martin Heidegger; he has also wielded the widest influence of any of the existentialists. Heidegger brings to his personal reflection a solid erudition in the whole range of the history of philosophy. He sees his own work as the correction, advancement, and completion of the metaphysical speculation of the past.

A student first of Rickert and then of Husserl (whose phenomenological method he adopted and transformed), Heidegger published his first important essay, *Die Lehre vom Urteil im Psychologismus* [The doctrine of the judgment in psychologism], in 1914 in Husserl's *Jahrbuch.* The following year saw the appearance of his first important study in the history of philosophy, *Die Kategorien- und Bedeutungslehre des Duns Scotus* [Duns Scotus' doctrine of the categories and of meaning]. Heidegger's most important work, *Sein und Zeit* (*Being and Time*), appeared in the *Jahrbuch* in 1927 and as a volume the following year. The work is incomplete; a "third section" of the part published and a "second part" were to follow but they never did. What has appeared must, consequently, be taken as a definitive statement of the most important phase of his thought.

Between 1927 and 1936 Heidegger published a number of interesting works centering about the problem of truth, which he conceives as the manifestation (*Unverborgenheit*) of Being which takes place only in the "existential" behavior of man. These works include: *Vom Wesen des Grundes* (*On the Essence of Reasons*), 1929; *Kant und das Prob-*

lem der Metaphysik (*Kant and the Problem of Metaphysics*), in the same year; and *Was ist Metaphysik?* (*What Is Metaphysics?*), also in the same year. In 1936 Heidegger read a conference at Rome which is considered to mark the opening of a second phase of his thought: *Hölderlin und das Wesen der Dichtung* [Hölderlin and the essence of poetry]; the conference was published the next year. To this second phase (which does not exhibit any strict unity) belong the works of the succeeding years: *Platons Lehre von der Wahrheit* [Plato's doctrine of truth], published as an essay in 1942 and as a volume in 1947; *Brief über den Humanismus*, [Letter on humanism], which appeared first as an appendix in the Plato volume of 1947 and in 1949 as a volume; *Vom Wesen der Wahrheit* [On the essence of truth], 1943; *Holzwege* [Forest paths], a collection of essays in 1950; *Erläuterungen zu Hölderlins Dichtung* [Elucidations of Holderlin's poetry], which brings together all his essays on that poet, 1951; *Einführung in die Metaphysik* (*An Introduction to Metaphysics*), 1953; *Was Heisst Denken?* (*What Is Called Thinking?*) 1954; *Vorträge und Aufsätze* [Lectures and essays], 1954; *Zur Seinsfrage* (*On the Question of Being*), 1956; and *Was ist das—die Philosophie?* (*What Is Philosophy?*), 1956. The year 1961 saw the publication of his two-volume study *Nietzsche;* 1962 saw *Die Frage nach dem Ding* (*What Is a Thing?*), while 1969 saw the English translation (*Identity and Difference*) of *Identität und Differenz* of 1957.

Heidegger's thought has given rise to extensive interpretations, varying much among themselves and frequently at variance with the line of exegesis which Heidegger himself has suggested. From the point of view of doctrine and interests, his thought falls into two phases. The line of demarcation is drawn (but not too sharply), as has been noted, by the Hölderlin lecture of 1936. The first phase centers about the great work of 1927: *Sein und Zeit*. This work is still considered as presenting the essential Heidegger. It most clearly exhibits his originality as a thinker in his "existential analysis" of human behavior with respect to the "unveiling of truth" and his "ontological" mode of treating phenomenology. It is the basis for the wide influence he has enjoyed. The second phase possesses no strict unity but shows Heidegger's concern with a number of themes, both historical and analytical, stemming from his main concern: being and truth.

a. *The Doctrine of* Being and Time. Early in his career Heidegger had voiced the complaint that contemporary philosophy, though claiming to be engaged in a "renaissance" of metaphysics, had completely forgotten the problem of being. His purpose in *Being and Time* is to take up anew, in systematic fashion, this ancient and absolutely central problem of western philosophy. His intention: the determination, as complete as it might be, of the meaning (*Sinn*) of being (*Sein*).

The question of being, like every other question, involves three elements: 1) what is being asked; 2) what is discovered through the asking; 3) to whom the question may be put. What is being asked is *being* itself; what should be achieved through the demand is the determination of the meaning of being (*Sinn des Seins*). The crucial point is: To whom can the question rightly be put? Obviously, the question can be meaningfully addressed only to *a being*, i.e., a principle or subject actually exercising the act of being, for being is always the property of some such principle. The objects of nature cannot be questioned on this point; they do not possess any knowledge of the meaning of being, or, if they possess it, they are silent. With man, the case is different. He alone, among all identifiable and describable "beings," can become the interlocutor, the "interrogated" (*Befragtes*), in this inquiry. The reason is clear. It is enough to look at man (his manner of conducting himself) or to listen to him (his words and gestures) to realize that he is unique among "beings" because he clearly possesses an implicit comprehension of being. Moreover, this possession is no "accident." On the contrary, man's "to be" (that which makes him a "being" and which makes him "this being," (different from all others) is this *comprehension of being*. Thus, he enjoys an *ontologically privileged status* in being in the sense that it is man who must be interrogated in the inquiry into the meaning of being.

This is not all. Man is not only the interrogated; he is also the *interrogator*. He alone can put the question of the meaning of being, just as he alone can respond to it. Even further, this is not a question he may or may not put to himself as he may choose. The question is an imperative of his being. It belongs to his being to put the question of the meaning of being.

For man in this dual character of interrogator and interrogated in the inquiry into the meaning of being, Heidegger has a special name: *Dasein*. He writes, "This existent which we ourselves always are and which possesses, among its other possibilities, the possibility of putting this question, we call *Dasein*" (*Being and Time*, sec. 2). *Dasein* is the human existent. Existence is man's specific mode of exercising being. That specific mode of exercising being is to comprehend it, i.e., to question it in order to determine its meaning.

From these considerations two things seem clear: that the basic task of the inquiry into the meaning of being is the construction of a *fundamental ontology*, that is, an analysis of existence, the mode of being of *Dasein;* and that only on this basis is a *general ontology*, concerning the meaning of being in its absolutely universal aspect, conceivable.

The part of *Being and Time* which we possess carries out the first project, i.e., the construction of the *fundamental ontology*. The unwritten part would ostensibly undertake the task of constructing a general ontology.

Heidegger is now faced with a second question: how to put this question to man, the method involved in this most delicate of inquiries. This method, in the widest sense, will be the *analysis of existence*. A preliminary distinction, however, is necessary. This is the distinction between the *existensive* or *ontic*, on the one hand, and the *existential* or *ontological*, on the other. To this distinction correspond the two modes in which the question of the meaning of being may be put to man. First, it may be put to him in his singularity; the existence of the singular subject may be analyzed. What will then ensue will be ontic and existensive. While possessing great intrinsic interest, this analysis is of limited value in the construction of the fundamental ontology.

The question may otherwise be put in such a way as to draw out in reply the fundamental structure of existence, as existence is exercised by *every singular man*. If this second mode of putting the question is fruitful, the reply will be existential and ontological. Heidegger insists, however, that the fundamental structure of existence obtainable in this way has nothing to do with an abstract "being-in-itself." Such a fundamental ontology refers always and only to the concrete singulars which actually exercise existence and being.

The two modes of putting this question are not, therefore, entirely distinct. They are, rather, interdependent. The existensive or ontic inquiry is initiated only with the further intention of making the existential and ontological analysis possible.

These reflections still leave the question of method undetermined. At this point Heidegger acknowledges his direct indebtedness to Husserl. The method of existential analysis must be phenomenological. Phenomenology, in Heidegger's view, is not a doctrine but a method. It concerns, not the *object* of philosophical inquiry, but its manner and mode. The phenomenon of which phenomenology speaks is not the mere appearance but the manifestation, revelation, or unveiling of what the thing is in its *being in itself*. That phenomenon is not opposed (as was the case with the phenomenon in Kant's *Critique of Pure Reason*) to a deeper but hidden reality. It is the *manifestation* of that deeper reality, as Hegel had said. Phenomenology is the *logos* of the phenomenon. It is a discourse which renders visible and present that with which the discourse is concerned. This discourse is *true* (a favorite point with Heidegger) in the etymological sense of the Greek term for truth—*a-lethes, a-lethia*, "unveiling"—when it makes apparent that which was hidden. The essence of phenomenology, therefore, "is making visible of itself that which is manifested, in the way in which it is

manifested by itself" (*Being and Time,* sec. 7c). When the phenomenological method is applied to the analysis of existence, the effect
would be that the being of that existence would manifest itself in its
fundamental structure without distortions or additions. Therefore, existential analysis must be phenomenological if it is to yield a fundamental ontology.

The fundamental trait of the fundamental ontology which Heidegger delineates in *Being and Time* is "being-in-the-world." The understanding of this trait depends on the concept of "transcendence."
Interpreters of Heidegger relate this concept to Husserl's notion of
"intentionality" and to that strain of phenomenology developed by
Hartmann and Scheler which has been called "realistic." Heidegger
develops the concept both in *Being and Time* and in *Vom Wesen des
Grundes.*

Transcendence is projection, passing beyond. Heidegger calls *the
transcendent* that which achieves such projection or "passing beyond"
and habitually maintains itself in that posture. Transcendence is characteristic of *Dasein. Dasein,* the human existent, is constitutively transcendent between the poles of its own existence and that of the *world.*
Transcendence is the first meaning of the phrase "being-in-the-world."
Transcendence is not merely a cognitive process; it involves the existent totally and integrally. The "world" in this sense is not to be
confused with the "world" as the totality of natural things, as in a naturalistic system, or with the "world" as the absolute community of persons, as in personalistic idealistic systems. The "world" is nothing else
than the *relational structure* of the existent, *Dasein,* as *transcendent.*

The "world" is the *project* of *Dasein.* As such, it is entirely derivative from and dependent upon *Dasein.* The world realizes the existent
in the world's own terms, according to its limits. Thus, the existent
both projects the world (in the sense that without this projection
there would be no world) and is "flung down" into the world (in the
sense that the project is realized according to the limits and conditions
of the world). Thus, "being-in-the-world" is both an act of liberty on
the part of the existent and a submission to necessity. This tension is
fundamental to *Dasein. Dasein* possesses a freedom which knows the
limitations of a necessity which is not "external" but is a part of its own
relational structure. Man is free in the act of projecting the world, but
this very projection immediately subordinates man to itself, making
him needy and dependent as well as free.

This "being-in-the-world" may also be examined from two points
of view which, though distinguishable, are mutually implicative: the
character of the world "in itself" as it were, and the character of man's
presence in it. For the basic sentiment of man's presence in the world,

Heidegger employs a number of terms, the most emphatic of which is "dereliction" (*Geworfenheit*), to which others such as "finding-oneself-there" (*Befindlichkeit*) and "facticity" (*Faktizität*) are appanages.

The world into which man is "flung down," viewed in its own character, is the world of things. These "things" have a special character. They are not "substances" but find their specific reality in serving as *instruments* for man, in being *usable*. This "usability" is not an adjunct character of things, but the very "being-in-themselves" of the things in the world. Heidegger employs the term *care* (*Sorge*) to indicate man's relation to these instrumentalities. Man is "careful" (*solicitous*) of the things of the world because his own project, i.e., his own self-realization, is dependent upon them and their usability.

From these considerations Heidegger concludes that the spatial character of the world is based on the usability (or non-usability) of things in the world. "Usability" involves "being-at-hand." Space is the complex of determinations of "being-at-hand" (near) or distant, measured in terms of usability. Thus, a complex radio instrument does not belong to the world of the savage though it may be lying beside him on the ground of his native compound, for he does not know how to use it. It is useless to him, hence *remote*. Heidegger suggests that the properly "intellectual" activities of man—understanding, judgment, science, etc.—are based on these relations of usability. He develops these ideas both in *Being and Time* (secs. 30–69) and in the later essay *Was heisst Denken?*

"Being-in-the-world" involves not only things but other existents, other subjects. For Heidegger, there is no "self isolated from other selves" just as there is no "subject without the world." The "substance" of man is to be constitutively open to the world and to other subjects. The attitude of the existent in the world of others is a variant of his attitude of "care" in the world of things. In the latter case, care is "taking care of"; in the former it is "solicitude for." The distinction may be made clearer if an allusion to Kant's distinction between treating "as ends" and treating "as means" is permitted. The attitude of "care" toward others corresponds to "treating as ends" and becomes the basis for the possibility of human relations among men.

Heidegger distinguishes two forms of such "care" for others, which he calls inauthentic and authentic coexistence. The first consists in relieving others of their care about things; the second, in helping them to be free to assume their own projects. Heidegger considers the first as inauthentic because the care is directed primarily, not toward the other as person, but toward the things which preoccupy him "carefully." The second is authentic because it is directed toward the other as other, i.e., as human existent. A patron who would pay for a young man's education illustrates the one form of "care" for others, a teacher the other.

Both care for things and care for others are instances of care in its transcendental sense. Transcendental care is directed not toward this or that dimension of the world, nor toward the world taken as a "whole." Transcendental care expresses the fundamental and pervasive condition of a being which, "flung down" into the world, constantly projects its possibilities forward onto being only to find them incessantly recoiling upon itself to reduce it to its original condition, i.e., its being "flung down" into the world. Man in the world does not *suffer* care; he *is* care. All the more specific forms of care are but determinations of this basic care.

The complexity of the structure of care appears at two levels, the psychological and the transcendental. At the first level appear all those forms of care which infect daily life: fear of loss of love, of loss of one's daily bread, etc. However, these are clearly not self-sustaining. They are specifications of transcendental care, which is man's constitutive sentiment of being in the world. These derivative modalities of care possess an inner complexity of their own. Immediately, they are introjective, referring only to the state of the subject, revealing only his transient condition. At a deeper level, however, they are revelatory of being and non-being. The phobia of a neurotic person is orientated toward an object or state but, at a deeper level, it is revelatory of the non-being or nothingness which the subject senses at the core of his being.

At the second or transcendental level, the complexity of care reveals the presence of many constitutive elements. Three upon which Heidegger places greatest emphasis are: dereliction, interpretation, and discursivity. Dereliction defines man's most fundamental sentiment toward being "flung down" into the world; it is the essence of care. Man senses himself as flung down into the world without *choice*, without *recourse*. The terms *Befindlichkeit* and *Faktizität* denominate dereliction in its other nuances: its finding itself *there* and its being a pure and irrevocable *given* to itself and not a constitutive liberty of choice. Dereliction accounts for the transcendental retrospectivity of man's being in the world; it is the basis of the "past." Interpretation, by contrast, is the basis of "future" for man; it is that dimension of care by which existence finds itself forever projected *outside itself*, issuing from itself toward the other in order to make itself by making the world. *Verstehen* defines the very notion of existence in its authentic etymological derivation: *ex-sistere*, to stand outside of. Interpretation has its roots in dereliction and facticity, for every project departs from and returns to this condition (cf. *Being and Time*, secs. 31–33).

Discursivity, as a transcendental characteristic of existence and of care, derives from the distention between retrospectivity and projection, past and future. Discursivity indicates the movement between these terms, which generates the dialectic of existence. Discursivity generates the present, the point at which past and future intersect.

Together, dereliction, interpretation, and discursivity generate the inward, transcendentally constitutive time of *Dasein* and of existence, the transcendental time over which human existence is distended.

The transcendental analysis of care is the basis for the distinction between authentic and inauthentic existence. In interpretation man can take as his point of departure either himself or the world of things and others. In the latter case, he is plunged into anonymous or inauthentic existence. This is the existence of the *all* and the *no-one.* Here the "one says" and the "one does" hold uncontested sway. Everything is leveled, rendered conformable, conventional, and without *direct* meaning (*official,* in Kafka's term). A man, the concrete individual, is at once everyone and no one, "one of the crowd." He is plunged into a fictitious and conventional mode of being which hides his real existence from him.

The inauthenticity of this existence is revealed in its language of anonymity. Language in its essence reveals being. In anonymous existence it veils meaning and is crystalized into set and meaningless phrases, maxims, philosophies. Such an empty existence inevitably seeks something with which to fill itself. It dissolves into curiosity which is directed, not toward reality, but toward the appearance of things. Its final mode is equivocation, for inauthentic existence, the prey of curiosity and idle language, ends by ceasing to understand even the meaning of "what is said" and "what is done." Everything is equivocal.

Authentic existence has its root in interpretation as it takes its point of departure in *Dasein,* man himself, consciousness (*Gewissen*). Heidegger employs the term *consciousness* in a manner properly his own. It means both "awareness" and "awareness of self"; it also means conscience, as "voice of conscience." He seeks to keep the term free from the psychological or metaphysical sense of turning back upon one's self, reflection on one's own interior and spiritual being. Human existence, he holds, is not closed within interiority and intimacy; it is openness to being in its ontic manifestations and ontological structures. This sets him apart from all forms of idealism and spiritualism. Consciousness both as awareness and as voice of conscience functions at the heart of authentic existence. It is the voice of conscience which calls man back to his authentic mode of existing. This conscience is ontological, however, and not moral. Ontological consciousness finds man immersed in the world, plunged into inauthentic existence, dominated by care in its worldly dimensions. Conscience calls him back to himself, to that which he is authentically.

Human existence, it has been noted, is constituted by *possibility*. All project and transcendence rests on possibility. Every project, every effort of transcendence, throws man back upon his original condition, his dereliction and facticity. Hence, it must be concluded that all human projects, all human possibilities are equal. What is it that makes them equal? It is the essential *nothingness* of them all. Every project is the project of nothingness. This is true of projects which "succeed" as well as of projects which "fail." "Existential nothingness," Heidegger says, "does not have the character of a privation, of deficiency with respect to an ideal proclaimed but not achieved. It is, rather, the being of this entity which is nothing antecedently to all that it can project and even more in what it can achieve, and it is already nothing as a project" (*Being and Time*, sec. 58). It is to this constitutive nothingness that the ontological voice of conscience recalls man. It is this nothingness which is authentic existence.

The ultimate and radical form of this nothingness is death. Authentic existence, therefore, is existence before death. Death is not, however, in Heidegger's view, man's end, the conclusion of his existence. It is rather, in his words, "the most proper, unconditioned, certain and, as such, undetermined and insuperable possibility of *Dasein*" (*Being and Time*, sec. 52). It is an unconditioned possibility because it belongs to man as an isolated individual; all other possibilities of *Dasein* place man in the midst of things or other subjects, but death isolates the man, places him by himself. It is an insuperable possibility because it is the extreme possibility of existence, its renunciation of itself. Finally, it is certain, not because it can be demonstrated as can assertions about situations in the world, but because it is identical with the most intimate awareness of *Dasein*. Existence becomes authentic, consequently, when it recognizes death in this manner, when it takes death upon itself in this character of its own ultimate possibility by an anticipatory decision. To live for death is the authentic form of existence.

This does not involve, Heidegger warns us, taking death as a project or seeking to *realize* it (as in suicide). Suicide, in fact, is a highly contradictory and futile gesture and demonstrates, not the acceptance of, but the final flight from, death. It is an act of banality. To live for death, to live in the presence of death, and thus to exist authentically, means to comprehend the impossibility of existence as such, the possibility of its impossibility. Death offers man nothing to realize. It is the intrinsic possibility of the impossibility of existence. Existence is radically impossible. What is possible, finally, is the comprehension of this impossibility. Authentic existence, living for death, is this comprehension.

Every form of existence is accompanied by an emotive state. The emotive state which accompanies authentic existence as the anticipatory decision for death is *anguish* (*Angst*). In Heidegger's words, anguish is the emotive state able to keep open awareness of the continuous and radical threat which emerges from the most intimate and isolated being of man. In anguish man senses himself in the presence of nothingness, the radical possibility of the impossibility of his own existence. Anguish reveals the totality of existence as something labile, accidental, and fugitive, in which nothingness is present through its power of nullification. The constitutive nothingness of man's existence is revealed by anguish to be no mere privation but an annihilating nothingness, a nothingness which cancels all possibility, all transcendence.

The analysis of the dimensions of *Dasein* reveals the origin of the *constitutive temporality* of man's existence. Past, future, present emerge from the penetration of the condition of being "flung down," of dereliction, of interpretation. Hence arises one of the most subtle themes of Heidegger's discourse, that of time and history.

His fundamental assertion is that, among these dimensions of time, the future is originative, giving rise to the others. This position accords with his other assertion that existence is possibility and transcendence, projection and anticipation. As such, it is constitutively directed toward the future. The essence of the future is that it generates that movement of being in which existence is "outside itself," projected. This moment he calls "ecstatic," in the radical sense of the Greek original. To be in the time dimension of existence is to be in this "ecstatic" posture which is pure and future time.

The problem of time is immediately correlated with the distinction between authentic and inauthentic existence. In *inauthentic* existence, time, the future, takes the form of attention; it is *protension* filled with care toward all that preoccupies one—the limited, but innumerable, projects in the world. By contrast, in *authentic* existence, orientated toward the only true and certain possibility, death, the future takes the form of anticipatory decision, of life for death. As a result, in *authentic* existence, man remains immune to all the solicitations of life in the world, its preoccupations and cares.

The past, in inauthentic existence, takes the form of *fear*. This is surprising at first because fear seems basically orientated toward the future. The fact is, however, that the object of fear is always related to man's fundamental condition, his being "flung down" into the world, to something, therefore, which he *has been*. Fear confronts man with his situation in the world, anchors him in it, and makes him forget the possibility of authentic existence. The past, for authentic existence, can only be *anguish;* it cuts off man's relation to the world, reducing the world to meaninglessness.

The present of inauthentic existence is the immediate presentation of the things of the world and their dominance over all other possibility. It exhibits a unity of forgetfulness and expectation upon which daily existence and senseless *routine* is founded. To this present as *now*, Heidegger contrasts the present as instant of authentic existence. In contrast to Kierkegaard, who employed the idea of *instant* to indicate the irruption of eternity into time, Heidegger employs it to indicate the opposite of the *now* of inauthentic existence, its nullification. Heidegger relegates to inauthentic existence all of the forms of time with which man is ordinarily concerned: chronology, measure of motion, etc.; these do not touch human existence. Authentic time *is* existence. Time, temporality, is the answer to the initial question of his inquiry, the *meaning* of being.

Heidegger's notion of time does not seem to lead to the analysis of *history;* history seems alien to both inauthentic and authentic existence and the time proper to each. Inauthentic existence has no history by reason of its very banality. Even less does the idea of authentic existence seem to tolerate that of history; for in authentic existence the subject is wholly concentrated in the instant, the moment of his stark presence before the ultimate reality of his existence, its possible impossibility, death. Heidegger takes another view. He tries to establish the *historicity* of existence precisely at the moment of *anguish.* Man is by his essential character historical. The future, which is the originative moment of his existence as project, self-projection, and transcendence, is always a "futurization of the past." The past is an essential moment of existence as ground of the future, which existence, as project, is. Taking account of the past (historiography) is an essential moment of man's existential consciousness. The structure of existence thus exhibits a historical character: the historiographic moment (taking account of the past), the future (the trajectory of project), the present (fulcrum of the project). The constitutive rhythm of being is the elliptical movement from past to future and future to past by way of the present.

It is precisely *anguish* which makes history possible. Anguish releases man from the inauthentic present. It permits him to transfer existence to the level of authenticity, being for death. Being for death is the starting point of the historical attitude, which involves detachment from the concerns of the world, the realization of the equivalence before possible nothingness of all the possibilities of the world, and commitment or recommitment to them. Man can do the work of the world best from the vantage point of death. Thence he is not deceived by the illusions of the world, but sees all transactions under the aspect of destiny. The destiny of the world toward which history moves in its transcendent dynamic is precisely that nothingness which is the engrossing present of authentic existence.

b. *The Second Phase of Heidegger's Thought.* The doctrinal lines of *Being and Time* come to a certain focus in the notions of history and destiny. The work, however, remains a fragment. Instead of advancing along the lines here projected, Heidegger turns to other speculative and analytic concerns, thus opening the second phase of his thought. This second phase has a complex relation to the first phase represented by *Being and Time.* Under one aspect, it is wholly dependent on what has been accomplished in *Being and Time;* under another aspect, it seems to derive wholly from the *failure* of that work, the negative conclusion to which it had led. *Being and Time* had sought to construct an ontology, that is, to determine the *meaning* (*logos*) of being. It had proceeded by way of the interrogation of man. The result of this interrogation had been to place in a clear light the nothingness of man's being. Hence it follows that an ontology, an intuition into the meaning of being, cannot be achieved by way of the interrogation of man or, for that matter, of any being. The being whose meaning must be sought in the ontological quest is not the being of any being. Heidegger draws this conclusion in *An Introduction to Metaphysics.*

Does this mean that Heidegger returns to the enterprise of classical metaphysics, which he had condemned: the discovery by reason of *being in itself.* To preclude such an impression, Heidegger in this work launched a frontal attack on the classical ontology. It is no metaphysics, no ontology at all, but a *physics.* It loses its way among entities, "beings," and loses sight of *being.* Plato is accused of setting the feet of western thought on this erroneous path, reversing the direction of pre-Socratic thought. Aristotle, Hegel, and Nietzsche are brought under the same charge. The pre-Socratics had taken the measure of truth to be being as revealing itself. (Again he alludes to the notion of truth as indicated by the etymology of the Greek word *aletheia*). Plato, instead, makes human thought, the idea, the measure of being. "Idealism" is the complete forgetfulness of being.

The essence or meaning of being cannot be reached by way of the analysis of the being of any being. Further, this meaning cannot be reached on the initiative of any being. *The meaning of being can only be revealed through the initiative of being.* (This course is not absolutely novel; its possibility had been mentioned in *Being and Time.*) Man has only to open himself to the self-revelation of being, dispose himself to be receptive of that revelation. But this is not a passive attitude. It is, on the contrary, an act of liberty, the highest the existent can achieve. Liberty means, from man's part, abandonment to the self-revelation of being. From the part of being it is the "permitting to be," the *laissez être* of being. This liberty cannot be conceived as a radical initiative on man's part. It is also a gift of being, the being which is in him and which makes him what he is.

The self-revelation of being is neither total nor direct. Being conceals itself at the same time that it reveals itself. There are moments of the illumination of being, moments of its concealment. Heidegger ventures a fresh notion of history. History is now the interplay of light and darkness in the process of the alternate self-revelation and self-concealment of being. These alternating periods he calls *epochs*. Being reveals itself by way of things, entities. The openness of man to the self-revelation of being means the openness to the manner in which being reveals itself and conceals itself in things, a subtle and delicate process of hermeneutic and dialectic.

This is the thematic of the rich literature which Heidegger produced in his second phase. From this new point of view a fresh notion of *existence* is ventured. Existence is "to stand in the light of being," as he remarks in the work *Platons Lehre von der Wahrheit*. In the same work, the notion of being "flung down" takes on a new value and meaning. Man is now thrown down by being into the truth of being in such wise that he becomes the "custodian," the "shepherd" of being. In a poetic passage in the *Brief über den Humanismus*, Heidegger says that in this way man reaches the total poverty of the shepherd, whose dignity consists in being called by being itself to be the guardian of its truth. Thought is always thought of being. In the essay *What Is Called Thinking?* he clarifies this point, noting that this is the work of being and not of man. For man, thinking is still maintaining openness to being, permitting being to be.

Heidegger indicates one exception to the statement that being never reveals itself directly. This exception is language. The consideration of the privileged status of language engages him in the work which, it was noted, marks the opening of his second phase: *Hölderlin und das Wesen der Dichtung*. There he recognizes in language, specifically in the language of poetry, what he calls the foundation or ground of being. He assigns to poetry (as many have done before in the history of philosophy) the role which reason is unable to enact, that of the ultimate witness to being.

Poetry is the primitive language. It is the primordial *naming* of things. This operation is not the creation of being by poetry. It is a gift to poetry from being itself. A primitive self-revelation of being transpires in the language of poetry. The attitude of man in language is not creative but attentive. It is not man who speaks in the language of poetry, but being itself. Man's role is to hearken.

Heidegger *suggests* that a new epoch in philosophy lies just beyond the horizon. It will replace the present epoch, dominated by metaphysics. The new epoch will be dominated by concern for language and will rest upon the power of language to reveal being directly. On this rather prophetic note his most recent pronouncements close.

B. *Existentialism in France: Marcel, Sartre, and Merleau-Ponty*

Paradoxically, existentialism in France both antedates and postdates existentialism in Germany. It antedates German existentialism in Gabriel Marcel. Marcel early embarked on a course of personal reflection, in opposition to idealism, which paralleled, though it never identified itself with, German existentialist thought. French existentialism postdates its German counterpart in Sartre and Merleau-Ponty. These men are inspired by the desire to rethink the ideas of Husserl, Heidegger, and Jaspers in the light of the conditions of contemporary French culture. In no sense, however, can the French thinkers be considered "disciples" of the German existentialists and phenomenologists. They develop the German line of analysis in a bold and original manner. Marcel, Sartre, and Merleau-Ponty are selected for consideration here for their representative value. Others might well deserve to be discussed if space permitted: Ricoeur, Dufrenne, Camus; only occasional reference to their work will prove possible.

1. Gabriel Marcel (b. 1889)

The classical form of expression for philosophy had become, in the course of a long tradition, the treatise. German existentialism continued this tradition, though profound changes in modes of thought and language were introduced. In France, this change is carried further. The treatise recedes in importance (though by no means disappears). It is supplemented and sometimes replaced by the drama, the journal, the novel. This movement is not to be considered superficial and irrelevant, as some writers, like Bochenski, have suggested. It responded to the deep need in existentialism for modes of expression more responsive to its own insights and affective states. The thought and the form of expression form a vital unity.

This departure from the tradition of the treatise begins with Gabriel Marcel. His first and most extensive contribution to philosophical literature is his *Journal métaphysique* (*Metaphysical Journal*), 1927. His plays are numerous. They are not theatrical pieces in the ordinary sense. They are situation pieces, evoked in response to the concrete character of his philosophical reflection, which needs the particular, concrete situation to give it full expression. In his more formal compositions Marcel continually draws illustration for his arguments from his plays. Marcel has written many essays and given many lectures; these, for the most part, furnish the material for his books. They are also more in the nature of meditations than argumentative expositions. Marcel gives the impression of admitting the auditor or reader to his inner personal reflections rather than addressing him directly. Among these books the chief are: *Etre et avoir* (*Being and Having*), 1935; *De refus a l'invocation* (translated as *Creative Fidelity* by R. Rosthal), 1940; *Homo Viator*, 1945; *Positions et approches concrètes du mystère ontologique* [Formulations and concrete approaches to the ontological mystery], 1933–49; and *Le mystère de l'être* (*The Mystery of Being*), 1951, his Gifford lectures. Marcel's thought lends itself best to a thematic treatment which is free to follow the interior movement of his thought.

Though his reflection is intensely personal, Marcel's philosophical formation is important for the understanding of his thought. This formation begins under the influence of idealism, with an especially strong exposure (for a European) to Anglo-American idealism; for example, he reflects the influence of Bradley, and one of his earliest essays concerns Royce's metaphysics. He soon revolted against this tradition in the name of an interior, personal experience. Nevertheless, though desiring to nourish this interior experience, he did not entirely trust the immediacy of its testimony. His thought seems polarized between an abstract dialectic (which, to achieve transcendentality of meaning, tends to dissolve all personal elements) and the pure immediacy of personal reflection (which sometimes seems unable to rise above itself to give testimony to any generally or universally significant truth). His effort to mediate this opposition gives rise to his "reflective empiricism," the preferred designation for his manner of proceeding.

Marcel's mediation of these opposites is achieved, not in methodological terms, but in ontological and ethical terms. Abstract impersonal rationalism and the pure immediacy of inner experience seem to him to be antecedent to the formation of the person. The person appears, from the ontological point of view, as a process of the auto-formation of the self, the effect of which is to integrate these elements. Marcel calls this process *faith*.

Faith is an ontological process in the strictest sense of the term. It is the process by which the self, transcending both the immediate particularity of its empirical existence and the abstract universality of logical thought, posits itself as a pure process of mediation. This libera-

ting and establishing affirmation is not reached by logical argumenta-
tion nor is it a given, a pure fact. It is a creative *act*—self-establishing,
self-grounded, and free. The person is always a living act which resists
any effort to reduce it to one or the other of the moments it mediates.
In symmetrical relation to his use of the term *faith,* he speaks of this
self-creative act of the person as an act of *grace.*

This manner of mediating the two immediacies of pure interior
personal experience and of pure transcendental logical process provides the frame of reference for the distinction, important for Marcel's
thought, of *problem* and *mystery.* To solve a problem is to resolve an
unknown by establishing, among its given elements, a functional relation unperceived until that moment. There are, however, difficulties of
another and superior order that are more significant to the philosopher.
These cannot be resolved in the manner of problem. The problem
stands before one; one is not involved in it. These higher difficulties
engage the person by his very act of becoming aware of them. They
cannot be contemplated; they precipitate one into participation. All
questions of being and existence are of the latter type. It is not possible for man to speculate with neutrality on being and existence. Any
question he puts to them, any affirmation or negation in their regard,
immediately engages him. Such questions cannot be resolved simply
by a reordering of their elements in a process of logical analysis or
construction. They possess a dimension in depth which endows them
with a quality of mystery and demands for them a manner of treatment entirely different from that of problems. By recognizing the character of this second order of difficulties, we achieve a certain intuition
of ourselves as *existents.* But our *existence* is not a simple empirical
reality, nor can its meaning be expressed and mediated by a concept.
Existence is incommensurate with the empirical and the logical orders.
The *aporias* of the latter orders are problems. Those of existence are
"mysteries" in the sense that they resist mediation by concepts or positing as facts. It is incorrect to say that the mystery can be *known* at all.
It can only be said that we perceive it, become aware of it. Resolution
and knowledge here are vain pretensions.

"Mystery" in this sense appears at different levels and in different
forms, though retaining this constant feature of the engagement of
the questioner in the question. It appears in the order of good and evil
where, clearly, no logical or empirical resolution can be given but the
participation of the subject determines all. It appears in art, where
the structure of meaning, though transcendental, always involves the
participation of artist, percipient, and world. A phenomenology of
mystery would involve the delineation of all these forms. But such is
not Marcel's concern. As he makes clear in *Positions et approches
concrètes du mystère ontologique,* he is seeking that mystery which

imparts the character of mystery to all others. This is the mystery of *being*.

The error of all prior, rationalistic ontologies, Marcel holds, has lain in treating being as a *problem*, in thinking it susceptible of resolution by processes of logical analysis, conceptualization, and functional reordering. Being is not a problem and hence is not subject to such resolution. Being is a *presence*. It surrounds and invades us and manifests itself within us as that which we are and at the same time are not but in some way must become. Its specific mode of presence corresponds to what he has described as mystery, and the only manner in which it can be treated as the object of philosophical reflection is the manner which he has described relative to mystery.

The basic relation of man to being is *fidelity*. Fidelity is the acceptance of being as a presence and a mystery, in much the way that one accepts another *person* as a presence and a mystery. Philosophy above all must recognize this character of being and man's basic relation to it. If philosophy does not, it will inevitably fall into pseudo-scientific postures. It will try to treat being as a mere empirical fact or as an abstract logical concept.

These considerations about problem, mystery, and being provide Marcel with an avenue of approach to the critique of modern society and culture. His vision of the human person, founded on his insight into being as presence and mystery, provides the cardinal principle of this social and cultural criticism. He isolates a "stifling sadness" as the prevailing spiritual quality of the modern and contemporary world. This sadness is the result of the suffocation of the person by the functionalism and technicism of modern life.

The concept of function is essential to Marcel's thought. It involves the dualism "person-function." The person is essentially autonomous and free. He *is*. His value as a person resides in *being* and *existing*, not in *doing* and *having*. With the acceptance of being and existing in and by the person, there goes an abiding joyousness, as Spinoza had already noted. This joy is the basic tonality of human existence when man is faithful to being, accepts it, and values it in himself and in others as an immediate positive and unconditioned value. This is the joy which is denied to man, to the individual person, in modern society.

Marcel accepts the principle that the basis of social organization in modern society is the division of labor. Man is valued not for *being*, for *existing*, but for *doing, performing, producing*. Life in society is organized, not on the basis of the human needs of its members and their satisfaction, but on abstract social operations. These operations are fundamentally, production and consumption. Within this overall pattern, however, they proliferate beyond number.

This operational or functional structure of society mediates between the individual and the group or totality. The individual enters society, not directly, by reason of his own presence as a person with others and to others, but by reason of his performance of one of the accepted functions and roles which the society has articulated and approved or valued. The interdependence of men, which should be based on direct recognition and response among persons, now is mediated by function and role performance. Gradually the person, in his own right as existent, is diminished and becomes identified with his role or function, becomes lost in it. Not only do *others* see the role before they see the man, or recognize the man only as the anonymous performer of the function, but the man comes to think of *himself* in terms of role performance rather than in terms of his authentic selfhood, his quality and value as a human person. He applies to himself the same criteria which society applies. He becomes anonymous, not only to society, but to himself. His image of self is based on role-success, and role-failure is equivalent to personal failure. Marcel's example of the ticket-taker whose personal life is wholly assimilated to and lost in his role has become quite famous.

Marcel seeks the most inclusive source of this dehumanization of the person through role substitution or surrogacy in modern society. He finds it in the prevalence and dominance of science and technology and the extension of their principles to the realm of the person and interpersonal relations. His manner of excoriating this dominance is novel and more subtle than that of other critics who have essentially agreed with him on this point. His criticism may be summarized by saying that the dominance of science and technology has transformed human existence from interior tension and presence to exterior spatial operation. The human universe is cut into a collection of bodies or corpuscles which are not existents but mere centers of energy, of possible effects or virtual action. Men are recognized only to the degree that they affect other bodies, to the degree that they produce work. But such outward effects are achieved only by the pouring out of the human existent as interiority and self into the world of public operations. Man thus becomes real for science and a technologically orientated society only to the degree that he is *not* himself, to the degree that he becomes other to himself. The methods and objects of science are extended to cover every level of reality, including the person and interpersonal relations. These are reorganized according to the schematizations which science enjoins. The sense of authentic existence is lost.

The human person must inevitably revolt against such an order. His spiritual principle, the sense of self and presence within him, must rise up against this oppressive imposition of matter and the all-embracing method of science. Marcel distinguishes a hierarchy of attitudes before this domination of science and technology. The lowest is that of animal resignation. Modern society seems to foster this attitude in its constituents. In this attitude men can be manipulated without fear of overt reaction and without diminution of their capacity for exterior effectiveness.

Suicide marks a direct emergence of the individual from this state of animal resignation, a direct revolt against the stifling conditions of spiritual negation. Suicide is at least an affirmation. The subject is no longer sunk in mere resignation. It expresses profound disgust with the world and may be taken as a kind of affirmation of a better, though unknown, condition; for not even suicide can be conceived as an option for nothingness. But suicide is a futile gesture. It indicates the evil but does not signalize the remedy. It is merely a blind affirmation of value, not an effective one.

True revolt against this spiritual oppression lies in prayer and hope. These offer the only true, opposing forces to the powers upon which science and technology rest. The latter rest on calculation and mathematical prevision, upon the calculable operations of matter; prayer and hope rest on the interior movement of man's sense of autonomous existence.

To *hope* is to think against what is objectively determinable and subject to prevision. Hope denies that the world of mechanical causes and effects, the movements of which can be calculated and predetermined, is the world which really *is*. Hope affirms the reality of that which is hoped for. It points to the reality of a world, an order of powers and value, which lies beyond the realm of appearance over which science and technology preside. *Prayer* offers the same testimony. To pray for the cure of one afflicted is to denounce the vanity of the world of appearance. It is to affirm and to appeal to the reality of powers of which the calculations of science and the organized procedures of technology can know nothing.

Marcel goes on to say that it would seem necessary to the full reality of prayer and hope that they not be answered or realized. If the reality of prayer were related directly to its results, prayer would enter into the order of technique. It would be but another technique for gaining ends, and it would cease to be an act with ontological meaning. The value of hope and prayer lies precisely in their possession of this last character. They are ontological. They enable man to throw off the suffocating blanket of matter and the determined. They are his means of affirming all that lies beyond that oppressive veil, without involving him in the pitfalls of a transcendental rationalism which simply translates into that higher realm the conditions which prevail

in the world. Prayer and hope are *acts of fidelity* to being. They are
witnesses to being. They alone can lift the enveloping sadness from the
shoulders of man in the modern world.

To speak of prayer, of hope, of miracle, inevitably leads to the
name of God. One can readily surmise, from what he has said about
prayer and hope what Marcel will be prepared to affirm about God,
what manner of God will solicit his prayer and be the object of his
hope. It is, after all, God who is invoked in prayer and upon whom
hope is directed; he is the agent of the miracle which gives the lie to
science and technology. This God is not, for Marcel, the absolute being
of the rationalistic philosophers, into whose presence we are ushered
at the end of a long process of logical argument and proof. Prayer and
hope and faith move, not toward the being of the outer world and its
source, but upward and inward within the subject toward the source
of that being which is in him as a person and which makes him to be
as a person. Prayer and faith move the subject beyond himself, not in
the direction of the physical world of things, but toward the other as
persons and beyond them finally to that "Thou" which transcends
alike the self and other selves and which is the God of faith, hope,
and prayer.

Miracle is a strange-sounding word in the world of philosophy
today, but Marcel does not hesitate to use it. Miracle is the correlative
of hope and prayer. Marcel rejects all those notions of miracle which
try to insert it into the order of nature and science. Rather, he accepts
a clear opposition between the world of miracle and that of science.
Miracle is the basic denial that the order mirrored in science and
technology is the ultimate and fundamental order of reality. Miracle
transcends the process of cause and effect, of statistics of prevision
and prediction, and the order of cause and effect cannot be introduced
into the relations between prayer, faith, hope, and miracle. Prayer,
for example, in no sense causes miracle. Causality has no reality or
meaning in the religious order, and to structure miracle causally
would be to deny its religious character. Miracle is a pure, voluntary,
and gratuitous response of God to the appeal of our hope and prayer.
It is the middle term in a pure dialogue of persons whose movement
is love. Prayer and hope reach their culmination in the experience of
mystics and saints, for whom God becomes, as the respondent of
prayer and hope, the pure other self, the "Thou" into which no element
of objectification enters.

The notion of the "thou," introduced in Marcel's discussion of God,
is important for his concept of the other as human person. Our ways
of speaking and thinking of the other at the human level are to be
ordered hierarchically. Along with the world, we may think and speak

of the other as the incarnation and symbol of a function. But the other as function is a social fiction. The other does not exist in this fashion. No man *is* a businessman, a doctor, a father, etc. At the functional level, men are abstract ciphers and are interchangeable. It is possible, however, and humanly necessary, to think in terms which this mundane mode denies: to pierce through this veil of function to the "who." As person, the other is transcendent to function. His being is his existence: he *is*. Compared to this reality, his social function is an abstract possibility which bears no intrinsic relation to him as person. This reality, his status as person, is shared with no one else. It is nonsubstitutable, a complete unitary value.

At this level of person, however, there still persists a degree of objectification which, in language, is revealed by the employment of the third person. A further stage of recognition is possible and humanly necessary. This is the passage beyond the third person, the "he," to the direct, not oblique, confrontation of the other as person, to the "thou." Only when thus confronted does the other stand before us in the full autonomy of his existential character. We express this recognition by the direct form of personal address, the "thou," the familiar form in languages of romanic origin. The inward reality of such a mode of address is full human recognition.

What is it that gives access to the "thou"? It is not science or social analysis. It is only love and charity. Between these a certain hierarchy exists. Love reaches to the reality of the person who is loved and may not extend to others. But charity reaches to the reality of the neighbor, as the Gospel indicates. But who is the neighbor? The neighbor is anyone in need to whom I offer succour. Even here a veil of anonymity hangs about the other. The need may come between the giver and the person. It is only when the need to which one ministers is wholly incarnated in and identified with the *person* of the needy as a pure "thou" that the recognition is complete and his status as a person is fully apprehended. In such a case, Christ does not hesitate to identify the *thou* with himself: What you do to the least of these my brethren, you do to me.

Communion among men takes place only through charity and love. The essence of love and charity, in their varying degrees, is the gift of self. Community and communion are born of the omnipresence and compenetration of being. Communion can only come about if I am willing to risk myself, to wager myself, to repress the tendency of my *ego* to turn back upon itself and to set up barriers between itself and the other. Communion demands participation. But we have the power to withhold participation. This happens with persons who remain attached only to themselves, who risk nothing. In place of communion they seek possession of the other.

These reflections give rise to Marcel's penetrating distinction between *being* and *having*. This distinction is the key to the entire complex of Marcel's ideas. *Having* and *being* are not pure states which can take form in man. They are, rather, the names of tendencies along a continuum between communion, as complete participation and gift of self, and self-enclosure. Being tends toward a participation and a communion which has its limit only in identification, though this term, needless to say, is not to be reached since the distinction between self and other is primitive. Indeed, identification cannot be proposed as an end to be attained; when this is proposed, Marcel contends, it inevitably turns out to be a form of exploitation of the other. *Having*, moving in the opposite direction along the same continuum, tends toward possessive dominance of the other. It exploits the other, i.e., dominates and uses the other, without being in any way engaged with or committed to it. This too is a limit-idea, for the self can never completely stand in this relation to things, not even to one's own body, which relates the self directly to the material world.

The body presents a special case of this distinction between being and having. It is not correct, in Marcel's view, to say either that I *am* my body or that I *have* a body. The relation of alienation, in which the self is dominated by things and the body, defines the situation even less accurately. Against the first possibility, identification, we have the testimony of interiority. But interiority does not warrant the conception of the body as complete instrumentality or exteriority. At this point the notion of "existence" is placed in special relief. It helps to define the special relation between myself and my body. The body is the mediator between the self and the world, the other. It could not fulfill this role if it fell completely outside the one or the other. It is the living bond which unites them. For this reason it enjoys a special ontological status which differentiates it from natural bodies. These are wholly exteriority. The human body looks both inward and outward, toward the self and toward the world; it is the mediating principle in the process through which each establishes itself toward the other.

Marcel treats this problem of the body under the rubric of the *ontology of sensibility*. He finds inadequate the traditional analysis which conceives sensible qualities as subjective states induced by the excitation of external stimuli and carrying an objective message; he rejects any comparisons designed to illustrate this concept. The body must be conceived as the exterior dimension of the self. The self *is* that dimension, though that dimension does not exhaust the being of the self. Sensible qualities are not messages from things which fall outside the self; they are the presence of those things to that dimension of man, his body, which is at once vitally linked with the self and yet situated wholly in the world of things as one among them. The body mediates the self and the world of things and of others, rendering the world and the other present to the self, and the self present to the world.

Mediation is one of the most profound notions Marcel employs. Some critics have regretted that he has not made greater use of it in dealing with social relations among men. They have detected in him a resistance to the mediating role of social institutions, a role which would have an analogue in his view of the role of the body. The only institution he recognizes is the family, and this he refuses to objectify, placing its essential note, rather, in the unity of interiority among its members. He senses the danger that the mediating principle, the institution, may become an end in itself—for example, the modern totalitarian state. It has also been indicated that this notion of mediation might mollify somewhat Marcel's evaluation of technology and science. These might well be conceived as mediating between man and the world under very important aspects.

Marcel has resisted all attempts to classify him as an "existentialist." He is entirely justified in doing so if the intention of such classification is to subordinate his work to an idea outside itself. This is not the intention here. Rather, the intention is to recognize that in his work, taken simply in itself, there is to be found one of the most powerful statements in which existentialist themes and attitudes may be illustrated.

2. Jean-Paul Sartre (b. 1905)

Sartre is, without doubt, the best known of the French existentialists; in the English-speaking world existentialism is, for many persons, identical with his thought. A writer of great facility, Sartre has employed many literary forms in the expression of his thought. His central interest, however, has always been philosophical, and his philosophical reflection is the life-giving element in all his writings, whatever their form.

Phenomenology offered Sartre his methodological point of departure. His chief work *L'être et le néant* (*Being and Nothingness*), 1943, is subtitled: an essay in phenomenological ontology. His contact with phenomenology antedates this work, however, and its influence is to be discerned in earlier and very characteristic works: the investigations into the self, the nature of the imagination and the imaginary, and the nature of the emotions. The point of departure of these investigations is the *intentionality of consciousness* as this notion is developed in Husserl. It is in the particular development of this intentionality, in which Sartre corrects and alters Husserl's view, that the basic meaning of his existentialism is to be found.

Sartre's earliest effort in phenomenological description is the essay "La transcéndence de l'égo" (*The Transcendence of the Ego*), published in *Recherches philosophiques*, 1936–37. This attempt to determine, in purely ontological terms, the ontological status of the "ego" or self opens by denying the "apodicticity" of the self as Husserl had presented it. Husserl had maintained that the self is given in consciousness with pure self-evident force *as existing*. Sartre maintains, on the contrary, that the self is no more certain for the subject of consciousness than is the ego or self of any other subject. The ego is neither formally nor materially in consciousness; it is a being *in the world*. The privileged ontological status of the self characteristic of idealism is denied. Sartre goes on to say that the ego and the world are both objects of an absolute and impersonal consciousness which is the first condition and absolute source of existence. In this early essay Sartre already exhibits that finesse in analysis and that powerful dialectical style which will never desert him.

The *Esquisse d'une théorie des émotions* (*The Emotions: Outlines of a Theory*), 1939, assumes the conclusions of the earlier essay without relying on them too directly for the force of its own arguments. Consciousness is "being in the world," existence. The emotions are identified as modes of consciousness. Emotion is an attitude which consciousness takes toward the world in which it finds itself. The world initially presents itself to consciousness as threat and obstacle; the corresponding attitude is to modify the world in such a way as to reduce this threat and obstacle. More specifically, however, emotion is the effort of consciousness to modify the world magically, i.e., without use of instruments or tools of any kind, by a direct effort which would alter the status of the world as a whole. Emotion in this sense is no accidental mode of consciousness; it is one of the constitutive modes in which consciousness comprehends its being in the world. Sartre's use of the work *comprendre* here would seem to depend directly on Heidegger's use of *verstehen*. Emotion would thus be opposed both to science and to technology. These, too, are modes of consciousness which seek to reduce the threat and obstacle of the world but in a very different manner, namely, by theoretical and instrumental procedures.

The theory of the imagination and of the imaginary which Sartre develops in the essays *L'imagination* (*Imagination*), 1936, and *L'imaginaire* (*Psychology of the Imagination*), 1940, is important for his phenomenological ontology, for he treats both from the point of view of their relation to being. What is the ontological condition for the formation of images by consciousness, for the evocation of the realm of the imaginary? To generate images, consciousness must be free with respect to every particular reality. The world cannot be given to consciousness by an intuitive representation which has apodictic force. Were this the case, the imaginary would be pure illusion and not the highly significant realm of being which it is, for example, in art. Consciousness both constitutes and annihilates the world. It is radically free with respect to the world, while the status of the world in being is somehow subject to the play of consciousness. The imaginary always involves the dialectical negation of the world and its being as apodictically given. The world evoked in a work of art is in no wise less real than the world imposed by direct sensibility or sensible intuition. Thus, consciousness seems to possess a certain ontological autonomy. Even more, consciousness, in its imaginative activity, is constructive of the world as significant. This is the key to the force of art and to Sartre's employment of art as a form of philosophical expression. The bivalent relation of consciousness to the world, apodictic and imaginative, opens the way to the notion of *situation*. This bivalency cannot be reduced by any dialectic but must be lived. This *living through* of such bivalency is situation.

The scope of Sartre's principal work, *Being and Nothingness*, is immense from the point of view of metaphysics. It involves the construction of the phenomenological ontology of consciousness as being-in-the-world. The structure of the essay is dialectical. It moves between the two poles of "being-in-itself" and "being-for-itself," consciousness and its suppositional object. The dominant role is consciousness since even the world of "being-in-itself" is projected from the world of consciousness. The point of view is reminiscent of Husserl. Consciousness is always consciousness *of something*, and this something is not consciousness. The specific way in which consciousness is conscious of this something is *as other*. This something, this other, is what Sartre calls "being-in-itself."

A first analytical effort to denominate this "being-in-itself" can have little success. It can only lead to some such statement as "being is that which is." Such statements place in relief only the opaque, impenetrable character of being. They involve its presence as a massive and static other. From this point the other is neither necessary nor possible. It is pure positivity, pure givenness. "Being-in-itself" *is*, simply.

In contrast to "being-in-itself" consciousness appears as "being-for-itself," presence to itself. The manner in which consciousness is present to itself, the kind of being involved in this presence, is the very nub of

Sartre's investigation and argument. It introduces the basic dialectical concept of his construction, nothingness (*néant*).

Consciousness becomes being-for-itself by negation, as that constitutive nothingness which is the basis of all positive being. This may be illustrated in the following way. The being-for-itself of consciousness can be achieved only by a scission within consciousness. Consciousness is consciousness of something. This something, under its global aspect, is being-in-itself. Under its concrete aspect, it is always a particular concrete being. The object of consciousness tends to absorb consciousness into itself, to *reify* it. To grasp that object as it is in itself, it is necessary to establish it in its own character, to separate it from the consciousness to which it is present. By what can that separation be accomplished? Clearly, not by another object and even less by the opposition to it of consciousness as being-in-itself. It can only be separated by *nothingness;* more precisely, by an act of *nullification.* The nothingness here involved is not, however, the nothingness of the object. It can only be the nullification of consciousness by itself. Consciousness is nothingness, i.e., the negation of the identity of the object with consciousness and the nothingness or negation of itself, consciousness, as something, being in itself *vis-a-vis* the being in itself of the object.

Hence emerges an ontological proposition about consciousness; or, more properly, a statement about the ontological status of consciousness. Consciousness is nothingness; it is nullification. This nothingness which consciousness *is* must be examined with care. Consciousness appears in a dual relation to the object of consciousness. As nothing, it is both more and less than that object. It is less in the sense that consciousness appears as being-for-itself only by denying that it is the object of which it is conscious. At the same time, it appears as more than that object, as more than any possible object, and this again under two aspects. By denying that it is the object of consciousness, consciousness establishes that it is more than the object since, whatever kind of being consciousness may have, it cannot be a being which can be exhausted by identification with an object, or any order of objects or all possible objects taken transcendently. Moreover, it is more than the object since it is the possibility of the object. The object could never be established as being-in-itself save by the nullification executed by consciousness. Finally, it may be added, the nothingness which is consciousness is not a static nothingness but an active nothingness, a *nullum nullificans.* Hence, in a strange manner, consciousness is more real than the being-in-itself of the object.

As soon as the pure nothingness of consciousness has been established in this way, that nothingness begins, for Sartre, to take on all the properties which had formerly been attributed by idealism and realism, in diverse but equally erroneous ways, to hypostatized consciousness. That nothingness which is consciousness is seen as the womb of all that is. The character of *plenum* first denied to consciousness as act or actuality, is now returned to it as *possibility*. Consciousness and object, being-in-itself and being-for-itself, are now seen in a sophisticated dialectical relation. Consciousness seeks being-in-itself to fulfill and realize its own being-for-itself by the projection of all possible objects—therefore, by a transcendental operation. In like manner, by a countermovement, the dynamic of all objects is toward presence for consciousness, for it is only by such presence (including the negation described above) that they become actual objects.

Beyond the opposition of being-in-itself and being-for-itself lies the higher synthesis of being-in-and-for-itself. This synthesis is not static but dialectical. In this synthesis, the dialectic of negation, which Sartre had placed as the ontological reality of consciousness, is not denied but reaffirmed. One is brought back, on the one hand, to the Idea of Hegel and, on the other, to the dictum of the schools, "intellectus aliquomodo omnia fit." The manner in which man grasps the being of the consciousness which he is lies in the possibility, through negation, of this dialectical synthesis of being-in-itself and being-for-itself. Ontologically, consciousness is the possibility of this synthesis, of which nothingness, active and positive negation, is the dynamic moment.

Sartre illustrates this process of synthesis and at the same time seeks to clarify basic life phenomena in many areas through reference to it. Desire is one such area. Desire is dynamism toward the unity of being-in-itself and being-for-itself. It involves an other which the subject of desire is not; it involves further the synthesis of this other in the being-for-itself of the subject of desire. (It has been noted that this would hold only for desire as *eros*, not as either *philia* or *agape* in the classical context.) Another area of illustration is knowledge. The object of knowledge is established as object only by the complex negation of the subject of consciousness, but the term of the process is the unity of presence in which subject and object are dialectically synthesized. A final illustration is to be found in human community. Here self and other appear in the perspective of negation (the other-as-other is established by negation of the other-as-self and the self-as-other) but are synthesized in the idea of communion and community, in which, without the deletion of selves, a condition of being in-and-for itself is established.

In *Being and Nothingness* Sartre places great emphasis upon the negative aspects of this dialectic. His later works, as we will presently see, seek to counterbalance this emphasis.

The idea of liberty is essential and central to Sartre's thought and grows directly out of the foregoing analysis. From his ontology of consciousness, Sartre concludes that man is *desire for being.* For what being? He has already answered this question. Not for any particular being or mode of being, but for that pure unity of in-itself and for-itself of which he has spoken. This unity cannot be the operation or work of any principle outside of man; for instance, of nature or of God. It is something which man must initiate and achieve by his own action. This is man's essential and constitutive liberty: his freedom before the object of his constitutive desire, the achievement of which is wholly contingent upon his own action and choice.

This liberty is fraught with risk. It carries with it an ineradicable possibility of failure. As there is no principle outside man which can initiate this synthesis, so there is no principle within him (such as the *reason* of Hegel's system) which will guaranteee the success of the venture once man has initiated it. This freedom is man's destiny. He cannot choose not to make this fundamental choice. He is not free to be free. The whole movement of his being is toward this synthesis, the realization of which depends on an initial decision which is never without the risk of failure.

His reflection on man's freedom (which is, at the same time, his destiny) leads Sartre to some arresting reflections upon man and God. Man, he says, is that being which has as its project to become God. The myths and rites of religion set apart, God is to man that which announces and defines man's fundamental project. God is the name for the actuality of being-in-and-for-itself. The "in-itself" of the world and the "for-itself" of consciousness present themselves to phenomeno-logical analysis in a state of disintegration with respect to an ideal synthesis which would, if realized, be that condition of being which is called by the name God. For this reason, God is, for man, an absent God, or, stated inversely, man is a God without Godhood. The synthesis toward which man tends is without the possibility of actualization. Nevertheless, it indicates the basic orientation of man's existence.

There thus appears in Sartre's thought a subtle blend of theism and atheism (always, of course, within the limits of the meaning he assigns to these terms and not with reference to any other employment of them). The God of whom he speaks is present within the basic movement of man's consciousness. The atheism in his position concerns the impossibility in the order of actualization of that ideal synthesis of which he speaks. His Godhead is the choice which man is freely con-strained to take as the fundamental project of his existence. The failure of this Godhood is the impossibility of the positive outcome of this elec-tion in the order of existence. From this situation Sartre sees no issue.

After *Being and Nothingness,* Sartre's thought undergoes a gradual reorientation in which his doctrine loses something of its original negative cast and takes on nuances which have led some of his followers to believe that it could be developed in a "positive" direction. This gradual reorientation is first apparent in the rather popular essay *L'existéntialisme est un humanisme (Existentialism),* 1946. In this essay Sartre advanced a definition of existentialism which gained considerable currency: Existentialism is the doctrine that "existence precedes essence." The gist of this formula is that man primarily *exists,* finds himself in the world and only then defines himself through that which he is, or better, *would be.* Linked to this is the assertion that man has no "nature" in the classical sense but only a history and a destiny which is in the power of his own decision.

The latter assertion opens the path to the reformulation of his existentialist doctrine as a theory of human action and history. Rather than possessing a "nature" (which, in Sartre's view, would delimit the range of his possibility and possible action), man *is* what he *makes of himself* in his fundamental project. He is free, but he also bears the full responsibility in this project. He also, in a sense, becomes responsible for all other men because the choices he makes in his basic project and its execution involve the existence of others and the values which inform the world which he inhabits in common with others.

These considerations alter the meaning of *anguish.* It now becomes the sentiment of one's own complete and profound responsibility. It leads, consequently, not to inertia, but to action. The subject is led to assess what depends on his own action and all the possibilities which make his action possible. This too implies a positive and active stance in the world. Although the basic cast of existentialism prevents the emergence of a confident belief in the realization of the projects to which the existent commits himself, Sartre can speak of it as an "optimistic doctrine"; more accurately, existentialism now appears as a doctrine which is pessimistic in theory and optimistic in action.

· The new path of development which the essay on existentialism as a humanism had opened eventually led Sartre to undertake the work which, if completed, may well counterbalance *Being and Nothingness* in the final accounting of his thought: *La critique de la raison dialectique* [The critique of dialectical reason], 1960. Some anticipations of this inquiry are to be discerned in the articles on communism, condemnatory in tone, which Sartre contributed to *Les temps modrens,* the existentialist organ, during 1952–54 and which carry the collective title *Les Communists et la paix (The Communists and Peace).* The influence of Marxian theory is very evident in the *Critique.* Sartre is rethinking the chief Marxian theses while seeking to subjugate them to his own insights. This marriage of existentialism and Marxism may seem a strange affair to an unjaundiced eye, but it appears to Sartre as a saving device which would infuse a new life in both members of the union.

The salient features of this new position may be presented briefly. The notion of *project* is partially revised. In *Being and Nothingness,* project is the expression of unconditioned liberty. In the *Critique,* project takes form within a given situation which defines the limits, conditions, and range of its possibility and imperative. To say what man is, is to say what he can do; the material conditions of his existence circumscribe the field of his possibilities. The field thus defined is the theater of man's action. The scope of his effort is to transcend his objective situation. But this field is strictly defined by social and historical reality.

This consideration provides the clue to a general theory of action. Action is essentially the movement of subjectivity to transcend the limits of its given objectivity in the direction of a wider objectivity as the field of a heightened subjectivity. Here, the earlier notion of man's freedom also undergoes considerable restriction. Man's absolute liberty is now submitted to limits; in the process, however, it gains force and direction. The structure of possibility within which it moves takes form. The project now has a basis in the given, that is, in the material, social, and historical conditions of our existence. Finally, the instruments available to man condition both the situation in which he acts and the situation toward which his action tends.

In the first form of existentialism, project, liberty, etc., had all been considered as transpiring within the consciousness of the singular subject. Now that position is seen to be fraught with the danger of solipsism. Sartre's effort is directed toward overcoming this solipsism without, on the other hand, depersonalizing action, i.e., making it an entirely exterior and determined process, as historical materialism, especially the dialectical materialism of Engels, had done. It is at this point that the problem of the dialectical reason enters most forcibly. Sartre must tame the dialectical reason, transform it from a force wholly external and transcendent to man's individual subjectivity to one which falls within the scope of individual action. The dialectic will become the supreme instrument of the individual for the ordering and structuring of his own action and, through it, the ordering and structuring of historical reality in its objective, social, material, and spiritual aspects. At this point it becomes clear what Sartre means by the *critique* of dialectical reason: its transformation from a force of transcendent and impersonal history into the instrument of individual action which possesses transcendent and totalistic reverberations. At this point, Sartre's thought seems to establish certain affinities with personalism.

Thus, the relation of man to the dialectic is twofold. On the one hand, he is subject to it; on the other, it is he who executes it, who is its subject. The dialectic becomes truly historical only to the degree to which these two aspects are united. It is clear that a certain element of paradox enters here. But what is gained is also clear: historical trans-cendentality is brought to human, individual action. Both the objec-tivity of historical and dialectical materialism and the solipsism of the earlier form of existentialism are overcome. History opens before the subject as the true transcendent and infinite field of the action which originates within him.

There is nothing destinarian or utopian in the history which Sartre sees as flowing from the dialectical action of the human subject. The open field of man's freedom is now rescued from that futility with which the earlier assertion of its absolute and subjective character had threatened it. Historical necessity appears as the delimiting force of history on the absolute liberty of the subject. Liberty is realized through historical necessity.

In this context, Sartre seeks to develop a concept of the group as an integrated whole. Its most important feature is the manner in which the individual within the group seeks himself in every other member and finds in the liberty of the other the realization of his own liberty. The basis of such integration is not a social contract but labor and struggle. The specific act by which the group is called into being is a vow, an oath. Despite the seemingly pacific character of the group, Sartre holds that its principle of internal cohesion is *terror*. Terror is initially evoked by the threats which the group faces from its external foes; eventually, however, it becomes a powerful instrument of internal social control. Despite this fact, Sartre finds it possible to speak of the sovereignty of every individual within the group. The group represents to his mind a higher synthesis, in concrete form, of liberty and neces-sity. The group gives form to liberty and meaning to necessity. It res-cues the former from the futility which attends its absolute state and it robs the latter of the irrationality which infects it when it is not seen as the ordering principle of absolute liberty.

History, Sartre suggests, must finally appear as the matrix of all "totalities." It is the final meeting place of necessity and liberty. But it must be recognized that this notion of history remains inchoate in Sartre. It awaits the perfecting promised by the architectonic plan of the *Critique*.

Sartre's most recent undertaking has been the composition of his autobiography. The first volume, entitled *Les mots* (*The Words*), has already appeared. Although it carries us but a short way along the course of his intense intellectual life, its value as a document has already become apparent. In it, Sartre repudiates nothing, but reevaluates everything, proving to be his own most severe and constructive critic.

3. Maurice Merleau-Ponty (1908–1961)

The radical negativism of Sartre would seem to have led French existentialism into an impasse from which, to borrow the title of one of his plays, there could be *No Exit.* This impression has been dissipated by the group of thinkers who, in the wake of Sartre, took up the task of existentialist analysis on phenomenological bases. These thinkers are sometimes referred to as the "School of Paris." The most important figure among them is Maurice Merleau-Ponty. His speculative and analytical powers were revealed in a number of works which have become fundamental and influential texts of existentialist thought. Among these works the chief are: *Le structure du comportement* (*The Structure of Behavior*), 1942; *Phénoménologie de perception* (*The Phenomenology of Perception*), 1945; *Humanisme et terreur* (*Humanism and Terror*), 1947; *Sens et non-sens* (*Sense and Non-Sense*), 1948; *Eloge de la philosophie* (*In Praise of Philosophy*), 1953; *Les aventures de la dialectique* [Adventures of the dialectic], 1955, and *Signes* (*Signs*), 1960.

The central motive of Merleau-Ponty's thought is his determination to avoid the negativity and irreconcilability of the dualisms—such as those between the "in-itself" and the "for-itself," between consciousness and being, soul and body, self and other, situation and freedom, truth and contingency, and history and reason—which have plagued existentialist thought. He seeks a positive issue from the negativity of existence and finite liberty. He constitutes the point of conversion within existentialism from negative analysis to positive speculative construction.

The central theme of his investigations is the relationship between man and the world under the specific aspects of consciousness and nature. This fact may be illustrated from his earliest work *The Structure of Behavior.* Examining the results of experimental research in psychology, he concludes that they have been reached in spite of, rather than because of, the naturalistic philosophy to which psychology subscribed; more specifically, that these results make any causal interpretation of the relation between body and soul impossible. Soul and body cannot be conceived as closed systems acting on each other *externally,* as it were. The action of soul on body and the action of body on soul can only be interpreted as two levels of behavior of an integral entity. The body involved in behavior is a *human* body, not a closed natural structure, and the soul is the soul of such a body. Together, in their integrity, they represent one field in which levels of structure and meaning can be discerned. This complex unity, so opposed to any naturalistic dualism, yields itself to phenomenological inspection and analysis.

The *Phenomenology of Perception* both assumes and fortifies the position of *The Structure of Behavior*. It shows a greater direct dependence on Husserl but also a greater power to employ the phenomenological method constructively. Merleau-Ponty first rejects the "spectator" view of consciousness which has been prevalent since Descartes. He indicates the true position of consciousness as "committed to the world," involved in the world, given to itself in and through its being in and for the world. Reflection delivers the self to the self, not as an idle subjectivity, but as identical with its presence in the world and to other selves. The self is an "intersubjective field" which is realized, not despite its body and its historical situation, but in function of them.

Therefore, the problem of perception is that of the relation between consciousness and the world. Having established this basic principle, Merleau-Ponty subjects the classical problems to fresh examination. These problems include sensation, our knowledge of things, the body, communication with others, space, time, liberty, and history. Among these, the problem of the body is most central, for body means the point of entry or emergence of consciousness into the world. It is our general means of having a world. At one level, the body limits itself to operations necessary to conservation of life. At another level, using these first operations but passing beyond their strict and proper meaning to a figurative meaning, the body manifests a whole new range of significance, as in the art of the dance. At a still further level, it is seen that the meaning intended cannot be achieved by the natural operations of the body alone. A cultural world must be projected and created, the instrument of which is *language*. Language, whether as word or discourse, reveals our basic relation to being.

Perception, consequently, can never be an isolated fact; it is a *world event* in the strict meaning of the term. The world of this event is an open world. The perception of this world and of all that is in it always tends to project perception beyond determinate manifestations to a dimension yet to be revealed. This openness of the world, this incompleteness in the meaning of things and persons, Merleau-Ponty calls *ambiguity*.

By *ambiguity* he does not mean to indicate any imperfection in

things, in consciousness or in the world; ambiguity is rather the definition of *existence*. It is impossible to conceive the world as a closed
system under any of its aspects. It is always an open world of ambiguity whose dimensions and perspectives at any moment can be organized and established only through the presence of the subject. The
subject is not the negation of that ambiguity but its perfection; it is the
point at which all determinable and determinate, but not conclusive,
meaning can emerge. Merleau-Ponty raises this ambiguity and openness of the world to the status of a transcendental principle; this is in
clear contrast to the transcendental principles of the great closed systems of classical rationalism and romanticism—Spinoza's substance,
Kant's *a priori forms,* Hegel's reason and Idea.

Within the existentialist context, Merleau-Ponty develops an interesting concept of liberty, which is in contrast to the idea expounded by
Sartre. Sartre offers a concept of liberty which is absolute but negative.
Merleau-Ponty defends the limited and conditioned freedom of man,
but with the purpose of endowing that freedom with a positive character. Rationalistic philosophy had set up a harsh alternative wherein
man's action either must derive from self, and hence be free with Sartre's absolute freedom, or must spring from the world or nature, and
hence be determined. Merleau-Ponty indicates a middle way, based on
his fundamental thesis of man's in-the-worldness. Man's freedom does
not deny man's situation in the world but *rests* upon it, because that
situation is open. This means that it invites man to preferential modes
of resolving the situation but has nothing in it sufficient to determine
those modes. From the situation, it is impossible to infer how the subject will act. Hence, consciousness is not the simple reflection of a situation, social or otherwise. (At this point, Merleau-Ponty is directing
his criticism against historical materialism.) Neither the element of
reason nor the element of risk can be eliminated from the structure of
action. Our freedom is circumscribed but, at the same time, given
structure and positive basis by our historical situation.

The openness of existence, its ambiguity, also provides the key to
Merleau-Ponty's view of history and of man's capacity for responsible
action in history. The two properties of history are contingency and
rationality. The former is the basis of human responsibility in history,
the latter of order. The movement of history is dominated by a dialectic between these properties. History is susceptible to rational ordering, but at every point it is open to contingency. This dialectic enjoys a
certain independence of man's action; it is, therefore, neither wholly
predictable nor able to be brought entirely under the sway of rational
action. The dialectic of history even possesses the power to convert
man's intentions into their opposites. At given points in history, how-

ever, man's intervention in history or his abstention from such intervention is decisive. While man cannot impose any order he may wish on history, he may intervene decisively according to the objective possibilities and induce an order commensurate with such decisive intervention. But every intervention of man in history is invested with risk. This view forbids dispair of history or of the power of human action; but it also forbids all utopianism, whether resting on the objectivity of reason or resting on the rightness of human intention.

C. *Existentialism in Italy: Nicola Abbagnano*

In Italy existentialism encountered a powerful, articulate, and culturally entrenched obstacle in the absolute historicism of Benedetto Croce and the actualism of Giovanni Gentile. Nevertheless, it made considerable headway through its influence on those thinkers who, like the Christian spiritualists, were in revolt against the absolute immanence which both historicism and actualism imposed. With the spiritualists, however, existentialism remained a secondary stream; their fountainhead was elsewhere. In only one Italian philosopher, Nicola Abbagnano (b. 1901), can existentialism be said to have become a basis for positive and autonomous speculative construction.

Abbagnano has given his position the appellation "positive existentialism" (*Esistenzialismo positivo,* 1948). The first indications of this position are discernible as early as his work *Le sorgenti irrazionali del pensiero* [The irrational springs of thought], published in 1923. This work antedates any mass influx of existentialist literature into Italy and indicates the independent origins of Abbagnano's views. His later writings show the influence of his reading of Husserl, Heidegger, and Jaspers.

La struttura dell'esistenza [The structure of existence], 1939, is recognized as Abbagnano's central work. It treats the central theme of existentialism: man in relation to being. The distinctive traits of Abbagnano's development of this theme are immediately apparent. His specific intention is to seek within existence its positive moment, the moment at which the drive toward nothingness, which Heidegger had stressed, is arrested and reversed toward being. He finds this moment in the notion of existence as *structure.* Structure is that form of existence in which the final situation of the movement toward being achieves essential unity with the initial situation of existence.

This initial situation is a certain possibility which *can be* realized in the final situation. Existence is justified as the *possibility* of its own *possibility,* in contrast to the *possibility* of its *impossibility* (death), as in Heidegger. The possibility of the possibility of existence takes the form of problem. Man can, by an existential option, recognize and accept himself in a continuous process of transcendence toward being; or, by an "inauthentic" option he may fall into "banal dispersion" of his being. The most authentic form in which the existent may realize itself is "coexistence," a process in which "the I and the Thou simultaneously constitute themselves" and each other.

Abbagnano subsequently reelaborates this line of thought in two other works: *Introduzione all'esistenzialismo* [Introduction to existentialism], 1942, and the work mentioned above, *Esistenzialismo positivo*. In the latter, he takes issue with the central point from which the negativity of French and German existentialism flows: the absolute equivalence of all of the possibilities which reveal themselves in human existence. For Abbagnano, not all possibilities are equal, and the form and positivity of human existence are established by a valuative discrimination among possibilities. The basis or principle of this valuative discrimination is *freedom;* not freedom as indiscriminate choice, but freedom as that choice which guarantees its own possibility. Abbagnano's *Critical Existentialism* (trans. N. Langiulli) appeared in 1968.

Readings

I. GENERAL WORKS

Barrett, W. *Irrational Man*. Garden City, N. Y.: Doubleday, 1962.
Blackham, H. J. *Reality, Man and Existence: Essential Works of Existentialism*. New York: Bantam Books, 1965.
Collins, James. *The Existentialists*. Chicago: Henry Regnery, 1952.
Sontag, Frederick. *The Existentialist Prolegomena to a Future Metaphysics*. Chicago: University of Chicago Press, 1970.

II. INDIVIDUAL PHILOSOPHERS

Karl Jaspers

Books
Allen, Edgar L. *The Self and Its Hazards: A Guide to the Thought of Karl Jaspers*. New York: Philosophical Library, 1951.
Schilpp, Paul A., ed. *The Philosophy of Karl Jaspers*. New York: Tudor, 1957.

Essays and articles
Gerber, Rudolph. "Karl Jaspers and Kantian Reason." *The New Scholasticism*, XLIII (1969).
Sablone, G. M. "Man Before God in the Philosophy of Karl Jaspers." *Philosophy Today*, XI (1967).

Martin Heidegger

Books

Frings, M. S., ed. *Heidegger and the Quest for Truth*. Chicago: Quadrangle Books, 1968.

Langan, Thomas. *The Meaning of Heidegger*. New York: Columbia University Press, 1959.

Marquarris, John. *Martin Heidegger*. Richmond, Va.: John Knox Press, 1968.

Richardson, W. J. *Heidegger: Through Phenomenology to Thought*. Preface by Martin Heidegger. The Hague: Martin Nijhoff, 1963.

Essays and articles

Adkins, H. W. H. "Heidegger and Language." *Philosophy*, XXXVII (1962).

Farber, M. "Heidegger on the Essence of Truth." *Philosophy and Phenomenological Research*, XVIII (1957–58).

Gray, J. Glenn. "Poets and Thinkers, Their Kindred Roles in the Philosophy of Martin Heidegger." In *Phenomenology and Existentialism*, edited by Edward Lee and M. Mandelbaum, pp. 93–113. Baltimore: Johns Hopkins Press, 1966.

Richardson, W. J. "Heidegger and the Origin of Language." *International Philosophical Quarterly*, II (1962).

Wild, John. "The Philosophy of Martin Heidegger." *The Journal of Philosophy*, LX (1963–64).

Gabriel Marcel

Books

Cain, Seymour. *Gabriel Marcel*. New York: Hillary House, 1963.

Gallagher, K. T. *Philosophy of Gabriel Marcel*. Foreword by Gabriel Marcel. New York: Fordham University Press, 1962.

Miceli, Vincent. *Ascent to Being*. Foreword by Gabriel Marcel. New York: Desclee, 1965.

Essays and articles

Hocking, W. E. "Marcel and the Ground Issues of Metaphysics." *Philosophy and Phenomenological Research*, XIV (1954).

Murray, J. Courtney. "The Structure of the Problem of God." *Theological Studies*, XXIII (1962).

Jean-Paul Sartre

Books

Bauer, G. H. *Sartre and the Artist*. Chicago: University of Chicago Press, 1969.

Cranston, M. W. *Sartre*. New York: Barnes & Noble, 1966.

Hartman, Klaus. *Sartre's Ontology*. Evanston, Ill.: Northwestern University Press, 1966.

Jolivet, R. *Sartre: The Theology of the Absurd*. Translated by Wesley Piersol. Westminster, Md.: Newman Press, 1967.

Warnock, Mary. *The Philosophy of Sartre*. London: Hutchinson, 1965.

Essays and articles

Kern, E. G., ed. *Sartre: A Collection of Critical Essays*. Englewood Cliffs, N. J.: Prentice-Hall, 1967.

Maurice Merleau-Ponty

Bannan, John F. *The Philosophy of Merleau-Ponty*. New York: Harcourt, Brace & World, 1967.

Langan, Thomas. *Merleau-Ponty's Critique of Reason*. New Haven: Yale University Press, 1967.

Rabil, A. *Merleau-Ponty: Existentialist of the Social*. New York: Columbia University Press, 1967.

Albert Camus

Onimus, Jean. *Albert Camus and Christianity*. Translated by Emmett Parker. University, Ala.: University of Alabama Press, 1970.

Thody, P. *Albert Camus: A Study of His Work*. London: H. Hamilton, 1957.

Nicholas Berdyaev

Davy, Marie Magdaleine. *Nicholas Berdyaev: Man of the Eighth Day*. Translated by Leonora Siepman. London: Bles, 1967.

CHAPTER IV

Philosophy as Analysis of Language

Introduction

The dominant current of philosophical thought in the English-speaking world today is called by a variety of names: neo-empiricism, logical positivism, logical empiricism, analytic philosophy, and linguistic analysis. There is sound reason for this variety of appellations, for this is not a strongly unified current but a mingling of richly diversified movements, each with strong characteristics of its own. Yet, through the entire range of these movements, there runs an element of unity which both justifies their being grouped together and serves as the basis for the intelligent distinction among them. This element is a certain view of philosophy—its nature, scope, and procedure. This is the view that the main concern of philosophy is the analysis of language.

At first glance, this would hardly seem to be enough to characterize this current or impart any great novelty to it. Nothing is more evident from the history of philosophy than the concern of philosophy for language and its analysis. From Plato to Vico and to the present, the analysis of language has been a main concern of philosophy. The Socratic dialogue, which has remained the perennial model of philosophical inquiry, is essentially an exercise in what today, in this new analytic philosophy, would be called "replacement" analysis: the examination, through linguistic and conceptual analysis, of a concept of dubious adequacy with the purpose of replacing it by a more adequate one. It might be added that what is called "exhibition" analysis is a phase of analysis never absent from the Socratic dialogue. Nevertheless, there is a difference which distinguishes the older, traditional concern with linguistic analysis from the new. It would seem to reside in this: Traditional philosophy looked upon linguistic analysis as a tool of philosophy, having only an instrumental value in the further speculative effort

301

of philosophical thought; linguistic analysis does not represent the total scope and range of philosophical inquiry. In modern linguistic analysis, by contrast, the analysis of language in all its forms is conceived to be the central and sole scope of philosophy. Linguistic analysis is *doing* philosophy, in the modern idiom, and nothing remains which is really philosophy when this task is accomplished.

The justification for this change must be sought in a transmutation of elements within the pattern of western intellectual culture. On the one hand stands the phenomenal growth of the positive sciences, not only in matter, but in clarity of method and ability to propound demonstrable theorems. The positive sciences are equipped with inbuilt means of rectifying their own errors and thus insuring their progress. For this reason, they seem gradually to be proving the only source of verifiable substantive knowledge. On the other hand stands the ostensible exhaustion of philosophical speculation—or, more accurately perhaps, the growing sense of its futility and sterility. This seems especially clear in the great idealist systems which held the stage at the end of the nineteenth and the beginning of the twentieth century. Within this perspective it was inevitable that the question should arise: What kind of inquiry is philosophy, what its scope and purpose, what its fruit? As Gilbert Ryle writes:

> Already surrendering its historic linkage with "mental science" or psychology and no longer remembering its former claim to be the science of things transcendental, philosophy looked like losing its credentials as a science of anything at all. Sterile of demonstrable theorems, sterile of experimentally testable hypotheses, philosophy was to face the charge of being sterile. [*The Revolution in Philosophy*, 1956, pp. 4–5]

The new conception of philosophy as analysis of language is an attempt to answer this charge; to redefine the nature, scope, and method of philosophy in such a way as to secure it a meaningful place in the contemporary scheme of the disciplines. In fulfilling this purpose it surrenders, on the one hand, the pretensions of philosophy to compete with the positive disciplines in the production of substantive knowledge; on the other, it rejects as alien to philosophy the "metaphysical" and "transcendental" pretensions of idealistic system-building. Instead, the attention of philosophy is directed to the common medium of all knowledge, language; and the purpose assigned it is that of determining the inner workings of language in the production of sound, verifiable knowledge. Its function is critical, in a way that is somewhat analogous to the Kantian use of this term; i.e., it is not the direct production of the theorems of science or the propositions of ordinary discourse which rules the lives of men, but the determination of the conditions of meaningfulness and truth in all forms of discourse. This is a task to which neither positive science nor speculative metaphysics directly addresses itself; yet it is a task which clearly needs to be done. Philosophy, moreover, by reason of its traditional, though instrumental, concern for language, is already in a position to take up this task. The new concern for the analysis of language thus links up with one of the soundest elements in the classical tradition of philosophy; it is not taking up a new task, but rather is taking up with new energy and seriousness one of the oldest tasks which philosophy has historically recognized as incumbent upon it.

Within this fresh conception of philosophy as the analysis of language, it has become customary to distinguish two main strains: 1) the analysis of *scientific* language, that is, of the languages proper to the individual sciences; and 2) the analysis of *ordinary* language, the language of common sense and of daily discourse. The former is usually called *logical positivism,* and it tends, beyond the determination of the actual processes of scientific discourse, toward the goal of constructing "ideal" languages for the sciences. The second is usually called simply *analytical philosophy* or ordinary language analysis and tends toward the clarification of such discourse, the removal of equivocations and ambiguities. This distinction is no doubt valid, but it does not seem ultimate. There is a unity between the two strands which would seem to indicate that they are but different aspects of a single inquiry. This deeper unity is to be found in the conviction that philosophical problems originate in the use of language and that the proper way to address them is, therefore, by way of the analytic and therapeutic treatment of language in all its forms, whether scientific or ordinary.

When this unity is recognized as central, it becomes clear that philosophy as the analysis of language is a cultural current with a geographical and time pattern which embraces the continent of Europe, England, and the United States over a period of about seventy-five years. It falls into a number of phases which are vitally related to one another. These include an anticipatory phase, which has diverse centers in America, in England, and on the Continent; a continental phase, at the center of which is the work of the Vienna Circle; an English phase, which has its center in the group which gathered about Wittgenstein upon his return to Cambridge; and, finally, an American phase, in which the center of activity shifts significantly back to America, due principally to the exile of numerous members of the continental movement but also to the indigenous American interests. The present treatment, instead of following the dichotometric pattern suggested by the distinction between logical positivism and ordinary language analysis, will follow this cultural pattern, finding within it the realities to which the members of that dichotomy refer.

A. *The Anticipatory Phase: Peirce, Moore, Russell, Wittgenstein as Pupil of Russell*

An authentic anticipation of the entire movement of philosophy as analysis of language is certainly to be found in the American, Charles Sanders Peirce (1839–1914). The germ of this approach may be said to be already present (independent of his specific pragmatical indications) in his famous article "How to Make Our Ideas Clear" (*Popular Science Monthly*, 1878, pp. 286–302). Peirce made important contributions to logic and to the general theory of signs. His influence was already felt in his lifetime, for example, on the work of the mathematician and logician Ernst Schröder and on Bertrand Russell's theory of relations and truth. It would be felt even more importantly in the third phase of the career of this movement, when his theory of signs would become the basis of the more elaborate system of Charles Morris, which would, in turn, have influence on and be influenced by the work of Carnap during his American period. Finally, Peirce's own writings contain passages of analysis, such as those in which he traces logical errors and confusions to the characteristics of language.

A more explicit anticipation of the conception of philosophy as analysis of language, if not the actual establishment of the concept in the effective form it would assume in the British phase of the movement, is to be found in the work of G. E. Moore (1873–1958). Moore, with Russell, is among the most important representatives of the reaction against idealism in England in the first decades of the present century; he is an authoritative exponent of common-sense realism. He develops the idea that the relation between consciousness and the object is a very particular one in that there is included in the consciousness of anything the consciousness that that thing is not an inseparable dimension of consciousness itself (cf. his *Philosophical Studies*, 2nd ed. 1948, p. 27). Moore's doctrinal position touching the value of common-sense concepts, the range of man's cognitive experience, etc., has abiding interest. His chief influence, however, lay not so much in these teachings as in his procedure in philosophizing. This procedure made him the model of later analysts of language. He enunciates the basic principle of the movement when he writes in *Principle Ethica*, that "it appears to me that in ethics, as in all other philosophical studies, the difficulties and disagreements, of which history is full, are mainly due to a very simple cause, namely, to the attempt to answer questions without first discovering precisely what question it is which you desire to answer"; what must be done is "the work of analysis and distinction" (Preface). He gives examples of this work in his treatment of such statements as that of idealism that the universe is *spiritual;*

in that term the idealist includes "quite a large number of different properties" which he fails to analyze and distinguish. Moore undertook to analyze "ordinary language," for in it, he believes, the theoretical confusions begin and at this point their resolution must be found.

A third anticipation of the conception of philosophy as the analysis of language is to be discerned in the early thought of Bertrand Russell (1872–1970), especially in the early system to which he gave the name "logical atomism." Russell, like Moore, had begun by reacting against the prevailing idealism. Like Moore, he reverted to a kind of realism, based ultimately on a belief in the meaningfulness of the statements of ordinary language. Ordinary language seemed to imply an implicit realism. That realism could be derived by an analysis of ordinary discourse. At this point, however, a difference appears. Moore, as Morton White points out (*The Age of Analysis*, 1955, p. 91), proceeds like a philologist; Russell, by contrast, actually initiates the logical analysis of language. This procedure led him to the position called "logical atomism," the essence of which is that the real world can be analyzed, not into psychological atoms (impressions, ideas), as Hume had held, but into logical units or atoms; also, that the world, as it actually appears and is spoken about, can be reconstructed on the basis of such logical atoms by the processes of logic. Russell did not persist in the position of logical atomism; but in its development he advanced a notion of philosophical activity, i.e., the logical analysis of language (in the first instance, of ordinary language, but ultimately of all discourse, including that of science, mathematics, ethics), which was to exercise very wide influence.

Closely linked with the name of Russell in the period of the formulation and gradual abandonment of logical atomism is that of the man who was to become the greatest influence in the later stages of the analytic movement, Ludwig Wittgenstein (1889–1951). An Austrian by birth and an engineer by early training, Wittgenstein came into contact with Russell and his ideas during a sojourn in England. He at first accepted Russell's ideas, but went on to develop and then to criticize and reject them. What he did not reject, however, was the living center of Russell's thought: the notion of philosophy as analysis of language. Wittgenstein was to develop this insight more elaborately and more acutely than any other figure in the movement. But before this development bore its first fruit in his immensely influential work *Tractatus Logico-Philosophicus*, Wittgenstein was to return to his native land, where he eventually formed certain relations with and exercised an influence over the Vienna circle (though he was never to become a formal member).

B. *The Continental Phase: The Vienna Circle and Its Adjuncts*

In its continental phase, the movement of philosophy as analysis of language is associated, above all, with the Vienna Circle and its work. The Vienna Circle can be treated most conveniently under the following rubrics: its origins and organization; its philosophical aims and ideals and the chief themes of its reflection; the chief phases of the thought of its chief figures.

1. Origins and Organization

The Vienna Circle was indirectly inspired by the philosopher-scientist Ernst Mach (1838–1916). As professor of the philosophy of the empirical sciences at the University of Vienna from 1895, he had instituted a tradition of criticism of contemporary idealistic and metaphysical philosophy and had begun a movement of reform directed to orientating philosophy toward the analytic task of establishing the bases and value of the empirical sciences.

In 1922 Moritz Schlick (1881–1936) succeeded to Mach's chair. He immediately began to form about himself the nucleus of the group which would become known as the Vienna Circle. Mach's influence is evident from the fact that the first name suggested for the group was the Verein Ernst Mach. The date of its inception may be placed as 1923. The movement was immensely strengthened by the arrival in Vienna of Rudolf Carnap (b. 1891), who was to become the guiding spirit of the group's discussions. In 1929 the configuration of the group became clearer and its name was fixed by the publication of a manifesto, "The Scientific World-View of the Vienna Circle," authored by Carnap, Otto Neurath (1882–1945), and the mathematician Hans Hahn. In the following year the group took over the journal *Annalen der Naturphilosophie,* which they rechristened *Erkenntnis.* Its editors were Rudolf Carnap and Hans Reichenbach (1891–1953). Reichenbach was a professor at Berlin, where he had formed a similar group with similar views and interests. To Reichenbach's group belonged such figures as Kurt Lewin and C. G. Hempel. It is worthy of note that Wittgenstein's *Tractatus Logico-Philosophicus* had first been published in the *Annalen* in 1921 and became the basis of many of the discussions of the Vienna Circle. Though Wittgenstein never formally associated himself with the group, his thought in this work forms an essential part of the picture of the Vienna Circle.

The years 1930–36 mark the height of the group's European activity. During this period, in addition to *Erkenntnis,* the group published a series of monographs under the general title *Einheitswissenschaft*

[Unified science] and a series of full-length books. The general editors of these efforts were Moritz Schlick and the philosopher of science Philipp Frank, who was a professor at the German University of Prague. Works of merit by authors who were not members of the Circle also appeared in this series. Throughout this period relations were maintained with philosophers in other countries—such as Poland, England, and Holland—who shared the interests and preoccupations of the group, and a number of international congresses were held.

The impending denouement of this phase of the movement was marked by the death of Moritz Schlick in 1936, at the hands of an enraged student. Political pressures had begun to mount which would make it impossible for many of the members of the group to remain in Austria. The country at that time was under the conservative rightist governments of Dollfuss and Schuschnigg, to whom the theories of the Circle and its adherents were unacceptable. This opposition was to increase when unification with Germany brought the Nazi party into power in Austria. As a result, many of the chief figures of the movement scattered abroad, some to other countries of Europe but most to the United States. Neurath took refuge in Holland, and Friedrich Waismann went to England. Carnap, Herbert Feigl, Gustav Bergmann, Hans Kelsen, and Kurt Gödel went to the United States, thus initiating the American phase of the movement. Neurath, from his place of refuge, first in Holland and then in England, sought to keep the continental phase of the movement alive. The journal *Erkenntnis* was renamed *The Journal of Unified Science* and published at The Hague. The war and Neurath's death brought even these efforts to a halt, and the continental phase of the movement closed.

2. Philosophical Aims and Themes of the Vienna Circle

The appellations applied to the central doctrine and method of the Vienna Circle include "logical positivism," "logical empiricism," "neo-positivism," and "neo-empiricism." All of these names are efforts to bring into relief the component elements of its position. The most basic component is a predeliction for the attitudes and methods of science. These are considered the only attitudes and methods which do not permit indulgence in mystical, metaphysical, and theological interpretations or falsifications of experience. According to Richard von Mises, a member of the group and author of an authoritative statement of its position, the scientific attitude is destined gradually, but inevitably, to displace all other attitudes and procedures in all fields of experience and inquiry. This emphasis on the exclusive validity of science was the basis for the application of the term "positivism," which linked it with the nineteenth-century movement of that name, of which Ernst Mach had been an exponent.

This position is the clue to the notion of philosophy entertained by the group. For the Vienna Circle, philosophy could only be the methodology of the sciences. The basis of this notion is the rejection, in the face of the indubitable positive achievements of science, of all pretentions of philosophy to establish itself as a "science" vis-a-vis the natural sciences. This is sometimes described as the opposition of the Vienna Circle to all forms of metaphysics. It is important to note that this attack on the scientific pretensions of philosophy was not directed at the excessively speculative character of those pretensions or at some basis for their erroneousness; this attack held the more radical ground that the statements expressing these pretensions lacked meaning, were, in fact, *non-sense*.

Philosophy then cannot be a "science" in its own right; that position is occupied exclusively by the positive sciences, those which can meaningfully make substantive statements concerning the form and content of experience. Philosophy can only exist and operate in function of this positive character of science. What, then, is the task of philosophy among the intellectual disciplines? It is to be the methodology of the sciences. The meaning of this statement would seem to embrace two operations which define the task of philosophy.

It might at first be supposed that this statement was intended to assign a wholly ancillary function to philosophy, the somewhat redundant task of analyzing after the fact, the methods by which science had achieved its success. This is by no means the case. Such an intention would have placed logical positivism out of contact with the advances of science, because those advances had been achieved through analysis of the conceptual and linguistic instruments of which it made use. Science, in a word, already practiced that form of self-analysis which some would call the task of philosophy as the methodology of science. On the contrary, the task of philosophy is still positive and even a bit surreptitiously "metaphysical." That task is to derive the *world view* implicit in the positive achievements of science. It was this notion of philosophy which led to the employment of the phrase "die wissenschaftliche Weltauffassung" in the manifesto of the Circle. The derivation of a world view is still the task of philosophy, but it is now a world view to be derived from science.

At this point two things become clear: 1) the difference between this "logical positivism" and the nineteenth-century positivism, and 2) the central place which logical positivism gives to the analysis of scientific language as the specific procedure of philosophy. The older positivism too had conceived its task as the derivation of a world view from science. It thought that this end could be achieved by a synthetic process, that of bringing together into a concrete unity the *substantive* results of the positive and empirical sciences. Nowhere had this purpose of the older positivism been better expressed than in the work of Spencer. The neo-positivism of the Vienna school rejects this view. It is not the *material* results of the sciences, however synthesized, which reveal the scientific world view. Rather, that world view is revealed by the analysis of the manner in which these results are formulated. But this mode of formulation is nothing other than the language of science. Therefore, the procedure for the derivation of the scientific world view must be the analysis of the language of science to determine the principles and the criteria of meaning on which its statements are formulated. The important thing to note is that this analysis is not redundant; i.e., it does not yield simply the arbitrary rules of scientific language; it yields, as Carnap says in the very title of one of his early works, the *logical structure of the world* and not merely the immanent structure of scientific discourse.

These reflections explain the "positivistic" element in logical positivism: the derivation of an empirically grounded world view from the analysis of the language of science. This, it should be noted, is a philosophical inquiry; it does not pretend to scientific construction nor is its function merely redundant and ancillary. The question now arises: What is the instrument of this analysis? The answer to this question yields the "logical" element in logical positivism. That instrument is found in the process of logic, especially the mathematical logic of the tradition of Frege and Russell. The *specific task of philosophy* is the logical analysis of the language of science. Philosophy will become the logic of science. But the proper end of philosophy, the derivation of the world view of science, will not be lost since it is identical with the logical analysis of the language of science. That world view is revealed as directly immanent to the positive statements of the sciences by the analysis of the conditions of the meaningfulness of its sentences. It will not be embodied in a separate system of statements which would have crypto- and pseudo-scientific status. There is no recurrence of the odious metaphysical structures of the past. The autonomous work of philosophy, the derivation of the *Weltauffassung* of science, is carried on within the orbit of scientific statements, and not through the creation of a transcendent body of propositions which would presumably obey laws of meaning different from those proper to science (the only valid ones).

3. Salient Ideas of Central Figures of the Vienna Circle

Although Ludwig Wittgenstein was not a member of the Vienna Circle in any formal sense, he exercised an important influence on its members and their views, principally through his work *Logisch-Philosophische Abhandlung*, published in German in 1921 and translated into English in the following year as *Tractatus Logico-Philosophicus*. In this work the members of the Vienna Circle saw clear indications of how the logical and empirical elements of science might be theoretically synthesized through the analysis of language. A difficult book, the *Tractatus* concerns two themes: the analysis of the nature of language and its power of symbolic representation, and the particular character of logical and mathematical language. Its fundamental ideas on these themes are expressed in a few basic propositions, upon which the remainder of the work elaborates.

The language which Wittgenstein considers is an ideal language (independent of spoken languages). The structure of this language reflects the logical structure of the real world; it has meaning as an image of the world. The configuration of simple signs and of propositional signs (nouns and sentences) corresponds to the configuration of objects in the real situation. The meaning of a proposition is, therefore, its power to describe possible facts. This conclusion implies the existence of simple facts (atom-facts) to which there correspond absolutely simple (atomic or elementary) propositions. The *Tractatus* implies that these "atomic facts" are the immediate data of sensible experiences. These data are neither subjective nor objective. The entire construction of language rests on these atomic propositions. Non-elementary (molecular) propositions result from the combination of atomic propositions by the use of logical constants: "and" "or" "if . . . then." Molecular propositions are truth functions of the atomic propositions, for their truth value depends on the truth value of the latter. The totality of atomic and molecular propositions with empirical meaning constitutes science. The propositions of logic and mathematics are without empirical meaning. They are transformations of linguistic signs; their validity depends, not on empirical verification, but on the intrinsic form of the signs. They are tautologies; this is especially true of the laws of logical inference. The propositions of traditional philosophy are not only meaningless (*sinnlos*) but non-sense (*unsinnig*). Philosophy is not a doctrine but an activity, that of showing the correspondence of facts and propositional images. This correspondence can be illustrated but not expressed. The office of philosophy is the clarification of obscure or dense ideas.

These basic notions of Wittgenstein's position in the *Tractatus* exercised a strong influence on the members of the Vienna Circle and consequently belong to any account of that movement.

The founder of the Vienna Circle, Moritz Schlick, was the most open-minded member of the group. In addition to embracing the chief positions of the Circle—opposition to metaphysics, reduction of philosophy to linguistic analysis, etc.,—he expressed a naturalistic world view which carried with it an optimistic ethics: Nature supports, though it does not supply, man's values. Before the establishment of the Circle and his contact with Wittgenstein's writings, Schlick had formulated a position that was founded principally on his reflections on the epistemological meaning of the theory of relativity. In this he anticipates certain positions later characteristic of the Circle. He developed a theory of knowledge based on the distinction between experiencing and knowing. According to this theory, the latter results from the coordination of the symbolic structures of the deductive sciences with immediate experience and its data.

When he came to know Wittgenstein's work, Schlick was led to transpose these earlier ideas into the idiom of the analysis of language. In addition to reformulating the characteristic Wittgensteinian theses, Schlick gave the earliest formulation of the "empirical principle of verification," which was to be the keystone idea of the first phase of the thought of the Circle. This principle said that "the meaning of a proposition is the method by which it is verified." The propositions of science alone are meaningful because they alone are verifiable through appeal to experience. Those of philosophy are either reducible to scientific propositions or are without meaning. This principle was later embarrassed by the fact that it did not fulfill the conditions of meaning which it formulated. Moreover, its appeal to the immediate data of experience seemed to other members of the Circle to have metaphysical overtones. Hence within the ranks of the Circle arose a controversy, involving chiefly Neurath and Carnap, who sought to replace the immediate expressions of sense data, which seemed metaphysically charged, with "protocol" sentences which carried no such charge. Schlick was the author of many works, most of them in the border area between physics and philosophy. Most interesting philosophically is his *Gesammelte Aufsätze* [Collected essays], 1926–36, because they reflect the most active period of his involvement in the work of the Circle. Other volumes were edited after his death: *Philosophie der Natur* [Philosophy of nature], 1948, and *Natur und Kultur* [Nature and culture], 1952.

Otto Neurath, another important early figure of the Vienna Circle, was a sociologist. His point of contact with the movement was his interest in the methodology of his science, which he sought to approximate as closely as possible to that of the empirical sciences of nature. He is considered an extreme nominalist in that he resolutely reduces science to language. The criterion of truth for linguistic propositions is, not their confrontation with immediate data of experience, but only the analysis of their position in relation to the other linguistic propositions and the total system of scientific language. There is no "reality" outside of language to which language can be compared; reality is the totality of propositions. This position has been called the "intranscendibility" of language. Neurath is also credited with the first formulation of the principle of "physicalism," which holds that, as language is identical with reality, it is, like all reality, a *physical* fact with the same status as all other physical facts. These views brought him into conflict with other members of the group on a number of points. He rejected Carnap's theory of original protocol sentences as well as his methodic solipsism, which held that such sentences could be proper to a single subject exclusively. A protocol proposition, as a linguistic structure (which it must be), is already universal and intersubjective. Every philosophical problem which does not admit of formulation in physical language is meaningless.

By far the most energetic and influential member of the Vienna Circle was Rudolf Carnap. His activity falls into a number of periods or phases. The chief division is between his European period and his American period. His passage to America must not be considered as a break in his activity, however, but as an extension of the horizon of his thought through contact with the active elements in the American scene.

Within his European phase, which alone is considered here, a number of lesser phases can be distinguished. The first of these is signalized by such publications as *Der logische Aufbau der Welt* [The logical structure of the world], 1928. In this work Carnap undertakes to reconstruct the entire domain of the concepts of human knowledge on purely logical grounds, independently of any metaphysical system or *Weltanschauung*, or, more precisely, with a view to replacing all such fanciful structures by a "scientific" world view which would meet the stringent conditions of science. In doing this he uses the results of the Machian position of "empirio-criticism" in conjunction with modern logical theories as developed by Bertrand Russell. In this view, concepts are constructible in a gradual order as classes of properties and relations, the meaning of which is guaranteed by the data of immediate individual and personal experience. What they would ensure would be, not an imaginary world view, but a scientific comprehension of the world. This effort placed him at the very center of the interests and activity of the Vienna Circle, for the establishment of a scientific understanding of the world to replace older philosophical constructions was the central goal of its activity.

Carnap proceeded to consolidate his position as the major spokesman of the Circle by a series of writings which constitute a radical criticism of traditional philosophy from the neo-positivist point of view.

These include the *Scheinprobleme in der Philosophie* [Specious problems in philosophy], 1928, and the "Uberwindung der Metaphysik durch logische Analyse der Sprache" [The dissolution of metaphysics through the logical analysis of language] in *Erkenntnis,* 1932. In these writings, traditional philosophy is considered as a complex of meaningless declarations or assertions. Only scientific language, insofar as its assertions refer to the immediate data of experience, in the sense he had elaborated, possesses meaning; and all philosophy which pretends to scientific stature ought to restrict its efforts to the analysis of such language.

In the phase centering on these writings, Carnap's concern with linguistic analysis may be called material; i.e., meaning is made to depend on reference to the immediate data of experience. From this he passes, principally in the work *Logische Syntax der Sprache (The Logical Syntax of Language)* 1934, to a more sophisticated analysis which places at its center the syntactical structure of language and the conditions it imposes on the concept of meaning. He begins by acknowledging the metaphysical residue present in the appeal, in the earlier phase, to the immediate data of experience as the basis of meaning and verification. Such extra-linguistic reference seems to violate the concept of philosophy as the analysis of language; this ideal of philosophy is maintained only by the formal analysis of language. Hence, his interest seems to move from a dominantly empirical phase to a more formalistic phase. In this phase, his effort is directed toward the analysis of language as the determination of its syntax—that is, the rules of formation of expressions and propositions in the language as well as the rules of transformation which establish the modes of inference, of logical movement, within the language. His greatest insistence is upon the formal character of such rules. They are established only on conventional grounds; i.e., they are selected and formulated on the basis of their usefulness and convenience for the purpose intended. There is no morality in logic, Carnap remarks (*Logische Syntax der Sprache,* p. 45). He does not envisage any problem concerning an ostensible privileged logical or linguistic form. The field of language is pluralistic in structure.

At this new juncture, Carnap finds himself somewhat embarrassed by the violently antimetaphysical position of his first phase, not because he has become any less antimetaphysical in intent, but because the grounds for this position had rested on the earlier empirical concept of verifiability and on Neurath's "physicalism." He therefore set about revising the method of confirming empirical propositions on the basis of the conventionalistic theory of language which he had developed in the *Logical Syntax of Language.* Meaning is now made to depend more on the "formal" or "syntactical" mode of language than on the "material." The chief text for this development is the essay "Testability and Meaning," published in the review *Philosophy of Science* in 1936–37.

In this phase Carnap also became interested in the problem of the unity of science. This concept had a dual aspect. In the first place, it tended to suggest the synthesizing role of philosophy in relation to the results of the sciences envisaged by ninteenth-century positivism. But this was not Carnap's idea, any more than it was that of Neurath, with whom he shared this interest (though it should be noted that Neurath's concern has its basis in his cultural and social interests, while Carnap's is more formal and philosophical). The new conception of the unity of science viewed it, not as material, but as resting on the unifying power of a common language for all sciences to which the specific language of each could be reduced. Carnap's long essay "Die physikalische Sprache als Universalsprache der Wissenschaft" [Physical language as the universal language of science], in *Erkenntnis* illustrates this interest.

Carnap's activity after he came to America not only kept alive the ideas of the Vienna Circle but added new dimensions to them. These developments will be considered briefly below when we deal with the American phase of the career of philosophy conceived as analysis of language.

C. *The British Phase*

The inception of the British phase of the movement is sometimes said to have begun with Wittgenstein's return to England. Despite the importance of this event for analytic philosophy, it should be recognized that significant developments in its career had taken place there prior to this event. The concept of philosophy as analysis of language cannot, therefore, be considered an import to England from the Continent. This idea has an independent history in England; it received fresh stimulus and direction from the Continent but not its origins. One of the important figures of this native English development of linguistic analysis is the Oxford philosopher Gilbert Ryle (b. 1900).

Ryle's thought reflects a rich and varied philosophical inheritance, judiciously assimilated and rethought into an original synthesis. Among the elements of this inheritance must be considered the philosophical atmosphere of Oxford in the early decades of the present century, in which a number of strains were present and interactive: the dissolution of idealism and the analytic activity of J. Cook Wilson; the classical tradition of analysis in Plato and Aristotle; the work of Russell, and the logical and phenomenological research of Brentano, Frege, and Husserl; finally Wittgenstein, in both the *Tractatus* and his later, English period.

Basic to Ryle's thought is his very conception of philosophical activity. Its function is to discover, correct, and prevent logical or "categorial" errors. These errors consist in the assigning of a concept to a category to which it does not rightly belong, classifying it with other concepts with which it has only superficial grammatical similarities. The "category mistake" is favored by the similarity, from the grammatical point of view, of propositions which, from the logical point of view, differ fundamentally. Such confusion leads, in turn, to the positing of meaningless or nonsensical questions. The categorial error manifests itself in a violation of the right use of language. Therefore, the logical analysis of language is the best means of laying bare and correcting category mistakes. But this procedure is only negative. More positively, analytic philosophy constructs a "logical geography" of concepts which would plot the logic of propositions in which concepts are used, show with what other propositions they are compatible, and indicate what processes of deduction are possible among propositions. The positive purpose is to establish the ways in which it is logically legitimate to operate with concepts.

Ryle applied this notion of philosophy extensively and organically in his work *The Concept of Mind* (1949). Although, on its first plane of meaning, this work is a criticism of the Cartesian "myth" of the "ghost in the machine" concept of the mind-body dualism, on a higher plane its true value lies in its reanalysis of the basic terms in which the problem appears and its selection of a "behavior" terminology for the adequate description and characterization of those operations which previously had been ascribed to hidden principles of the mind. Thus, the mind-body dualism is resolved in operational terms.

Ludwig Wittgenstein returned to Cambridge University in 1929 to pursue philosophy as a Fellow of Trinity College. Ten years later he was elected to succeed G. E. Moore in his professorial chair, but the Second World War broke out before he could assume his duties. He remained at Cambridge until he resigned this chair in 1947 and only returned there again to endure his last illness before his death in 1951.

When he came to Cambridge for the second time, his stature in the field of philosophy was already authoritative, and his influence on the general movement known as logical positivism was both wide and great. This authority and influence rested on one thing, the *Tractatus Logico-Philosophicus*, in which his position would seem to have been definitively established. The interesting fact is that his Cambridge career was marked by a steady withdrawal from this position. The process was gradual and was worked out in the course of the tortuous sessions which he held with his never numerous students. No published record of the process appeared before his death. The documentation for this process became public only with the posthumous publication of the *Philosophical Investigations,* 1953, and of the *Blue* and *Brown Books,* 1958. The latter were composed between 1930 and 1934 and trace the first stages of this withdrawal from his earlier position; the former is the master document of the mind of the later Wittgenstein. The thought of the first Wittgenstein, as it took form is the *Tractatus,* has already been touched upon. The question now is: How does the position of the later Wittgenstein, as it appears in the *Philosophical Investigations,* differ?

It must be noted that the position of the *Philosophical Investigations* is not merely a revision of that of the *Tractatus.* There is a complete break between them, and the doctrine of the *Investigations* constitutes not only something new in Wittgenstein's thought but, according to some, something absolutely new in the history of philosophy. Thus Georg von Wright says: "Wittgenstein's later philosophy is . . . entirely outside any philosophical tradition. . . . The author of the *Philosophical Investigations* has no ancestor in philosophy" (*Logik, Filosofi och Språk,* p. 176 ff.) More accurately, one might say that the treatment is entirely original and, hence, so are the results; however, the theme is continuous. This theme is language—the theory of what it is and the theory and practice of its analysis for the solution of philosophical problems. This continuity of theme makes it possible to characterize the original doctrine of the *Philosophical Investigations* against the background of the *Tractatus.*

What had been Wittgenstein's view of language in the earlier work? Language, in the *Tractatus,* is a *picture* of reality; it depicts the logical structure of facts, of states of facts. Meaning, in language, is corrsepon-dence between language and the facts or states of affairs which langu-age indicates. The primary function of language is the naming of the objects which, in their relations, constitute the state of fact or of affairs; a meaningful proposition is one made up of the names of objects and which serves thus to depict the world. Language, in the *Tractatus* (following Frege and Russell and in kinship with logical positivism), meant an ideal language which was logical in structure and which reflected the logical structure of the situations of fact which constitute the world. Philosophy reveals the logical structure of the world through the analysis of language in this sense. Its task is to analyze sentences to unveil the elementary propositions of which they are truth-functions; it must then proceed to the analysis of these elementary propositions to reveal their logical form. In doing so it will lay bare the logical form of the states of affairs which constitute the world.

The doctrine of the *Philosophical Investigations* begins to develop its original direction at this fundamental point of the basic operation of language, at the point of the meaning of meaning. In the *Tractatus* the fundamental meaning of meaning had been naming; this operation linked language and the state of affairs to which it referred. In the *Philosophical Investigations* the key to meaning is *use*. Wittgenstein writes: ". . . the meaning of a work is its use in the language" (*Philosophical Investigations,* sec. 43). This does not constitute complete rejection of the doctrine of the *Tractatus;* naming is still one use to which words are put. The doctrine of the *Tractatus* is now put in a larger context, that of *use.* Naming alone will not give the meaning even of a name completely; the name too must be taken in the context of its use.

The concept of meaning as use gives rise to the basic notion of *language-game.* The language-game may, with some accuracy, be described as a pattern of use of words. Such uses, which become the bases of language-games, are, in addition to naming: asking questions, giving orders, describing things and events, evaluating, etc. The term "game" as used here should not distract from the serious purpose involved. Wittgenstein writes: ". . . the term 'language-game' is meant to bring into prominence the fact that speaking of language is part of an activity, or a form of life." (cf. *Philosophical Investigations,* sec. 64 ff.). The language-game is a serious use of language; what Wittgenstein seems to want to indicate by calling it a *game* is that the use is not governed by any overarching logic of the world or of reality, but is free in this respect, although within each game a rigid logic of the game (say, naming within a language) prevails. The notion of game is best described here as a logical and operative term. Any given language is made up of the language-games which it is possible to "play" in that language. One has learned a *language* when one can use the various language-games which make up the language. Among the language-games which constitute a language, there is no priority of one over another. This would include the language of science, which does not any longer have a privileged place for Wittgenstein but forms one of the possibilities of use in the phenomenon of language. The various uses have a basic autonomy, although in the language they develop certain relations and even dependencies which further complicate the picture of the language.

There is, however, a certain danger in speaking of *the* language. This might give the impression that the language is first and that the use or the language-games are derivative. This is not Wittgenstein's view. The language is not prior to the language-games which make it up; it is wholly immanent in them. Therefore, it is not possible to define language as over and above the language-games. There is no common concept of language; or, to say it in another way, language-games do not all possess one trait in common which can become the basis of a general definition of language. There exists instead, among the language-games which compose a language, what Wittgenstein calls family resemblances (*Philosophical Investigations,* sec. 67). Language-games form a family, and it is the family which is the language. The number of language-games which make up a language-family is at any moment *de facto* limited, but this is not so in principle. The number of language-games possible is indefinite, even within one family. Uses, which are the basis of the family structure of the language, can be multiplied, refined, etc.; the language family can grow and develop. This growth need not be irenic; it can be creative of tensions within the family group of language-games.

The family group of language-games is expressive in character. It expresses, in a complex way, the form of life of a people, i.e. of those individuals and groups which share its use or can play the same family or language-games. But the language-games do not tell us something *about* the form of life of that people. They *express* that life so that that life is wholly contained within those language-games and is made concrete and limited by the language-games which are actually available. If the language family has developed only certain uses, then it lacks the dimensions of the other uses as a form of life. With the development of language, the very form of life of a people develops. Thus, for example, within the Greek language western philosophy was born, through the development of that language-game in which philosophical inquiry takes form. By this development not only the Greek language but the life of the Greeks was immensely enriched and, through it, the life of the system of culture which includes Greek philosophy as one of its bases.

This mention of the development of the language-game of philosophy leads to what may be the final point in this brief characterization of the doctrine of the *Philosophical Investigations,* the concept of philosophy which Wittgenstein now entertains in view of his further reflections on language.

The function of philosophy in the *Tractatus* was *therapeutic;* it was to discover and correct errors in the use of language. This notion was possible because, in the *Tractatus,* there existed the notion of the *logically correct* use of language, which provided a therapeutic norm. This notion of correctness is not viable in the view of language in the *Philosophical Investigations.* Here, every use, every language-game is correct as it stands. The task of philosophy is, therefore, also changed. It should not attempt to correct but to *understand* the way of words in the language. To understand does not mean to know what the language pictures, as it did in the *Tractatus,* but to see how it functions, what purpose it serves, what work it does. Philosophy arises at the point of the possibility of misunderstanding a sentence in language or in a language-game. If there were no possibility of misunderstanding, there would be no philosophy. It would not arise. Philosophical problems arise from confusing one language-game with another, from supposing that different language-games are the same, or from thinking that only one language-game is legitimate and trying to make all others conform to it (as he had done in the *Tractatus*). But philosophical misunderstandings are not *lapses,* like other forms of mistake or error. They are misunderstandings which arise in the very forms of the language. Thus, the solution to a philosophical problem lies in discovering how and why such a misunderstanding has arisen. It responds to the need for a deeper insight into the actual function of the language being examined, through the understanding of the language-game actually being used. The *task of philosophy* is not to correct that use, but to describe it as it actually is. It is, therefore, descriptive in function. It cannot alter the discourse which it is examining with a view to understanding. "Philosophy may in no way interfere with the actual use of language; it can, in the end, only describe it" (*Philosophical Investigations,* sec. 124).

In the last analysis, it would seem clear that there is a tendency to exaggerate the distance between the *Tractatus* and the *Philosophical Investigations,* between the earlier and the later Wittgenstein. There is a basic continuity of theme; what is original is the theory of language in the later work and the manner in which the analysis of language is put to philosophical use. But even these original elements have a certain genetic relation to the *Tractatus;* they are born of insight into the shortcomings and the arbitrary positions taken up in the *Tractatus.* With no desire to minimize the striking originality of the doctrine of the *Philosophical Investigations,* it is still possible to see the entire thought of Wittgenstein as possessing a deeper basic unity within which the differences are significant and intelligible.

The closest link between the logical positivism of the Vienna Circle and the English phase of philosophy as the analysis of language lies, after Wittgenstein, in the work of Alfred Jules Ayer (b. 1910). Ayer had personal contact with the work of the Vienna Circle through a period as student in Vienna in the early thirties when the Circle was most active. He opened his own exposition of the position with an essay in the journal *Mind,* entitled "Demonstration of the Impossibility of Metaphysics"; this appeared in 1934. Two years later he published the book which was to bring him some measure of authority in the field: *Language, Truth and Logic,* 1936. This is considered one of the most complete and incisive expositions of the general position and principal theses of neo-positivism or logical positivism. It gained much in authority from the clarity and brilliance of its style. The fulcrum of the argument is the emphasis on the verification principle as it has been stated by the thinkers of the Vienna Circle and the consequent insistence that empirical propositions are the sole source of meaning. *A priori* statements or propositions are considered pure tautologies which say nothing about reality. Philosophical propositions and metaphysical statements, since they are neither tautologies nor empirical hypotheses, are pseudo-propositions without meaning. (This point had already been made in the article referred to above.)

The task of philosophy is altered in the light of this position. Its work now is linguistic and consists in the clarification and analysis of propositions on the basis of the verification principle of meaning. Ethics and religion have either to be reduced to psychological or sociological propositions or to be recognized as verbal expressions of emotional states. In later works, Ayer was to temper the extreme position taken here. These later works include *The Foundations of Empirical Knowledge,* 1940, *Thinking and Meaning,* 1947, and *The Problem of Knowledge,* 1956. Always clear and incisive, Ayer attracted attention by his treatment of such complex problems as that of other minds. In his later statements, he tended to assign a merely conventional status to the verification principle of meaning, though he never relinquished the empirical viewpoint to approach the formalistic point of view which others, like Carnap, were proposing. It is dubious, in the light of his later statements, that Ayer has ever withdrawn substantially from the position taken in *Language, Truth and Logic.*

Von Wright has been quoted as saying that the philosopher of the *Philosophical Investigations* has no ancestors; Wittgenstein himself, however, did not fail to acknowledge his indebtedness. Among those whose contribution he did acknowledge (cf. *Philosophical Investigations,* preface) was Frank Plumpton Ramsey (1903–1930). Ramsey died very prematurely, and the few years of his active career were devoted to economics, mathematical logic, and philosophy. He did not write any major work, but his essays and fragments were collected and edited by R. B. Braithwaite as *The Foundations of Mathematics,* 1931. If a general direction of development can be assigned to the essays and pieces which compose the volume, it might correctly be said that Ramsey had in view a revision of the *Principia Mathematica* of Russell and Whitehead, under the influence of suggestions from the *Tractatus* of Wittgenstein. His purpose then was to construct a rigorously deductive system which would demonstrate the identity of mathematics, considered in all its different branches, with logic. In carrying out this project, and in his treatment of such themes as "Truth and Probability" in the essay of that name, Ramsey also shows the influence of the American, C. S. Peirce. Thus, he maintains that induction, though not reducible to rigid logical form, is pragmatically justified; but this is a *rational* justification, and not, as Wittgenstein had said, a merely psychological one. Ramsey thinks that the activity of philosophy gives rise to a particular class of statements: elucidations, clarifications, classifications, definitions, and descriptions of the ways in which terms could be used. Elucidation may be said to be the key work in his philosophical lexicon. Nevertheless, he is not entirely sanguine about the prospects of this philosophical activity, for elucidations involve one another, and the argument ends, seemingly, in a circle, when it should be proceeding in a straight line. The danger of a philosophy dedicated to elucidation, he suggests, is "scholasticism," which means treating what is vague as if it were precise and could be put in an exact logical category.

John Wisdom (b. 1904), professor of philosophy at Cambridge, is author of *Problems of Mind and Matter,* 1931; *Other Minds,* 1952; and *Philosophy and Psychoanalysis,* 1953. He is noted among the analysts for his wide range of interests and for his readiness to recognize as significant or meaningful ethical, metaphysical, and aesthetic propositions, each with a language which must be distinguished both from scientific language and from "ordinary" language. Perhaps the most interesting and original of Wisdom's reflections are those touching on the problem of "other minds" (cf. the work of that title). He differs from Ryle in this matter. Ryle, in the *Concept of Mind,* had argued for the dissolution of the dichotomy between interior and exterior and the reduction of both to a common, "public" plane. But Wisdom not only recognizes interior experience but tends to give it a privileged place as the only form of certain and authentic knowledge. The very emphasis on the authenticity of interior experience gives rise to the problem of other minds. These, obviously, cannot occupy a public plane; they too must possess the depth dimension of interiority. Hence, the question of how they are to be known arises.

Wisdom seeks to meet this problem with the theory that such other minds are known by being reconstructed on the basis of certain symptoms which we discover in our own experience of ourselves. This accounts for Wisdom's interest in psychoanalysis. It also makes it clear that the prohibition which has been imposed on speaking of objects which lie beyond direct experience does not hold for Wisdom. Discourse about other selves is possible, though these lie, by definition, beyond experience. In his essay "Gods," contributed to the book *Logic and Language,* edited by A. G. N. Flew, 1955, Wisdom even admits to discovering symptoms of the existence of God in the religious behavior of men.

John Langshaw Austin (b. 1911), who is coming to exercise greater influence among those devoted to linguistic analysis, is known principally for a number of essays, the first of which was contributed to the *Proceedings of the Aristotelian Society.* These include: "Other Minds" (1946), "Truth" (1950), and "How to Talk" (1952). Austin is known especially for the extreme finesse and delicacy of his analyses and for the fact that he proceeds with a clear understanding of the philological, as distinct from philosophical, problems involved; or more precisely, he understands the subtle manner in which these two orders of problems are interwoven and interdependent.

Especially illustrative of Austin's skill is the essay on "Other Minds." He believes that the act of belief in other persons, in authority, and in testimony is an essential part of the act of communication and is an act which we perform regularly. It is an irreducible part of our experience. This essay is noteworthy for drawing attention to a special class of speech-actions, which Austin calls "performatory utterances." It has ordinarily been assumed by philosophers that language is descriptive. Thus, statements such as "I know that S is P" are explained by reference to a special act of knowing which is described in various ways. But Austin says that in such a statement "I know" is not a description; it functions like a promise, stating a performance; it makes a commitment. It is like saying "you can rely on me" or "take my word for it." Austin has carried the initial undertaking of language analysis to an extreme degree of grammatical and philological refinement, and his results have begun to have considerable appeal for younger philosophers, who tend to feel that older forms of this analysis reveal serious deficiencies.

Particular attention is given to the language of ethical and moral discourse in the work *The Language of Morals,* 1952, by R. M. Hare (b. 1919). Hare's argument in this work and the meaning he is prepared to assign to ethical imperatives turns about the distinction between imperative and descriptive propositions, a distinction which had already been recognized as early as Hume. These kinds of statements, he holds, are clearly not derivable from each other; no descriptive statement is ground for inference to an imperative. Therefore, all the older types of metaphysical-ethical systems, which sought to draw their imperatives from ontological situations which could first be rendered descriptively, are rejected.

But the two orders of propositions are not entirely divorced. They do have a common content. This he calls *phrastic*, that is, indicative or designative. Thus, two propositions such as the imperative "close the door" and the descriptive "I am about to close the door" share a common element—"close the door"—which is the *phrastic* element. The two kinds of propositions involve different attitudes and interpretations with reference to this common element. The first or descriptive order of propositions implies belief in that element; assent to the imperative order of propositions involves doing or performance or commitment to do or perform. The basis from which imperative statements with respect to this common phrastic element are derived are themselves prescriptive statements, the origin of which, in their concrete character, Hare tends to assign to the society of which one is a part. It goes without saying, of course, that such prescriptive principles are not themselves fixed and immutable. But the system of discourse based on them has clearly discernible meaning in the order of doing and performing and does not express mere subjective and emotive states, but reflects a relatively objective prescriptive order (based on society), which is translated into the imperatives and ought sentences of ethical and moral discourse. The significant point is that the person uttering such statements is indeed speaking of his own state, but, even more importantly, he is speaking of that state relative to an objective order which he translates into the language of commitment and performance. Ethical discourse is clearly meaningful.

In a recent book, *Freedom and Reason*, 1963, Hare has advanced the position of *The Language of Morals* in a very significant manner. He has taken under consideration two important problems: the possibility of *universalizing* imperative propositions and that of testing them. In the first, he takes a hint from Kant, who raised this same problem in the *Critique of Practical Reason*. He comes to the conclusion that moral imperatives and propositions can be universalized as well as descriptive propositions. Unlike Kant, however, he does not make this universalization rest upon a categorical imperative which the individual subject enunciates under some rubric such as that which Kant had suggested (*So act*, etc.), but finds the universalizing force in the social basis of the prescriptive principles from which, as he has held, the imperatives are derived. Regarding the testability of such imperatives, he follows a pattern derived from science: One proves or tests such propositions by trying to refute or confute them. Just as science seeks hypotheses and tests them by the effort to falsify their particular consequences, so moral science seeks principles and puts them to the test by seeking to confute them in particular cases. The discipline of rational moral thought is to put to the test the principles of action which are suggested to us, by drawing out their consequences and deciding on their acceptability. Thus, he takes a further step from that position which sees moral discourse as referring to emotive states; it is now clear that moral discourse shares the same properties as scientific discourse: universality and testability.

The men referred to in these brief paragraphs do not exhaust the roster of those in England actively practicing linguistic analysis as the authentic mode of philosophizing. They are, however, representative both of the strongest examples of this kind of exercise and of the different forms it can take. The fact that they are cited in their individual endeavors, each with his own preoccupations, makes it clear that this current of thought and this mode of practicing philosophy must not be conceived in too rigid a fashion. It is more a persuasion than a movement, and each of these writers follows out this persuasion in response to personal discernments.

D. *The American Phase*

One of the most interesting phenomena of recent history is the cultural migration westward from Europe both before and after the Second World War. This was a migration of both men and ideas. Among the migrant elements was the current of philosophy as analysis of language in both the form which it had taken on the Continent and that which it had taken in Great Britain. Under the political pressures which had built up in central Europe in the late twenties and the thirties, the Vienna Circle was dispersed and its chief adherents removed. Some went to other cities in Europe, but its chief figures, among them Carnap, migrated to the United States. No such violent force motivated the movement from Great Britian to the American shores. The motive force here was supplied by the cultural attraction and interaction which had always persisted between England and America. The migration of the language analysts was part of this traditional cultural movement between England and America. In America, both branches of this current struck new roots and continued to flourish, both in the work of the migrant philosophers themselves and in the work of native Americans whom they inspired. Thus, a natural pattern for the study and consideration of this "American phase" suggests itself. It seems natural to look first at the fresh developments of each branch of this current, logical positivism and linguistic analysis, giving due attention to the work of both the transplanted European representatives and the native Americans.

1. American Developments of Logical Positivism

Logical positivism of the Vienna-Berlin type, upon migrating to the United States, came into contact with two other movements which were to affect its interests and teachings in the thought of such representatives as Carnap. Of these movements, one, pragmatism, was native to the United States. The other, the Polish school of logic, had, like logical positivism itself, migrated to the United States. Both of these movements were to enter into contact with logical positivism on the ground of a problem which had been maturing within the context of logical positivism even while it still remained European. This was the problem of the adequacy of the syntactical position which logical positivism had assumed and the necessity of extending its analysis to include the semantic dimension of language.

The problem of the semantic dimension of language was not foreign to logical positivism. Schlick, the founder of the movement, had developed a theory of "empirical semantics." This had meant that the language of the sciences was controlled in its reference to actual objects by a rigid system of empirical control and that all propositions which could not meet these conditions were rendered meaningless. The canon of this process of empirical control was Schlick's criterion of meaning and verification, and the propositions which had suffered most from its application had been philosophical propositions, for these seemed to meet neither of the sets of conditions foreseen and administered by the criterion of meaning and verification. This early semantical position had been weakened significantly by the fact that the verification principle of meaning, as a proposition, could not itself find a place in either of the two classes of propositions which it had rendered acceptable: synthetic or analytic.

As Carnap's position had developed, he had tended to withdraw from the implications of this early empirical semanticism to a position of pure logical syntax. In this position it was the internal syntax of the language alone which was the basis of its meaning and significance. At first glance, this position seemed to be immune from the particular problems which had troubled the empirical semantics of Schlick. But this illusion did not endure for long. It too developed clear indications of insufficiency and of the need to be supplemented by a new attack on the problem of the semantic dimension of language. This inadequacy became very clear when logical syntax moved from the ground it first occupied, that of the construction of the ideal language of science, to the more concrete ground of the logic of science; for it could not be questioned that concrete scientific discourse involved a direct semantic reference to the world of experience with which it dealt. But the purely formal syntactical analysis of language, on which Carnap, in his last European phase, was placing the main emphasis, could supply no clue to the nature of this relation. It tended to end up in an empty formalism and to lose contact with the very problems out of which it had arisen, namely, the understanding of the procedure of science and the derivation of the "scientific conception of the world," which was its basic philosophical interest.

In his American phase, Carnap revealed a great sensitivity to these new demands. Many of the most important works of his American period are dedicated to the semantic problem; among these are *Introduction to Semantics*, 1942, and *Meaning and Necessity*, 1947. In the development of these semantic dimensions of his analysis of the language of science, Carnap underwent two influences: that of the Polish logician Alfred Tarski, also living in America, and that of the pragmatist and behavioralist, Charles Morris, who had developed a rich theory of signs upon behavioristic and pragmatic bases. These two forms of contact in the new cultural environment led respectively to the formation, in interaction and interrelation between these thinkers, of a "logical semantics" and of a "pragmatic and behavioral semantics" based on Charles Morris' theory of signs or general semiotic.

The "logical semantics" cultivated by Tarski and Carnap during this period was a technical rather than a philosophical development. (Tarski's main contribution is the essay, based on an earlier European study, entitled "The Semantic Conception of Truth," now to be found in *Readings in Philosophical Analysis*, edited by Feigl and Sellars, 1949.) It concerned problems which had already arisen in the construction of the logical syntax of language in the continental period. In this logical semantics, the relation between the symbol and what it symbolized is not posited as a problem; the distinction between them is introduced only for the sake of its logical-technical utility. In syntactical analysis, language had been interpreted as a calculus, entirely enclosed within its formal structure. In logical semantics, this calculus is "interpreted," but only by means of rigid postulated rules which indicate the entities designated by the symbols. It thus became possible to define "truth" in this context. This had not been possible within syntax alone. But logical semantics did not concern itself with the nature of the entities designated or with the conditions under which a particular assertion could be declared true according to the definition it had determined. The semantic definition of truth was only a technical arrangement which made it possible to determine more clearly the axiomatic structure of a language and to define concepts, such as analytic and contradictory, which are employed within it.

The chief effects of logical semantics were felt in the area of mathematics. Tarski himself clearly recognized that it had no value for deriving that "scientific conception of the world" which had concerned logical positivism from its inception. Carnap recognized this fact too in the works which are to be considered his chief contributions to the development of logical semantics: *The Logical Foundations of Probability*, 1950, *The Continuum of Inductive Methods*, 1952, and those mentioned above.

The stimulus provided by contact with the position that Charles Morris had been developing led to results with greater philosophical resonance. As early as his work of 1937 entitled *Logical Positivism, Pragmaticism and Scientific Empiricism*, Morris had been aware of the affinity between his own investigations into language and the general theory of signs and the investigations of logical positivism. The two positions seemed to complement each other; the formalism of logical positivism would provide logical rigor, while his own pragmaticism and behaviorism would supply the material dimension of reference needed for science. This contention was based on the more complete analysis of the linguistic and sign operation which he was prepared to offer.

The linguistic sign, for Morris, possesses significance in three dimensions inextricably related to each other and based on the conception of the sign as an operation of the living organism; these dimensions are: the relation of the sign to the organism using it (*pragmatic dimension*), the relation of the sign to the object which it signifies (*semantic dimension*), and the relations between signs taken in themselves but still in view of the other dimensions (*syntactic dimension*). The study of all these dimensions in their complexity and their singularity constitutes the science of semiotic. In this analysis the semantic dimension assumes great importance; it is indeed the crucial dimension, for without semantic reference to an existing world the other functions of signs would be without meaning (cf. *Signs, Language and Behavior*, 1946, p. 229.) By way of this semantic dimension all of the philosophical problems, which purely formalistic analysis of language had presumably banished, appeared with new force. Carnap and other logical positivists, for example, Philipp Frank in his important work *Philosophy of Science*, 1950, received this fresh apparition of these philosophical problems as in line both with their interest in providing a valid philosophy and logic of the sciences and with the primary desire of logical positivism to derive the "scientific conception of the world."

In this same line of development of logical positivism in the new American context, should be noted the activities of other members of that school transported to America. Among these are Herbert Feigl

(*Existential Hypotheses,* 1950; *Major Issues and Developments in the Philosophy of Science of Logical Empiricism,* 1956); Gustav Bergmann (*The Metaphysics of Logical Positivism,* 1954; *Philosophy of Science,* 1957), and Hans Reichenbach (*The Rise of Scientific Philosophy,* 1951). The work of the American Willard van Orman Quine possesses a special importance in this context. In his works (*Methods of Logic,* 1950; *From a Logical Point of View,* 1953; *Word and Object,* 1960), Quine makes important contributions not only to logical theory but to philosophical problems. Especially interesting is Quine's contention that the minimal unity which can be said to have empirical meaning is the totality of science. The margins of the system of science, he says, must square with experience; the rest, with all its elaborate myths and fictions, has the simplicity of laws as its concern.

2. American Developments of
British Analytic Philosophy

Despite the new force it took on in the American context, logical positivism must be considered something of a phenomenon of the past. Its influence has definitely waned. The influence of British analytic philosophy, on the contrary, must be recognized as definitely on the ascendant in the American scene. It would not be too much to say that, with phenomenology, it tends to dominate the field of academic philosophy in America, and its influence promises to increase before it diminishes. Nevertheless, the historian is at a loss to point to any truly original work in the line of development of British linguistic philosophy in the United States. What one witnesses is a vast process of assimilation and reelaboration. It would seem that original work lies in the future. The truth of this statement is not negated by the appearance in 1945 of such a work as the celebrated *Language and Ethics* of Charles Stevenson. For all its power of exposition and keeness of analysis, this work remains an elaboration of things already said in England and shows especially the influence of Ogden and Richards in their early work on the *Meaning of Meaning,* 1923.

Many promising names stand out among the explicit adherents of this movement in the United States. But it would seem as yet premature to speak of solid original works which mark a clear advance over the work of the British practitioners of this method. From the ferment caused by the introduction of British analytic philosophy into the American cultural scene, there can be no doubt that original work will inevitably arise for the historian to record.

Readings

Books

Angelelli, Ignacio. *Studies in Gottlob Frege and Traditional Philosophy.* Dordrecht: D. Reidel, 1967.

Anscombe, G. E. M. *An Introduction to Wittgenstein's Tractatus.* London: Hutchinson University Library, 1959.

Ayer, A. J., et al. *The Revolution in Philosophy.* London: Macmillan, 1956.

Bergmann, G. *The Metaphysics of Logical Positivism.* Madison, Wisc.: University of Wisconsin Press, 1967.

Blandshard, Brand. *Reason and Analysis.* LaSalle, Ill.: Open Court Publishing Co., 1964.

Copi, I. M., and Beard, R. W., eds. *Essays on Wittgenstein's Tractatus.* New York: Macmillan, 1966.

Dufrenne, Mikel. *Language and Philosophy.* Translated by H. Veatch. Bloomington, Ind.: Indiana University Press, 1963.

Griffin, J. *Wittgenstein's Logical Atomism.* Oxford: Clarendon Press, 1964.

Kraft, V. *The Vienna Circle.* New York: Philosophical Library, 1953.

Küng, Guido. *Ontology and the Logical Analysis of Language.* Dordrecht: D. Reidel, 1967.

Malcolm, N. *Ludwig Wittgenstein: A Memoire.* New York: Oxford University Press, 1958.

Pears, David F. *Bertrand Russell and the British Tradition in Philosophy.* New York: Random House, 1967.

Pitcher, G., ed. *The Philosophy of Ludwig Wittgenstein.* Englewood Cliffs, N. J.: Prentice-Hall, 1964.

Pole, D. *The Later Philosophy of Wittgenstein.* London: Athlone Press, 1958.

Russell, B. *My Philosophical Development.* New York: Simon & Schuster, 1959.

Stenius, Erik. *Wittgenstein's "Tractatus": A Critical Exposition of its Main Lines of Thought.* Ithaca: Cornell University Press, 1960.

White, A. *G. E. Moore: A Critical Exposition.* Oxford: Blackwell, 1958.

Wood, Alan. *Bertrand Russell: The Passionate Sceptic.* New York: Simon & Schuster, 1957.

Essays and articles

Dwyer, Peter J. "Thomistic First Principles and Wittgenstein's Philosophy of Language." *Philosophical Studies,* XVI (1967), 7–29.

Jorgensen, J. "Development of Logical Empiricism." In *International Encyclopedia of Unified Science.* Chicago: University of Chicago Press, 1951.

Medlin, Brian. "Ryle and the Mechanical Hypothesis." In *The Identity Theory of Mind,* edited by C. F. Presley. New York: Humanities Press, 1967.

CHAPTER V

Contemporary Spiritualism

Introduction

The spiritualist tradition, it has been noted, is one of the oldest and deepest in western philosophy. It has found expression in every period of the history of philosophy, reflecting in each period the particular conditions which evoked the fresh affirmation of the basic spiritualistic insights: the interiority of truth and the radication of man's being in the plenitude of the divine being. This pattern appears again in contemporary philosophy. The present century, in fact, has seen a reaffirmation of these insights which has seemed to gain clarity and force from the very strength of the movements against which it defined itself: positivism and naturalism.

The reaction against positivism and naturalism, especially strong in France and Italy, has given rise to a spiritualistic climate which has expressed itself in many currents. In some of these currents the spiritualistic element appears as only one motif among others; this is true, in neo-scholasticism, voluntarism, neo-idealism, and other movements. It has reached its clearest expression and its fullest elaboration in two movements which have explicitly assumed the designation "spiritualism" to characterize their doctrine. These are the movement of the "philosophy of spirit" in France and "Christian spiritualism" in Italy. While these movements have had their centers in the countries named, they are in no way national in character. Both have arisen in response to conditions and demands which characterize European thought as a whole and the idioms in which they express themselves reflect, not any nationalistic character, but the idiom of classical western spiritualism. From their centers in France and Italy, moreover, they have awakened resonances in many other countries of the West. Their appearance in these countries is due to the fact that, for historical and cultural reasons, the inevitable reaction against the extremes of positivism, naturalism, and scientism, found there readier soil and a more favorable climate.

A. *The Philosophy of Spirit in France*

The "philosophy of spirit" in France is associated both with the impressive series of books collectively entitled *Philosophie de l'esprit*, edited jointly by Louis Lavelle and René Le Senne, and with the review *Esprit*. The books brought out under this rubric are not, however, all representative of one point of view. The "philosophy of spirit," in a strict theoretical sense, can be identified principally with the thought of two men, Louis Lavelle and René Le Senne, and with those who sought to continue their initiative.

In the essay "De la philosophie de l'esprit," Le Senne remarks that the movement had its beginnings as the renewal of a *psycho-metaphysical* current, ultimately derivative from Descartes. In another essay, "Epitome metaphysicae spiritualis," in the *Giornale di metafisica* of Genoa (1947, p. 397 ff.), Lavelle identifies the philosophy of spirit with the perennial movement in western thought which has set itself against all forms of materialism and naturalism. After pointing out its affinity under certain aspects to existentialism, Le Senne (in *Obstacle et valeur*, 1934, pp. 9–55) distinguishes between these movements, indicating that, by reason of its unrepentent theism, the philosophy of spirit opens to man the possibility of an escape from finite existence and its spatio-temporal situation. In the same work, he indicates the method which the philosophy of spirit finds most congenial: that of a rational mediation *within spiritual experience* that is integral and total. This method, he points out, demands an initial *metaphysical experience* of being as act or actuality. Lavelle, in his important work *De l'acte*, formulates this point even more explicitly (pp. 9–13). The being thus intuited is spirit; spirit, in turn, is the negation of every determination, "*surdétermination*," or *value*, and is act in the sense of *causa sui* (cf. Le Senne: *Introduction à la philosophie*, 1939 ed., p. 253 ff.; Lavelle: *De l'acte*, p. 111 ff.). The central problem of this spiritualism, from the metaphysical point of view, is the relation between finite and infinite spirit and the status of the world of nature. The first part of this problem is resolved by Le Senne ethically, through a dialectic between *obstacle* and *value*, while Lavelle resolves it through a theory of the participation of the finite in infinite spirit through liberty. Both agree in identifying nature, the world, as the phenomenal product of spirit, the necessary condition for the exercise of the act of spirit's own being (cf. Lavelle, *De l'acte*, pp. 311–317; 341–342). Within this common area, each of these men develops a position characteristically his own.

1. Louis Lavelle (1883–1951)

Lavelle developed his philosophical position in a long series of books and many articles. It is difficult to declare any of these more representative than the others, for he made each of them carry the full weight of his insights. The most imposing of his undertakings and the most elaborate exposition of his thought is the four-volume series *La dialectique de l'éternal présent* [The dialectic of the eternal present]. The composition of this work engrossed him for over twenty-five years and resulted in the component titles: *De l'être* [On being], 1928; *De l'acte* [On act], 1937; *Du temps et de l'éternité* [Of time and eternity], 1945; *De l'âme humaine* [Of the human soul], 1951. Equally illuminating are such individual volumes as *La conscience de soi*, [Consciousness of self], 1933; *Le moi et son destin* [The ego and its destiny], 1936; *De l'intimité spirituelle* [Of spiritual intimacy], 1955 (posthumous). For the background of his reflection, the essay "La philosophie française entre les deux guerres" [French philosophy between the two wars], 1942, is almost indispensable. A fine summary statement of his personal position, "Métaphysique de la participation," appeared in the collective volume *La mia prospettiva filosofica* [My philosophical perspective], 1950.

Lavelle's basic purpose was to unite the old and the new; his thought possesses the splendid architectonic structure of older systems combined with an openness to that problematic structure of experience which weighs so heavily on the modern sensibility. From a historical point of view, he prolongs the *ontologism* of western thought, which runs from Plato to Malebranche, and renews the spiritualistic tradition of Augustine, Pascal, and Maine de Biran. He shares the modern concern with the antihumanistic implications of science and establishes immediate contact with the themes of existentialism, especially its strong sense of the singular and the person. But he cannot share the tragic sense of life, the sense of *angst* of German and Danish existentialism. He does sense an anguish, but it is the Augustinian and Pascalian longing for the divine. He does not feel that anguish is the ultimate moment of human life and experience; the ultimate is rather that in which the Absolute reveals itself to us in the profound calm born of interior conflicts which have been suffered and lived through, but overcome. The truth, he says, does not wish to be taken by storm or violence but to be hearkened to with a docile and receptive ear.

His basic philosophical undertaking is the restoration of metaphysics. Philosophy which is not metaphysics has no real character. But what is metaphysics? Metaphysics is the effort to lay bare the profound meaning of the universe. In this effort metaphysics begins, not with the external world to mount thence to an abstract *concept* of being, but with being as revealed to a privileged form of experience, which places us, in a stroke, at the eternal center. The experience of which Lavelle speaks has been compared to Bergsonian intuition, with the important difference that, while the latter situates man in duration, the former places him in the eternal. This difference far outweighs any similarity between them. Bergson's intuition sets itself in opposition to reason, while, for Lavelle, it is reason which develops and prolongs this basic intuition. Metaphysics lays bare universality at the heart of singular, spiritual interiority. The capacity of each individual being to establish his own personal existence is in direct ratio to his power of discovering the universal in himself. The task of philosophy as metaphysics is to place us at the eternal center, to lay bare the dialectic between the individual and the whole, between man and God. Lavelle believes that this collocation actually transpires in exceptional moments of our experience. When our vital activity and sensibility is at its height, the awareness of time fades, and we find ourselves at the eternal center which coincides with the presence of being in us.

Thus the fundamental experience of philosophy is simultaneously a *personal* and a *universal* experience. This experience is *participation*. I am present to Being and Being is present to me, not as pure other, but as reciprocally establishing principles. The mystery of existence is revealed when we discover our point of contact with the absolute (cf. especially *L'erreur de Narcisse*, 1939, p. 26, and *La conscience de soi*, p. 163 ff.).

These reflections lead Lavelle to the heart of the metaphysical problem, to which he assigns the name "dialectic of the eternal present" (whence the collective title of his *magnum opus*). This is the problem of determining the manner in which the eternal and the divine are immanent in us. Lavelle discovers that the tension between these terms does not permit any unilateral resolution. Being, the absolute, the divine, God, is both immanent and transcendent to us. While the human subject is both wholly enclosed within the divine being, it is also conscious in the most intimate moment of its awareness of the divine that it is subjectivity which cannot be dissolved without the dissolution of its object. The resolution of these tensions lies in the direction of the *dialectic of participation*. The task of this dialectic is to trace that double movement by which the human subject is placed in relation to the transcendent and by which God offers himself, as absolute being, to man. This is the movement of *vocation* and *invocation*. God's call to man, man's reply to this call.

The locus of this process of the dialectic of participation is *diremption* (to use the term which Hegel made classical), which Lavelle refers to as the *interval* between God and man, an *ontological defect* (*De l'acte,* p. 101), a fracture between essence and existence. There is no deterministic means by which this interval can be closed. Its very existence establishes man in his autonomy before God and makes it clear that this interval can be closed only by his own free and personal response to his *vocation,* the call to respond to the call of God. In this profound sense, the situation of man is freedom or liberty.

But Lavelle does not see this "interval" as an accident, as something fortuitous and contingent. This "interval" between essence and existence, between God and man, was necessary in order that the subsequent union between them be whole, that is, a union in and through the presence of diremption and not a union through indifferentiation. By participation man returns freely to being, takes it upon himself through an act of liberty which is the warrant of his own actuality (*De l'être,* p. 9 ff.). Through this process of free participation in the absolute, the existent is established as *person.*

Thus, liberty is the basic concept in Lavelle's metaphysics, the very heart of the process of participation. For this reason, it is necessary to clarify his notion of liberty. In the first place, liberty is not an *endowment* of man; but a *conquest* by man. To act is to consent to an activity which is proposed to us, to make an option, to respond to a call or vocation. Thus, authentic existence is vocation and invocation, gift and choice. Each has his vocation to being; but to each this vocation comes, not as a determination from without, but as a call or invitation within. This call to being is imperative, but it has no coercive element. Any coercive element would negate its character as call. It can be fulfilled only by a free response, an act of liberty; yet the failure to respond to this call is the negation of the self, its eternal abortion. Thus, liberty and necessity reveal themselves as constitutive components of the dynamic situation between the individual and the absolute. As such, they reveal themselves as one and the same. The tension between them is one of dialectical opposition, not ontological scission. God and Being call and must call; man answers freely but through the most profound constitutive necessity of his being.

This, however, is from a strictly metaphysical point of view. Existentially, man's response to the appeal of the absolute marks a path of freedom as choice, a path of true self-establishment of the person as the self, grounded in the absolute, based on the intimate self-revelation of the absolute in the depths of the self-awareness of the individual human subject. The spell of Narcissus, as Lavelle says, is broken. Looking into himself man sees, not himself, but the absolute, God. Hearkening within himself, he hears, not the call to be himself, but the call to find his authentic selfhood in his participation in the absolute.

2. René Le Senne (1882-1954)

Within the general framework of spiritualistic ideas and purposes, it was noted above, Lavelle and Le Senne developed highly individual positions. Much of the diversity stems, without doubt, from the difference in preparation which they brought to philosophical reflection. In his earliest period, Le Senne had been under the philosophical influence of the idealist O. Hamelin. But his first interests lay in psychology; he read extensively in William James and at the Ecole Normale Supérieur followed the courses of the psychologist and moralist Frederic Rauh. It was, by his own testimony, the experience of the First World War which led him to philosophy, by way of an impression of the existential situation of man engendered by the terrible contradictions of that conflict. The fruit of his philosophical reflection, which led eventually to a chair in philosophy at the Sorbonne and the presidency of the International Institute of Philosophy, resides in a series of penetrating works. Among the most important of these are: *Introduction à la philosophie* [Introduction to philosophy], 1924, 1939, 1947, *Obstacle et valeur* [Obstacle and value], 1943, perhaps his most characteristic work; *Traité de caractérologie* [Treatise on characterology], 1946; *La destinée personelle* [Personal destiny], 1951; and *La découverte de Dieu* [The discovery of God], 1955.

Le Senne's thought is dense and concentrated. In a brief presentation it is most useful to limit consideration to a number of essential points: the "ideo-existential" notion of philosophical synthesis; *fêleur* or rupture; obstacle and value, and the characteristics of value; "metaphysical existential" unity of finite and infinite, Man and God; and some traits of the characterology.

It was noticed above that Le Senne's early formation was subject to two influences: the positive interest in psychology, wholly grounded in the concrete and finding in that order the ultimate reference of all science and reflection, and the idealism of the type of Hamelin, which, while rich in psychological insights, still tended toward the abstract model of classical idealism. The "ideo-existential" idea of philosophy and of philosophical method which Le Senne developed is an effort to meet and to transcend these partial demands and influences. Philosophy is unique among disciplines precisely because it seeks to meet these diverse exigencies. It seeks to remain in close contact with experience in its variety and openness; at the same time, its particular task is to go beyond the mere givenness of experience to discover in it some perspective of understanding which would generate an ideal and rational order within that empirical richness. Classical idealism had fallen victim to the seductive idea of *system* and had eventually discovered that the openness of experience mocked this ambition. Yet the essential purpose of idealism, *synthesis,* could not be abandoned. Hence, the notion of the "ideo-existential," a mode of synthesis which, while generating order within experience (interpretative order, ultimately), claimed for its ordering principles no absolute and transcendental value which would enclose experience in a range of possibility determined *a priori* (Kant, Hegel). Respecting the openness of experience, it nevertheless created within it ideal perspectives which both ordered the initial chaos of experience and revealed further dimensions of its openness.

The primitive ideo-existential insight upon which Le Senne builds is that of *fêleur,* rupture, diremption. The fact that he places this insight at the basis of his constructive efforts marks his philosophy as a "philosophy of crisis," for it is impossible not to interpret *fêleur* as the translation into ideo-existential terms of the deep shock induced by his experience of the Great War. That historical crisis, along with numerous evidences of personal and social psychological and moral trauma, raise the possibility that in these outward and relatively superficial manifestations of "fracture" one is encountering the signs of a more radical and even constitutive diremption—not in man alone but in the very structure of being. It is this ultimate fracture, in itself, ontologically, and as it manifests itself in man's experience of himself and of his world, that concerns Le Senne.

What is the ultimate character of this rupture, *fêleur?* Le Senne's reply is, in essence, the classical spiritualistic reply: It is the radical diremption between finite and infinite, relative and absolute, man and God, being and existence. Moreover, *fêleur* is not a static condition; it has a dynamic structure; it is a tension toward the closure of this diremption, toward the union of these opposed elements or dimensions. In his own words, it is a "red signal of alarm which emerges from among the fogs" of experience (*Obstacle et valeur,* p. 47). The radical testimony of this *fêleur* is to the transcendent; a transcendent which does not remain an absolute and alien *other,* but which, in its character of transcendent and absolute, becomes the goal of finite striving, though without hope of an ultimate unification which would dissolve the fracture definitively. The unity between man and this transcendent reality, God, is *value.*

In the context of Le Senne's thought value cannot be considered apart from its dialectical opposite, obstacle. Obstacle is both the impediment and the condition of value. It is obstacle which generates the very notion of value, that is, unity with the absolute, for it is through obstacle that the idea of the transcendent emerges and the tension toward unification with it is created. The concept of obstacle is itself complex and many-sided. Obstacle is related, in the first instance, to *fêleur.* By the sense of *fêleur,* man is opposed and thrown back upon his own finiteness; he appears as obstacle to himself. It is above the barrier of obstacle as *fêleur* that vision of the transcendent emerges.

The transcendent, in its turn, presents a dual aspect. By reason of its absoluteness, it appears as necessary term, and hence as goal, of the finite; the inner reality of finiteness is the infinite, the absolute, by which that limit is determined and measured. But by reason of its absoluteness, the transcendent also appears as the unapproachable, the unattainable toward which it is nevertheless necessary that the finite strive and tend.

As a consequence, value too, reveals a double aspect. Viewed from the vantage point of the absolute, which is the prime determinant of value, every value is relative and, indeed, contains a negative element—its infinite distance from the absolute. Viewed from the vantage point of value itself, every value appears limited and none can claim to be dominant. But this limited, and even negative, character of every value is overcome by another consideration. Every value is also absolute, not by reason of its intrinsic character, but by reason of the fact that all value is implicit in every value. It is impossible to seek any value in isolation; the effort to realize any one reveals itself at the same time as the effort to encompass all. Le Senne rejects the view of the world as a theater of conflicting and mutually canceling values; at the same time he rejects the notion of a hierarchy of values. Every value is autonomous because it aspires, not to itself or to other values, but to the ground and principle of all value, the absolute. At the same time, every value draws with it all values because these are already implicit in its own term, the absolute. Nevertheless, none of these aspects of value cancels the basic incommensuration between all value and the absolute, God, toward which it aspires.

In the last analysis, Le Senne seems to place man in an ambiguous and frustrating position: He is moved by the dynamism of his existence toward an absolute to which he can never attain, but he is condemned to an inauthentic existence, a non-existence, if this quest of the absolute under the form of the pluralism of finite values is not pursued. Le Senne's thought seems to suggest, with a romantic intonation, that it is the quest which is the ultimate value. This implication has been criticized, especially from the Christian point of view; yet it is reconcilable with the most traditional and orthodox type of Christianity when it is noted that the area which separates aspiring man from the absolute, from God, is precisely the area of the activity of grace.

Le Senne protested many times that in the development of his theory of value and of values he was proposing neither a metaphysical nor a psychological axiology. He calls this area of his work the "existential metaphysical" area and his theory of values an "existential metaphysics." By this he meant to say that the purpose of his theory was neither abstractly constructive nor concretely descriptive; it was, in the last analysis, ethical and moral: to supply the absolute principle on which human aspiration and will might be concretely structured. The values of which he speaks are not reports of what men seek; at times they are in direct opposition to what men seek. Neither, however, do they represent a heaven of Platonic ideas, fixed and immaculate in themselves. The values which he treats arise only within and from the concrete dialectic of human action and aspiration; but they arise in that context in response to a movement which compels such action always to transcend itself in the direction of an absolute which is present fundamentally as a term of its own dynamics. His discourse, therefore, is at once Platonic and empirical, and at the same time neither. Its real purpose is ethical: to place at men's disposal the dialectical ideas which might make it possible for them to orientate human desire and action toward this transcendent term.

Le Senne's "characterology" reflects this basic notion of his "existential metaphysics." This theory has two primary aspects: the phenomenology and typology of character and the concept of character as the true form and term of the ethical life. The latter is most interesting philosophically and reflects the structure of his existential metaphysics of value. Character is nothing other than the concrete locus of value in the existential metaphysical sense. Character is personal existence structured on principles of transcendent value. Its seat is the concrete human person. It is present in him only under the aspect of his dynamic toward the transcendent. It resides precisely in the qualitative transformation of his life of thought and action which is induced by the orientation of that life toward a transcendent principle, ultimately toward God. When this is established, it is readily seen that Le Senne can attribute to character in all its aspects, ethico-psychologico-metaphysical, all of the properties which classical characterology and ethical theory since Plato have assigned it. At the same time he can and does enrich this basic structural concept with all of the insights which modern psychology and psychological methods have made available. In the last analysis, there always remains in Le Senne a hint, or at least an echo, of the "toughness" of William James; but at all points it is united with a vision of the absolute and an aspiration toward the unity of the finite and infinite which is of a very different and more ancient provenance.

B. *Christian Spiritualism in Italy*

The historical context in which the Italian movement called "Christian spiritualism" developed was that created by the dominance of the historicism of Croce and the actualism of Gentile. With respect to these philosophical positions, Christian spiritualism exhibited a complex attitude. On the one hand, its chief purpose was to overcome the intransigent immanentism of Crocean and Gentilean thought in order to reestablish the basis of the theistic transcendence essential to Christianity. On the other hand, it sought to achieve this end, not by abandoning this type of idealism, but by developing its historical and speculative dimensions from within, thereby demonstrating that, on the basis of its own historical antecedents and in the implication of its own major theses, this idealism, especially in its actualistic form, demanded to be developed into a spiritualistic metaphysics of transcendence.

In this context, the term *Christian* sustains a double meaning. In the first place, it means the reaffirmation of the classical philosophical purpose of developing a philosophical system consonant with and reflecting the vision of the world and of life characteristic of Christian theism. It seeks to achieve this end basically by Blondel's method of immanence: by showing that the dual principles of faith and reason coincide to create the integrality of man's nature and that the enterprise of a Christian philosophy, consequently, is not extrinsic and quixotic but rests on the inner demands of the integral nature of man. (For this reason, some Christian spiritualists, Sciacca in particular, prefer to call their position "integralism.") In the second place, the term *Christian* has a historical meaning. It indicates that this movement is prepared to appeal, in establishing its position, to the long historical tradition of Christian thought which has been one of the mainstreams of western speculation.

As in all forms of spiritualism, the basic theme of Christian spiritualism is "interiority." In developing this concept, it is concerned above all to avoid the absolute immanence of Gentile and to demonstrate that the penetration of man's interiority leads inevitably, by a rigid logic, to the projection and recognition from this ground of the transcendence of the Absolute (God), the real multiplicity of finite spirits and minds, and the reality of the external world. Its preoccupation with transcendence under these various aspects has led it to form various patterns of affinity with classical scholasticism and its modern counterparts, neo-scholasticism, and neo-Thomism. These affinities do not, however, obscure the basic difference in point of departure of the two systems: For spiritualism this point of departure always remains the interiority of the spiritual act, while for the scholastic tradition it

is the notion of being. This difference in point of departure immediately involves a difference in method; the method of spiritualism is the
development of the implications of interiority, while that of scholasticism is conceptual abstraction. But the two movements share the basic
conviction that the development of a Christian philosophy is a philosophical enterprise and not merely a historically or apologetically
justified undertaking. Both are integralistic in this sense.

Within the framework of this purpose and problematic, Christian
spiritualism exhibits various lines of development and emphasis. Among
the most representative figures we may cite Armando Carlini, Michele
Sciacca, Felice Battaglia, Augusto Guzzo, and Luigi Stefanini.

1. Armando Carlini (1878–1959)

Although he began his career in the area of literary criticism, Carlini was irresistibly attracted to philosophical themes and even in his
earliest efforts in this direction exhibit a keen critical intelligence.
Drawn into the pattern of Italian idealism, he became a contributor
both to Croce's *La critica* and Gentile's Critical Journal of Italian Philosophy. Of these two philosophers, it was undoubtedly Gentile who
exercised the greater influence over Carlini. It was by way of an
interior development of Gentilean actualism that Carlini was to become, as Sciacca called him, "the first of the Christian spiritualists, the
man who laid down its problems and its doctrinal principles."

The basic lines of Carlini's original reflection begin to emerge with
the volume *La vita dello spirito* [The life of spirit], 1921. Ostensibly
devoted to the exposition of actualism, Carlini reveals the purpose of
defining within the pattern of this system a clear basis for objectivity
and, in this way, of rescuing both God and the individual from that
complete submergence in the absolute unity and immanence of the act
of thought to which Gentile's philosophy seemingly led. This line of
thought is pursued in a subsequent work, *La religiosità dell'arte e della
filosofia* [The religious character of art and of philosophy], 1934. Here
Carlini declares forthrightly that actualism had exhausted its possibilities and that it was no longer able to meet the needs of the times. The
problem which demonstrated this exhaustion was that of religion. The
autonomy of religious experience seemed manifest, whereas immanentism could do nothing more, despite Gentile's gestures toward religion,
than dissolve it into the omnivorous unity of the act of thought. To fulfill itself actualism had to be transformed itself into a new system
which would respond to the intellectual, moral, and religious needs of
the time. He undertook to effect this transformation.

This new system would be both idealistic, in the actualistic sense, and Christian. Essentially, this meant, in speculative terms, that he had to reverse the inner dynamics of the "act" of actualism. From the movement toward absolute immanence, that dynamic had to be redirected toward transcendence. It had to be shown on the basis of the inward and constitutive movement of the act that the *autoctisis,* the self-positing of the human spirit, implied the positing of the absolute transcendent (God) as its ground. It is to the development of this argument that two works, very central to his thought, are devoted: *Mito del realism* [The myth of realism], 1936 and the *Lineamenti di una concezione realistica dello spirito umano* [Outlines of a realistic conception of the human spirit], 1942. Within the limits of a "naturalistic" realism, this effort of Carlini's seemed to achieve reasonable success. That is to say, he seemed confident in demonstrating that in positing its own act of existing, of being, the human spirit, at the same time and in the same act, posits the necessity of the world of experience which confronts it and exhibits a characteristic "independence" of it. This world is necessarily posited under two aspects, that of its "otherness as exterior" (the world of physical nature) and its "actuality as other interiorness" (other minds or spirits and, eventually, God). To this point Carlini seems, without having violated the inner logic of actualism, to have moved beyond its absolute immanence to the reconstitution of the world of nature, of other spirits, and of God and thus to have prepared the way for the readmission of religion into the life of spirit as the supreme act of recognition of the other absolute interiority (God).

But Carlini could not rest content with this notion of religion. It had to mean something more concrete to him: historical and institutional Christianity, Catholicism. This led him eventually to confront the problem of reason and dogma. At this point, his inner transformation of actualism falters. This new confrontation seemed to demand that the act of assent to dogma must itself be grounded in the inward dynamic of spirit. But to reach this conclusion it would be necessary to deny the absolute character of the transcendence which marks dogma as revelation and which precludes any absolute commensuration between reason and dogma. In his latest works such as *Perché credo* [Why I believe], 1951, and *Cattolicismo e pensiero moderno* [Catholicism and modern thought], 1953, Carlini seems to surrender his original undertaking and to move toward a fideistic position. The entire content of supernatural revelation could not be grounded in the act of thought but demanded of the human spirit a certain self-abnegation, which, in moral terms, might be rendered as humility but which broke the continuity of consciousness on which his reconstruction of actualism rested. In a word, he seemed to surrender that ideal of "integrality" which was a principle of Christian spiritualism. For this reason, while still acknowledging him as the founder of Christian spiritualism, later thinkers in this current could not rest their case on the position he had achieved nor follow him in the direction his last works seemed to be taking.

2. Augusto Guzzo (b. 1894)

Guzzo's thought has followed substantially the same path of development as Carlini's, with the important difference that, through a very deft employment of an Augustinian dialectic, Guzzo has avoided the impass into which Carlini was led. A disciple of Gentile, Guzzo never intended to leave the precincts of idealism and actualism, but rather, working within them, to achieve that synthesis of idealism and Christianity which marks Christian spiritualism. The clue to the manner in which this synthesis might be achieved, as the early historico-critical work *Agostino dal "Contra Academicos" al "De vera religione"* [Augustine from the "Contra Academicos" to the "De vera religione"], 1925, indicates, is to be found in the work of that great Father of the Church. Thus, Guzzo may be credited with giving Italian spiritualism that Augustinian orientation which it has never subsequently lost. The essential line is that Augustine indicates how it may be possible, without violating the basic principle of actualism, i.e., the ultimate character of thought, to conceive the act of thought, not as the all-devouring void (which it has threatened to become in Gentile), but as the *plenum,* thought which contains and attests to the existence of the world, of other minds, of God. This line of progress from the absolute immanence of Gentilean actualism to a developed and coherent spiritualism under the guidance of Augustine inspires the early works *Verità e realtà* [Truth and reality], 1925, and *Giudizio e azione* [Judgment and action], 1928.

Guzzo spells out the three principles of spiritualism with unusual clarity in an important work, *Idealismo e Cristianesimo* [Idealism and Christianity], 1936. These are: 1) There is nothing outside thought; nevertheless knowledge does not impugn, but rather confirms the objectivity of the object. 2) Spirit is essentially ethicity; it has reference to a universal and obligatory ideal which it is free to realize or not in its acts. 3) This universal and obligatory ideal represents the truth of the interior man; indeed, it is the very voice of God in man's conscience. This voice orientates us toward values and, through the pursuit of these values, to closeness to God. Fidelity to this inward truth endows man with truly human existence.

From these principles it is clear that, for Guzzo, idealism and Christianity actually call upon each other, imply and demand each other.

Idealism does not endanger or threaten the affirmation of the absolute. Correctly understood, it is the only firm testimony of the absolute. And it affirms the absolute as transcendent, unlike actualism, which asserts that the inner need for the absolute implies the immanence of the absolute to human experience. In his own words, "in his need of the absolute, man is not the absolute, and if certain idealists identify him with the absolute, they are mistaken; but man comes from the absolute and the idealists who insist on the incomparable and unique dignity of man in the universe are right" (*Idealismo e Cristianesimo*, 1936, II, 255). God, as other, invokes man by his inward voice. Man's dignity lies in the power to respond to this invocation. God is thus an immanent transcendence. He speaks, as absolute other, from within the consciousness and conscience of man.

Beginning about 1940, Guzzo set himself the task of giving more systematic expression to his thought. Two volumes of this system have appeared: *L'io e la ragione* [The ego and reason], 1947, and *La moralità* [Morality], 1950. These volumes eloquently attest to the firmness of outline and inner coherence of Guzzo's mature thought. While adding nothing new to its basic structure, they enrich it with a wealth of detailed analysis of metaphysical and moral problems, firmly establishing Guzzo as one of the most authoritative voices of Christian spiritualism.

3. Felice Battaglia (b. 1902)

Battaglia, rector of the University of Bologna and an authority in the philosophy of law, was another who came to Christian spiritualism through an internal criticism of the actualism of Gentile. Battaglia viewed actualism as implying an all-inclusive humanism, and it was the quality of this humanism and its consequences which led him to move in the direction of a Christian spiritualism. The chief mark of this humanism is its absolute immanentism. This immanentism seems to Battaglia to imply or to be equivalent to an unabashed naturalism. For by that immanentism, man is nothing but man. But a humanity which cannot transcend the logical necessities which arise from its nature is no longer spirit, freedom, and transcendence but nature and natural necessity. Although Battaglia directs this criticism primarily against Gentilean actualism, he notes pointedly that it applies with equal force to all contemporary forms of immanentism and humanism—neo-positivism, existentialism, Marxism, and historicism. These are all philosophies of finitude and worldliness; they enclose man within himself and within the necessities, logical or otherwise, of his situation. But in doing so they make absolutes of finiteness and of the world. Their humanism amounts to a reduction of man to what is least characteristically human about him (cf. Battaglia's contribution to the collective work *La mia prospettiva filosofica* [My philosophical perspective], Padova, 1950).

What is, by contrast, most characteristically human about man? Precisely this: that he can never be sufficient to himself. What is most specifically characteristic of man is the élan to transcendence; his profoundest movement is to surpass his own limits. He is essentially openness to the infinite; not in any merely passive way, but dynamically, in that he moves with all his concrete being toward transcendence. (ibid.).

At this point Battaglia introduces an important disjunction. His criticism has been directed toward immanentistic humanism, which had been implied in actualism and, in general, in idealism. But is such immanence, and the kind of humanism allied to it, really to be identified with idealism as a method in philosophy? Battaglia, like Carlini and Guzzo, believes not. A rejection of immanentistic and reductive humanism does not directly or completely involve a rejection of idealism. On the contrary, it is necessary and useful to retain both the point of departure and the method of idealism, for "there is no theoretical or practical process save that which is attested and guaranteed by consciousness" (ibid. p. 59). In order to correct the extravagance which leads idealism to immanentistic extremes, it is necessary to note that the act which is rooted in consciousness is never complete and perfect; at every instant it encounters the limits of error and of sin, limits for which immanentistic idealism provides no place. These limits, as he notes, are of both the theoretical and the practical orders; and the vital center of the human spirit lies in its élan to transcend these limits. It is indeed *act*, as Gentile had insisted, but act of transcendence.

The élan of the human spirit toward transcendence opens the horizon of value. This is perhaps the idea to which Battaglia has given the greatest attention. Within the self-enclosed system of immanentism, there can be no value in any true sense. Everything is given; all is equal to all, and what is, as Hegel had recognized, is necessary in its givenness. Value appears with transcendence, for transcendence opens the perspective of possibility which is the basis of oughtness. Value is precisely the rule of oughtness which gives determinate structure to possibility. Thus, the horizon of transcendence provides man with a norm and measure by which to evaluate the world and his immediate existence and by which to direct his effort to transcend himself in the direction of values. Even more, it is only in the presence of the transcendent that human existence, the world, and human life can be evaluated, and hence *become* a value.

The concrete presence of the transcendent, as valuing principle and as value, is religion. For this reason, Battaglia asserts in this same essay

(p. 69) that religion is the ultimate solution which philosophy offers for the problems of life. In the first place, the presence of the transcendent is abstract, i.e., as a rule of valuation; ultimately, however, the transcendent takes concrete form as the value toward which spirit directs itself. Transcendent values are the norms on the basis of which the world is transformed; but as values they are also the direct object of that transcendent act. In this way religion passes, in Battaglia's thought, from a first stage in which it appears as a transcendent axiology, to a second, in which it takes the form of an overt theism.

But in the ultimate analysis, the theater for the realization of value is history. History is the meeting ground of the transcendent and the immanent; it is the locus of that transformation of the world in the light of transcendent values. A thorough understanding of value, consequently, must involve a reexamination of the concept of history under this specific aspect. This reexamination, which provides the theme of one of Battaglia's most important books, *Il valore nella storia* [Value in history], 1948, takes the immanentistic historicism of Croce and Gentile as its point of departure. Both these positions and indeed all forms of immanentistic historicism involve a denial of value and, consequently, of the moral and juridical orders which rest on the notion of value. And they do so, not accidentally, but necessarily, as the logical consequence of immanentism. The exclusion of the dimension of the transcendent excludes the dimension of value, of the possible and of the *ought* as the rule for the preferential reduction of possibility. Both Gentilean and Crocean historicism involve moral and juridical positivism.

By contrast, Battaglia offers a dynamic view of history as the locus for the process of valuation. Valuation is the transformation of the given of experience in the light of the transcendent. This process is the very essence of the life of spirit. Spirit is the generation of value, the point of intersection of the given and the transcendent and of the qualitative transformation of the former in the light of the latter. The valuative process, the process of the creation of values in history, may be viewed under the aesthetic, the moral, or the juridical aspect; ultimately, however, it is religious in character. History is thus seen essentially as a providential process—not in any schematic sense, such as characterized the older "philosophies of history," but in a concrete, processive and dynamic sense, in that the actuality of history is the temporal form of the incursion of the transcendent, as qualitative transforming principle, into the process of life. This process is illustrated supremely in the moment of the Incarnation and it is continued in history, which, since that event, is indelibly Christian; not, to be sure, in any dogmatic or doctrinal sense merely, but in the far more basic sense that Christianity reveals the very structure of history, value, and human existence.

In addition to those already cited, Battaglia is the author of many important works both in the area of his own specialty, the philosophy of law, and in that of the general problems of spiritualistic philosophy. Among them are: *Il problema morale nell'esistenzialismo* [The moral problem in existentialism], 1947; *Filosofia del lavoro* [Philosophy of work], 1951; *Moralità e storia nella prospettiva spiritualistica* [Morality and history in the spiritualistic perspective], 1954; *La lezone spiritualistica di Gentile* [A spiritualistic reading of Gentile], 1955; *Heidegger e la filosofia del valori* [Heidegger and the philosophy of values], 1967.

4. Michele Federico Sciacca (b. 1908)

Sciacca is the representative of Christian spiritualism in Italy who is best known outside that country. His influence has been felt in all the Latin countries, in both Europe and South America, and a number of his works have been translated into English. Within Italy, too, he represents the aggressive promotion of Christian spiritualism as the cultural counterweight to the influence of Crocean historicism and Gentilean actualism, as well as to other currents of divers origins, such as existentialism and phenomenology. While Sciacca is a keen critic, and measures nicely the positive and negative elements of other positions, he sees Christian spiritualism as the philosophy of human integralism *par excellence*, the philosophy in which the integrity of man's nature and existence is expressed and respected. Consequently, he views all others as suffering from some form of unilateralism. A very prolific writer and editor, he is the founder and director of the influential review *Giornale di metafisica*.

Sciacca, as has been noted, also underwent an initial phase, in which the influence of Gentile was dominant. His earliest works, *Linee di uno spiritualismo critico* [Outlines of a critical spiritualism], 1936, and *Teoria e practica della volontà* [Theory and practice of the will], 1938, show him struggling to extricate himself from the Gentilean network and to define a position more in accordance with his own personal insights, which were increasingly religious. At the same time, he was discovering influences which were to help him shape his personal thought more firmly. These influences included the thought of Rosmini (which was to become a pillar of the spiritualism of Sciacca [cf. *La filosofia morale di A. Rosmini*, 1938]), Blondel, and the French philosophers of spirit: Lavelle and Le Senne, as well as the fountainhead of all spiritualism, Augustine (to whom Sciacca devoted an ample, though never completed, study). This process of spiritualistic development comes to a head in the critical study *Il problema di Dio e della religione nella filosofia attuale* [The problem of God and religion in contemporary philosophy], 1944–47. This last work may be considered the definitive point of departure for Sciacca's positive philosophical construction, the program and principles of which are clearly defined in the work *Filosofia e metafisica* [Philosophy and metaphysics], 1950. The understanding of this work is essential.

The problem of the guarantee of self-consciousness (the Gentilean interpretation of which he rejects but which remains the principle of all philosophical inquiry) is clearly posited. Rejecting the term and concept of existence as a pure abstraction, he affirms the primacy of the *existent*, the concrete human subject and person; his task becomes that of discovering within the existent, by a critical process, being itself. He denies, against existentialism, that the existent can be pure possibility or nothingness; he affirms, rather, that it is concrete reality which seeks its own consistency and coherence, its own plenitude. Thus he accepts the existent as project and affirms that "every project of being in itself is the perpetual project of establishing oneself in oneself, autonomously; at the same time, it is the perpetual failure of this effort. The tendency of the existent toward the other (the transcendent) is invincible, it is the tendency toward God. Existence is not the end, but the means of subjectivity: God is the end of every subject. Consistency, coherence, comes to the person from, and resides in, his relation to absolute Being (God)" (*Filosofia e metafisica*, p. 122).

The proof of the existence of God takes its point of departure likewise in the existent, in thought and self-consciousness. The problem of God is basically anthropological and only secondarily cosmological. Within the very structure of the thinking subject there exist at once the fact of doubt and the possibility of judgment; both of these point to the same thing, the presence of a norm which legitimizes both the possibility of doubt and the validity of the judgment. From this norm to the affirmation of the existence of God, it seems to Sciacca, the step is short: "there is nothing in man nor in the world superior to mind; but the mind intuits immutable and absolute truths, which are superior to itself; therefore there exists Immutable Truth, both absolute and transcendent, which is God" (*Filosofia e metafisica*, p. 164). All the other proofs for the existence of God are reducible to this one because the proof "from truth" is the center of reference for the whole problem, since it is situated in the very structure of thought and of the actuality of the existent.

This form of the proof of the existence of God leads Sciacca directly to the formulation of the central concept of his spiritualism, "objective interiority." The elaboration of this concept occupies the work which constitutes the speculative center of his thought *L'intériorité objective* (It. *Interiorità oggettiva*) [Objective interiorness], 1951. Here he takes up again the classical problem of all spiritualism, in order to give it his own formulation (which is, at the same time, directly influenced by the insights of Augustine, Pascal, Rosmini, and Blondel).

He begins with a critique of the notion of interiority as it had existed in idealism, in Gentilean actualism in particular but in all forms of immanentism as well. Interiority had been conceived as a void, a nothingness, even though, with romanticism, the pretension had been maintained that from this void the whole of reality was engendered. But, for Sciacca, interiority has meaning only as it refers to a transcendent and objective reality which defines the horizon of interiority. The subject achieves interiority only through the apperception of the indwelling truth, which is ultimately discovered to be absolute truth. This is one of the clearest reaffirmations of the classical Augustinian dictum; but it goes further to affirm clearly that the indwelling truth is not present to an anterior interiority, but constitutes man's interiority. By reason of its objectivity, its transcendent reference, this indwelling truth does not enclose the subject within itself, as the transcendental notion of truth had done, but constitutes an opening upon the absolute realm of being. The crux of the entire theory lies in the point that the subject constitutes itself as subject only in the act of achieving and affirming the presence of this absolute transcendent. Sciacca lays great emphasis on the fact that this is a single constitutive act. On this point, it would seem, the influence of Gentile is not only persistent but ultimately triumphant. These insights are enriched and elaborated, without substantial alteration, in Sciacca's later works *Atto ed essere* [Act and being], 1956; *L'uomo, questo squilibrato* [Man, this unbalanced being], 1956; *Morte e immortalità* [Death and immortality], 1959; *La libertà e il tempo* [Freedom and time], 1965.

5. Luigi Stefanini (1891–1956)

Among spiritualists, the name of Stefanini is associated most closely with the development of personalism. His personalism, however, represents the terminus of a long process of development which retraces all of the phases of the passage of spiritualism from the Gentilean matrix to its own affirmations. This process is, as a matter of fact, reflected in the very order and succession of Stefanini's works. His early study of Blondel (*L'azione*, 1913) already gives a clue as to the point at which he will eventually arrive: the assertion of transcendence against the pretensions of the method of immanence. Decisive in this process is the *Idealismo cristiano* [Christian idealism] of 1930; this work undertakes to submit idealism to a serious criticism in order that he might use its valid insights in the spiritualism which he was formulating. The fruit of this process is contained in his doctrinal work: *Spiritualismo cristiano* [Christian spiritualism], 1942. This work provides the solid basis of Stefanini's whole speculative construction; it does not, however, close the process of development. This is capped by his characteristically personalistic interpretation of spiritualism, which is treated extensively in the work *La metafisica della persona* [The metaphysics of the person], 1948.

Three points characterize Stefanini's personalism. The first is the opposition between personalism and subjectivism. In his thought, these concepts, far from implying each other, stand in firm opposition. The existent subject achieves personal status, status as person, only by transcending its pure subjectivity by relating itself to the transcendent. The second point is the character of this transcendent. It may be said to possess both vertical and horizontal dimensions. Vertically, it relates to God, to the absolute. The person is constituted as person by his relation to God, to absolute being and truth. Horizontally, the transcendent relates the person to other persons. The person in isolation, even when in vertical relation to God, is incomplete and unfulfilled. He finds the plenitude of his self-affirmation and of the affirmation of his vertical relation to God in the recognition of, and cooperation with, other persons. This has been called the social dimension of Stefanini's personalism and its document is his brief work *Personalismo sociale* [Social personalism], 1951. Finally, the third point is the essential constitutive note of personality, of the status of person. This is not merely ontological but ethical for the person resides in an act, that of the generation of values. But the range of values in question is not viewed in any narrow way; Stefanini sees value not as narrowly moral but as embracing all fields.

The extensive range of the field of value led Stefanini into the philosophy of art. As a matter of fact, art had been an early preoccupation as evidenced by such works as *Problemi attuali d'arte* [Contemporary problems concerning art], 1939, *Arte e critica* [Art and criticism], 1942, and the more ambitious *Metafisica della forma* [The metaphysics of form], 1949. Not until the concept of the person had been clarified, however, did this interest find complete expression. In the *Estetica* [Aesthetics] of 1953, he offers a definition of art which is made possible and comprehensible only through the notion of the person; art becomes for him "the absolute word [utterance] in the sensible order" and hence wholly personalistic and spiritual in its essence. The word, in turn, is defined in the rather scholastic formula: *ens declarativum et manifestativum sui* [being, in that aspect under which it declares and manifests itself] (cf. pp. 66–67, 75). The completion of the still more elaborate *Trattato di estetica* [Treatise of aesthetics] was interrupted by Stefanini's death, but the first volume did appear in 1955 and a second edition of this same volume in 1960. The position taken in this work reaffirms the personalistic character of art. In an interesting article G. Santinello, who is intimately acquainted with Stefanini's thinking, sought, on the basis of the few notes which the author had left, to complete the trajectory of the ideas of this first volume (cf. *Rivista di estetica*, 1956, pp. 147–160).

Readings

Very little material is available in English on contemporary European spiritualism. The following items, however, offer some indications of the main directions of this current. Some basic foreign references are added for completeness.

Caponigri, A. R. "Italian Philosophy: 1943–1950." *Philosophy and Phenomenological Research*, XI (1951), 489–509.

—————. "The Proof for the Existence of God 'From Truth' in the Philosophy of M. F. Sciacca." In *Studi in onore di M. F. Sciacca,* edited by M. T. Antonelli and M. Schiavone, pp. 53–78. Milan: Marzorati, 1959.

Chaix-Ruy, Jules. "France." In *Les grands courants de la pensée mondiale contemporaine: Panoramas nationaux*, I, 535–644. Milan: Marzorati, 1958.

Forest, Aimé. "Louis Lavelle." *Les grands courants de la pensée mondiale contemporaine: Portraits*, II, 831–860. Milan: Marzorati, 1964.

—————. "René Le Senne." In *Les grands courants de la pensée mondiale contemporaine: Portraits*, II, 907–936. Milan: Marzorati, 1964.

Jolivet, Regis. "Le courant neo-augustinien." In *Les grands courants de la pensée mondiale contemporaine: Les Tendances principales*, I, 709–793. Milan: Marzorati, 1961.

Jolivet, R., and Roggerone, G. "Michele Federico Sciacca." In *Les grands courants de la pensée mondiale contemporaine: Portraits*, II, 1379–1413. Milan: Marzorati, 1964.

Lavelle, Louis. "Epitome metaphysicae spiritualis." *Giornale di metafisica*, II (1947), 397–408.

—————. *La philosophie française entre les deux guerres.* Paris: Aubier, 1942.

Nabert, Jean. "Experience of the 'Fault.'" *Philosophy Today*, XI (1967), 213–221.

Piersol, Wesley. "Introductory Notes on Jean Nabert." *Philosophy Today*, XI (1967), 208–212.

Sciacca, M. F. "Philosophie de l'esprit." In the same author's *Philosophical Trends in the Contemporary World,* pp. 555–629. Notre Dame, Ind.: University of Notre Dame Press, 1964.

_____. "Present-Day Italian Philosophy." *The New Scholasticism,* XXXIX (1965), 69–87.

Smith, V. E. "Lavelle and Le Senne: University Philosophy in France." *Thought,* XXIII (1948), 245–280.

NAME INDEX

Abbagnano, Nicola, 249, 254, 297–300
Alexander, Samuel
  critique of Kantian categories, 95
  deity
    discourse of, negative, 96
    generation of, by time, 95–96
    nature of, 95
  mind, self-knowledge of, 94–95
  realistic monism, 94–95
  space-time as matrix category, 95
  time as mind of space, 95
Aliotta, Antonio, 62
Austin, John L., 322
Ayer, Alfred Jules, 329–330

Baeumker, Clemens, 129
Balmes, Jaime, 123
Balthasar, Nicolas, 127
Bañez, Domingo, 121
Barth, Karl, 248
Battaglia, Felice, 343–345
Battaglini, Francesco Cardinal, 122
Bellarmino, Roberto Cardinal, 122
Berdyaev, Nikolai, 249
Bergmann, Gustave, 328
Bergson, Henri, 4, 6, 8, 14, 183–194
  creative evolution, 189–191
  élan vital, 188
  intuition, 192–193
  matter and memory, 186–187
  morality and religion, 193–194
  and positivistic evolution, 184–185
  spirit as interiority, 187
  time and freedom, 185–186
Billot, Louis Cardinal, S. J., 128
Blondel, Maurice, 201, 202, 212–219
Bourke, Vernon, 132
Boutroux, Emile, 183
Boyer, Charles, S. J., 128, 138

Brentano, Franz, 135, 155–156
Broad, C. D., 93–94
Buchner, Ludwig, 69, 71
Buzzetti, Vincenzo, 121

Caird, Eduard, 44
Calderoni, Mario, 62
Camus, Albert, 276
Carlini, Armando, 340–342
Carnap, Rudolf
  American phase, 326–328
  European phase, 312–314
Cassirer, Ernst, 24
Chiocchetti, Emilio, 128, 129
Clifford, William K., 71, 73
Cohen, Morris Raphael, 113, 114–115
Copleston, Frederick, S. J., 138
Coreth, Emerich, 144–146
Cornoldi, Giovanni, S. J., 3, 14, 26, 133
Croce, Benedetto, 223–237
  "absolute historicism," 236–237
  ethical liberalism, 234–237
  later aesthetic doctrine, 233–234
  philosophy of spirit, 226–233
    internal relations of moments of spirit, 231–232
    meaning and structure of spirit, 228–231
    role of, 232–233
    spirit of system, 227–228
    works comprising, 226–227
  seminal phase, 224–226
Curci, Carlo Maria, 121, 122

De Raeymaeker, Louis, 127
Derisi, Octavio, 130
Deschamps, Marie-Leger Cardinal, 127

Dewey, John, 44, 53–57
De Wulf, Maurice, 127
Dezza, Paolo, S. J., 128
Dilthey, Wilhelm, 14, 24, 26–29, 33
Dopp, Joseph, 127
Dostoevski, Fëdor, 249
Dreisch, Hans, 6, 8, 10–11
Dufrenne, Mikel, 249

Ehrle, Franz Cardinal, 129
Engels, Friedrich, 64, 79–82

Fabro, Cornelio, 136
Farber, Marvin, 180–182
Fechner, Gustave, 69–71
Feigl, Herbert, 327
Feuerbach, Ludwig, 66–68
Fichte, Johann Gottlieb, 25
Fink, Eugen, 180
Fonseca, Pedro de, 120
Frank, Philipp, 306, 307, 327
Frege, Gottlieb, 309

Gemelli, Agostino, 128
Gentile, Giovanni, 26, 237–245
    and Aristotle, 238
    chief works, 238
    educational theories, 238–239
    God, in actual idealism, 243
    historicity of spirit, 241
    history, temporal and ideal, 241
    law, theory of, 243
    nature and spirit, 242
    originality, 238
    pure act, concept of, 241–242
    reformation of Hegelian dialectic,
        239–241
    and St. Augustine, 238
    Sistema di logica, doctrine of,
        242–243
    society, theory of, 244–245
Gilson, Étienne, 129, 136, 138
Gioberti, Vincenzo, 131
Gobineau, Joseph Arthur de, 40
Goethe, J. W. von, 13, 24, 25, 37, 38
González, Ceferino, 123
Goudin, Antoine, 121
Grabmann, Martin, 129
Gramsci, Antonio, 88
Grassi, Francesco, 121
Greene, Thomas H., 44

Guardini, Romano, 129
Guyau, Jean-Marie, 14, 15–16
Guzzo, Augusto, 342–343

Haeckel, Ernst, 73–74
Hahn, Hans, 306
Hare, R. M., 322–323
Hartmann, Nicolai, 173–176
Hartshorne, Charles, 97
Hegel, G. F. W., *passim*
    and Gentile, 239–241
Heidegger, Martin, 263–276
    attention, 276
    Being and Time, doctrine of, 264–
        265
    being-in-the-world, 267
    care, concept and forms of, 268–
        269
        transcendental analysis of, 270
    Dasein, concept of, 265
    death, 271–272
    dereliction, 268
    existence, authentic and inauthen-
        tic, 270–271
    facticity, 268
    formation, 263
    history, 273
    language, 275–276
    man, theory of, 264–265
    method, 266–277
    ontic and ontological distinguished,
        266
    phenomenology, concept of, 266
    poetry, 275–276
    second phase, 274–276
    temporality, constitutive, 272–273
    truth, theory of, 266–267
    two phases, 262
    "usability" and space, 268
    works, 263–264
    "world" as project of *Dasein*, 267
Helmholtz, Hermann, 69
Hempel, C. G., 306
Herder, Johann Gottfried, 12
Hertz, Heinrich, 69
Hoenen, Petrus, S. J., 128
Holt, Edwin B., 106
Husserl, Edmund, 153–170
    antecedents and relations, 154–155
    chief works, two categories of,
        153–154

formation, 153
phenomenological doctrine, 155–170
See also: phenomenology

James, William, 49–53
formation and character, 49
ideas, 51–53
and Peirce, compared, 50
works, 50–51
See also: pragmatism
Jaspers, Karl
communication, 260–261
Dasein, concept of, 259
Existenz, defined, 259
properties of, 260
formation and relations, 254
and Hegelianism, 257
"limit-situations," 261
"metaphysics," 261–262
necessity and choice, 260
philosophy, function and method, 259–260
"physician" of existence, 255
selves, other, 260
shock, 261, 263
thematic, 256
works, 255–256
John of St. Thomas, (Juan de Poinsot), 121
Jourdain, Charles, 123

Kallen, Horace, 43
Kierkegaard, Søren
and Engels, 81
and German existentialism, 248
and Marx, 81
and Newman, 206
Klages, Ludwig, 14, 16–17
Kleutgen, Josef, 123

Laberthonnière, Lucien, 219–221
Laín Entralgo, Pedro, 250
Lavelle, Louis, 332–335
anguish, concept of, 332
diremption, 333–334
eternal present, dialectic of, 333
and existentialism, 332
God, 334
liberty, 334
metaphysical experience, 333

metaphysics, 333
Narcissus, spell of, 334
ontologism, 332
participation, dialectic of, 333
person, 334
tragic sense of life denied, 332
vocation, 334
works, 332
Lenin, Nicolai, 82–85
Leo XIII, Pope, 122, 125
Le Senne, René, 335–339
"characterology," theory of, 338
chief works, 335
"existential metaphysics," theory of value as, 338
experience, openness of, 336
fêleur, concept of, 336
ideo-existential philosophy, concept of, 335
obstacle, concept of, 336
transcendent, dual aspect of, 337
value, concept of, 336
Lessing, Gotthold, 24, 26
Lessius, Leonardus (Lenaert Lys), 121
Lewin, Kurt, 306
Liberatore, Matteo, 121, 122
on the human composite, 132
Lombroso, Cesare, 70
Lonergan, Bernard, S. J., 146–149
on *a priori* principles, 147
and common sense knowledge, 147
"dynamism" of thought, 148
isomorphism between "real" being and thought, 149
and Kant, 146
"levels" of knowledge, 148
and Maréchal, 146
"recurrent structure," 149
and science, 147
Lotz, Joseph, 135
Lovejoy, Arthur O., 45, 108–109
Lukačs, Georg, 87–88

Mach, Ernst, 306–307
Macintosh, D. C., 106
Mandonnet, Pierre, O. P., 129
Marcel, Gabriel, 276–285
and American idealism, 277
being, having, and *body,* 284–285
communion and society, 283

existence and existents, 278
faith, 278
"fidelity to being," 279
function, 279
grace, 278
hope, 281
mediation, 285
mystery and problem, 278–279
person, 277, 280, 281
philosophy and literary form, 276
"reflective empiricism," 277
rejects characterization as "exist-
    entialist," 285
sensibility, 284–285
suicide, 281
"Thou" and God, 282–283
works, 276–277
Maréchal, Joseph, S. J., 139–142
dynamism of mind and thought,
    141
and Kantianism, 140–141
"Maréchalian Thomism," 140
mind as "act," trajectory of, 142
theoretical and practical reason,
    division of, 141
works, 140
Mariana, Juan de, 121
Marías, Julián, 14, 22, 250
Maritain, Jacques, 129, 137–138, 139
Martinetti, Piero, 223
Marvin, M. T., 104–105
Marx, Karl, 74–78
alienation, 76
determinism and revolution, 77–78
expropriation, 76
historical dimension of matter, 75
and "humanistic materialism" of
    Feuerbach, 74–75
man
    discovery of, in history, 75–76
    as productive agent, 75
matter, concept of, 74–75
moralism of, 77
and romanticism, 75
work, transitive and intransitive,
    75
Masnovo, Amato, 129
Mattiussi, Guido, 134
Maxwell, James Clerk, 71, 73
Mead, George H., 57–59

Meinecke, Friedrich, 26, 38–39
finite and infinite, dialectic of, 39
Kratos and Ethos, 38
and romanticism, 38
"temporalizing" of reason, 38
Meinong, Alexis, 171–173
Melchior Cano, Francisco, O. P., 121
Mercier, Désiré Cardinal, 127
Merleau-Ponty, Maurice, 294–296
Mises, Richard von, 307
Moleschott, Jacob, 69–70
Molina, Luis de, 121
Montague, W. P., 103–104
Moore, George E., 91–94, 304–306
Morris, Charles E., 326–327
Mounier, Emanuel, 249
Muck, Otto, 139, 140
Murray, John Courtney, S. J., 139

Neurath, Otto, 306–309, 311–312
Newman, John Henry Cardinal,
    204–208
Nietzsche, Friedrich, 13, 14, 248
Nys, Désiré, 127

Olgiati, Francesco, 129
Ollé-Laprune, Léon, 204, 208–212
Ortega y Gasset, José, 14, 20–22
Ostwald, Wilhelm, 8, 9–10, 71

Padovani, U. A., 138
Papini, Giovanni, 61
Pasteur, Louis, 8
Peano, Giuseppe, 98
Pecci, Giuseppe Cardinal, 122
Pecci, Vincenzo Gioachino (Pope
    Leo XIII), 122, 125
Perera, Benito, 120
Pesch, Tilmann, S. J., 123
Peirce, Charles S., 43, 44, 46–49
abstraction, hypostatic, 49
action, nature of, 48
belief, theory of, 48
categories, theory of, 49
interpretation, modes of, 47
and logic, 46
meaning, definition and criterion,
    48
sign, conceptual meaning of, 47–
    48

truth, theory of, 48
tychism, 49
works, 46
Perry, Ralph Barton, 104–106
Piemontese, F., 138
Pieper, Josef, 129
Pius IX, Pope, 125–126
Poinsot, Juan de. *See* John of St.
   Thomas
Pratt, James B., 109, 110
Prezzolini, Giuseppe, 63
Prisco, Giuseppe, 122

Quine, Willard van Orman, 328

Rahner, Karl, S. J., 142–144
Ramsey, Frank Plumpton, 320–321
Ranke, Leopold von, 38
Rankins, W. J., 71
Reichenbach, Hans, 306, 328
Reinke, Johannes, 6, 8–9
Renan, Joseph-Ernest, 16, 73
Renoirte, Ferdinand, 127
Richert, Heinrich, 31
Ricoeur, Paul, 180
Riet, Georges van, 132, 140
Rogers, Arthur K., 107
Roselli, Salvatore Maria, 121, 123
Rosmini-Serbati, Antonio, 131
Rousselot, Pierre, 140
Royce, Josiah, 44, 102
Ryle, Gilbert, 314–315
Russell, Bertrand, 97–102
   early Hegelianism, 98
   early realism, 98
   ethical discourse, 102
   knowledge, theory of, 100–101
   language, theory of, 101–102
   logical theories, 98–100
   and Whitehead, 101

Sanseverino, Gaetano, 121–122
Santayana, George, 110–113
   dualism, 113
   faith, animal, 111
   materialism, monistic, 112–113
   realm
      of essence, 111
      of matter, 111–112
      of spirit, 112–113
      of truth, 112

Sartre, Jean-Paul, 285–294
   Being and Nothingness, doctrine
      of, 287–291
   ego, the, 286
   emotions, theory of the, 286
   imagination, theory of, 287
   intentionality, central role of, 286
   La critique de la raison dialectique
      and *Being and Nothingness,* 291
      doctrine of, 292–294
      Marxian influence in, 291
   Les Mots (autobiography), 294
Scheler, Max, 176–179
   community, idea of, 179
   emotive experience, 177
   emotive intuition, 177
   ethics, concept of, 177
   God, concept and function of, 178
   and Kant, 178
   person, concept of, 178–179
   self, concept of, 178
   sociology, philosophical, 180
   sympathy, concept and role of,
      180
   values, hierarchy of, 177–178
Schelling, F. C. S., 60–61
Schlick, Moritz, 310–311
Schopenhauer, A., 14
Schröder, Ernst, 304
Sciacca, Michele Federico, 346–348
   integrality, philosophy of, 348
   interiority, objective, 346
      as horizon of transcendent, 347
Sellars, Roy Wood, 107
Sertillanges, A. D., 129
Shestov, Lev, 249
Signoriello, Nunzio, 122
Simmel, Georg, 14, 26, 29–30
Soloviëv, V. S., 249
Sordi, Domenico, 121
Sordi, Serafino, 121
   and Rosmini, 128
Sorel, Georges, 201
Soto, Domingo de, 121
Spaventa, Bertrando, 223
Spaulding, E. G., 103, 105
Spengler, Oswald, 17, 26, 35–37, 39
Stalin, Josef, 85–87
   anti-evolutionism, 87
   dialectic of matter, laws of, 86

materialism, dialectical and historical, 87
"ought," nature of, 87
psycho-physical dualism, 85
"seven theses," 85
spiritual values, 87
Stefanini, Luigi, 348–352
and actualism, 348
art, theory of, 351–352
personalism, 349
social, 349–350
and value, 351
Stein, Edith, 136, 180, 131
Stevenson, Charles, 328
Strong, A. C., 103
Suarez, Francisco, 121

Taine, Hippolyte, 16, 71–73
Talamo, Salvatore, 122
Taparelli d'Azeglio, Luigi, 121, 122
Tarski, Alfred, 326–327
Toledo, Francisco de, 120
Troeltsch, Ernst, 33–35
Toynbee, Arnold, 26, 39–41
challenge and response, 40
Christianity, privileged place of,
41
civilization, units of, 39
empiricism of, 39
and Spengler, 39

Unamuno, Miguel de, 14, 18–20
Christ, 20
conatus, interpretation of, 18
death, view of, 19
immortality, 19
God, 20
Socratism, 18
and Spinoza, 18
Urraburu, Juan José, 128

Vailati, Giovanni, 62
and Peirce, 62
Vanni Rovighi, Sophia, 129
Veblen, Thorstein, 43
Vera, Augusto, 223
Vico, Giambattista, 12, 301
Vogt, Karl, 69, 71

Wagner, Rudolf, 71
Wahl, Jean, 248
Weber, Max, 26, 30–32
history, object of, 30
meaning in, 31
possibility as category of, 31
science, problematical character
of, 31
three directions of thought of, 30
types, ideal, 32
understanding (*verstehen*), 31
value, and meaning, 31
Whitehead, Alfred North, 96–97
extensive abstraction, method of,
96
epistemological realism, 97
pluralism, dynamic, 97
"prehension," theory of, 96–97
substance, reexamined, 96
theodicy, 97
theology, 97
Wilson, Cook, 314
Windelband, Wilhelm, 28
Wisdom, John, 321
Wittgenstein, Ludwig, 305, 309–310,
314–321
early career, 305
relation to Vienna Circle, 309
Tractatus Logico - Philosophicus,
310
Woodbridge, F. J. F., 113–117

Ziegler, Leopold, 17
Zigliara, Tommaso, O. P., 122

SUBJECT INDEX

abstraction
  eidetic (Husserl), 157, 159, 160
  extensive (Whitehead), 96
  hypostatic (Peirce), 49
  and hylomorphism, 131
  Sordi's interpretation of, 132
  Thomistic doctrine of, 131–132
  in transcendental Thomism, 139–140
Accademia di Filosofia Tomista (Naples), 122
Accademia Tomistica (Bologna), 122
act
  and potency, theory of, 133
  Mattiussi's statement of, 134
  mind as pure act, 142, 241–242
action, philosophy of, 201–222
  characteristics of, 201–203
  as Christian philosophy, 202
  and fideism, 201
  and pragmatism, 202
  polarity in, 204
  and voluntarism, 201
  See also: Blondel; Ollé-Laprune; Newman; Laberthonnière
actualism
  autoctisis in, 241
  historical derivation of, 237–238
  history in, 241
  interiority in, 239
  logos, abstract and concrete, in, 243
  retrospective dialectic in, 240
  state in, 244
Aeterni Patris (encyclical), 125–126
Alberoni, Collegio, 121, 129
alienation
  and bourgeois society, 76, 77
  in existentialism, 248–296
  in historical materialism, 76

"all-givenness," theme of, 160
Aloisianum, Collegio, 127
analysis
  "exhibitive," 301
  instruments of, 309
  ordinary language, 303
  "replacement," 301
Angelicum (Ateneo Angelico), 128
anthropology, Thomistic, 131–132
"apriorism," Kantian, and neo-scholasticism, 135
Apollonian/Faustian dichotomy (Spengler), 36–37
art
  as existentialist theme, 254
  and neo-scholasticism, 137–138
anguish, concept of (Lavelle), 382
assent
  and inference, 207
  notional, 207
  real, 207
  and will, 207
Ateneo Angelico (Angelicum), 128
atomism, logical, 305

being
  "bracketing" (phenomenology), 159, 160–163
  question of, three elements in, 265

care
  concept of (Heidegger), 268–269
  transcendental analysis of, 270
category (-ies)
  evolutionary, 24
  historical, defined, 24
  natural, 24
  theory of (Peirce), 49
"category mistake" (Ryle), 315
Catholic University of Milan, 128

challenge and response (Toynbee), 40

Chantilly (Jesuit house of studies), 129

characterology (Le Senne), 338

Christian doctrine, development of (Newman), 205

Christianity, privileged status of (Toynbee), 41

cipher (Jaspers), 262–263

Civiltà cattolica (review), 122

civilization, units of (Toynbee), 39

colloquy, theme of, in existentialism, 253

communication
  and *Existenz*, 260
  theme of, in existentialism, 253

communism, Marxian, 77

community
  Marcel's theory of, 283
  Scheler's theory of, 179

conatus, interpretation of (Unamuno), 18

Concept of Mind (Ryle), 314–315

concepts, "logical geography" of, 315

consciousness, intentionality of, 157

constitution
  generic concept of, 165
  problem of, 164
  subgeneric modes of, 166

contingency, status of, in existentialism, 252

Cours de philosphie de Louvain, 127

creation and philosophy of life, 7

"critical problem," 131

Dasein
  Heidegger's concept of, 265
  Jaspers' concept of, 259

death
  Heidegger's idea of, 271–272
  Unamuno's idea of, 19

deity, generation of, by time (Alexander), 95

dereliction, concept of, 268

dialectic
  of the eternal present (Lavelle), 333
  Hegelian, Gentile's reformation of, 238

"retrospective" (Gentile), 240

dialogue, interpersonal (Jaspers), 259

diremption, concept of (Lavelle), 334

discourse
  ethical (Russell), 162
  moral and scientific compared (Hare), 323

Divus Thomas (review), 129

dominants, theory of (Reinke), 8–9

doubt, concept of (Newman), 206

ego
  autoexposition of, 167
  Sartre's analysis of, 286

élan vital, 6, 188

elucidation, notion of (Ramsey), 321

emotion, theory of (Sartre), 286

emotive experience, phenomenology of (Scheler), 177

emotive intuition (Scheler), 177

empathy (Husserl), 167

empiricism
  historical (Toynbee), 39
  reflective (Marcel), 277

energeticism (W. Ostwald), 9–10

energy
  conservation of, and entelechy, 10
  free, and concept of life, 9–10
  as fundamental category (Ostwald), 10

entelechism (Driesch), 10–12

epoché (Husserl), 159, 160–163

Erkenntnis (review), 306

erlebnis
  active character of, 11
  finality of, 12
  "interiority" of, 11
  and value, 12

Erscheinung, Jaspers' concept of, 256

Essay in Aid of a Grammar of Assent (Newman), 204–208

Essay on the Development of Christian Doctrine (Newman), 204–206

essence, concept and status of (phenomenology), 157

eternal present, dialectic of (Lavelle), 333

ethics, existential, 252

Ethos (Meinecke), 38

existence
  analysis of method in, 266
  authenticity of (Heidegger), 270–271
existential, defined, 266
existentialism, 248–300
  French, 276–298
  German, 254–276
  inception and geographical distribution, 248
  method in, 250
  moral theme in, 252
  and neo-scholasticism, 135–137
  theistic and atheistic, 252–253
  thematic and problematic, 251–252
Existenz
  defined (Jaspers), 259
  properties of, 260–261
expropriation in historical materialism, defined, 76

facticity, defined (Heidegger), 268
faith
  animal (Santayana), 111
  as disposition (Marcel), 278
  philosophical, 262
fêleur
  defined (Le Senne), 336
  role (Le Senne), 337
fidelity, concept of (Marcel), 279
finitude (finiteness), dialectic of, 252

game, concept of, 317
generation, spontaneous, and neovitalism, 8
"generation of '98," Spanish, 8
God
  Christ as (Unamuno), 20
  as direct object of assent (Newman), 206
  "function" of (Scheler), 178
  as "Thou" (Marcel), 282–283
Gregorian University, 128
Gregorianum (review), 129
"grounding," defined, 162
guilt, as limit-situation, 261

historical, locus of the, 24
historicism, 24–41
  absolute (Croce), 236–237

defined, 24
open-ended, 25
pluralistic, 25
relativism in, 25
and romanticism, 25–27
historicity, properties of, 170–171
history
  divine meaning in, 254
  in existentialist thought, 253
  meaning in (Weber), 31
  in neo-scholasticism, 138
  possibility as category in (Weber), 31
human composite in Thomistic anthropology, 131–132
Husserl Archives, 154
hylomorphism
  and act and potency, 133–134
  Cornoldi on, 132
  Liberatore on, 132–134
  and science, 133

idealism
  revival of, in Italy, 223
  transcendental, 168
Ideas (Husserl), 161–168
imagination, theory of (Sartre), 287
immanence, method of
  in Blondel, 214
  in Gentile, 238
immortality
  concept of (Unamuno), 19
  as proof of God's existence (Unamuno), 20
inference, theory of, in Newman, 207
Institute of Mediaeval Studies (Toronto), 129
Institute Supérieur de Philosophie de Louvain, 126–127
integralism, Christian
  aspects of, 201–203
  in Newman, 207
  in Ollé-Laprune, 208
  philosophy of action as, 203
  in Sciacca, 348
intentionality
  in neo-scholasticism, 135–136
  in phenomenology, 157–158
  in Sartre, 286
interiority
  in Bergson, 186

in Jaspers, 256
objective, in Sciacca, 346–347
in Ollé-Laprune, 210
interpretation, theory of (Peirce), 47
"intranscendibility" as property of
    language, 312
intuition and metaphysics (Bergson),
    192
isomorphism, ontic-epistemic (Lon-
    ergan), 149

Kantianism
    and Maréchal, 140
    and Thomistic neo-scholasticism,
        135
    and transcendental Thomism, 139
knowledge
    levels of (Lonergan), 148
    recurrent structures in (Lonergan),
        149
Kratos (Meinecke), 38

La critica (review), 224
language
    as expression of life-form, 317
    expressive character of, 317
    game(s), 316–317
    "ideal," construction of, 301
    and metaphysics (Jaspers), 261
    philosophy as analysis of, 301–329
    semantic dimension of, 324
    therapeutic view of, 303
    traditional and modern views of,
        301
Language, Truth and Logic (Ayer),
    320
Leonardo (review), 61
"Leonine Edition" of works of St.
    Thomas Aquinas, 125
Le Saulchoir (Dominican house of
    studies), 129
liberalism, ethical (Croce), 234–236
liberty as property of *Existenz*, 260
life, philosophy of, 5–23
    aesthetic structure of, in Reinke, 9
    aestheticism and, 14
    and creationism, 8
    and development of biological sci-
        ence in nineteenth century, 5
    earlier history of, 12–13

Goethe and, 13
Herder and, 13
humanism and, 14
"irrationalism" and, 15
Nietzsche and, 13
primitivism and, 14
romanticism and, 16
Schelling and, 13
Schopenhauer and, 13
two speculative tendencies in, 11–
    12
Vico and, 13
life experience, 297
life-force, 6
limit-situations (Jaspers), 261
Logische Syntax der Sprache, Der
    (Carnap), 313

materialism, 64–87
    dialectical, 78–87
    evolutionary monistic, 73
    historical, 74–78
    methodological, 8, 86
    monistic, 71
    psychophysical, 68
    radical humanistic, 65
    types of, 64
matter
    and form, Thomistic theory of,
        132–133
    historical character of (Marx), 75
    realm of (Santayana), 111–112
meaning
    criterion of (Peirce), 48
    defined (Peirce), 48
    as naming, 316
    as use of language, 317
    and verification, 320
mediation, concept and role of (Mar-
    cel), 285
metaphysics
    existential (Le Senne), 338
    in Jaspers, 261–262
    redefined (Lavelle), 333
    restoration of (Lavelle), 333
    and science, in neo-scholasticism,
        137
    and transcendental Thomism, 139–
        143

mind as (pure) act
  in Gentile, 237–248
  in transcendental Thomism, 140–141
minds, other (Ayer), 320
monism, realistic (Alexander), 94

natural attitude (phenomenology), 159–160
naturalism
  American, 102–117
  English, 91–102
  general characteristics, 90
  as reaction to idealism, 90
  as reaction to pragmatism, 90
necessity and liberty (Jaspers), 259–260
"neo" movements in philosophy, 3
neo-romanticism, German, 309
neo-scholasticism, 118–151
neo-vitalism, 5–11
noema, defined (phenomenology), 169
noesis, defined (phenomenology), 158, 169

objects, constitution of, 159
ontic, notion of (Heidegger), 266
ontological, notion of (Heidegger), 266
ontology, fundamental and general (Heidegger), 265
order, theory of (Dreisch), 10–11

pan-objectivism, defined, 103–105
participation
  dialectic of (Lavelle), 333
  notion of, 253
Pascendi Domenici Gregis (encyclical), 126
perception
  immanent, 166
  transcendent, 166
person, concept of (Scheler), 178–179
personalism
  realistic, 109
  social (Stefanini), 349–350

perspectivism (Weber), 31
phenomenology, 152–182
  continuing influence of, 180–182
  developments of, 170–179
  Husserlian, 153–170
  preliminary definition, 152
philosophia perennis, 118
Philosophical Investigations (Wittgenstein), 314–323
philosophy
  as analysis of language, 301–329
    American phase, 324–328
    anticipatory phase, 304–306
    British phase, 314–324
    continental phase, 306–313
    general characteristics, 301–303
  as comprehension (Wittgenstein), 319
  concept and work of (Jaspers), 258
  "function" of, 318
  history of, and neo-scholasticism, 119–120
  ideo-existential concept of (Le Senne), 335
  as methodology of historiography (Croce), 225
  as methodology of science, 308
  of spirit, in France, 331–338
  as therapy (Wittgenstein), 318
  as understanding of language-use, 318
  and world views, 308–309
"phrastic" elements of language, 323
Piacenza (seminary), 121
poetry
  and existence, 254
  and metaphysics (Heidegger), 275–276
positivism
  countermovements against, 297–298
  logical, defined, 303
potency and act, theory of, 133–134
pragmaticism (Peirce), 45
pragmatism(s), 43–65
  American character of, 43
  and classical empiricism, 46
  European dimension of, 43
  five masters of, 46–61
  influence of, 43

Italian school of, 61–64
metaphysical aspect of, 45
methodological aspect of, 45
origin and history of the term, 44–46
and "situation in the world," 45
thirteen, of Lovejoy, 45
unifying constants among, 45
propositions, types of (Newman), 206–207
psychiatry, phenomenological, 255–256
psychologism of Husserl, 154–156
psychology in Thomistic neo-scholasticism, 131–132

realism, American, 102–113
"critical" phase, 106–107
first constructive phase of, 102–103
genesis of, 102
new, 105–106
systematic phase, 109–113
realism, English, 91–102
reason, "temporalization" of (Meinecke), 38
reduction
epistemological, 160
phenomenological, 158
religion, defined (Newman), 207
"retorsal" method in transcendental Thomism, 140
Revista neo-scholastica (review), 129
Revue Philosophique de Louvain (review), 127
Roman Academy of St. Thomas, 126

Sapientia (review), 130
scholasticism
defined, 118
dimensions of, 119
persistence of, 120
second, 120–122
science
Jaspers' critique of, 257–259
and metaphysics, 129
philosophy as rigorous (Husserl), 103
unity of, 314
Weber's critique of, 31
self, spurious (Jaspers), 258

selves, others (Jaspers), 260
semantics
logical and mathematical, 326
and logical positivism, 324
pragmatic and behavioral, 326
semiotic dimensions (Morris), 327
sensism, Lockean, and neo-scholasticism, 131
shock, defined (Jaspers), 261
"signified" and "thing as known," the, 156
signs
Morris' theory of, 326
Peirce's theory of, 47
singularity, defined, 252
situation
defined, 252
limit, defined (Jaspers), 261
"Six" in American realism, the, 104–105
society, theme of, in existentialism, 253
space-time as matrix category (Alexander), 95
spirit
as interiority (Bergson), 187
realm of (Santayana), 112–113
spiritualism, contemporary
in France, 331–338
in Italy, 339–351
statements, prescriptive
universalization of, 323
verification of, 324
Studiorum Ducem (encyclical), 126
suffering as limit situation (Jaspers), 261
Syllabus of Errors, 125
sympathy, concept and role of (Scheller), 180
syntax, logical (Carnap), 325–326

thermodynamics, second law of, 10
Thomism, transcendental method in, 139–151
thought, dynamism of
Lonergan on, 141
Maréchal on, 141
time
consciousness of, 160
existential, 254
and freedom (Bergson), 185–186

as mind of space (Alexander), 95

Tractatus Logico-Philosophicus (Wittgenstein), 309–310

truth

Heidegger's theory of, 266–267

historical character of (Newman), 205

"living" character of (Newman), 206

Peirce's theory of, 48

realm of (Santayana), 112

semantic definition of, 326

tychism (Peirce), 49

types, theory of ideal (Weber), 32

understanding *(verstehen)*, Weber on, 31

utterances

imperative and prescriptive, 323–324

performatory, 322

value

concept of, 336

hierarchy of (Scheler), 177–178

and meaning (Weber), 31

verifiability of imperative and prescriptive statements, 323

verification, criterion of, 324

Vienna Circle, the, 306–313

vitalism and neo-vitalism distinguished, 6

vocation, concept of (Lavelle), 334

will and assent (Newman), 208

work, transitive and intransitive (Marx), 75

world

logical structure of, 308

as project of *Dasein* (Heidegger), 267